The Great Depression in America

The Great Depression in America

A CULTURAL ENCYCLOPEDIA
Volume 2: N–Z

WILLIAM H. YOUNG
and
NANCY K. YOUNG

GREENWOOD PRESS
Westport, Connecticut • London

Library of Congress Cataloging-in-Publication Data

Young, William H., 1939–
  The Great Depression in America : a cultural encyclopedia / William H.
Young and Nancy K. Young.
    2 v.
  Includes bibliographical references and index.
  ISBN 0-313-33520-6 (set : alk. paper) — ISBN 0-313-33521-4 (v. 1 :
alk. paper) — ISBN 0-313-33522-2 (v. 2 : alk. paper)
    1. Popular culture—United States—History—20th century—
Encyclopedias. 2. United States—Civilization—1918–1945—
Encyclopedias. 3. United States—Intellectual life—20th century—
Encyclopedias. 4. United States—Social life and customs—1918–1945—
Encyclopedias. 5. United States—Biography—Encyclopedias. 6.
Depressions—1929—United States—Encyclopedias. I. Young, Nancy K.,
1940– II. Title.
E169.1.Y595   2007
973.91′003—dc22   2006100693

British Library Cataloguing in Publication Data is available.

Copyright © 2007 by William H. Young and Nancy K. Young

Library of Congress Catalog Card Number: 2006100693
ISBN-10: 0-313-33520-6 (set)   ISBN-13: 978-0-313-33520-4 (set)
       0-313-33521-4 (vol. 1)   978-0-313-33521-1 (vol. 1)
       0-313-33522-2 (vol. 2)   978-0-313-33522-8 (vol. 2)

First published in 2007

Greenwood Press, 88 Post Road West, Westport, CT 06881
An imprint of Greenwood Publishing Group, Inc.
www.greenwood.com

Printed in the United States of America

The paper used in this book complies with the
Permanent Paper Standard issued by the National
Information Standards Organization (Z39.48–1984).

10 9 8 7 6 5 4 3 2 1

In memory of Gary Sederholm,
whose spirit inspired us all

Contents

Alphabetical List of Entries

Guide to Related Topics

ART
Advertising
American Gothic
Art Deco
Benton, Thomas Hart
Century of Progress Exposition
   (Chicago World's Fair)
Comic Books
Comic Strips
Design
Disney, Walt
Fashion
Federal Art Project (FAP)
Hopper, Edward
Illustrators
Marsh, Reginald
Photography
Regionalism
Rockwell, Norman
Sculpture
Sheeler, Charles
Social Realism
Streamlining
Wood, Grant
Wyeth, N. C.

ARCHITECTURE
Architecture
Art Deco
Century of Progress Exposition
   (Chicago World's Fair)
Chrysler Building, The
Empire State Building, The
International Style
New York World's Fair
Rockefeller Center
   (Radio City)
Wright, Frank Lloyd

AVIATION
Airships
Aviation
China Clippers
Douglas DC-3
Earhart, Amelia
Lindbergh Kidnapping
Transportation
Travel

COMIC BOOKS & STRIPS
Apple Mary
Big Little Books
Blondie
Comic Books
Comic Strips
Dick Tracy
Flash Gordon
Gumps, The
Hillbillies
Illustrators
Li'l Abner
Little Orphan Annie
Prince Valiant
Serials
Superman
Tarzan
Terry and the Pirates

EXPOSITIONS/FAIRS
Century of Progress Exposition
   (Chicago World's Fair)
Circuses
Fairs & Expositions
New York World's Fair

FADS/GAMES
Contract Bridge

Comic Strips
Dick Tracy
Flash Gordon
Gumps, The
Li'l Abner
Little Orphan Annie
Newspapers
Prince Valiant
Roosevelt, Eleanor
Tarzan
Terry and the Pirates
Winchell, Walter

ORGANIZATIONS
Alcoholics Anonymous (A.A.)
Civilian Conservation Corps (CCC)
Federal Art Project (FAP)
Federal Bureau of Investigation (FBI)
Federal Music Project (FMP)
Federal Theatre Project (FTP)
Federal Writers' Project (FWP)
Political Parties

RADIO
Advertising
Amos 'n' Andy
Grand Ole Opry
Hillbillies
Little Orphan Annie
March of Time, The (Radio & Film)
Radio
Radio Networks
Rockefeller Center (Radio City)
Roosevelt, Franklin Delano
Science Fiction
Serials (Radio & Movies)
Smith, Kate
Soap Operas
National Barn Dance, The
Welles, Orson
Winchell, Walter
Your Hit Parade

SOCIAL ISSUES
Crime
Dionne Quintuplets
Lindbergh Kidnapping
New Deal
Prohibition & Repeal (1920–1933)
Race Relations & Stereotyping
Religion
Roosevelt, Eleanor
Social Consciousness Films

SONGWRITERS & LYRICISTS
Berlin, Irving
Fields, Dorothy
Gershwin, George, & Ira Gershwin
Kern, Jerome
Porter, Cole
Rodgers & Hart (Richard Rodgers & Lorenz
    Hart)
Songwriters & Lyricists

SPORTS
Baseball
Basketball
Bowling
Boxing
Football
Golf
Horse Racing
Ice Skating & Hockey
Miniature Golf
Motorsports
Olympic Games
Polo
Roller Skating
Seabiscuit
Skiing
Softball
Swimming
Tennis

THEATER
Berlin, Irving
Federal Theatre Project (FTP)
Gershwin, George, & Ira Gershwin
Kern, Jerome
Musicals (Stage & Screen)
Porgy and Bess
Porter, Cole
Operettas
Rockefeller Center (Radio City)
Rodgers & Hart (Richard Rodgers & Lorenz
    Hart)
Stage Productions (Drama)
Welles, Orson

TRAVEL
Airships
Auto Camps
Automobiles
Aviation
Buses
Century of Progress Exposition (Chicago
    World's Fair)
China Clippers

N

NATIONAL BARN DANCE, THE. Country **music**, both live and recorded, began to make its first appearances on **radio** stations in the mid- to late 1920s. WLS, a Chicago-based station owned by merchandising giant Sears, Roebuck and Company (the call letters stand for World's Largest Store), first broadcast a program called *The Barn Dance* in 1924. The creation of George Dewey Hay (1895–1968), one of the early promoters of country music for radio, the show proved a commercial success. *The Barn Dance* would continue its run on WLS until 1933, when the National Broadcasting Company (NBC radio) picked it up for network transmission. NBC, with its coast-to-coast hookups, changed the name to *The National Barn Dance* and retained the show until 1942. During the Depression years, Alka-Seltzer, a popular pain remedy, provided continuous sponsorship, which suggests a sizable listenership and continuing sales. Hay, in the meantime, moved on to Nashville, Tennessee, in 1925. There he created **Grand Ole Opry**, another successful and long-running country music show modeled on *The National Barn Dance*.

Many sources provided the music played on *The National Barn Dance*. A true variety show, country tunes dominated, but **swing** and pop numbers had their place, along with plenty of silliness, Regulars on the show included, among many others, the vocal duet of Lulubelle (b. Myrtle Cooper, b. 1913; active 1930s) and Scotty Wiseman (1909–1981), her husband; Henry Burr (active 1930s), a crooner; and the Hoosier Hot Shots, a comedy quartet that enjoyed considerable regional popularity. Originally in vaudeville, the Hot Shots came to prominence in 1933 after their exposure on *The National Barn Dance*, and soon ranked as one of the top musical novelty acts of the day. In addition to vocalizing and onstage antics, they employed a slide whistle and clarinet as their lead instruments, with a washboard for rhythm, creating a sound that might be classified as hillbilly hokum. Their repertoire included such numbers as "From the Indies to the Andes in His Undies," "I Like Bananas Because They Have No Bones," and "The Coat and the Pants Do All the Work." Audiences loved them all, making the Hot Shots the precursors of groups like Spike Jones (1911–1965) and His City Slickers.

The show billed itself as a "barn dance," and it lived up to its title. Inside the studio, callers provided instructions to onstage square dancers, and stations broadcast the action into homes everywhere. For those raised in the age of **television**, such a radio concept may be difficult to imagine, but the dancers' invisibility proved no problem to the listening audiences of the day. In addition to the musical acts and the dancing, various comedians performed their routines, and everyone appeared in costume for the studio audience. The show soon outgrew WLS's limited facilities and had to move to a large Chicago theater, but it continued to be associated with the radio station.

Movie tickets cost only a dime in the 1930s (roughly $1.50 in contemporary money), but it took 90 cents (about $14) to gain entrance to *The National Barn Dance*, making it both expensive and one of the few radio programs of that era to charge admission. Even in the dark days of the Depression, it required months of waiting to obtain a reservation to the popular show.

See also Advertising; Hillbillies; Movies; Radio Networks

SELECTED READING

Dunning, John. *On the Air: The Encyclopedia of Old-Time Radio.* New York: Oxford University Press, 1998.

Peterson, Richard A. *Creating Country Music: Fabricating Authenticity.* Chicago: University of Chicago Press, 1997.

NEW DEAL. March 4, 1933, saw **Franklin D. Roosevelt** (1882–1945) inaugurated as the 32nd president of the United States. Prior to taking office, he had assembled an administrative staff with a wide range of expertise and backgrounds—college professors, lawyers, businessmen, social workers—people who generated an unending stream of ideas and plans for addressing the crises of the Great Depression and its aftermath.

When first elected president, Roosevelt pledged to all Americans a "New Deal." Although evidence shows that this term had been employed politically in the Civil War era by a North Carolina journalist, a more direct etymology probably links the phrase to two other presidents, his cousin Theodore Roosevelt's (1858–1919) "Square Deal" and Woodrow Wilson's (1856–1924) "New Freedom." Plus, when one's luck runs poorly in cards, a "new deal" can be requested, and certainly the nation had hit a run of bad luck in the early 1930s.

During Roosevelt's first two weeks of office, his administration engineered banking and economic legislation that ended the banking crisis and drastically reduced federal expenditures by lowering government employees' salaries and veterans' pensions, money that a couple of months later would help underwrite unemployment relief programs. Also, in anticipation of the repeal of Prohibition, the Beer-Wine Revenue Act (1933) paved the way for additional monies through the sale of beer and light wines. For the next hundred days, March 9–June 16, Roosevelt and his team furiously worked to draft legislative proposals that offered relief to those experiencing the greatest hardships under one of the worst depressions in the country's history. Nothing less than a national effort to respond to

Frances Perkins (1882–1962), secretary of labor, the first woman to hold a U.S. cabinet post. (Courtesy of the Library of Congress)

basic human needs while preserving the American economic system, Roosevelt's New Deal made him more central to the life of the country than any previous president.

Government activities during the years 1933–1935, often referred to as the First New Deal, concentrated on the immediacy of relief to the unemployed and impoverished; they attempted to get nonworking Americans back to work, and to achieve economic recovery through national planning and controls. Roosevelt's so-called Second New Deal, which ran from 1935 until 1937, focused on social reform issues. The delivery system designed to carry out the phases of both New Deals consisted of new federal agencies that shifted power to the national government and away from local and state governments. Sometimes called "alphabet agencies" because of the frequent use of just the first letters of each word in their full name, these groups brought about increased scrutiny and regulation of nearly every aspect of American life.

The chart below lists some of the agencies that provided immediate relief for many, along with others that established reform policies and procedures affecting Americans long after the end of the 1930s.

Program	Description	Dates
AAA (Agriculture Adjustment Administration)	A part of the U.S. Department of Agriculture, it subsidized farmers for reducing crops and also provided them loans to avoid bankruptcy, particularly for those living in the Dust Bowl. In 1936, the Supreme Court found some parts of the Agriculture Adjustment Act unconstitutional. With some changes, the act remained in effect until 1945, when other government programs assumed its functions.	1933–1945
CCC (Civilian Conservation Corps)	One of the New Deal's most successful programs, this public works/environmental effort put 2.5 million unmarried, unemployed men to work maintaining and restoring forests, as well as constructing roads, bridges, buildings, parks, and the like.	1933–1942
CWA (Civil Works Administration)	It provided jobs building or repairing roads, parks, playgrounds, airports, schools, etc., and received its funding from the PWA (Public Works Administration). By early 1934 it had put 4.2 million men and women to work. The WPA (Works Progress Administration), founded in 1935, absorbed many of its functions.	1933–1934
DRS (Drought Relief Service)	This service bought cattle from designated counties and gave those fit for human consumption to the Federal Surplus Relief Corporation to be used in food distribution to families nationwide.	1935
FCA (Farm Credit Administration)	Established by executive order, the FCA extended relief to debt-ridden farmers, coordinated loans to refinance farm mortgages, and offered credit. It saved tens of thousands of farms from foreclosure, and nine existing farm agencies came under its control.	1933–present
FCC (Federal Communication Commission)	A replacement for the Federal Radio Commission, the FCC had jurisdiction over **radio**, telegraph, wire, cable operations, and, by extension, **television** and other forms of new communication.	1934–present

Program	Description	Dates
FDIC (Federal Deposit Insurance Corporation)	The federal government insured individual bank accounts for the first $100,000.	1933–present
FERA (Federal Emergency Relief Administration)	A work relief program, it sent $3 billion to depleted local relief agencies and also funded public works programs.	1933–1935
FHA (Federal Housing Administration)	This long-lived program provided federal insurance for private mortgages to protect creditors against default and encouraged banks to loan money for new construction, renovation, and repairs. The FHA also rated neighborhoods as to level of risk, which resulted in areas with high concentrations of racial minorities being designated too risky to receive assistance. In 1965, it became HUD (Housing & Urban Development).	1934–1965
FNMA (Federal National Mortgage Association)	Still in existence and popularly known as Fannie Mae, it tried to increase the availability of mortgage credit to stimulate home construction and ownership.	1938–present
FSA (Farm Security Administration; see also Resettlement Administration [RA])	Succeeding the Resettlement Administration, the FSA functioned as a division within the Department of Agriculture. It financed farm improvements and maintained migrant labor camps. As a public awareness effort, the FSA sponsored photographers who captured a pictorial record of the hardships created by the Great Depression.	1937–1943
FWA (Federal Works Agency)	The result of a wide-ranging administrative reorganization by President Roosevelt to bring public works projects under one entity, the FWA combined the PWA (Public Works Administration) and the WPA (Works Progress Administration) into a single organization, although the WPA continued with many of its projects.	1939–1943
HOLC (Home Owners Loan Corporation)	This agency enabled people to refinance their mortgages under supervision of the Federal Home Loan Bank Board and save their homes from foreclosure. At the time of its closing, it had provided money for some 1 million mortgages.	1933–1936
NLRB (National Labor Relations Board)	Created by the Wagner Act, it provided government protection for laborers to exercise their right to organize and engage in collective bargaining.	1935–present
NRA (National Recovery Administration)	Organized under terms of the NIRA (National Industrial Recovery Act) to stimulate competition & benefit producers, the NRA implemented various codes to establish fair trade. It addressed unemployment and inadequate income by regulating the number of hours worked per week and setting a minimum wage. The program ended when declared unconstitutional by the U.S. Supreme Court. Its Blue Eagle logo may be the most famous icon of the Great Depression.	1933–1935

Program	Description	Dates
NYA (National Youth Administration)	Implemented by the WPA, this program kept young men and women in school or college through apprenticeships or work. It held camp and resident programs to teach homemaking and vocational skills to those who had dropped out of school.	1935–1943
PWA (Public Works Administration)	This agency launched public works projects across the United States, such as post offices, schools, dams, tunnels, airports, and bridges. It also supported conservation practices of farmers in the Dust Bowl. The PWA merged with the FWA (Federal Works Administration) in 1939.	1933–1939
RA (Resettlement Administration; see also Farm Security Administration [FSA])	Designed to help farm families relocate and furnish them with loans, its programs became better known under the name FSA.	1935–1937
REA (Rural Electrification Administration)	Created by executive order to help bring electricity to areas where it was previously unavailable. Once installed, rural families could buy and use small appliances such as irons and radios.	1935–1994
SEC (Security Exchange Commission)	By regulating security transactions, it protected the public against fraudulent actions in the securities markets.	1934–present
TVA (Tennessee Valley Authority)	The authority built dams and power plants along the Tennessee River to bring electric power, and with it industry, to rural areas in seven states.	1933–present
WPA (Works Progress Administration; in 1939, name changed to Work Projects Administration)	The era's most famous program, it affected many people's lives as it addressed both the country's infrastructure and cultural activities. Its construction and repair projects included roads, bridges, schools, hospitals, airfields, etc. One division, Federal Project Number One and its affiliated programs, the **Federal Art Project**, **Federal Music Project**, **Federal Theatre Project**, and the **Federal Writers' Project**, provided employment for artists, musicians, actors, & writers.	1935–1943

In 1933, Congress passed the National Industrial Recovery Act (NIRA), which had as its administrative arm the National Recovery Administration (NRA). The NRA stands as one of the most ambitious undertakings of the 1930s. It met with vociferous opposition as it attempted to oversee the implementation of codes and agreements restricting competition, control working conditions and sales, and boost declining prices. For many, the NIRA represents the signature agency of the First New Deal. Numerous opponents charged this agency with being un-American, socialist, even Communist. During early 1935, opposition to the policies of the NRA increased, and in May 1935 the U.S. Supreme Court entered the fray. It ruled that Title I of the NIRA gave an invalid delegation of legislative power to the president and thus served as an

Editorial cartoonists delighted in lampooning President Roosevelt (1882–1945) and New Deal policies. (Courtesy of the Library of Congress)

unconstitutional regulation of intrastate commerce. The court's ruling brought an end to the program.

A stylized Blue Eagle patterned on Native American thunderbird designs, along with the legend, "We Do Our Part," served as a symbol of compliance with NRA codes during its brief history. Displayed everywhere, it became a famous Depression-era logo. Roosevelt, more than any president before him, understood the power of media and regularly used **newspapers** and radio broadcasts to communicate with the American public. He introduced the Blue Eagle in one of his famous Fireside Chats at the end of July 1933, urging consumers to shop only at businesses **advertising** the symbol.

Another contentious issue revolved around the public ownership and regulation of utilities. The arguments date back to the World War I era. Congress approved, with little hesitation, the Tennessee Valley Authority (TVA) in 1933, and the project immediately had its critics. Although it provided many Americans with electricity for the first time, created jobs for thousands of unemployed construction workers, and brought electricity and industry to an impoverished part of the country, the program outraged private power companies.

The New Deal suffered unending criticism on many fronts. For example, Father Charles E. Coughlin (1891–1979), a Catholic priest who broadcast weekly over an independent network, at first supported the New Deal. In time, however, he became a vocal critic of the alphabet agencies, particularly the Agricultural Adjustment Administration (AAA) and its tactics of limiting overproduction by plowing under crops and slaughtering livestock.

Many politicians were numbered among the nay-sayers. Huey Long (1893–1935), governor of Louisiana and later a U.S. senator, initially endorsed the New Deal, but he soon found it too conservative and believed that Roosevelt had given in to big business. Governor Floyd B. Olson (1891–1936) of Minnesota declared himself a socialist and tried to build a third political party that advocated collective ownership as the best means of production and distribution. But criticism seldom discouraged Roosevelt; he liked to say, "Do something. And when you have done that something, if it works, do it some more. And if it does not work, then do something else." In the long run, Roosevelt's supporters outvoted his critics, electing him to a record four terms as president that ran from 1932 until his death in 1945.

The "something else" did occur regularly. Of all the alphabet agencies, the Works Progress Administration (WPA), formed in 1935 during the Second New Deal, gained the reputation as the most famous and far-reaching. It promoted both economic relief and reform. Although by law it could not compete with private business, the WPA, over its seven-year history, employed about 8.5 million Americans and made work available through a multitude of construction and cultural projects.

The Farm Security Administration (FSA), charged with enabling sharecroppers and migrants to purchase land, came into existence in 1937 when the already-existing Resettlement Administration (RA) moved to the Department of Agriculture. The FSA wanted to increase public awareness about the problems faced by migrants, and to accomplish this, it sponsored a documentary **photography** program. The agency hired photographers like Walker Evans (1903–1975), Dorothea Lange (1895–1965), Ben Shahn (1898–1969), and Arthur Rothstein (1915–1985) to document pictorially the consequences of the Great Depression on American life in specific geographic areas of the country. Their stark black-and-white photographs provide a moving record of hardship and deprivation.

The New Deal addressed economic issues and the provision of relief and reform at a time when many struggled with unemployment and others feared they would be the next ones out of work. But despite these uncertainties, Americans continued to be optimistic about the future and went about "life as usual." The New Deal played a significant role in the life of the nation, but it cannot be called a revolution, nor did it end the Great Depression. It told farmers what they could and could not plant; it permitted laborers to vote in federal elections for union representation; it collected income taxes for the federal government for the first time; it closely monitored banking and securities operations; and it told employers what they had to pay their employees and, for a short time, how much could be produced. Almost every U.S. community has a lasting New Deal artifact: an improved public park, a public housing project, a high school stadium, a bridge, a post office with murals depicting a local historic event, a city symphony.

The New Deal set the tone for social change, causing the federal government to play an increasingly active role in the nation's social welfare. The program called for fundamental reforms in society, not just relief of the symptoms of social and economic problems. Although critics of the New Deal saw it as interference, a strongly Democratic Congress passed controversial legislation that strove for an improved future, assisted both business and labor, and altered the relationship between government and private enterprise.

See also Alcoholic Beverages; Automobiles; Education; Fads; Political Parties; Racial Relations & Stereotyping; Radio Networks; Prohibition & Repeal; Transportation; Travel; Youth

SELECTED READING

Kennedy, David M. *Freedom from Fear: The American People in Depression and War, 1929–1945.* New York: Oxford University Press, 1999.

Leuchtenburg, William E. *Franklin D. Roosevelt and the New Deal.* New York: Harper & Row, 1963.

Perkins, Dexter. *The New Age of Franklin Roosevelt, 1932–1945.* Chicago: University of Chicago Press, 1957.

Schlesinger, Arthur M., Jr. *The Age of Roosevelt.* 3 vols. Vol. 1, *The Crisis of the Old Order, 1919–1933.* Vol. 2, *The Coming of the New Deal, 1933–1935.* Vol. 3, *The Politics of Upheaval, 1935–1936.* New York: Houghton Mifflin, 1957–1960.

NEWSPAPERS. Throughout the nineteenth century and on into the twentieth, newspapers ruled supreme; they functioned as far and away the primary American mass medium. **Magazines**, important to be sure, occupied a distant second place. With the onset of the 1930s, new media—**radio**, and to a lesser degree, **movies**—arose to challenge that supremacy, and for the first time the press felt the sting of real competition. Readership and circulation, however, remained strong during the decade, even showing increases during that difficult time. Not until after World War II did these and other electronic media significantly cut into newspapers' seemingly impregnable lead.

During the 1920s, the nation boasted over 2,500 daily newspapers. By 1930, it could still claim 1,942 dailies at a time when the nation's population stood at more than 123 million people. By 1940, the newspaper figure had fallen to 1,878 dailies, whereas the population had risen to nearly 132 million. So, the actual number of daily newspapers had been steadily falling, albeit slowly. Some of this loss could be accounted for by mergers or consolidation, but some papers failed because of the economy, a situation that caused **advertising** revenues to fall. Readership, however, continued to climb, rising from 40 to 41 million throughout the decade. Over 33 million households received or purchased at least one paper a day. The apparent difference between 41 million (readers) and 33 million (households) means that many individuals or families received more than one daily paper. If two or three people read each issue, more than half the nation looked at a newspaper on a regular basis. Thus, although newspapers themselves declined in number, their readers remained faithful to the medium throughout the decade, apparently finding it an essential source of news and entertainment.

An additional set of figures paints another story: in 1940, the population had risen to almost 132 million, an increase of roughly 8 million over 1930, or about 7 percent. The circulation increase from 40 to 41 million readers totals less than 3 percent. Taking circulation and population together, even the gradual population growth rose at a faster rate than readership. Despite their modest gains in circulation, newspaper readership on the basis of total population in reality went through a slow but steady decline.

Other factors also affected the newspaper industry. With the country falling more deeply into the Depression, the effects of the calamity quickly became apparent as the number of advertisements appearing in papers plummeted: 15 percent fewer in 1930, 24 percent in 1931, and then whopping drops of 40 and 45 percent in 1932 and 1933, the two bleakest years of the economic turndown. Statistics like these made still more advertisers retreat, either by reducing the number and kind of ads they ran, or, as was often the case, finding other venues or ceasing to advertise at all.

In 1929, newspapers made a record-setting $860 million in advertising revenues (roughly $10 billion in contemporary dollars). By 1933, that figure had shrunk to $470 million ($7 billion). A slow comeback began in mid-decade, then stalled during the 1938 recession. By 1939, advertising expenditures of $552 million ($8 billion) meant they had risen only to 1920 levels, figures nowhere close to those of 1929. Generally, smaller papers suffered most from this decline in advertising, both in numbers of ads and revenues.

A recovery of sorts took place in the remaining years of the decade, but it could not equal the successes of the late 1920s. In many ways, the newspaper business changed significantly during the Depression. The flush times of the twenties had imbued American newspapers with a sense of never-ending prosperity, a feeling that readership and advertising volume would continue to rise with each passing year.

Nevertheless, 1939's advertising figure of $552 million remains a significant sum. Newspaper ads took well over a third of what American firms spent for advertising in all media during the decade. Such large numbers demand a certain perspective: in 1930, newspapers took about 48 percent of the national advertising dollar; by 1940 their share had fallen to 36 percent, but that still translates as more than one-third of the total. During the same period, magazines consistently averaged 8 to 10 percent of the ad dollar. The relatively new—and growing—electronic medium of radio can be blamed for most of this decline for newspapers. In 1930, radio could claim only about 3 percent of the advertising dollar; by 1940 its share had soared to 20 percent, and most of that at the expense of newspapers.

Radio probably did more damage to the newspaper business than did the Depression. Newspapers might have once been the average citizen's first choice for news, but omnipresent radios provided a ready source for late-breaking stories. Radio took up an increasing portion of ad revenue, gave instantaneous updates of the news, provided live sporting events, consistently entertained—and it came into homes for free. Radio's popularity skyrocketed during the 1930s, going from 14 million home receivers in 1930 to over 44 million by 1940. No commensurate gains occurred in the newspaper industry. Many newspapers acquired radio stations as a way to stay profitable. Publishers saw their erstwhile rival as a surefire moneymaker, and invested in stations accordingly. In 1930, newspaper interests owned about 90 stations; by 1940, 250 stations claimed affiliations with newspaper publishing companies.

Other forces also conspired to affect newspaper profitability. During the 1930s, most cities of over 100,000 population claimed at least two rival papers; by 1940, 25 cities had lost that kind of lively competition and had become one-newspaper towns. Even New York City, that most competitive of newspaper sites and home to many famous papers, felt the change. Early in the century, it had boasted some 20 dailies. It still possessed nine at the onset of the 1930s, but by 1940 the number had fallen to seven. Those places that continued to have two or more papers usually claimed both morning and evening editions. The majority came out in the evening (or late afternoon); the morning newspaper did not achieve dominance until the 1980s.

Unlike most other developed nations, the United States never published a true national newspaper until the rise of the *Wall Street Journal* and *USA Today* in the latter part of the twentieth century. Whereas most books and magazines enjoy nationwide distribution, the vast majority of newspapers claim at best a limited regional audience. For the 1930s, that meant that while countless people across the country read a newspaper and shared world and national stories, the state and local articles, along with ads and features, that someone in St. Louis saw would surely differ from the choices in Seattle or Philadelphia. Although journalism scholars classify newspapers as a mass medium, in their individual formats they go through changes both obvious and subtle.

Coupled with all the different local editions came chain ownership. A chain consists of several papers linked in a financial relationship that allows for savings in materials and labor, and can even mean sharing staff and facilities. In 1900, eight American chains existed, controlling 27 papers; by the mid-1930s, some 60 chains exerted control over 300 papers, mostly large enterprises that accounted for 40 percent of total circulation.

As a rule, most of these linked papers could be found in populous urban areas, and names like Scripps-Howard, Gannett, Hearst, and Cox became leaders in chain ownership. The days of the independent daily, free of any outside influences, were numbered. Hearst, the largest of the chains at the time, owned 26 dailies and 17 Sunday papers in 1935 (or 14 percent and 24 percent of total circulation, respectively). The Hearst endeavors also encompassed 13 magazines, 8 radio stations, 2 movie studios, and 2 wire services. William Randolph Hearst (1863–1951), one of the last great press lords and the founder of this empire, had a personal worth of about $250 million (or roughly $3.6 billion in today's dollars), making him one of the richest men in the world.

Newspapers increasingly began to feature briefer, more compartmentalized stories in the 1930s, an acknowledgment of the success of newsmagazines like *Time*, *Life*, and *Newsweek*. And, despite their drops in revenue, most big-city papers expanded their operations. With considerable controversy raging in the nation's capital about President **Franklin D. Roosevelt** (1882–1945) and the **New Deal**, newspaper bureaus located in Washington experienced rapid growth. As a new war in Europe loomed, a similar expansion occurred in overseas coverage.

Given the excitement in Washington and foreign countries, smaller papers immediately felt themselves at a disadvantage. They could ill afford to staff bureaus in cities far from their home bases. Thus news syndicates like the Associated Press (AP) and United Press (UP) enjoyed tremendous growth. For a subscription fee, they could supply the reporters and detailed stories a small, independent newspaper could not hope to provide. Although both the AP and the UP trace their beginnings to the late nineteenth century, not until the 1930s did they come into their own. With more and more national and international news to cover, only the far-flung syndicates could consistently file stories for their growing lists of subscribers.

Widespread syndication brought about a certain amount of standardization in the American press. The syndicated features found in one paper could easily be found in another. This lessened the insularity of small-town dailies, bringing them more into the mainstream of American life. Standardization occurred not just with news stories; **comic strips**, horoscopes, crossword puzzles, **contract bridge** columns, the latest Hollywood gossip, advice columnists, box scores, financial pages—these features appeared because of syndication. In fact, the comic pages gained the enviable reputation of being the single most popular feature in American dailies during the 1930s.

Driven by popular series like **Apple Mary**, **Blondie**, **Dick Tracy**, **Flash Gordon**, **The Gumps**, **Li'l Abner**, **Little Orphan Annie**, **Prince Valiant**, **Tarzan**, and **Terry and the Pirates**, the comics drew readers as never before. A mix of entertainment and escapism, their daily antics and adventures proved a perfect antidote to the dreary realities of the Depression.

The success of syndication led to the rise of the appropriately named "syndicated columnist." Consisting of writers who spurned reportorial objectivity and instead gave readers a lively, colorful style coupled with a subjective point of view, their pieces usually appeared on or near the editorial page. Not all syndicated columnists, however, shared space with editorials; many wrote nonpolitical pieces, and a mix of humorous, satirical, and even poetical writings resulted. A fair number commented on the passing scene. For example, O. O. McIntyre (1884–1938), one of the most widely syndicated writers of the decade, wrote a column he called "New York Day by Day." Although the title might suggest otherwise, his unpretentious approach seemed to appeal most to those living outside big cities. Franklin P. Adams (1881–1960), who signed his columns FPA, presented his many fans bits of poetry and urbane trivia in *The Conning Tower*, a much-quoted column he wrote for many years.

Some columnists relied on gossip and celebrity-watching for their appeal. **Walter Winchell** (1897–1972) probably ranks as the most famous (or notorious, depending on point of view) of this group. Over 1,000 papers, most a considerable distance from the Great White Way, carried his "On Broadway." Close on Winchell's heels, at least in popularity during the 1930s, were Louella Parsons (1884–1972) and Hedda Hopper (1890–1966). Both women contributed widely syndicated columns that focused almost exclusively on Hollywood and its stars. Their success helped spawn a number of movie magazines, ranging from the purely gossipy *Screen Romances* to the slightly more serious *Silver Screen*.

In addition to their newspaper work, both columnists could be heard on radio. Parsons hosted two productions, *The Louella Parsons Show* and *Hollywood Hotel*. The first, mainly interviews, ran intermittently from 1928 until 1931; the second, a mix of talent and gossip, premiered in 1934 and remained on the air until 1941. Not to be outdone, Hopper parlayed her fame and influence into the popular *Hedda Hopper Show*. A 15-minute mix of chatter and celebrities, it began in 1939 and ran until 1951.

Other columnists mixed gossip and political rumors, such as Drew Pearson (1897–1969) and Robert S. Allen (1900–1981) with their *Washington Merry-Go-Round*. This widely circulated column grew out of a book by the same name that they published anonymously in 1932. The success of the book, a collection of articles rejected by their respective newspapers, led to quick syndication by United Features, and even some radio time for the two men. From 1935 to 1940, they appeared on the Mutual Network with their investigative reports.

Other types of writers also enjoyed significant syndication. For example, First Lady **Eleanor Roosevelt** (1884–1962) penned a long-running column titled *My Day*. It began in 1935 and chronicled her thoughts and activities for many appreciative readers. The folksy Will Rogers (1879–1935), "the cowboy philosopher," wrote a daily paragraph on some current topic. The poet Edgar Guest (1881–1959) began contributing verse to his syndicate at the turn of the century. Over the next 60 years, he composed over 11,000 poems. By the advent of the 1930s, hundreds of papers subscribed to his wit and wisdom. Generations of newspaper readers enjoyed his poetry, usually lightly humorous and sentimental ("It takes a heap o' livin' in a house t' make it home"). It might be doggerel and damned by critics, but the audience seemed not to notice. Guest's immense readership testified to the roles simplicity and sentiment often play in popular culture.

Emily Post (1872–1960) provided the last word on etiquette; her column could be found in over 200 papers and she even had a radio show that premiered in 1931. Dorothy Dix (b. Elizabeth M. Gilmer, 1870–1951) and Beatrice Fairfax (b. Marie Manning, 1873–1945) wrote advice-to-the-lovelorn columns. Dix had the distinction of being the highest-paid woman columnist of the decade, while Fairfax got memorialized in song. In 1930, **George (1898–1937) and Ira Gershwin** (1896–1983) composed "But Not for Me." In the number, lyricist Ira Gershwin contributed the witty, "Beatrice Fairfax, don't you dare / Ever tell me she will care," probably the only mention of an advice columnist in the annals of American popular **music**. All three women grew into unofficial arbiters of manners and mores, their words anxiously studied by millions of readers who wanted to know about proper dining and dating etiquette.

Over time, American popular culture has reflected attitudes about newspapers by focusing on reporters, those individuals most associated with the medium. Neither journalistic standards nor writing ability play much role in these representations. Throughout the decade, Hollywood released a string of movies, some good, some bad, about newspapers and reporters, creating the stereotype of the fast-talking, wise-cracking reporter who always gets the story. Starting in 1931 with *The Front Page*, a film version of the Ben Hecht (1894–1964)–Charles MacArthur (1895–1956) play of the same name, the image of the busy newsroom, the harried editor, the race to make a deadline, and the constant chatter of all involved became the standard. *Platinum Blonde* (1931) features the most noted platinum blonde of the era, Jean Harlow (1911–1937), in a comedic romance with an ambitious reporter.

Over a dozen other newspaper/reporter pictures came tumbling out of the movie studios during this time. Titles like *Shriek in the Night* (1933), *Libeled Lady* (1936, and again starring Harlow), *Nothing Sacred* (1937), *The Thirteenth Man* (1937), *Too Hot to Handle* (1938), and *His Girl Friday* (1940) created a virtual genre of motion picture. The final film, *His Girl Friday*, brings the list full circle because the studio simply remade *The Front Page*, but this time featuring Cary Grant (1904–1986) and Rosalind Russell (1907–1976), whereas the original stars Adolphe Menjou (1890–1963) and Pat O'Brien (1899–1983). The newspaper reporter made a convenient character, and audiences obviously responded positively to such impersonations.

The 1930s revealed some chinks in the armor of the once mighty medium, although most editors and publishers would probably have denied it. Still the dominant source for news, advertising, and considerable entertainment, the loss of a handful of papers and a statistical decline in readership provided hints of things to come. For the decade, however, circulations remained strong and people looked to their daily papers for information and escape during the Great Depression.

See also Games; *Life* & *Fortune*; Radio Networks

SELECTED READING

Emery, Michael, Edwin Emery, and Nancy L. Roberts. *The Press and America: An Interpretive History of the Mass Media*. Boston: Allyn & Bacon, 1999.

Mott, Frank Luther. *American Journalism: A History, 1690–1960*. New York: Macmillan, 1962.

Schudson, Michael. *Discovering the News: A Social History of American Newspapers*. New York: Basic Books, 1978.

Wallace, Aurora. *Newspapers and the Making of Modern America: A History*. Westport, CT: Greenwood Press, 2005.

NEW YORK WORLD'S FAIR. Two world's fairs—one celebrating progress despite a debilitating economic depression, the other looking optimistically to the future amid the gathering shadows of war—anchor the beginning and the end of the 1930s. Both held in the United States, the 1933–1934 **Century of Progress Exposition** (Chicago World's Fair) and the 1939–1940 New York World's Fair rank as true extravaganzas, the greatest shows of the decade. Other **fairs and expositions** were held in the intervening years, but nothing equaled these two.

New York's World of Tomorrow commenced in the spring of 1939 and ran until the fall of 1940. Not even the German invasion of Poland in September 1939 caused its gates to close. Eventually some 45 million people would pay 75 cents apiece (roughly

$11 in contemporary money) for the privilege of attending, a stiff admission fee in those times. At the urging of New York's parks commissioner **Robert Moses** (1888–1981), planners sited the event on over 1,200 reclaimed marshland acres in an area called Flushing Meadows. Adjoining New York City and Long Island, the locale served as the Valley of Ashes in F. Scott Fitzgerald's (1896–1940) acclaimed novel *The Great Gatsby* (1925). Just the clearing and reclamation of the land took three years.

Officials laid out the entire festival in "zones," an idea much in vogue among futurists at the time. Visitors could choose among Commerce and Industry, Communication, Production and Distribution, Government, and **Food**. In addition, the promoters established an Amusements area; not actually a zone, this attraction gave people a respite from all the high-minded exhibits and allowed them a chance to see entertainment more on the level of a carnival sideshow.

Chicago's Century of Progress had starred Sally Rand (1904–1979) and her notorious fans; New Yorkers deserved at least as much. The midway featured animal freaks and lots of flesh and hokum, along with showman Billy Rose's (1899–1966) Aquacade, a showgirl-filled spectacle that featured swimmers Esther Williams (b. 1921), Eleanor Holm (1913–2004), and Johnny Weissmuller (1904–1984) plunging into a pool daily. In 1940, Buster Crabbe (1908–1983), replaced Weissmuller. Both Weissmuller and Crabbe had been Olympic swimmers, and later moved to acting. No strangers to celebrity, Weissmuller had achieved fame in a number of ***Tarzan*** movies, and Crabbe had attempted the role of the Ape Man in one also, as well as starring as space heroes Buck Rogers and ***Flash Gordon***.

In addition to the **swimming** shows, attendees could try the parachute jump, a 250-foot tower in the amusement area. Some 2 million daring visitors paid 40 cents apiece (almost $6.00 in contemporary money) to ascend the steel frame and then float to earth in colored parachutes.

Enthusiasm for the fair and its myriad offerings ran high. The Long Island Railroad delivered fairgoers to an ultramodern terminal where huge, 160-passenger Greyhound **buses**, designed by the renowned Raymond Loewy (1893–1986), ferried them to the various zones. To accomplish this, investors formed Exposition Greyhound Lines. All in all, workers paved over 65 miles of streets and footpaths to accommodate various modes of **transportation**. At night, the cool white glow of fluorescent tubes bathed the event, among the first large-scale public demonstrations of that form of lighting.

Upon entering, crowds encountered the towering, pure white Trylon and Perisphere, the official Theme Center for the event and the ubiquitous symbols of the Fair. The Trylon, a 700-foot needlelike pyramid, earned its name because of its derivation from a triangle and a pylon. The Perisphere, a giant, 200-foot hollow sphere that sat beside the Trylon, contained within its cavernous interior Democracity, a vast diorama of the utopian city of tomorrow. Conceived by industrial designer Henry Dreyfuss (1904–1972) and sponsored by U.S. Steel, Democracity gave visitors a glimpse of an ordered, prosperous future, one that might frighten a contemporary viewer with its legions of marching workers and their automaton-like precision. But in a nation still reeling from a depression and with the threat of World War II increasing almost by the minute, a picture of a strong, albeit militarized, America probably reassured many.

Visitors exited the Trylon and Perisphere via the "Helicline," a sloping walkway that placed them inside the fairgrounds; from there they could choose from endless exhibits.

Much of the fair served as a celebration of the American automobile, and so the Commerce and Industry Zone included, as a broad topic, "transportation."

General Motors, Ford, and Chrysler responded by mounting enormous displays. Noted designer Norman Bel Geddes (1893–1958) fashioned "Futurama" for General Motors, creating a technological landscape circa 1960. Viewers relaxed in moving chairs that took them past a vast network of half a million miniaturized buildings and 50,000 motor vehicles, 10,000 of which actually moved. This utopian vision placed the automobile in a position of dominance, a rather accurate prognostication that enthralled over 10 million visitors and turned out to be the fair's most popular attraction.

Not to be outdone, the Ford Motor Company sponsored "The Road of Tomorrow," the work of architect Albert Kahn (1869–1942) and designer Walter Dorwin Teague (1883–1960). Although it drew significant crowds, the Ford pavilion never approached the numbers that rival General Motors achieved.

If an urban, automotive culture turned out to be a major element of the fair, **Streamlining** certainly served as the primary motif. It translated as leaving the roughhewn past behind, of progressing into the sleek, smoothly running future. Streamlining emerged as an economic metaphor. A "sticky" economy gives way to a "frictionless" one, and urbanity replaces rusticity. With the aid of "consumer engineering," science and technology could bring an end to underconsumption. People would flock to carefully designed products that looked ahead and symbolized an end to drudgery. This vision embraced consumerism, a future filled with new appliances and the blessings of industry.

The New York World's Fair profoundly influenced cultural thinking, especially in the areas of **architecture** and **design**. The extravaganza represented the work of some of the fields' most distinguished professionals, and almost without exception the corporate might of the country—Du Pont, General Electric, the Pennsylvania Railroad, AT&T, Shell Oil, IBM, and many others—underwrote their efforts. On a scale never before seen, the entire operation signified a three-way marriage among industry, commerce, and the arts. Promoters proclaimed, lest there be any doubt, that they hoped to bring together architecture and commerce, to show that modernity, industrial design, and popular culture could coexist. As a result, virtually nothing in the fair escaped commercialization. Observers noted that the merchandising of souvenirs alone exceeded anything attempted in previous fairs. Over 25,000 different items bore the festival's official imprint of the Trylon and Perisphere, ranging from a dainty Heinz pickle to a pin proclaiming "Time for Saraka," a popular laxative that somehow gained space at the exposition.

The U.S. Post Office issued a 3-cent commemorative stamp (in contemporary money, the stamp would cost roughly 40 cents), and the illustrious songwriting team of **George** (1898–1937) **and Ira Gershwin** (1896–1983) penned an "official" song of the Fair, "Dawn of a New Day." George's part consisted of scraps of **music** written before his death and pieced together by Ira with the assistance of Kay Swift (1897–1993). Hardly the greatest song of the decade, several of the era's leading bands nonetheless recorded it, given the interest and enthusiasm surrounding the proceedings. With the fair's second year and the world at war, the naive optimism of "Dawn of a New Day" seemed inappropriate, and officials commissioned a new anthem. Taking a cue from the event's 1940 slogan, "For Peace and Freedom," the musical director, Eugene LaBarre (active 1930s and 1940s), hastily composed a song of the same name.

More important than trinkets or baubles or lyrics, however, were the global products and world cultures promoted during the fair's two-year run. Despite the bow to world-wide customs, the emphasis remained on American themes, and designers presented them employing the rhetoric of spectacle, especially the mastery of the machine. A mammoth cash register, a giant typewriter, Democracity, the Trylon and Perisphere themselves—nothing escaped exaggeration and enlargement. Big equaled better. The many futuristic pavilions celebrated American corporate might; their symbolism presented American technocracy as the savior of the world. And with that world falling hopelessly and helplessly toward World War II, it provided a message that audiences very much wanted to hear.

By focusing on America's strengths, the New York World's Fair suggested that neither the Depression nor the threat of war could challenge the fundamental optimism generated by the exhibits. At the fair's conclusion, officials tore down the bulk of the displays and sold the scrap materials to lessen the debts incurred. Ironically, for an exhibition that claimed to stand "For Peace and Freedom," much of its scrap went for munitions and armaments.

See also Art Deco; Automobiles; Comic Strips; Olympic Games; Science Fiction; Trains

SELECTED READING

Appelbaum, Stanley. *The New York World's Fair, 1939–1940*. New York: Dover Publications, 1977.

Gelernter, David. *1939: The Lost World of the Fair*. New York: Avon Books, 1995.

Harrison, Helen A. *Dawn of a New Day: The New York World's Fair, 1939–1940*. New York: New York University Press, 1980.

Meikle, Jeffrey L. *Twentieth Century Limited: Industrial Design in America, 1925–1939*. Philadelphia: Temple University Press, 1979.

New York World's Fair. http://xroads.virginia.edu/w1930s/DISPLAY/39wf/taketour.htm

OLYMPIC GAMES. Over the span of the decade, two separate sets of Olympic games took place, each consisting of winter and summer events. In 1932, the Tenth Olympiad, the proper term for the games, took place with the United States serving as the host country. Four years later, Germany served as the site for the Eleventh Olympiad. The twelfth round had been scheduled for 1940 in Japan, but by then the Axis powers had plunged the world into war, blocking any festivities that year. Not until 1948 would the Olympic torch again be lit.

The Tenth Olympiad played Lake Placid, New York, for winter sports, and Los Angeles for summer events. Sonja Henie (1912–1969), a Norwegian figure skater who had competed in 1928, electrified crowds with her finesse on ice, making her a celebrity at the winter gathering. Several months later, despite the Depression and gnawing unemployment, another woman, Mildred "Babe" Didrikson (1911–1956), captured the summer spotlight with her skills in track and field. The anchor of the U.S. women's team, she won medals in the javelin throw, hurdles, and the high jump.

Henie's and Didrikson's victories occurred at a time when the press and various sports-related organizations questioned women's participation in sporting events. Of all the athletes assembled in Los Angeles for the 1932 games, only 120 women took part, compared to some 1,300 men. Numerous newspaper and magazine articles claimed that strenuous, highly competitive activities were "unladylike" and thus unbecoming to women. These old-fashioned attitudes would persist, albeit less vociferously, with the passage of time. Women like Henie and Didrikson led the way toward gender equality.

In the days prior to World War II, Olympic officials followed much stricter guidelines regarding the amateur status of competing athletes, both men and women, than they do today. If even the slightest hint of non-amateur activity surfaced, such as pay, gifts, endorsements, and the like, players would be disqualified and not allowed to participate in any events. For example, following Didrikson's Olympic victories, she allowed her name to be used in a sales promotion. When informed of her indiscretion, officials banned her from any future participation in the Olympics, a harsh punishment, but one that upheld the high standards of amateurism the games demanded.

By the time 1936 rolled around, the rules about amateur status remained firmly enforced, but the world's political realities had changed dramatically. Germany welcomed the Olympics with a new National Socialist, or Nazi, government in power, a

Track standout Jesse Owens (1913–1980) electrified audiences at the 1936 Olympics. (Courtesy of the Library of Congress)

change that signaled the intrusion of politics into the supposedly neutral games. The winter activities took place in Garmisch-Partenkirchen, a mountainous part of Bavaria. Racism and anti-Semitism overshadowed **skiing** and ice skating when Nazi officials attempted to ban non-Aryan (i.e., Jewish or nonwhite) athletes. The German efforts failed, but that did not prevent Chancellor Adolf Hitler (1889–1945) and his supporters from casting ugly slurs on those they opposed, providing a grim foretaste of the upcoming summer events in Berlin.

Despite the unpleasantness, the overwhelming majority of athletes had come to Germany to test their skills, not to represent ideologies. Sonja Henie again dominated on the ice. After her performances, she announced her retirement from active competition, a move that would allow her, at the peak of her fame, to go to Hollywood and pursue a lucrative career in **movies** built on her skating talents.

In the meantime, many nations threatened a boycott of the Berlin meet unless Hitler and the National Socialists toned down their rhetoric. Some parties even proposed a change in venue to Rome, Italy, but it failed to materialize when a substantial number of countries balked at the move. Nazi spokesmen piously promised improved behavior, although the world should have known better.

Amid politically tinged spectacle—swastikas everywhere, uniformed and regimented party members, martial music, nonstop Nazi propaganda—the August games got under way in Berlin. Numerous Jewish athletes had been denied participation, not by the Germans, but by their own tremulous coaches and governments, fearful of German hostility and criticism. The American team happened to include some outstanding Jewish and black athletes, and Nazi authorities tried to have them banned. Their ploy failed, however, and one black American in particular, Jesse Owens (1913–1980), stole the show.

Owens, a track and field star from Ohio State University, and already a world record holder in several events, collected individual gold medals in the 100-meter, 200-meter, and long jump, and as a member of the 400-meter sprint relay team. He not only won, but he also set world records in two of the events (long jump and 200-meter) and tied the world record in a third (100-meter).

This public blow to the Nazis' theories of Aryan superiority delighted everyone but the Nazis themselves. In a show of petulance, Hitler would not meet Owens, nor would he present him his medals, and so the 1936 Berlin Summer Olympics closed under rapidly darkening political clouds. For the world at large, the Nazis stood exposed, a party of racists and anti-Semites, but the failure of most nations to take a strong stand against this bullying behavior encouraged Hitler and his followers to continue such policies.

Out of all this came a masterful documentary movie about athletes and the Olympics. Leni Riefenstahl (1902–2003), a German filmmaker, created *The Olympiad* (1938), a two-part record of the 1936 Berlin Olympics. Much criticism has been leveled at Riefenstahl's work, most of which revolves around the charge that her documentary contains too much pro-Nazi propaganda. *The Olympiad*, however, has outlasted Nazism and much of the rhetoric of World War II, and it can be seen today as a remarkable celebration of the human form and athleticism.

The obvious propaganda in the film—massed flags and Nazi emblems, a beaming Hitler and his followers, the adoring crowds—remains, but seems more muffled, a kind of theatrical background that disappears before the magnificence of the Olympic events themselves. Even Jesse Owens, perhaps the bête noire of Hitler and the National Socialists, has his day, running and jumping, the perfect foil to all the Aryan hatred that Nazism espoused. Riefenstahl made no attempt to belittle Owens's, or anyone else's, victories, and in fact, *The Olympiad* salutes athletes of all nations and all races.

Most American **movies** that deal with the Olympics during the 1930s fall short when compared to Riefenstahl's epic work. They tend to focus on melodrama or comedy and miss much of what the Olympics really are about. *Charlie Chan at the Olympics* (1937) says it all; Swedish-born Warner Oland (1879–1938) plays the popular Asian detective in makeup, just as he had done more than a dozen times during the decade. A potboiler, this film does at least use the Berlin games as its background. *Million Dollar Legs* (1932) features comedian W. C. Fields (1880–1946) performing as the president of Klopstokia, a small, fictitious European country. Klopstokia wants to participate in the Olympics, and the rest of the plot involves wacky stratagems to achieve that goal; it may be good comedy, but it has little to do with the Olympic spirit.

See also Ice Skating & Hockey; Magazines; Newspapers; Race Relations & Stereotyping

SELECTED READING
Brant, Marshall. *The Games*. New York: Proteus, 1980.
Coote, James. *A Picture History of the Olympics*. New York: Macmillan, 1972.
Guttmann, Allen. *The Olympics: A History of the Modern Games*. Urbana: University of Illinois Press, 1992.
Olympics. http://www.ushmm.org/museum/exhibit/online/olympics

OPERETTAS. Although the operetta (or "light opera") form has seldom generated much enthusiasm in the United States, for a few brief years Jeanette MacDonald (1903–1965) and Nelson Eddy (1901–1967) made it their personal cinematic property. MacDonald, already a minor musical star, had attracted attention costarring with Dennis King (1897–1971) in a 1930 film adaptation of *The Vagabond King*, an operetta penned by Rudolf Friml (1879–1972) for a Broadway show in 1925. She followed that with a 1934 movie of *The Merry Widow*, a worked originally written by Franz Lehar (1870–1948) for a 1925 stage production. Both **movies** apparently exceeded expectations, because filmmakers decided to try more of the same.

MacDonald and Eddy commenced their collaboration with a surprisingly successful 1935 version of Victor Herbert's (1859–1924) *Naughty Marietta*, a vehicle he had composed for the stage in 1910. A box-office hit, the pair teamed up again in 1936 for a Hollywood interpretation of Rudolph Friml's *Rose-Marie*, another operetta that Friml had composed for the stage in 1924. Possibly their most successful outing, the film includes "Indian Love Call" (lyrics by Otto Harbach [1873–1963] and Oscar Hammerstein II [1895–1960]), the number most often associated with the "singing sweethearts."

For whatever reason—the **music**, the lavish costumes, the frothy plots, the escapism from the workaday world—Americans flocked to theaters showing these adaptations of traditional light opera. And so a new MacDonald-Eddy production became almost an annual event. In 1937, they appeared in Sigmund Romberg's (1887–1951) *Maytime*, which had first appeared on stage in 1917. The following year, 1938, saw them in Victor Herbert's *Sweethearts*, originally a 1913 stage presentation. MacDonald and Eddy also starred in *The Girl of the Golden West* (1938), a film scored by Sigmund Romberg, and loosely based on a 1910 opera, *La Fanciulla del West*, by Giacomo Puccini (1858–1924), which in turn had been taken from a 1905 play by David Belasco (1853–1931). In its cinematic form neither an opera nor an operetta, but more a Western drama with music, *The Girl of the Golden West* was one of their less successful endeavors.

The two vocalists graced theater screens in 1940 for *New Moon*, another Sigmund Romberg creation, this one originally produced in 1928 for the stage. By now, however, the magic had begun to wear thin. They nevertheless gave the format another try in 1940 with *Bitter Sweet*, a picture based on a 1929 stage operetta by Noel Coward (1899–1973). Unfortunately, the production finds both stars ill suited to the material, and *Bitter Sweet* marked the end of the brief period of popularity enjoyed by operettas. Undaunted, MacDonald and Eddy would reunite in 1942 for the limp *I Married an Angel*; and its lack of success spelled the end of their musical and cinematic collaboration.

Although both Jeanette MacDonald and Nelson Eddy possessed reasonably good voices, neither could claim outstanding acting abilities. Eddy, in particular, always seems wooden in front of the camera, redeeming himself only when he sings. As a result, MacDonald tends to get much more screen time, often carrying the wafer-thin plots for long periods without Eddy in sight. But for a time audiences overlooked these weaknesses, and the operetta briefly boasted two champions and innumerable fans.

See also Musicals; Western Films

SELECTED READING

Mordden, Ethan. *Sing for Your Supper: The Broadway Musical in the 1930s.* New York: Palgrave Macmillan, 2005.

Springer, John. *All Talking! All Singing! All Dancing! A Pictorial History of the Movie Musical.* Secaucus, NJ: Citadel Press, 1966.

P

PHOTOGRAPHY. By the 1930s, advances in the technologies of photography, coupled with a growing interest among consumers, spurred the increased home and commercial use of simple, easy-to-use cameras. Eastman Kodak, the nation's largest camera and film manufacturer, sensed a readiness for personal ownership of a small, inexpensive camera, and in 1934 introduced its point-and-shoot Baby Brownie. With a casing created by the distinguished designer Walter Dorwin Teague (1883–1960), Kodak marketed the Brownie as suitable for children and sold it for the rock-bottom price of $1 ($15 in contemporary dollars). The Brownie experienced strong sales and made amateur picture-taking more popular than ever. Throughout the 1930s, Kodak offered specialty editions, including Boy Scout and **New York World's Fair** models.

Kodak's promotion of amateur photography did not stop with still pictures; it had already introduced the first 8-mm motion picture camera, along with film and projector, in 1932. Four years later, the firm offered another home movie camera, the 16-mm Cine-Kodak, which featured film in magazines instead of rolls.

On another front, the amateur photographer traditionally had to rely on black-and-white film. In 1935, however, Kodak brought out Kodachrome transparency film in a 16-mm format for motion pictures. Color film for 35-mm slides and 8-mm home movies came on the market the next year. RCA, a competitor, led the way to sound photography by unveiling its sound-on-film in 1935, making talking home movies possible for the first time. Kodak entered the field in 1936 by offering its first 16-mm sound-on-film projector. Finally, for the serious hobbyist or photojournalist, improvements in flash techniques made picture-taking in low light a more reliable procedure.

While these developments advanced photography for the home enthusiast, the Associated Press initiated a wirephoto service in 1935 that allowed **newspapers** fast access to innumerable photographs of news events At the same time, an increasingly sophisticated use of photography occurred in the publishing field; about half of all American **magazines** employed photography as part of their **advertising** layouts, relying less and less on traditional painted illustrations. The high level of detail and realism found in most photographs conveyed strong impressions to consumers, suggesting to them what clothes they should wear, what they should eat, and the best car to drive. Edward Steichen (1879–1973), an important American photographer, worked during the 1930s as a **fashion**

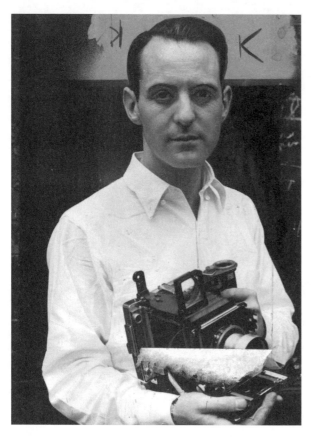

Sheldon Dick (active 1930s), one of the many photographers with the Farm Security Administration. (Courtesy of the Library of Congress)

photographer for magazines such as *Vogue, Harper's Bazaar*, and *Vanity Fair*. He made a name for himself and helped popularize photography for advertising purposes.

In 1936, Henry Luce (1898–1967), a leading magazine publisher, banked on the growing public interest in photojournalism by introducing *Life*, a weekly pictorial periodical. For the premiere issue, Margaret Bourke-White (1904–1971), the first woman photographer hired by the periodical, provided a picture essay that told the story of the lives of workers constructing Montana's Fort Peck Dam, a **New Deal** project. One of the pictures, a striking picture of the enormous dam in black-and-white, appeared on the cover. The magazine struck a chord with the public, and enjoyed immediate success. Many of the first photographers hired by Luce found a comfortable environment to pursue their craft, with the result that people like Alfred Eisenstadt (1898–1995) remained on *Life's* staff from 1936 to 1972, establishing a reputation as one of the primary figures in photojournalism as he did so.

While *Life*, after only four months of production, could claim sales of over a million copies weekly, in Washington, D.C., an even bigger photography story was unfolding under the management of Roy Stryker (1893–1975). The Resettlement Administration (RA; 1935–1937), established as one of President **Franklin D. Roosevelt**'s (1883–1945) New Deal alphabet agencies, assisted struggling farm families to relocate. Stryker, as chief of the RA's Historical Division, oversaw exhibits such as the 1938 First International Photographic Exposition at New York's Grand Central Palace and *The Way of the People* at **Rockefeller Center** in 1941, as well as a huge, ongoing agency-supported photojournalism project that resulted in publications, posters, and billboards.

When the name of the Resettlement Administration changed to the Farm Security Administration (FSA; 1937–1943), Stryker continued to hire and organize people, including both established American photographers and some new to the trade. He instructed them to take photographs that would document the agency's work and progress, and through their pictures endeavor to explain and define the conditions of the Great Depression. They photographed ordinary Americans in their everyday settings, portraying the spirit, strength, and courage displayed by people experiencing various hardships because of the economic crisis.

The FSA photographers hoped their black-and-white pictures of coal miners, sharecroppers, migrant mothers, farm couples, child laborers, immigrants, urban street scenes, and the destitute would convince government officials and others of the need to actively assist in easing the suffering being experienced by so many. This kind of photojournalism, sometimes called "social documentary," served to raise public awareness, and it also attempted to secure continuing funding for various New Deal efforts.

In addition to the FSA's Historical Division, other government groups, particularly the Department of the Interior and the Department of Agriculture, used photographs for a variety of purposes. Three factors distinguished the FSA photographers and their work from that of most other agencies. First, the FSA hired employees on the merits of their professional ability, not a need for a job. Second, agency pictures showed real problems and frequently hinted at solutions. Third, the FSA group worked to capture images that would be preserved as a permanent record of American history. Since 1944, the FSA photographs have been held by the Library of Congress in the Prints and Photographs Reading Room in Washington, D.C. The collection consists of approximately 77,000 images from the RA and the FSA years, as well as those from the Office of War Information (OWI; 1942–1943) and other government agencies.

Stryker started with a small number of photographers, but over his eight-year reign approximately 130 individuals participated in the project. Some of the most famous included Lewis Hine (1874–1940), Russell Lee (1903–1986), Carl Mydans (1907–2004), Gordon Parks (1912–2006), and Ben Shahn (1898–1969). Arthur Rothstein (1915–1985), another successful FSA photographer, eventually published a comprehensive overview of the country during the crisis with a mix of rural and urban images in *The Depression Years* (1978). In contrast to the desperate straits shown in a majority of the FSA work, Marion Post Wolcott's (1910–1990) pictures of Miami revealed that even in the Depression a few citizens had enough wealth for mansions and leisure time activities.

Some of the FSA photographers joined with writers to give an added dimension to their work. For example, Walker Evans (1903–1975) and critic James Agee (1909–1955) created *Let Us Now Praise Famous Men* (1939; revised 1941). For this landmark publication, the two focused on farm families and the dual hardships of the Dust Bowl and economic chaos. The husband-and-wife team of labor economist Paul Schuster Taylor (1895–1985) and photographer Dorothea Lange (1895–1965) worked on *An American Exodus* (1939), a record of human displacement on the Midwestern plains. Archibald MacLeish (1892–1982) published *Land of the Free* (1938), a book containing a poem by him and 88 photographs by Dorothea Lange, Walker Evans, Arthur Rothstein, and Ben Shahn. Most of the pictures came from the FSA project and address rural poverty and child labor.

Photographers outside government circles also actively participated in photojournalism. Margaret Bourke-White, like Walker Evans, photographed farm families dealing with hardships brought on by drought and economic difficulties. She collaborated with her husband, novelist **Erskine Caldwell** (1903–1987), to present these families' stories in *You Have Seen Their Faces* (1937). Photographer Berenice Abbott (1898–1991) received funds in 1935 from the Works Progress Administration (WPA, 1935–1943; name changed to Works Projects Administration in 1939) and its **Federal Art Project** (FAP, 1935–1943) to photograph New York City and published *Changing New York* in 1939. She joined fellow photographer Paul Strand (1890–1976), a committed socialist, to establish in 1936 the Photo League, a nonprofit organization for amateur and professional photographers. She and Strand worked to provide the radical press with pictures of trade union activities and political protests, and working class communities. Collectively, all these publications helped establish photojournalism as a legitimate literary form.

Even the movie industry became involved in photojournalism. Pare Lorentz (1905–1992) directed *The Plow That Broke the Plains* (1936), a documentary that deals with soil erosion and the resulting Dust Bowl. Paul Strand also assisted with this film. Another Lorentz film, *The River* (1938), addresses the importance of the Mississippi River to the United States and looks at the environmental effects when farming and industrial practices cause large amounts of topsoil to wash into the river. It features an outstanding musical score by the noted composer Virgil Thomson (1896–1989), as does *The Plow That Broke the Plains*.

A number of the photographers active during the 1930s gained recognition as artists in their own right. In 1932, several living on the West Coast—Edward Weston (1886–1958), Ansel Adams (1902–1984), Imogen Cunningham (1883–1976), Sonya Noskowiak (1900–1975), Henry Swift (1891–1962), Willard Van Dyke (1906–1986), and others—founded f/64, a group interested in presenting sharp images and maximum depth of field, which they called "pure" or "straight" photography. The name of the group refers to the smallest aperture on the lens of a large-format camera, which in turn gives the greatest depth of field. Members presented their work in many collective and one-person shows. Edward Weston also took photographs for the Federal Art Project in New Mexico and California in 1933 and received the first Guggenheim Fellowship for Photography in 1937.

Alfred Stieglitz (1864–1946), famous as a photographer long before the 1930s, operated a gallery in New York City called An American Place. He supported f/64 member Ansel Adams, with a one-man show in 1936. The decade saw art museums add photographic prints to their collections and the Museum of Modern Art in New York mounted a show of Walker Evans's photographs of **architecture** in 1934, following it with a second show in 1938. The Baltimore Museum presented Edward Steichen's noncommercial work in a 1938 exhibit. During 1940, the second year of the Golden Gate International Exposition in San Francisco, Ansel Adams organized a large retrospective show, The Pageant of Photography, which presented an overview of the craft as both science and art and featured changing exhibits of 17 artists including Paul Strand, Margaret Bourke-White, and Edward Weston.

Americans experienced a transition from a reading culture to a visual one during much of the decade. Newly founded magazines like *Look*, **Life**, and **Fortune**, with their many photographs, altered the country's reading habits. Also, technological advances introduced more people to amateur photography and cheaper printing techniques allowed for the mass production and increased availability of picture books and illustrated reading materials. Most important of all, professional photographers, both those with the FSA and others, left for future generations a graphic story of human events described by Roy Stryker as work that "introduced America to Americans."

See also Automobiles; Design; Fairs & Expositions; Illustrators; Music; Charles Sheeler; Social Realism

SELECTED READING

Guimond, James. *American Photography and the American Dream.* Chapel Hill: University of North Carolina Press, 1991.

Hulick, Diana Emery, with Joseph Marshall. *Photography: 1900 to the Present.* Upper Saddle River, NJ: Prentice Hall, 1998.

Hurley, F. Jack. *Portrait of a Decade: Roy Stryker and the Development of Documentary Photography in the Thirties.* Baton Rouge: Louisiana State University Press, 1972.

Peeler, David P. *Hope among Us Yet: Social Criticism and Social Solace in Depression America.* Athens: University of Georgia Press, 1987.

POLITICAL PARTIES. Throughout the twentieth century, the two major political parties—Democratic and Republican—dominated American politics. Opposing groups gained at best a tiny following and had little impact on legislation. From 1932 on, following the sweeping victory of **Franklin D. Roosevelt** (1882–1945), Democrats controlled both the executive and legislative branches of government. They greatly expanded the role of the federal government through **New Deal** legislative activities, and their actions generally met with broad popular approval. Only as the Depression lessened in severity during the late 1930s did their electoral support begin to decline, and then only gradually. In addition, the growing threat of war made many people want to "stay the course" with a trusted leader, an important factor in Roosevelt's 1940 victory.

Ideologically, most people viewed the Republican Party as more socially and financially conservative than the Democrats. When Republican **Herbert Hoover** (1874–1964) won the 1928 presidential election against Democrat Al Smith (1873–1944), the U.S. Congress divided as follows along party lines: 56 Republican senators and 39 Democrats; 267 Republican representatives and 163 Democrats. Hoover inherited a strongly Republican Congress, the party that had controlled the Senate since 1917 and the House since 1914. Hoover would continue enjoying a Republican-led Congress until the decisive, Depression-era presidential election of 1932, when Roosevelt easily defeated him. At the same time an overwhelming number of Democratic candidates for Congress beat their Republican counterparts.

Roosevelt took 57 percent of the popular vote in 1932, and 472 of the 531 available electoral votes. The makeup of Congress reflected this victory: 59 Democratic senators and 36 Republicans; 313 Democratic representatives and 117 Republicans. In four years' time, the party representation in both the executive and legislative branches of the federal government had undergone a complete reversal.

Roosevelt would repeat his landslide victory in 1936 when he campaigned against Republican Alfred M. Landon (1887–1987). This time around, he garnered 61 percent of the popular tally and 523 electoral votes, and again the results in Congress followed suit: 75 Democratic senators faced 17 Republicans, and 333 Democratic representatives faced 117 Republicans, thereby creating one of the most lopsided Congresses ever.

In 1940, running against Wendell Willkie (1892–1944), Roosevelt won an unprecedented third term with 55 percent of the popular vote and 449 electoral votes. Congress divided as follows: 66 Democratic senators against 28 Republicans, and 267 Democratic representatives against 167 Republicans. Although the Republicans had made some significant gains in 1940, they remained very much the minority party, a position they would retain until 1947, when they finally regained control of Congress.

Minority & Splinter Parties. While the Democrats and Republicans battled one another, a handful of other parties attempted to make their voices heard. No real third party emerged during the turbulent 1930s, despite the cries of many for change.

The Communist Party of the United States (CPUSA, or simply "the Party"), which had functioned in the country since the days of World War I, attained its greatest visibility during the Depression era, but it never seriously challenged either the Democrats or Republicans. With unemployment running high, many disaffected workers looked to the Party for support, but that support could not be translated into victory at the polls. Labor found some of the Party's promises—unemployment assistance, jobs for all, improved workers' rights—enticing, but the thought of Communist-led unions and any concomitant rise of socialism frightened management and government, with the result that those in power harshly put down any swings to the left.

William Z. Foster (1881–1961) served as titular head of the CPUSA in the early 1930s; after a heart attack, he was replaced by Earl Browder (1891–1973), who remained as chair until 1940. Although the Party continued its efforts to infiltrate the trade union movement throughout the decade, events abroad led it also to embrace Roosevelt and the New Deal as time went by. The outbreak of the Spanish Civil War in 1936 and the rise of fascism in Europe placed Communists everywhere on the side of most Western democracies, employing the theme of a "popular front" against their enemies.

The Spanish conflict found the Communists supporting the existing Loyalist government, whereas various fascist groups—especially Nazi Germany—rallied behind the right-wing revolt of General Francisco Franco (1892–1975). Often called a rehearsal for World War II, the bitter civil war drew hundreds of idealistic young Americans into the fray, and most of them fought with the Loyalist forces under the name of the Abraham Lincoln Brigades.

Part of the larger International Brigade, a group composed of volunteers drawn from many countries, the Abraham Lincoln fighters struck an emotional chord among citizens back home. Romanticized in popular media, their doomed efforts and high casualties only added to their mystique as "freedom fighters" against fascism. When the Loyalists ultimately lost to the Nationalists in early 1939, the disheartened young volunteers returned to the United States, certain that a new world war would soon follow.

While the Lincoln Brigades fought in Spain, at home both Foster and Browder, along with most of their associates, fell under the scrutiny of the **Federal Bureau of Investigation** (FBI). Many members of Congress ardently supported any investigations of Communist activities, and most media coverage of the Party tended to be negative. As a result, the Communist Party of the United States never rose to any real prominence, and many of its supporters found that Party membership meant imprisonment, loss of jobs, social ostracism, and harassment. Even when Russia and the United States stood together as allies in World War II, people looked askance at any open support for the American Communist Party, and in the 1940s and 1950s, the dark days of the Cold War, those who had once belonged, for whatever reasons, suffered relentless investigation.

The American Socialist Party, another labor-oriented group, lingered on the political sidelines throughout the 1930s. Not as controversial as the Communist Party, but also never a power in American politics, it boasted a number of mayors in Midwestern cities and little else. Formally organized in 1901, the party featured Eugene V. Debs (1855–1926) as one of its early leaders, and in five unsuccessful runs for the presidency (1900, 1904, 1908, 1912, and 1920) Debs gave voice to the organization in the first quarter of the twentieth century, drawing almost a million votes in each of his last two attempts. A reform-minded party, but lacking much of the radicalism associated with the

Communists, it espoused socialism. The organization almost disintegrated until Norman Thomas (1984–1968) assumed leadership and ran for president in 1928. Despite his losing candidacy, Thomas ran again in 1932, a time when some of the party's positions held considerable appeal.

In 1936, the American Socialist Party found itself adrift amid the liberal policies of the New Deal and actually came out in support of Roosevelt and many Democratic candidates for Congress. World War II saw most American Socialists united in their opposition to fascism but disorganized as a political entity, and the party failed to regain any popular strength in the general prosperity that followed the conflict.

An offshoot of the Socialist Party called itself the Farmer-Labor Party, and it claimed the upper Midwest, particularly Minnesota, as its stronghold. Formed in 1918, the group gained prominence when Floyd B. Olsen (1891–1936) became governor of Minnesota in 1931, an office he would hold until his death. A strong believer in state ownership of many businesses, most of his dreams failed to materialize; nonetheless he remained a popular politician. Despite Olsen's limited success, the Farmer-Labor Party never achieved national prominence and remained a regional phenomenon.

In neighboring Wisconsin, another Socialist-aligned party grew under the leadership of Robert "Fighting Bob" M. La Follette, Sr. (1855–1925). Nominally a Republican in his younger years, La Follette, with other liberal Republicans, formed the Progressive Party in 1924 when he ran for the presidency. Despite a strong showing, he lost. Although the party itself went out of existence, La Follette continued to battle for his principles.

His son Robert M. La Follette Jr. (1895–1953) carried on his father's traditions, and in 1934 revived the Progressive banner, calling it the Progressive Party of Wisconsin. His brother, Philip La Follette (1897–1965), became Wisconsin's governor that year, and in 1938 strove to widen the influence of the Wisconsin group still further when he formed the National Progressive Party of America, but the movement went nowhere. By the early 1940s, this attempt at a third party had disappeared.

Many other groups tried to make their political voices heard in the nation, but none met with any long-term success. In California, author Upton Sinclair (1878–1968) created a momentary wave of publicity in 1934 with his EPIC (End Poverty in California) crusade. The Great Depression, coupled with the Dust Bowl, had hit California hard, and Sinclair, a gubernatorial candidate, campaigned on a platform that promoted the idea of the state taking over idle factories in order to create jobs. Accused of being a socialist, or worse, a Communist, Sinclair nonetheless captured 37 percent of the vote. Following his defeat, he returned to private life, and EPIC faded away, a momentary reminder of that difficult time.

The Prohibition Party, born in 1869 with the avowed purpose of encouraging temperance, enjoyed its greatest moment in 1919 and the formal enactment of Prohibition throughout the country. After slightly more than a decade of enforced temperance, however, the nation rejected the restrictions on alcohol, and the party suffered from irrelevancy with the passage of the Twenty-first Amendment, or Repeal, in 1933. Since those high-flying days of Prohibition, the party has been a footnote in most political discussions, although it continues to soldier on, dutifully nominating a candidate for president every four years.

Not in the 1930s, nor in any other decade of the twentieth century, have any minority parties achieved any real political importance. They bring a certain amount of diversity to elections, and sometimes have served as spoilers in tightly fought contests. Their candidates usually offer significantly different approaches to issues, but seldom if ever do they win elections. Basically they alert people to alternatives, but occasionally irony comes into play when their disparaged ideas reappear in the platforms of mainstream Democrats and Republicans.

See also Alcoholic Beverages; Federal Theatre Project; Eleanor Roosevelt; Prohibition & Repeal; Social Consciousness Films

SELECTED READING
Election Results. http://www.uselectionatlas.org
Reichey, A. James. *Life of the Parties: A History of American Political Parties*. New York: Simon & Schuster, 1992.
Schlesinger, Arthur M., Jr. *History of United States Political Parties*. New York: Chelsea House, 1987.

POLO. Since it enjoys at best a limited (but growing) following today, it may come as something of a surprise to learn that many remember the 1930s as the golden age of American polo. An ancient game, with roots in Asia and the Middle East, it came belatedly to the U.S. in 1876. Since its introduction, the sport has been associated with wealth and leisure, with country clubs and ladies and gentlemen, and with long summer days. This image made polo an unlikely choice for popularity in the midst of an economic downturn, but it nonetheless attracted large crowds and considerable enthusiasm in those limited areas that welcomed the sport.

Humorist Will Rogers (1879–1935), a popular star of **movies** and **radio** and an expert horseman, campaigned tirelessly in the 1920s and 1930s for the game and raised public awareness about it. A ranked player himself, Rogers encouraged equestrians in the West to try what until the 1930s had been an Eastern activity, especially at Newport, Rhode Island, and on Long Island. The Meadow Brook Club in Westbury, which boasted eight playing fields, long reigned as the center of U.S. polo. During the Depression years, a number of Hollywood celebrities also took up the game, leading to a strong West Coast presence.

Throughout the 1930s, the press followed the sport, and several competitions emerged as newsworthy events. The Westchester Cup, which pitted the United States against England, became a prestigious contest, as did the U.S. Open. The first meeting of the Westchester Cup attracted 45,000 spectators, evidence of the level of public interest in the game. Several East-West All-Star matches increased the geographic spread of polo, and the U.S. Army, in the days before mechanization, mounted teams representing its best cavalry riders. Reflecting this expansion, over 80 polo clubs could be counted around the nation, and they achieved new membership highs, with almost 3,000 participants in the early years of the decade. The rolls dropped as the Depression wore on, and World War II effectively removed the cavalry presence, when tanks replaced horses. Only recently has polo again seen rising numbers, both in clubs and players.

Inevitably, several polo stars emerged. Tommy Hitchcock ("Ten Goal Tommy"; 1900–1944) and Cecil Smith ("The Texas Cowboy"; 1904–1999) dominated the game. Both Hitchcock, the poised Easterner, and Smith, the horseman from Texas, were superlative players and earned the highest possible ranking. They enjoyed a friendly rivalry and helped immeasurably to popularize the game.

Polo players in action. (Courtesy of the Library of Congress)

Despite charges of elitism and snobbery from many opposed to polo, the growing interest in the game attracted the movie industry's attention. At least a dozen or so features, most of them forgettable, include polo elements in their plotting and action sequences. Movies like *Lucky Larrigan* (1932); *This Sporting Age* (1932); *The Woman in Red* (1935), a Barbara Stanwyck (1907–1990) vehicle, not to be confused with two identically named movies from 1945 and 1984; *Polo Joe* (1936), a silly romp with comedian Joe E. Brown (1892–1973); *Wild Brian Kent* (1936); and *The Spy Ring* (1938) reflect some of the enthusiasm the game engendered. Edward G. Robinson (1893–1973), star of many **gangster films**, brings his acting talents to *The Little Giant* (1933), an offbeat comedy that involves wealth and polo. *The Adventures of Rex and Rinty*, a 1935 12-part serial, features Rex, king of the wild horses, and Rin Tin Tin Jr., the son of the famous canine star Rin Tin Tin. The two overcome obstacles in each cliff-hanging episode, many of which feature polo in their plotting. Even **Walt Disney** (1901–1966), by this time a major force in American cinema, released a polo-related cartoon, *Mickey's Polo Team* (1936). For a brief moment in sports history, polo had its day.

See also Games; Horse Racing; Serials

SELECTED READING
Aldrich, Nelson W., Jr. *Tommy Hitchcock: An American Hero*. New York: Margaret Mellon Hitchcock, 1984.
Peplow, Elizabeth. *Encyclopedia of the Horse*. San Diego: Thunder Bay Press, 1998.

PORGY AND BESS. The title given an extended 1935 work composed by George Gershwin (1898–1937) that combines elements of traditional opera and the classic American musical. Critics and musical historians have never been able to agree on a precise definition for *Porgy and Bess*. The debate revolves around the question of whether *Porgy and Bess* should be seen as musical theater posing as opera, or opera that contains elements of popular musical theater. Some have settled on the term "folk opera." Whatever the case, producers have long approached it as they would a traditional musical, with the result that this unique composition has usually been performed in theaters, not in opera houses or symphony halls.

Gershwin first entertained thoughts of attempting an opera in the early 1920s; nothing came of the idea, but he never abandoned it. At about the same time, DuBose Heyward (1885–1940), a writer from South Carolina, in 1925 published a novel titled *Porgy*. Loosely based on characters in and around Charleston, as well as local folklore, *Porgy* tells a tale of love, jealousy, revenge, and violence—just the makings for opera.

Shortly after the novel's publication, Gershwin read it and began discussing with Heyward the possibility of *Porgy* as an operatic vehicle. Despite the composer's early enthusiasm, other commitments kept Gershwin from pursuing the project, and it would take almost a decade for him to bring the idea to fruition. In the meantime, Heyward's wife, Dorothy (1890–1961), oversaw a straight dramatic production of *Porgy* in 1927–1928. Other parties also expressed interest in *Porgy*. **Jerome Kern** (1885–1945) and Oscar Hammerstein II (1895–1960), the team that had brought *Show Boat* to the stage in 1927, hoped to convert *Porgy* into a musical starring Al Jolson (1886–1950) in the title role, but complications blocked their plans.

In the early 1930s, Gershwin finally began work on his operatic dream after securing the needed agreements. He worked closely with the author, and *Porgy and Bess* slowly took shape. Although Heyward gamely tried to create the lyrics to the composer's songs, Gershwin wisely called on his more experienced brother Ira (1896–1983) to assist in crafting them. Ira Gershwin and Dubose Heyward, from all reports, made for a unique writing team. They shared generously with one another, and egos seldom clashed. Final attributions for a number of songs read "lyrics by Ira Gershwin and Dubose Heyward," with neither writer claiming more credit than the other.

The Gershwins and Heyward finished their work in the summer of 1935. They took *Porgy and Bess* to Boston for its first public performance toward the end of September. It received generally favorable reviews, although it proved too long. George pared it down slightly, and *Porgy and Bess* had its formal premiere two weeks later at New York's Alvin Theater. The gala opening rivaled that enjoyed in 1924 by *Rhapsody in Blue*, George's popular and much-lauded blending of **jazz** and classical **music**. The black-tie audience consisted of critics, opera buffs, Gershwin fans, and much of New York's high society.

As in Boston, the audience received the work warmly. As for reviewers, most drama critics liked it, whereas most music critics gave it lukewarm reception, with some remaining skittish about calling it a bona fide opera. The show ran for 124 performances—not much for a musical, but an extended run for an opera. Never a robust financial success, *Porgy and Bess* just broke even.

On stage, *Porgy and Bess* demands a large cast of 65 actors, and the libretto requires that they be black performers. Gershwin selected Todd Duncan (1903–1998) as Porgy, and Anne Brown (b. 1912) as Bess. John W. Bubbles (b. John William Sublett, 1902–1986), a popular black vaudevillian, took the role of Sportin' Life and gave a memorable performance. Rouben Mamoulian (1897–1987), who had directed Dorothy Heyward's 1927 stage version of *Porgy*, served as director. He had already established himself in Hollywood with a number of films, including **musicals**, and he proved a capable director.

Set on Catfish Row, a run-down fishing village on the South Carolina coast, a range of characters populate the show. From the crippled Porgy to the virtuous Clara to the villainous Crown, everyone in this microcosm has numerous interconnections. Gershwin's memorable score of course links them all with songs like "Summertime," "It Ain't Necessarily So," "Oh Bess, Oh Where's My Bess?" "I Got Plenty o' Nuttin'," and "I Loves You, Porgy." Much of the music has become a part of the standard American repertoire, and the show itself has entered the annals of classic theater.

Ironically, the first major commercial **recordings** of music from the score feature Lawrence Tibbett (1896–1960) and Helen Jepsen (1904–1997), two white artists from the Metropolitan Opera who also performed for RCA Victor, the company willing to undertake a substantial recording of music from the show. In 1940, Decca Records issued highlights from *Porgy and Bess* and used members of the original cast, a breakthrough for black performers at the time. The archaic idea that somehow recordings by black artists—called "race records" in those days—would not sell to white consumers still held sway until Decca's pioneering anthology. Eventually, such concepts fell by the wayside and the show has long since been recorded innumerable times by black and white performers, both in its entirety and as individual songs.

Porgy and Bess, finally made it to film in 1959, has gone on tours and successfully straddled the difficult line between high art and popular entertainment. Whatever its proper definition, the music remains George Gershwin's, not adaptations of folk or local music. But credit must also be extended to both DuBose Heyward and Ira Gershwin for their lyrics, especially to Ira, since he ended up editing or rewriting most of Heyward's efforts. Because of George's premature death in 1937, *Porgy and Bess* would be the Gershwin brothers' last joint theatrical production.

See also George & Ira Gershwin; Movies; Race Relations & Stereotyping; Songwriters & Lyricists

SELECTED READING

Hyland, William G. *George Gershwin: A New Biography*. New York: Praeger, 2003.
Jablonski, Edward. *Gershwin*. New York: Doubleday, 1987.
Rosenberg, Deena. *Fascinating Rhythm: The Collaboration of George and Ira Gershwin*. New York: Penguin Books [Plume], 1991.

PORTER, COLE. Heir to a large family fortune, Cole Porter (1893–1964), born in Peru, Indiana, experienced a lonely childhood. Educated at private schools and Yale, he early on showed a prodigious talent for **music**, especially the writing of clever lyrics to accompany his tunes. Rejecting a career in law, he went to Paris in World War I, flirted with the expatriate community, and attempted his first Broadway play, *See America First*, in 1916. It flopped, but he continued to write and compose, honing his skills throughout the 1920s. He enjoyed several early hits with "I'm in Love Again" (1925; from *Greenwich Village Follies of 1924*) and the suggestive "Let's Do It" (1928; from the revue *Paris*), and he stood poised to take on the 1930s.

Composer and lyricist Cole Porter (1893–1964).
(Courtesy of the Library of Congress)

In November 1929, Porter premiered "You Do Something to Me," for the musical *Fifty Million Frenchmen*. People took notice, and Porter's name next graced marquees in December with *Wake Up and Dream*, just a month after *Fifty Million Frenchmen*. Few songwriters or lyricists have two **musicals** going at once: Porter opened *Wake Up and Dream* in London that spring and debuted in New York at the end of the year. It featured "What Is This Thing Called Love?" destined to become a Porter chestnut.

With all his activity, it took only a short time before Hollywood took notice of Porter. In 1930, First National, a small movie studio, produced *Paris*, a film version of Porter's 1928 revue. The picture served as a breakthrough and, for the remainder of the decade, he would shuttle between East Coast and West, working within both theater and film.

The New Yorkers opened on Broadway during the 1930 Christmas season. A forgettable play, it contained an unforgettable song, "Love for Sale." A controversial description of a prostitute's life, "Love for Sale" has entered the standard repertoire. **Radio** stations at the time found its risqué lyrics unsuitable for broadcasting, but it achieved hit status anyway, in large part thanks to a recording by Fred Waring (1900–1984) and the Pennsylvanians. Apparently offending no one, the record sold well. As a result, broadcasters dropped their restrictions on airplay. In light of contemporary lyrics, listeners might wonder about the concerns expressed in the early 1930s.

Almost two years passed before the opening of Porter's next play, *Gay Divorce* (1932). It starred Fred Astaire (1899–1987) before he began devoting most of his time to **movies**, and he sang the memorable "Night and Day." Producers adapted *Gay Divorce* for film two years later, changing the name to *The Gay Divorcee*. Astaire again got the lead male role and performed with Ginger Rogers (1911–1995), the second pairing for them—the first had been in *Flying Down to Rio* in 1933. Hollywood, in its infinite wisdom, worried about the play's title, and feared censor problems with the connotation of "happy divorce," and thus the unusual compromise of "Divorcee" for "Divorce."

Other problems also plagued *The Gay Divorcee*. Unlike his stage version, Porter contributed little to the film adaptation. RKO Pictures dropped most of the original score for new material, and only Porter's pulsating "Night and Day" survives. Con Conrad (1891–1938) and Herb Magidson (1906–1986), two professional **songwriters and lyricists**, took on the remaining score. They contributed "A Needle in a Haystack" and the delightful "Continental," but the deletions and substitutions resulted in a new and different musical. These highhanded studio tactics probably soured Porter on Hollywood, helping to explain his greater devotion to musical theater.

In 1934, the musical *Anything Goes* opened on Broadway and it contains one of Porter's most inspired scores. Standards like "I Get a Kick Out of You," "All through the Night," "You're the Top," "Blow, Gabriel, Blow," and the title song adorn the show. The original stage version starred Ethel Merman (1908–1984). She gave such a strong performance that the 1936 movie adaptation cast her in the same part, rather than substituting a Hollywood star.

Aside from Ethel Merman, however, the movie *Anything Goes* (1936) bears little resemblance to its Broadway counterpart. Once again much of the original music, such as "All through the Night" and "Blow, Gabriel, Blow," has disappeared. Merman does team up with costar **Bing Crosby** (1903–1977) for a spirited, but rewritten, rendition of the sophisticated "You're the Top," but why the producers chose to cut so much of the original Porter score remains a mystery. The substituted songs, while adequate, do not do justice to this outstanding musical comedy.

Jubilee came to the stage in 1935. A so-so play with some memorable music, it features "Why Shouldn't I?" "Just One of Those Things," and a number most people initially dismissed, "Begin the Beguine." Fortunately, bandleader Artie Shaw (1910–2004) heard Porter's tune, and recorded it in 1938. Shaw's interpretation of "Begin the Beguine" resulted in one of the biggest hits of that or any decade, a song that will always be associated with the clarinetist and one that helped epitomize the **swing** era.

Keeping to a demanding schedule that seemingly required a new musical each year, Porter premiered *Red Hot and Blue!* in 1936. It contains one of his clever, sophisticated numbers much loved by cabaret singers, "Down in the Depths (on the Ninetieth Floor)." A recital about the problems of love, it never managed to be a big hit but instead has achieved a devoted following and illustrates Porter's mastery of lyrics. *Red Hot and Blue!* also showcased "It's De-Lovely." A rising young actor named Bob Hope (1903–2003) sang the song with costar Ethel Merman, by that time one of Broadway's leading lights.

Movie theaters showed *Born to Dance* that same year. This picture marked Porter's return to film musicals, his first since the challenges he faced with *The Gay Divorcee* in 1934. Since *Born to Dance* had not first played on Broadway, it features a score written for film and boasts a topnotch Hollywood cast that includes James Stewart (1908–1997) and Eleanor Powell (1912–1982). Two Porter classics, "Easy to Love" and "I've Got You under My Skin," grace the proceedings.

Eleanor Powell appears in another Porter film vehicle, *Rosalie* (1937). Although Sigmund Romberg (1887–1951) and George Gershwin (1898–1937) had collaborated on a 1928 Broadway play of the same name, the two works share nothing other than identical titles. The movie *Rosalie* stars not just Powell, but also the popular Nelson Eddy (1901–1967), doing the vocals. The movie resembles the frothy **operettas** then so much in vogue, which means that *Rosalie* lacks much of a plot. But that seemed to matter little to Porter; he managed to compose the memorable "In the Still of the Night" and "Who Knows?" for the picture.

You Never Know opened the 1938 Broadway season. Not every show can be a hit, and *You Never Know* proved it, closing after just 78 performances. "What Shall I Do?" and "At Long Last Love" have endured far longer than the play. Undeterred, Porter redeemed himself one month later with *Leave It to Me!* A fine score that included "Get Out of Town" and "My Heart Belongs to Daddy" pleased audiences. Mary Martin (1913–1990), just starting out, performed the latter number. Her rendition, a combination of innocence and sophistication, made her an overnight sensation.

For the 1930s, *DuBarry Was a Lady* (1939) proved to be Porter's final Broadway effort. Two standards emerged from the production, both humorous: "Friendship" and "Well, Did You Evah?" Just a few months later, MGM released *Broadway Melody of 1940*, a big-budget screen musical that features a fine Porter score and the superlative dancing talents of both Fred Astaire and Eleanor Powell. Two new classics emerged from the movie, "I've Got My Eyes on You" and "I Concentrate on You." In addition, he contributed the witty "Please Don't Monkey with Broadway," a sharp commentary on his own allegiances to musical theater and tradition. Probably at the insistence of producers, he also resurrected "Begin the Beguine," such a phenomenal recorded hit for Artie Shaw just two years earlier.

Despite his bumpy relationship with Hollywood, Cole Porter would continue to contribute original music to the movies and adapt his shows to the film medium for the rest of his life. Motion picture producers apparently deemed much of what he wrote too sophisticated or "too adult," and Porter himself clearly preferred New York City and its clubs and urbanity. As a result, a good percentage of his most memorable music comes from stage productions, not films.

Like his contemporaries, especially **Jerome Kern** (1885–1945) and Lorenz Hart (1895–1943), Porter's view of the world had little to do with economic crises or New Deals, but he was not above making topical references in his remarkable catalog of songs. Thanks once again to movies, radio, and **recordings**, he became widely known and his music has come down to the present as some of the best of the era.

See also Fred Astaire & Ginger Rogers; George & Ira Gershwin; Rodgers & Hart

SELECTED READING

Eells, George. *The Life That Late He Led: A Biography of Cole Porter.* New York: G. P. Putnam's Sons, 1967.

Kanfer, Stefan. "The Voodoo That He Did So Well." http://www.city-journal.org/html/13_1_urbanities-the_voodoo.html

Kimball, Robert, and Richard M. Sudhalter. *You're the Top: Cole Porter in the 1930s.* 3 CDs. Indianapolis: Indiana Historical Society, 1992.

McBrien, William. *Cole Porter: A Biography.* New York: Alfred A. Knopf, 1998.

PRINCE VALIANT. First appearing on the Sunday newspaper comic pages in early 1937, *Prince Valiant* is generally recognized as one of the most beautifully crafted strips of that or any era. Artist Harold R. Foster (1892–1982) had already made a name for himself in the comic strip industry by illustrating ***Tarzan***, a series he intermittently worked on from 1929 until the end of 1936. But the cartoonist harbored dreams of a series of his own, from artwork to story lines, and *Prince Valiant* realizes that dream.

Dissatisfied with the pay he received for drawing *Tarzan*, Foster in 1935–1936 undertook a new adventure series that he called *Derek, Son of Thane.* His syndicate, United Features, turned down his samples, but the Hearst Syndicate promptly signed him to its roster of artists. In the process, Foster's new associates renamed the strip *Prince Valiant in the Days of King Arthur.* An immediate hit with readers, the tales transported them back to the fifth century, to the days of Arthur and his fabled Knights of the Round Table. Immaculately drafted, the series took adventure comics to a new level. A Sunday-only strip, it gave Foster greater space than would a daily, plus it allowed the use of color.

These two elements combined to create what many have called the most beautiful of all newspaper strips.

In an era looking for escapism, *Prince Valiant* celebrated heroism and bravery, presenting images of characters meeting and overcoming all challenges. The legends of Arthur and his knights have never died out, and Foster built on this reservoir of shared familiarity, creating a body of characters that continue to live on in the imagination. Prince Valiant himself, or "Val," starts as a young squire who quickly rises to knighthood and in 1938 gains the mythic "singing sword," his fearsome weapon of choice. From then on, the series focuses on his adventures, a kind of contemporary serial, but one of epic proportions, set in the dusty pages of history.

Meticulously researched, the drawings display an almost fanatical attention to detail. Foster would be the first to admit that he took several centuries of English and northern European history and blended them, but each frame nonetheless remains a treat for the eyes. No speech balloons interrupt his pictures; he instead scrolled the plot details across the bottom of each frame, a technique he had employed on *Tarzan*. Foster's drawing encourages comparison with that being done by Alex Raymond (1909–1956) at the same time in **Flash Gordon**, but Raymond creates **science fiction** fantasy whereas Foster contributes historical realism. Each has its merits, and each helps explain why the 1930s can be called the golden age of American newspaper **comic strips**.

In the last years of the decade, with Hitler and the Nazis moving Europe to the brink of war, Foster commenced a famous storyline about Val encountering Attila the Hun. When Germany invaded Poland in the fall of 1939, this adventure struck a particularly timely note. The Huns, portrayed as rapacious invaders, need to be stopped, and it will take warriors like Prince Valiant and his fellow knights to do the job. Bloody violence, no stranger to the strip, is a price that must be paid to ensure freedom. It would be difficult for anyone to miss the message in this particular episode, one of the few times *Prince Valiant* ever spoke directly to contemporary events.

After 1970, Foster required assistance in drawing *Prince Valiant* until his retirement in 1980. The series continued in the capable hands of John Cullen Murphy (1919–2004), and with his death new artists and writers inherited the strip. It can still be found in over 1,000 Sunday newspaper comics sections. In retrospect, *Prince Valiant*, a product of the 1930s, will be remembered as one of the best-drawn comics of the twentieth century.

See also Newspapers; Serials

SELECTED READING

Goulart, Ron, ed. *The Encyclopedia of American Comics*. New Rochelle, NY: Facts on File, 1990.
Horn, Maurice, ed. *100 Years of American Newspaper Comics*. New York: Gramercy Books, 1996.
Marschall, Richard. *America's Great Comic-Strip Artists*. New York: Stewart, Tabori & Chang, 1997.

PROHIBITION & REPEAL (1920–1933). In December 1917, the U.S. Congress passed the Eighteenth Amendment to the Constitution, which, if ratified by three-quarters of the then-48 states, would make unlawful the manufacture, sale, transport, import, or export of intoxicating beverages within the nation's boundaries. As the amendment worked its way through state legislatures, the 1919 Volstead Act, a federal

Bottles and a barrel of confiscated liquor. (Courtesy of the Library of Congress)

law named for Minnesota congressman Andrew J. Volstead (1860–1947), defined beer, wine, and liquor as such beverages if they contained more than .5 percent alcohol by volume. By January 16, 1919, the Eighteenth Amendment, familiarly called Prohibition, had been ratified by the required 36 state legislatures. Enforcement of the new constitutional amendment went into effect January 16, 1920. It would remain the law of the land until December 1933, when the Twenty-first Amendment, or Repeal, overturned it.

President **Herbert Hoover** (1874–1964; in office 1929–1933) called the challenging Prohibition era a "noble experiment." It had been a long time coming. Efforts toward restricting the sale of liquor can be traced back to the mid-1800s, when Maine forbade it. Most of the South followed suit after the Civil War. The Prohibition Party, organized in 1869, ran candidates in several presidential elections. Although they never received a large percentage of the popular vote, their participation contributed to the growing influence of the "dry" (i.e., no alcohol) movement. The conservative Midwest joined the ranks at the time of World War I (1914–1918), insisting that its grain should be used for making bread for soldiers, not liquor, thereby linking the prohibition of alcohol to patriotism.

Family, not love of country, became the loudest, most persuasive and intense reason for controlling alcohol. Members of the temperance movement, a wide-ranging crusade that included men and women, churches, employers, and social and political reformers, moralistically argued that the damaging effects of alcohol on the drinker also hurt the family, society, and nation. Two groups, the Women's Christian Temperance Union (WCTU), organized in 1874 in Cleveland, Ohio, and a Washington, D.C., lobbying group known as the Anti-Saloon League, founded in 1893, played major roles in gaining passage of the Eighteenth Amendment.

After Prohibition became a reality, saloons around the nation had to close, with the result that another kind of public place prospered—the soda fountain. Before Prohibition, some soda fountain drinks contained alcohol, and these now had to be dropped from menus. Rich egg and malted milk beverages often served as their replacements. Soda fountains also expanded their business by selling light lunches, something most had not done in the past. Since Prohibition had forced the closing of saloons, places that had traditionally served **food** to a mostly male clientele, the fountains saw a good business opportunity. They added menu items attractive to both men and women, creating a gathering place. The rise of lunch counters in all forms started with Prohibition and continued through the Depression and the remaining years of the decade. After Repeal in 1933, saloons never made a real comeback.

By the time of the Great Depression, Prohibition had many foes and support for Repeal had markedly increased. Two groups, the Association against the Prohibition Amendment, a leading political pressure group founded in 1918 and revived and reorganized in 1927, and the Women's Organization for National Prohibition Reform, founded in 1929, actively worked toward abolishing the Eighteenth Amendment. Others also voiced concerns, adding to the growing chorus of support for Repeal. Some disliked the power given to federal and state authorities to control an individual's choice of drink; others cited increased acts of violence and other **crime** associated with the restrictive law. People complained of the enormous costs to implement Prohibition coupled with an even larger loss of tax revenue. They saw a decline in respect for laws, lawmakers, and law enforcers, and claimed the jammed court system and increasing prison population testified to the futility of Prohibition.

With the onset of the Depression, Repeal supporters said it pointed the way to returning many unemployed Americans to work. In 1931, the successful federal prosecution of Al Capone (1899–1947), a well-known bootlegger and gangster, helped the cause. Ironically, Capone went to prison not because of the Volstead Act, but on charges of income tax evasion.

In 1929, President Hoover established the Wickersham Commission and charged them with investigating the administration of justice throughout the nation's jails, prisons, courts, and prosecutors' offices. The commission had instructions to report its findings both to him and to the American public. It produced 14 volumes of detailed information, one of which dealt with Prohibition. This section recommended that Congress consider a more effective means of controlling abuses of laws dealing with alcohol. A detailed minority report from the commission flatly stated that the Volstead Act had failed and should be abandoned.

With the Wickersham findings fresh in mind, Republicans and Democrats differed on the Prohibition issue during the 1932 presidential campaign. The Republican platform pledged continued enforcement, while the Democratic platform called for immediate repeal. In the election, the Democratic Party's candidate, **Franklin D. Roosevelt** (1882–1945), reaped a landside victory. Although the Democratic sweep came about on a variety of issues, with Prohibition being only one of many, the government quickly reacted. The 72nd Congress met in a remarkable lame duck session that ran from December 1932 to March 1933.

Most congressional discussions focused on how to aid the failing economy, but this special session also passed, by more than a two-thirds margin in each house, a resolution mandating passage of the Twenty-first Amendment. This new addition to the Constitution would overturn 1919's Eighteenth Amendment prohibiting the sale of **alcoholic beverages**. The states responded by promptly convening constitutional conventions between April and November 1933 to consider ratification. Repeal—acceptance of the Twenty-first Amendment—occurred on December 5, 1933, when the 36th state, Utah, voted for ratification. Clearly, most Americans by then viewed the Eighteenth Amendment and its accompanying Volstead Act with disdain. Only six Southern states, along with Kansas and North Dakota, chose to remain dry.

Although Prohibition officially ended in 1933, it profoundly influenced the popular culture of the entire decade. For example, the **gangster films** of the early 1930s celebrate criminals, most of whom make their fortunes in bootlegging and related activities. The subsequent G-man pictures likewise use Prohibition as a background for their plots. Speakeasies, nightclubs, and free-flowing liquor make up the imagery of these **movies** as they chronicle the crime waves and drinking life of the times. Even the stage and film comedies of the 1930s reflect these shifting mores. Actors like Mae West (1893–1980) and W. C. Fields (1880–1946) built their careers on anti-Prohibition attitudes. Their popularity suggests significant changes in public attitudes toward alcohol, along with challenges to traditional American values and beliefs.

Through the imposition of Prohibition, political and religious conservatives attempted to solve what they believed to be the country's social problems. The ban did reduce the per capita consumption of alcoholic beverages between 1919 and 1933, but it hardly ended drinking. Instead, Prohibition spawned new economic problems, established a violence-filled environment for the illicit importation and sale of alcohol, and helped entrench a network of organized crime. Significant opposition began almost immediately following passage of the Eighteenth Amendment; it grew throughout the 1920s and came to a climax with the beginning of the Great Depression. Repeal did indeed bring a great economic boost. It restored countless jobs in the beer, wine, and liquor industries, along with various supporting businesses, and it returned lost tax revenues to the economy. Amid widespread celebrating, Prohibition came to an end in late 1933. The "noble experiment" had failed.

See also Political Parties; Soft Drinks

SELECTED READING

Sinclair, Andrew. *Era of Excess: A Social History of the Prohibition Movement.* New York: Harper Colophon, 1962.

Smith, Andrew F., ed. *The Oxford Encyclopedia of Food & Drink in America.* New York: Oxford University Press, 2004.

Young, William H., with Nancy K. Young. *The 1930s: American Popular Culture through History.* Westport, CT: Greenwood Press, 2002.

PROPAGANDA & ANTI-AXIS FILMS. Movies sometimes provide a mirror to society, and many American motion pictures of the 1930s accurately reflected the nation's state of mind. They offered escape—escape from the realities of ongoing world events. Not until the last years of the decade did a handful of films begin to depict the specter of impending war. Throughout most of the period, the United States wrapped itself in a mantle of isolationism, ignoring, as best it could, the reality of totalitarianism expanding throughout much of the world, and Hollywood dutifully followed suit. People might have sensed that a conflagration would eventually break out, but no one offered concrete solutions to the growing menace, and certainly no one wanted to get involved.

As early as 1930, director Lewis Milestone (1895–1980) warned American moviegoers about the horrors of war, using World War I as his example. In a splendid screenplay, playwright Maxwell Anderson (1888–1959) adapted Erich Maria Remarque's (1898–1970) stirring antiwar novel, *All Quiet on the Western Front* (1929), and Milestone visually captures the slaughter and futility that characterize modern warfare. Lew Ayres (1908–1996) plays a young German soldier trapped in the European killing fields; neither Anderson nor Milestone attempted to change Ayres' character to an American doughboy because Remarque's story makes its point that war respects no nation. Featuring some of the most harrowing combat reenactments ever put on film, *All Quiet on the Western Front* doubtless sparked feelings of isolationism for those who saw it. If America could stay out of Europe's wars, so much the better.

In 1932 the producers of *A Farewell to Arms*, another film set in World War I, gave in to official Italian government complaints about depictions of their nation's army. Based on the 1929 novel of the same name by Ernest Hemingway (1899–1961), and historically accurate, Paramount Pictures nevertheless altered the script so it would not show the Italian army in retreat. This avoidance of any hint of political controversy characterized much American moviemaking in the years prior to World War II.

One film series defied the prevailing wisdom of not taking political positions when discussing, or portraying, international events. **The March of Time**, a documentary approach to the news, had its theatrical debut in 1934 (a **radio** version had preceded it by several years). Very much on the side of the Western democracies, from its inception it warned against the dangers of growing fascism.

The March of Time notwithstanding, Hitler (1889–1945) in 1936 marched into the demilitarized Rhineland and no one moved to stop him. He formalized already close relations with Italy and Japan that same year, thus creating the Axis alliance, and neither the impotent League of Nations nor any Western country attempted to block this dangerous growth of fascist power. The world looked on, but did nothing, thus setting the stage for World War II.

As the international scene worsened, an unusual British motion picture, *Things to Come* (1936), received wide U.S. distribution. The film proves almost uncanny in its predictions of modern, mechanized warfare. Directed by William Cameron Menzies (1896–1957), who would later gain considerable fame as the production designer on 1939's **Gone with the Wind**, another film dealing with war, the movie had been adapted from *The Shape of Things to Come* (1933), a dystopian work by the popular writer H. G. Wells (1866–1946). It stars Raymond Massey (1896–1983) and Ralph Richardson (1902–1983), both well-known actors of the day.

For *Things to Come*, Menzies needed to create a recognizable future, one that had come through a terrible war and emerged regimented and dependent on science and rationality. Certainly he succeeded in depicting modern warfare; his menacing squadrons of bombers and the destruction of civilian targets suggests nothing so much as the 1940 London blitz, an event that followed the picture by just four years. As an antiwar protest, however, *Things to Come* seems primarily a curiosity piece. Wooden acting and stilted dialogue detract from the movie, and Wells's heavy-handed philosophy comes across more as a rant than as a coherent warning to audiences. The scenes of devastation, however, remain powerful, and its prophetic qualities—the "things" of the title truly were to come—have an eerie fascination about them, making *Things to Come* something of a cult classic in the years since its release.

The Spanish Civil War, a bloody, mid-1930s conflict between those loyal to the existing government and those wishing to overthrow it and establish a more dictatorial state, energized the emotions of many Americans. Most favored the Loyalists, but Hollywood practiced a studied neutrality in films that alluded to the war.

Spanish Earth (1937), a documentary, enlisted the aid of a number of distinguished American writers and musicians. John Dos Passos (1896–1970) wrote and narrated part 1, and Ernest Hemingway wrote and narrated part 2. Poet Archibald MacLeish (1892–1982) and playwright Lillian Hellman (1905–1984) also contributed to the script, and composers Marc Blitztein (1905–1964) and Virgil Thomson (1896–1989) shared honors for the musical arrangements of the score.

More a recounting of the tragedy of the conflict than a propagandistic attack on one side or the other, *Spanish Earth* allowed moviegoers to see the war up close, reminding them of the unstable conditions in Europe that made it ripe for still more fighting. Filmed amid the destruction rained on Spain by both Loyalists and Nationalists, it served to preview similar dangers then facing the world.

That same year, Paramount released *The Last Train from Madrid*. Despite its provocative title, this Dorothy Lamour (1914–1996)/Lew Ayres romantic drama provides little insight into the war, instead focusing on a group of attractive people fleeing any possible battles. Pure soap opera, the background war depicted in the movie could have been occurring anywhere.

In a similar fashion, MGM adapted another novel by Erich Maria Remarque, *Three Comrades* (novel, 1937; film, 1938). A disappointing movie, despite a screenplay by F. Scott Fitzgerald (1896–1940), *Three Comrades* hints at life in post–World War I Germany, but fails to pay adequate attention to the rise of Nazism. Tinkering by **Hollywood Production Code** staff removed a number of topical scenes. By robbing the picture of any anti-Nazi references, the changes gave audiences a gloomy picture of contemporary Germany but little explanation of any causes.

Yet another American motion picture about the Spanish tragedy came out in 1938. Titled *Blockade*, United Artists marketed the movie as an exciting drama about espionage. With the Spanish Civil War as its setting, and starring Henry Fonda (1905–1982) and Madeleine Carroll (1906–1987), *Blockade*, albeit quietly and unobtrusively, sides with the Spanish Loyalists through the respected Fonda and takes a small stand against the rising forces of fascism. Writing credits go to John Howard Lawson (1894–1977), a man who openly embraced the Communist Party during the earlier 1930s, the same party that supported the Loyalists during the civil war.

Given its roster of stars and promotion, *Blockade* heightened awareness of the brutal civil war ravaging Spain. By 1938 most Americans knew enough about current events to separate the fascists (i.e., the Nationalists) from the Loyalists. Even so, the picture remains scrupulous in its neutrality, fictionalizing place-names, clothing the players in virtually identical uniforms that betray no allegiances, and carefully avoiding any mention of Russia, Germany, or Italy, the principal international players in the conflict.

Despite this cloak of seeming objectivity, Fonda, looking directly into the camera, makes a closing speech condemning fascism. *Blockade* may not have been an outspoken anti-Axis film, but it cautiously moved into territory almost no commercial American movies had yet explored.

In the years following World War II, the U.S. Congress, acting through its House Un-American Activities Committee (HUAC), launched a lengthy investigation into purported Communist influences in American movies, especially those made during the 1930s and on into the early war years. Numerous Hollywood personalities found themselves hauled into hearings about their pasts, and earnest lawmakers cited both *Blockade* and John Howard Lawson as evidence of subversion. For Lawson, it meant blacklisting and the end of his Hollywood career; he eventually went into self-exile in Mexico. For *Blockade*, however, the hearings gave it a reputation, undeserved, of being sympathetic to Communism. If any pro-Communist sympathies evidence themselves in *Blockade*, they remain so muted that they must be adjudged more imagined than real.

In the early 1930s, Warner Brothers had addressed social issues with hard-hitting films like *I Am a Fugitive from a Chain Gang* (1932), *Heroes for Sale* (1933), and *Black Fury* (1935). As the threat of a world war increased, the studio again led the way, releasing *Confessions of a Nazi Spy* and *Espionage Agent* in 1939. Given its title, *Confessions of a Nazi Spy* leaves little or no doubt about who the enemy will be, and both pictures reflect the growing national concern about foreign agents and spies. *Confessions of a Nazi Spy* prompted a protest from the German consulate, but the studio stood firm.

Veteran actor Edward G. Robinson (1893–1973), who had made his name playing criminals, but could be equally convincing as a law officer, commands *Confessions of a Nazi Spy* as a government agent who ferrets out a vast Nazi conspiracy within American borders. Whereas *Blockade* may have been muted in its allegiances, *Confessions of a Nazi Spy* blatantly takes sides. The Nazis, depicted as zealots determined to undermine American morale, attempt to infiltrate all aspects of life. Melodramatic propaganda by any standards, the picture nonetheless touched many a nerve in the tense days leading up to World War II. Immediately banned in Germany and Japan, as well as much of South America, it came out shortly before the September 1939 invasion of Poland by German forces.

In *Espionage Agent*, the studio cast one of its big stars, Joel McCrea (1905–1990), as an American diplomat who must uncover German spies in order to save his marriage and protect his name. He of course accomplishes these things, and the picture focuses as much on romance as it does on espionage. Produced in early 1939, it came to theaters shortly after the outbreak of war. Like *Confessions of a Nazi Spy*, *Espionage Agent* cautioned American audiences that the enemy would be Germany and its allies.

A short documentary film, *Lights Out in Europe* (1939) covers the German invasion of Poland and the beginning of World War II. Filmmaker Herbert Kline (1909–1999) directed, and James Hilton (1900–1954), a well-known screenwriter and best-selling novelist (*Lost Horizon*, 1937, *Good-bye, Mr. Chips*, 1939), created the script. Fredric March (1897–1975), a popular, respected actor, serves as narrator. The title, *Lights Out in Europe*, says all that has to be said. Any chances for peace had disappeared, and the continent—and shortly the world—would be plunged into darkness and chaos.

Although it would be another two years before the United States entered the war as a combatant, the invasion of Poland shook the nation and the film industry out of any remaining complacency. The following year saw films like *The Fighting 69th, Four Sons, Escape, Foreign Correspondent* (with Joel McCrea again battling Nazis), *The Mortal Storm*, and *The Man I Married*. Even comedian Charlie Chaplin (1889–1977) entered the growing fray with *The Great Dictator*, a hilarious spoof of Hitler and totalitarianism. Sporting a little black moustache, Chaplin mimics the Nazi leader to devastating effect. By then, most studios had lost their reticence and clearly began taking sides against the Axis powers, although not everyone supported this move. Some patrons and studios continued to press for nontopical entertainment. Not until the sneak attack on Pearl Harbor in December 1941 did the sleeping giant called Hollywood truly awake. Then the propaganda and war movies poured out of the studios as fast as they could be filmed. The neutrality of the 1930s quickly became a memory.

See also Best Sellers; Crime; Music; Political Parties; Social Consciousness Films; Songwriters & Lyricists; *Terry and the Pirates*

SELECTED READING
Blockade. http://www.classicfilmguide.com/index.php?s=links
Manvell, Roger. *Films and the Second World War*. New York: Dell Publishing Co. [Delta Books], 1974.
Morella, Joe, Edward Z. Epstein, and John Griggs. *The Films of World War II*. Secaucus, NJ: Citadel Press, 1973.

PULP MAGAZINES. Sensational, garish, tawdry, trashy—all that, and more, but the pulp magazine has long existed as a singular part of American popular culture. Born in the nineteenth century—in England their equivalents bore the name "penny dreadfuls"; in the United States people called them "dime novels"—these cheap periodicals enjoyed enormous audiences. They gained their name from their low price and the cheap paper on which they were printed. Coarse, grainy pulp-based paper served as the technological innovation that allowed inexpensive mass reproduction of printed materials. That, plus rising literacy rates and a ready readership, guaranteed success for publishers.

In the United States, periodicals of all types flourished in the later nineteenth and early twentieth centuries, and they frequently displaced dime novels in popularity. Although **magazines** for every taste could be found, tales of action and adventure found a ready audience. Somewhat akin to **comic strips** in their simplicity and aimed at males of all ages, they became a standard part of newsstand displays and enjoyed huge sales.

In 1919, Bernarr Macfadden (1868–1955) launched *True Story*, the first of a long line of confessional magazines that eventually displaced the earlier action tales in popularity. Best known for his own colorful personality—physical culturist, bodybuilder, health-food faddist—Macfadden established a publishing empire that never shied away from controversy or sensationalism, provided it kept circulations up. He had entered the magazine field in 1899 with *Physical Culture*, which sold for a nickel (about $1 in today's money). It made him rich and famous, and endeared him to millions of readers anxious to improve their health.

With *True Story*, Macfadden unearthed an untapped lode in popular culture, the desire to read the supposedly truthful, but usually undocumented, stories of others. Tabloid **newspapers**, led by the *New York Daily News* (also founded in 1919), likewise mined this vein, making front-page stories out of **crime** and tragedy, and never shying away from sensational pictures to accompany them. Thus the 1920s gained a reputation for tabloid journalism and pulp magazines, and the two genres shared many affinities.

Both featured low cover prices, aimed for a mass readership, and sought to excite and arouse their audiences. In the case of *True Story*, Macfadden and others quickly launched a host of look-alikes: *True Detective Mysteries, True Experiences, True Ghost Stories, True Lovers,* and *True Romances*. Since Hollywood at the time offered endless celebrity gossip and occasional scandal, this segment of the magazine industry adopted the film capital as a source of factual, not-so-factual, and utterly fictitious publicity designed to entertain readers. Along with all the "true" titles, publishers offered *Click, Hollywood, Modern Screen, Motion Picture, Movie Classic, Photoplay, Screenland, Screen Romances,* and *Silver Screen*.

What truly defined the pulp category, however, were the action-adventure periodicals. Shunned by critics and librarians, but adored by fans, these collections of thrilling tales bore such titles as *Action Stories, Air Stories, Amazing Stories, Astounding Stories, Battle Aces, Battle Birds, Battle Stories, Black Mask Magazine, Nick Carter, Crack Detective, Crime Busters, Detective Classics, Detective Story, Dime Detective, Dime*

Modern Screen magazine cover (1938) depicting Katharine Hepburn (1907–2003) and Howard Hughes (1905–1976). (Courtesy of Photofest)

Mystery, Doc Savage Magazine, Exciting Sports, Fantastic Stories, The Feds, G-8 and His Battle Aces, G-Men Detective, Hollywood Detective, Master Detective, New Detective, The Shadow, Speed Adventure Stories, Spicy Adventure, Spicy Detective, Spicy Western Stories, The Spider, Startling Stories, Strange Tales, Super Detective, Ten Detective Aces, 10-Story Magazine, Terror Tales, Thrilling Detective, Thrilling Love, Thrilling Mystery, Thrilling Wonder, Underworld, Weird Tales, Western Story, Western Trails, and *Wonder Stories*. Easily found at the neighborhood newsstand, they provided the perfect distraction for people with a little time on their hands and a desire to escape from the harsh realities around them.

As might be expected, the magazine titles usually promised more than the pages within contained. The "spicy" and "thrilling" titles suggested adult or edge-of-your-seat fiction, but more often than not the stories turned out to be as pedestrian as anything else on the market. Strong self-censorship by the publishers to avoid controversy or newsstand banishment, meant that little overt sexuality appeared in the magazines. And the thrills simply could not be maintained, issue after issue, by harried, overworked writers cranking out material at pennies per word.

What initially attracted the consumer's eye for these magazines were their bold, provocative covers. They soon came to characterize pulp fiction in general. Most of the artists who churned out these illustrations remain anonymous, although a few, such as Hannes Bok (1914–1964), Rafael De Soto (1904–1987), John Newton Howett (1885–1958), Frank R. Paul (1884–1963), George Rozen (1895–1974), and Norman Saunders (1907–1989), attracted some notice during their active careers and have become the subjects of considerable interest more recently. In general, whether executed by artists known or unknown, pulp covers feature an attractive woman—frequently scantily clad—in a seductive pose that also suggests menace or some melodramatic situation. Regardless of merit, the covers helped mightily to sell millions of magazines.

Traditional magazine fiction, especially short stories, abounded during the 1930s, and "big name" periodicals like *Redbook* and the **Saturday Evening Post** often paid over $1,000 (about $14,200 in current dollars) for a submission by a well-known author. Many of the most popular writers of the decade eventually wrote for magazine publication, such as Rex Beach (1877–1949), Corey Ford (1902–1969), MacKinlay Kantor (1904–1977), Kathleen Norris (1880–1966), Mary Roberts Rinehart (1876–1958), Raphael Sabatini (1875–1950), and P. G. Wodehouse (1881–1975).

But for those authors who ground out fiction for the pulps, obstacles blocked the road to riches for virtually all of them. They usually wrote in obscurity; publishers often employed pseudonyms; and even if one's real name appeared in a byline, the author seldom garnered any recognition except from the most diehard of fans. And the going rate remained a meager 3 or 4 cents a word, sometimes less for the many low-circulation publications. A 3,000-word story might fetch $90 to $120 (about $1,275 to $1,760 in current money), and rarely did anyone retain rights to their work. But such hard-nosed economics were in keeping with the genre, from the cheap printing and paper to the garish illustrations and melodramatic stories.

Despite the numerous hardships, the writers listed below developed a following and made significant contributions to the pulp genre:

Name (dates)	Genre
Edward Anderson (1905–1969)	Mainly detective stories
Dwight V. Babcock (1909–1979)	Gangster tales
Fredric Brown (1906–1972)	**Science fiction**
John K. Butler (1908–1964)	**Crime**
Hugh B. Cave (1910–2004)	Various
Walt Coburn (1889–1971)	Westerns
Carroll John Daly (1889–1958)	Detective stories
Lester Dent (1904–1959)	*Doc Savage* tales, usually under the name Kenneth Robeson
Walter Gibson (1897–1985)	*The Shadow* stories often under the name as Maxwell Grant
Robert J. Hogan (1897–1963)	G-8 **aviation** tales
John H. Knox (1905–1983)	Various
H. P. Lovecraft (1890–1937)	Fantasy & horror

Name (dates)	Genre
Talbot Mundy (1879–1940)	Adventure
Frederick Nebel (1903–1966)	Mainly detective stories featuring an investigator named Cardigan
E. Phillips Oppenheim (1866–1946)	Spy stories
Norvell Page (1904–1961)	Various genres under different pseudonyms
Sax Rohmer (1883–1959)	Thrillers, especially Fu Manchu tales
Luke Short (1908–1975)	Westerns
Clark Ashton Smith (1893–1961)	Exotica
Emile C. Tepperman (active 1930s)	Various genres under different pseudonyms
W. C. Tuttle (1883–1969)	Westerns
Raoul Whitfield (1897–1945)	Gangster tales
Cornell Woolrich (1903–1968)	Crime
Richard Wormser (1908–1977)	Writing primarily as detective Nick Carter

The subjects these writers covered ran the gamut from "true stories" to cliché-ridden adventure yarns to sadistic, psychological thrillers. For readers eager for some vicarious excitement and titillation, the pulps supplied their wants and more. Tremendously popular throughout the two decades between World Wars I and II, they saw their influence slacken after 1945, especially with the rise of a new amusement, **television**.

See also Best Sellers; Gangster Films; Horror & Fantasy Films; Illustrators; Movies; Mysteries & Hard-Boiled Detectives; Race Relations & Stereotyping; Serials; *Superman*; Western Films

SELECTED READING
Goulart, Ron. *Cheap Thrills: An Informal History of the Pulp Magazines.* New Rochelle, NY: Arlington House, 1972.
Gruber, Frank. *The Pulp Jungle.* Los Angeles: Sherbourne Press, 1967.
Lesser, Robert. *Pulp Art: Original Cover Paintings for the Great American Pulp Magazines.* Edison, NJ: Castle Books, 2003.
Server, Lee. *Encyclopedia of Pulp Fiction Writers.* New York: Checkmark Books, 2002.

R

RACE RELATIONS & STEREOTYPING. Race relations in the 1930s made some progress, albeit at a snail's pace. Many white Americans suffered during the Great Depression, but the country's primary minority groups—black Americans, Native Americans, and Mexican Americans—endured equal or greater hardships. For minorities, life had been difficult enough during the prosperous 1920s, and bad situations became worse with the Depression. When banks foreclosed on the owners of southern cotton fields, for example, the poorly educated, poorly paid, and badly treated black tenant farmers and sharecroppers found themselves driven off the land and without work.

Blacks and Mexicans working in cities and the industrial sectors of the country experienced increased discrimination. Given a choice between firing a minority or a white, employers routinely dismissed the minority. The Meriam Report, a 1928 investigation of federal policies toward Indians, confirmed what many suspected: rampant poverty and disease on all reservations and the use of physical intimidation, robbery, and murder to take Indian land. These situations persisted after the stock market crash of 1929.

By the mid-1930s, the proportion of blacks, male and female, on relief had doubled that of whites. Everywhere, north and south, east and west, black citizens found themselves "last hired, first fired." In addition, high mortality rates among black males, coupled with unemployment, removed many of them as the breadwinners of their families, causing more and more black women to become the heads of households. Traditionally the providers of domestic work for others, these women soon found themselves unemployed when white families, **hotels**, and other sources of domestic service could no longer afford them.

The Depression forced many school districts across the country to shorten the academic year. Localities and states, especially those in the segregated South, had historically allocated less money and resources to black schools, and now many faced closure, not merely a reduced calendar, leaving a large percentage of black **youth** in dire straits.

In the presidential election of 1932, the Democratic candidate, **Franklin D. Roosevelt** (1882–1945), won by a landslide and immediately embarked on ambitious programs designed to tackle economic and social problems. He and his **New Deal** advisers viewed black poverty as only one of the many challenges facing the country. Because of political realities and fear of losing the support of Southern Democrats President Roosevelt moved cautiously and quietly in providing assistance to black Americans. But the steps taken did acknowledge black poverty for the first time, a turning point in American race relations. Minority citizens may have felt that Roosevelt offered weak support of their civil rights, but most appreciated any efforts on their behalf, and in 1936 they voted overwhelmingly for the Democratic ticket.

Before the Depression, state and local relief agencies had not been penalized for turning blacks away. In a significant turnaround, Roosevelt, during his first one hundred days in office, oversaw the creation of a number of government agencies, including the Federal Emergency Relief Administration (FERA, 1933–1935), the National Recovery Administration (NRA, 1933–1935), the Agricultural Adjustment Administration (AAA, 1933–1945), and, later, the Works Progress Administration (WPA, 1935–1943; name changed to Work Projects Administration in 1939)—programs that provided **food**, shelter, and clothing for many blacks.

Other government agencies, such as the **Civilian Conservation Corps** (CCC, 1933–1942) and the National Youth Administration (NYA, 1935–1943), offered both jobs and job training and displayed minimal favoritism. Unfortunately, local authorities, especially in the South, frequently ignored executive orders from Roosevelt that forbade discrimination in federal programs. Often blacks found themselves either denied enrollment or recipients of lower monthly relief checks, situations that federal officials, reluctant to antagonize Southern support, tolerated.

Despite his cautious approach to providing assistance for minorities, Roosevelt did appoint blacks to important positions within his administration. Mary McLeod Bethune (1875–1955), educator, confidante and associate of First Lady **Eleanor Roosevelt** (1884–1962), and perhaps the most influential black woman in the United States in the 1930s, served on the National Advisory Committee for the NYA and in 1939 became director of the Federal Council on Negro Affairs. Bethune encouraged black teenagers to return to high school and continue with a college **education**.

Along with Bethune, William Henry Hastie (1904–1976), a civil rights attorney and law professor, and Robert C. Weaver (1907–1977), an academic, became known as the "black cabinet." Although these three did not hold official posts, they had opportunities to influence presidential decisions. Roosevelt also appointed Clark Foreman (active 1920s and 1930s), a white civil rights activist, to serve with Weaver in ensuring fair treatment for blacks by his administration.

For Native Americans, poverty and ill health, along with inadequate education, became more severe during the Depression. Tuberculosis caused the death of seven times as many Indians as the general population; infant mortality rates ran at twice the national average; and untold numbers of children and adults lived disease-ridden lives.

Roosevelt's appointment of John Collier (active 1920s & 1930s), a founder of the American Indian Defense Association, as commissioner of Indian Affairs for Native Americans offered some hope. Collier supported the preservation of native cultures, introduced bilingual education in the schools, and ended requirements that children living at federal boarding schools attend Protestant church services. Under his leadership, Congress passed the 1934 Indian Reorganization Act. This law restored tribal authority, allowed each tribe to draft its own constitution and assume ownership of all reservation lands, and recognized tribal ceremonies and practices. Also, the federal government designated a fund of $10 million (roughly $150 million in contemporary money) to help Indians move toward self-sufficiency and an additional $2 million ($30 million) to be used annually by the secretary of the interior to buy new land for Indian use.

Prior to the 1930s, Mexican immigrants, both legal and illegal, had become an integral part of the labor force for farms in the Southwest and in factories in other parts of the country. Although many held U.S. citizenship, they often lost their jobs to white Americans, mainly those escaping the poverty of the Dust Bowl in Kansas and Oklahoma. Some 400,000 people of Mexican descent, accused of failure to assimilate into the larger white population, were unjustly deported or repatriated to Mexico between 1929 and 1934. This departure of people from the United States during the 1930s did not involve only Mexicans. Many others, most of them citizens, left the country of their own accord in search of better economic conditions. In fact, during the federal government's fiscal year that ended June 30, 1932, emigration exceeded immigration for the first time in the nation's history.

The use of ethnic stereotypes in American popular culture and the portrayal of minority groups as inferior can be traced back to the nation's beginnings. In the 1800s minstrel shows flourished. White performers dressed up as black men and women, using exaggerated makeup. They sang, danced, and joked in stereotypical ways, reinforcing disparaging imagery. Musical and dance routines from vaudeville also contributed to the injustices, as did commercial **advertising**; distorted black stereotypes became a mainstay of variety acts, songs, and skits well into the twentieth century.

Hollywood **musicals** followed the example of minstrel shows and vaudeville; in comedies and dramas, the **movies** tended to cast blacks either as faithful servants or comic buffoons. Through endless entertainment and advertising, a devoted mammy-type character became the best-known racial caricature of black American women. First found on the vaudeville stage and later in novels, plays, and films, Mammy appeared as a happy and faithful worker who loved her white family. In the 1930s, two black actresses, Louise Beavers (1902–1962) and Hattie McDaniel (1895–1952), portrayed maids in countless movies, frequently without credit, but they still managed to achieve success and recognition, especially for their Mammy performances.

Beavers performed in 102 films during the 1930s alone. Although blacks generally did not secure serious roles, Beavers costarred with Claudette Colbert (1903–1996) in *Imitation of Life* (1934), a sentimental film that became a box office hit. Hollywood perpetuated the usual stereotype by casting Beavers as Aunt Delilah, a black maid, who works for Colbert's Miss Bea. The twist comes when both women find themselves in financial difficulties and Delilah agrees to work as a housekeeper in exchange for a room for herself and her daughter, Peola, played by Fredi Washington (1903–1994). Bea then devises a successful plan to market Delilah's unique pancake recipe. The two share the profits and develop a deep friendship. But the movie becomes more than a "rags to riches" story. Ashamed of her mother, Peola searches for a new life by "passing" for white, and the movie pulls out the emotional stops by depicting the conflict between a submissive mother and a rebellious daughter torn apart by a nation's racism.

Hattie McDaniel acted in 73 movies during the decade. She experienced the height of success when she earned the first Academy Award given to a black performer. Her role as Mammy, Scarlett O'Hara's loyal servant in **Gone with the Wind** (1939), garnered her Best Supporting Actress recognition.

An aspiring actress, vocalist Nina Mae McKinney (1913–1967), signed a contract with MGM after her appearance as a member of the chorus line of *Lew Leslie's Blackbirds* (1928) and a role in the largely black *Hallelujah* (1929). But she found little work because of an absence of roles for black performers. Despite her potential, McKinney spent most of the decade in cheap, little-known productions such as *Safe in Hell* (1931), *Kentucky Minstrels* (1934), *St. Louis Gal* (1938), *The Devil's Daughter* (1939), and *Pocomania* (1939).

Black male movie actors could usually play one of two stereotypical roles: Uncle Toms or coons. Uncle Tom, the docile, happy, nonthreatening servant or train porter, evolved as a black caricature from antebellum America; virtually every film of the 1930s that dealt with the South included Toms. Bill "Bojangles" Robinson (1878–1949), a Broadway dancer and perhaps the most notable personality to play an Uncle Tom role, appeared in several films during the 1930s, including four with white child star **Shirley Temple** (b. 1928). In *The Littlest Rebel* (1935), Robinson plays Uncle Billy, a good-natured, well-mannered Tom, and in *The Little Colonel* (1935), not only does he play the loyal servant, he also dances with Temple, breaking a long-held racial barrier. Since Temple was only seven years old at the time, audiences probably did not see their routine as threatening.

The coon caricature, a slow-talking, slow-walking, self-demeaning figure with large, exaggerated eyes, comes from the days of American slavery and stands as one of the most insulting of all black caricatures. Lincoln Theodore Monroe Andrew Perry (1902–1985), using the stage name Stepin Fetchit, arrived in Hollywood in the mid-1920s, having decided to leave his two-man vaudeville act called "The Laziest Man in the World." He performed in 14 movies during the 1920s, followed by 29 in the 1930s. His career peaked when he costarred in several movies with the popular Will Rogers (1879–1935), including *Steamboat Round the Bend* (1935). The coon stereotype had existed before Perry adopted it. Ironically, his popularity with white audiences quickly made him a millionaire. Others followed suit. Willie Best (1913–1962) and Mantan Moreland (1902–1973) made successful careers out of playing comic coon characters, acting in many films during the decade.

Hollywood even cast black children in stereotypical roles, with Matthew Beard (1925–1981) and Billie Thomas (1931–1980) perhaps being the best known. Beard started acting at age five in a comedy group of ever-changing children first known as *Our Gang* and then as *The Little Rascals*. He played Stymie from 1930 to 1935 and true to caricature presented a slick-tongued, self-assured, nonchalant, con artist always ready with a sly comment. In 1935, Thomas at age four replaced Beard and took the name Buckwheat. Despite their racial typecasting, these young actors shared equal billing with their white counterparts.

Other films carried even more extreme and belittling portrayals of blacks. The successful ***Tarzan*** pictures, eight in all during the 1930s, presented black characters performing either as savages or porters who relieve their white masters of physical burdens. Their roles also demanded that they face unimaginable dangers, saved only by the intervention of the white Johnny Weissmuller (1904–1984) as Tarzan. In ***King Kong*** (1933), black tribal members appear primitive as they worship a giant ape, Kong, as a god and make human sacrifices to him. King Kong himself, many critics have suggested, symbolically represents black masculinity and, as such, needs to be repressed and ultimately destroyed by fearful whites.

Featuring an all-black cast but aimed at a mass market, *The Green Pastures* came out in 1936. Based on Marc Connelly's (1890–1980) Pulitzer Prize–winning 1930 play, this fantasy has the characters reenact scenes from the Bible; it depicts life in a heaven set in the plantation-era South. Rex Ingram (1895–1969) plays "De Lawd" in memorable style, but the exaggerated dialect creates yet another film filled with clichés and racial stereotyping. Nevertheless, the commercial success of *The Green Pastures* opened hitherto closed doors for black performers.

One member of *The Green Pastures'* cast, Eddie "Rochester" Anderson (1905–1977), became a famous star, especially in the medium of **radio**. At age 14, he had performed as a member of "The Three Black Aces," a vaudeville act. He quickly moved to motion pictures, playing bit parts in 44 films during the 1930s. This phase of his career included minor roles in two Oscar-winning movies in the Best Picture category—*You Can't Take It with You* (1938) and *Gone with the Wind* (1939). Beginning in 1937, Anderson intermittently acted as a Pullman porter on *The Jack Benny Program*, a long running radio and, later, **television** show (1932–1958; 1950–1965). Anderson quickly advanced to the permanent role of "Rochester," Jack Benny's (1894–1974) gravel-voiced valet, a part that cemented his future and made him one of a very small number of blacks featured regularly on network radio.

In 1938, some black leaders, concerned about stereotyping in the movies, publicly requested that roles other than doormen, maids, and porters be made available to blacks, but their demand produced little change. In addition to the discrimination they experienced both through their casting in movies and the people their characters represented, blacks often had to sit in separate sections of the theater and sometimes even enter by doors marked "For Colored," especially in the South. This segregated labeling covered other aspects of life in the Jim Crow South—water fountains, public restrooms, **restaurants**, and lodging when traveling.

With blacks relegated to roles as maids and butlers, Native Americans for their part had to play savages in endless **Western films**; most of the time they were mercilessly eliminated in order for the West to be won by whites. The popular depictions of Indians carrying bows and arrows, beating on drums, and stomping around in buckskins, moccasins, and head feathers while raiding white settlements to capture women originally came from Wild West shows and dime novels. Hollywood perpetuated this imagery throughout the 1930s, and it did not fade out until many years later.

Stagecoach (1939), a classic Western directed by John Ford (1894–1973) that stars John Wayne (1907–1979), illustrates this convention: hostile Indians go on the warpath, pursuing and attacking the stagecoach through much of the journey. The picture presents a simplistic plot and thrilling action in which a white male hero defeats Indians and other bad guys. To compound the indignity, the industry frequently did not use Native Americans at all, but white actors in Indian makeup.

The Lone Ranger, first introduced as a radio program in 1933, came out as a full-length movie feature in 1938. This first effort starred Lee Powell (1908–1944) as the masked Ranger, with Chief Thundercloud (1899–1955) costarring as the faithful Tonto (which means crazy in Spanish). A second picture, *The Lone Ranger Rides Again* (1939), kept Chief Thundercloud, but Robert Livingston (1904–1988) replaced Powell. The radio show, created by George W. Trendle (1884–1972), with writing assistance from Fran Striker (1903–1962), employed the same story line and stereotyping of the movies—the team of the heroic white Lone Ranger and his subservient Indian companion righting injustices throughout the mythic West.

In the popular culture arena, opportunities for blacks and Native Americans on radio remained limited, but the medium contributed to the shaping of stereotypical images of minorities. In 1929, the National Broadcasting Company (NBC radio) added **Amos 'n' Andy** to its network offerings, a program with overtones from minstrel shows and black-face comedies. Freeman Gosden (1899–1982) and Charles Correll (1890–1972), two white performers, provided dialogue in a stereotypical dialect, not only for Amos and Andy, but for a large cast, including Kingfish, a dishonest and lazy confidence man who massacres the English language, and Sapphire, his loud, abrasive, and bossy wife.

In 1931, a black newspaper journalist named Robert Vann (active 1920s & 1930s) obtained 740,000 signatures on a petition requesting *Amos 'n' Andy* be taken off the air. But the program had captured the imagination of millions of listeners both black and white, enough to convince the network and the sponsor to retain the show; it easily became the most popular radio program of the decade. Conversations among fans about the previous night's episode usually included a reenactment of some of the lines in the approximate dialect, apparently without an acknowledgment of what should have been an issue of racial stereotyping.

Juvenile radio **serials** such as *The Tom Mix Ralston Straight Shooters* (1933–1951) also contained some stereotyped characters, a situation influenced by *Amos 'n' Andy*. For example, one of the workers on the Mix ranch was Wash, the "colored cook" and man-of-all-work. Native Americans also appeared in Western radio shows, usually approximating the roles given their cinema counterparts. In many radio adventures, the villains also bear evil-sounding foreign names, a form of electronic xenophobia.

Advertising and sponsors supported the absence of minorities, especially blacks, on radio. By the mid-1930s, the **radio networks** received millions in advertising revenues and prime-time shows often had more than one backer. Sponsors did not want to fund programs starring blacks for fear their product would be perceived as black-oriented and thus be shunned by white consumers.

Organized labor also supported the exclusion of blacks on radio. The American Federation of Musicians (AFM), the Radio Writers Guild (RWG), and the American Federation of Radio Actors (AFRA) did not accept blacks into membership. Some radio executives occasionally attempted to employ prominent blacks on their shows but quickly aborted their efforts when their good intentions came under fire. Three shows serve as examples: NBC's *Ethel Waters Show*, starring actress and singer Ethel Waters (1896–1977), closed in 1933 after only a few weeks because of a boycott threat from Southern affiliates; the network also curtailed *Quizzicale*, starring bandleader Cab Calloway (1907–1994), when it failed to secure a sponsor. The Columbia Broadcasting System (CBS radio) in 1937 cancelled *The Louis Armstrong Show*, starring **jazz** trumpeter Louis Armstrong (1901–1971), after 13 weeks when it received poor ratings. This show suffered the added challenge of airing opposite the very successful *Jack Benny Program*, which ironically featured Eddie Anderson as Rochester.

An occasional show did manage to cross the racial dividing lines erected by radio stations. Chicago's WSBC managed to air the *All-Negro Hour* from 1929 to 1935. It featured black performers exclusively and at first ran weekly and later expanded to 10 hours a week. Jack L. Cooper (active 1920s–1960s), a vaudeville performer and pioneering disc jockey, served as host for the program, which featured **music**, comedy, and serial dramas.

Even a seemingly innocuous medium like **comic strips** reflected the endemic racism of early twentieth-century America. Humorous series like *Thimble Theater* (better known as *Popeye* to many) featured demeaning caricatures of wide-eyed, grinning natives, as did *The Katzenjammer Kids* and its look-alike *The Captain and the Kids*. Family strips, such as the enormously popular *Gumps*, had their stereotyped black servants and cooks, while adventure serials featured white heroes like Mandrake the Magician, a tuxedoed man of magical powers, accompanied by Lothar, a faithful but clearly subordinate black companion. The Phantom, the mysterious "ghost who walks," a white male who commands instant respect from primitive tribesmen, roams "the Dark Continent" freely, a symbol of racial supremacy decked out in purple tights. The 1930s may have been a banner decade for comic strips, but many of them persisted in portraying blacks in a style more befitting the crude drawings of the nineteenth century.

As in the media, discrimination occurred in athletics and sports too, but some black athletes achieved scattered recognition during the 1930s. Nonsouthern colleges, especially in track and field and **football**, began to integrate their teams and much Negro League **baseball** equaled anything then being played in the all-white major leagues. **Boxing** fans, black and white, followed over national radio the exploits of Joe Louis (1914–1981), nicknamed "the Brown Bomber." Louis became the world's heavyweight champion in 1937 and reigned, undefeated, until his 1949 retirement.

At the 1932 Summer **Olympic Games** held in Los Angeles and the later 1936 games in Germany, black participants from the United States won medals. In the California events, black Americans gained a total of five medals, more than in any previous games. In 1936, 19 black athletes, an increase from 1932, qualified for the U.S. track and field team. One participant, Jesse Owens (1913–1980), earned lasting fame by winning three individual gold medals and a fourth one as a member of a sprint relay team. He also set three world records. In a subtle note of prejudice, the press, in reporting any sporting accomplishments by black athletes, usually reminded the public whenever the winners were "colored."

In the music world, many performers, both black and white, found themselves unemployed during the Depression. As economic hardships spread, the sales of **recordings** dropped dramatically, although **jukeboxes** and radio provided a wealth of music for listening and dancing. The failure of small, independent recording companies hit black musicians especially hard since many of these businesses produced what the industry called "race records," music recorded by blacks and sold in predominantly black neighborhoods.

Broadway saw occasional revues featuring black performers, but stage opportunities proved few and far between. In 1935, *Porgy and Bess*, with music and lyrics by **George (1898–1937) and Ira Gershwin** (1896–1983) and based on a book by DuBose Heyward (1885–1940), premiered with an all-black cast. True to the segregated atmosphere of the times, the 1936 commercial recording of the score featured Lawrence Tibbett (1896–1960) and Helen Jepsen (active 1930s), two white artists. Producers feared that a recording by black artists would not sell to white buyers.

Marian Anderson (1897–1993), an accomplished contralto, gained recognition during the 1920s and 1930s in both the United States and Europe. In 1935–1936, she appeared for the second time in concert at New York's Town Hall, gave two concerts at Carnegie Hall, and then toured the country from coast to coast. But in the spring of 1939, the

Daughters of the American Revolution (DAR), with their policy of "concerts by white artists only," refused to let her perform at Constitution Hall in Washington, D.C. Many people voiced outrage, including First Lady Eleanor Roosevelt, who immediately resigned from the DAR and helped arrange a free, open-air concert at the Lincoln Memorial on April 9, 1939. Anderson sang for an audience of 75,000 people, as well as millions of radio listeners, in what can be remembered as one of the most dramatic civil rights spectacles ever.

On a brighter note, the Negro Theatre Project, a part of the **Federal Theatre Project** (FTP, 1935–1939) of the WPA, provided opportunities for black actors and actresses. John Houseman (1902–1988) and **Orson Welles** (1915–1985), two white producers, headed the New York branch of the nationwide project. The FTP produced several innovative dramas, including an all-black *Macbeth*, directed by Welles, that used Haiti as its locale in 1936. *The Swing Mikado* (1939), a black version of the 1885 Gilbert and Sullivan operetta, attracted 250,000 people in Chicago alone, and went on the road. Its success inspired impresario Mike Todd (1909–1958) to mount a similar production, *The Hot Mikado*, that same year.

By 1936, economic conditions and employment possibilities had improved for whites and minorities and the country's popular music reflected a new optimism. **Swing,** with its lively tempos and easy rhythms, pulled dancers out on the floor and bookings increased rapidly for musicians and their bands. But segregation still flourished in many parts of the United States, which meant that, commercially, white musicians benefited the most from this popular development in the music industry.

Restricted to inferior venues, most black performers received lower pay and less recognition for their accomplishments. Exceptions included **Duke Ellington** (1899–1974), Cab Calloway, and **Count Basie** (1904–1984), who achieved some success in the industry. Marking a step forward in race relations, clarinetist **Benny Goodman** (1909–1986), arguably the most popular swing musician of the day, in 1937 added two black musicians, Teddy Wilson (1912–1986) and Lionel Hampton (1908–2002), to his quartet and no one raised any significant objections.

Black performers in the music world, as well as in movies and radio, began to serve at least in small ways as ambassadors of equality. Some, such as **Paul Robeson** (1898–1976), took an active stand for civil rights. A college graduate with a law degree, as well as a singer and actor, he performed on Broadway (*Showboat*, 1932) and starred in a number of films, including *The Emperor Jones* (1933) and *Song of Freedom* (1936). His rendition of Earl Robinson's (1910–1991) "Ballad for Americans" (1938), on both CBS radio and at the **New York World's Fair**, became legendary. Robeson, a political activist, and the first major black artist to refuse to perform before segregated audiences, served as a spokesperson for a variety of causes especially equal rights for black Americans.

By 1939, annual record sales had once again attained their pre-Depression levels, about 50 million discs. That same year vocalist Billie Holiday released "Strange Fruit" (music and lyrics by Lewis Allen [pseudonym of Abel Meeropol, 1903–1986]), a controversial condemnation of lynching. The major recording companies and radio networks refused to touch the song, fearing a consumer backlash. Lynching as a means of mob rule and intimidation had become almost commonplace and closely associated with race relations in the South following the Civil War. The number of reported incidents began to fall at the beginning of the twentieth century and significantly decreased during the 1930s. By the end of the decade, such reports had become rare. White people, it seemed, increasingly viewed violence like lynchings as unconscionable and repulsive, but "Strange Fruit" reminded listeners of its continued existence.

Radio and movies perpetuated unflattering images of minority groups, and consumer products, especially foods, had long used blacks in stereotypical ways as part of their advertising and labeling. In the late 1800s, a Missouri mill owner used the mammy image along with the name Aunt Jemima, taken from a popular vaudeville song, to promote a pancake mix. He then sold the pancake recipe and the Aunt Jemima marketing idea to the R. T. Davis Mill Company, which developed an advertising plan to use a real person to portray Aunt Jemima.

In 1933, the Quaker Oats Company, the owner of the Davis Mill Company since 1926, employed Anna Robinson (d. 1951) to play the role of Aunt Jemima. She prepared and served pancakes at Chicago's 1933 **Century of Progress Exhibition** and for several years made appearances at county fairs, food shows, and local **grocery stores and supermarkets**. Packaging before and during the 1930s usually consisted of a picture of Aunt Jemima and often a message in dialect, such as "Don't you fret, Honey! Jus' festify dem wif my pancakes!" Billboards featuring her smiling face would announce "I'se in town, honey." Similarly, Uncle Rastus, Aunt Jemima's male equivalent, appeared throughout the 1930s in print ads for Cream of Wheat, a hot cereal.

Even products like chewing gum used demeaning tactics in their advertisements. A 1933 cartoon for Beech-Nut Gum shows a white adult male and an adolescent boy and girl getting captured by black cannibals. But thanks to Beech-Nut Gum and some silly magic tricks, which could be obtained for five gum wrappers, they gain their freedom. Certainly the image of white superiority over bloodthirsty savages added support to much of the racial stereotyping so rampant in the United States during the first half of the twentieth century.

Along with the abundance of such imagery throughout all facets of popular culture, one event and the subsequent trial associated with it further reveals the deep racial divisions that plagued the country during the 1930s. A group of white teens got into a fight with some black youths on a train passing through Alabama on March 25, 1931. All hobos, the whites lost the fight and subsequently got thrown off the train. Two young white girls, also transients, claimed they had been raped by the blacks. At that point, local law officers arrested and jailed the blacks, aged 12 to 21, in the town of Scottsboro, Alabama. Following a quick trial that began 12 days after the event, and despite evidence to the contrary, eight of the young men—including one who suffered severe retardation—received convictions for rape and accompanying death sentences. The court spared the life of the 12-year-old.

This highly publicized event drew outraged reactions from across the country and letters poured into Scottsboro pleading for pardons. Ministers preached sermons; jazz artists like Duke Ellington and Cab Calloway held fund-raising events; the distinguished black poet Langston Hughes (1902–1967) wrote about visiting them in the penitentiary; and blues singer Leadbelly (b. Huddie Ledbetter, 1888–1946) immortalized them in song. Eventually, the U.S. Supreme Court overturned the initial verdicts, and after a series of retrials lasting until 1937, only five of the nine received convictions. Appeals dragged on; in 1948 one escaped from prison and the remaining four received paroles in 1950.

But the 1930s experienced a slow awakening of the country's social conscience, as evidenced by the reaction to the Scottsboro case, the continuing popularity of groups like the integrated Benny Goodman Quartet, the acceptance of black athletes in some sports, and racially blind New Deal legislation and programs. The 1929 stock market crash severely disrupted the lives of those who already lived at or below the poverty line and, as usual, minorities suffered the worst consequences. Their conditions improved only slightly after the Depression, but some racial barriers had been weakened and small steps taken toward equality and respect.

See also Children's Films; Fairs & Expositions; Fletcher Henderson; Hollywood Production Code; Leisure & Recreation; Motels; Prohibition & Repeal; Religion; Travel

SELECTED READING

Benshoff, Harry M., and Sean Griffin. *America on Film: Representing Race, Class, Gender, and Sexuality at the Movies*. Malden, MA: Blackwell, 2004.

Bogle, Donald. *Bright Boulevards, Bold Dreams: The Story of Black Hollywood*. New York: Ballantine Books, 2005.

————. *Toms, Coons, Mulattoes, Mammies, and Bucks*. New York: Continuum Publishing Co., 1989.

Brown, Gene, ed. *Ethnic Groups in American Life*. New York: Arno Press, 1978.

Olson, James Stuart. *The Ethnic Dimension in American History*. New York: St. Martin's Press, 1979.

Verney, Kevern. *African Americans and U.S. Popular Culture*. New York: Routledge, 2003.

RADIO. Although somewhere between 60 and 75 million Americans attended the movies at least once a week during the 1930s, untold millions more listened to radio *each* and *every* day. The most pervasive form of communication ever developed up to that time, radio broadcasting leveled regional and social differences and barriers by its very ubiquity. Everyone could share in the same programming through national networks.

At the beginning of the decade, slightly over 600 AM (amplitude modulation) stations broadcast to almost 14 million receiving sets, or 46 percent of American homes, a remarkable statistic in itself, given that radio as a mass medium had been around only since 1920. Its phenomenal growth did not slow down with the Depression. By the mid-1930s, the actual number of active stations had dropped slightly because of the economic situation, but people continued buying new radios without any significant letup. In 1935, over 21 million sets could be found in 67 percent of homes. At the close of the 1930s, the industry had recovered from its slump, and 765 stations sent their signals to over 51 million receivers in 81 percent of homes. In addition, many families had multiple sets, a clear reflection of radio's vast popularity.

The purchase of a radio would not have been undertaken lightly during the Depression. Small, table model receivers cost $40 and more in the early 1930s (over $450 in contemporary dollars), although prices declined throughout the decade; a cheap plastic "pee-wee" radio could be had for about $10 in 1939 (or roughly $145 today). Many of the larger, floor model receivers served as fine pieces of furniture. Often done in exotic veneers with striking **Art Deco** and Streamlined styling, a top-of-the-line radio could cost hundreds of dollars. Since much American family life in the evenings revolved around the living room radio, people seldom begrudged this significant investment if their budgets allowed it. Manufacturers like Atwater-Kent, Crosley, Emerson, General Electric, Magnavox, Philco, RCA, and Zenith pitched their products as much for their aesthetic elegance as they did for their electronic excellence.

Radio served as an important piece of furniture in many American homes; this 1939 floor model receiver dominates the living room. (Courtesy of the Library of Congress)

As radio became part and parcel of the everyday lives of Americans, the medium assumed a unique importance. Unlike movies and print media, it gave the illusion of being free. Radio entertained continuously, from **music** to drama to comedy, provided instant news, weather, and sports, and educated with endless self-help and instructional shows. A twist of the dial brought in just about anything a listener might want, and detailed schedules in **newspapers** and **magazines** informed the public about favorite shows. Most Americans considered radio a necessity, right along with **food** and shelter. Even in the worst of the Depression, very few people defaulted on their receiver payments.

Car radios, introduced to the driving public in 1927, initially met some resistance. Less than 1 percent of all vehicles boasted a receiver in 1930, but interest in them grew, despite the Depression. Over 2 million vehicles had radios by 1935, and that number jumped to 7 million—a quarter of all **automobiles**—by the close of the decade. A grow-ing percentage of consumers no longer viewed the car radio as a luxury; it had become just as necessary as one in the home. Amid continuing economic woes, the radio had succeeded in becoming "Depression-proof." Advertisers quickly grasped the importance listeners placed on radio and willingly put their dollars into commercials; ad spending went from slightly over $3 million in 1932 (roughly $44 million in contemporary dol-lars) to well over $100 million by 1940 ($1.5 billion).

American radio acquainted an avid listening public with hundreds of personalities who grew to be household names. Some of these entertainers moved directly to radio from vaudeville, others came from movie careers and sometimes mixed radio with film, and still others started in radio and stayed there. Whatever route they followed, those who found a niche in broadcasting often rose to an unparalleled level of popular fame.

In addition to the array of stars, American radio during the 1930s offered a variety of programming hitherto unseen in entertainment. Not even the movie industry, churning out hundreds of feature films yearly, could approach radio's output of dozens of shows each day, hundreds each week, thousands by the end of a year. The quality may have been wildly uneven, but the selection was unparalleled.

Selected Programming on American Radio during the 1930s
(arranged chronologically by category)

Category	Selected Artists/Performers and Shows	Dates
Music and Variety	Vaughn De Leath, *Vaughn De Leath* (and other titles)	1920–1939
	Billy Jones and Ernie Hare, *The Happiness Boys*	1921–1940
	Wendell Hall, *The Red-Headed Music Maker*	1922–1937
	Harry Horlick, *A & P Gypsies*	1923–1936
	(Various hosts), *The Clicquot Club Eskimos*	1923–1936
	(Various hosts), *The Eveready Hour*	1923–1930
	(Various hosts), *The Ipana Troubadors*	1923–1934
	Joe Kelly (and others), **The National Barn Dance**	1924–1970
	Whitey Ford (and others), **Grand Ole Opry**	1925–present
	Billy Hillpot and Scrappy Lambert, *The Smith Brothers*	1926–1934
	Rudy Vallee, *The Fleischmann Yeast Hour; The Royal Gelatin Hour*	1928–1939
	(Various hosts), *The Old Gold Hour* (and other titles)	1929–1948
	Lanny Ross, *The Lanny Ross Show* (and other titles)	1929–1952
	Gene Arnold, *The Sinclair Wiener Minstrels*	1930–1939
	Ben Bernie, *Ben Bernie, The Old Maestro*	1930–1943
	Bing Crosby, *The Music That Satisfies, Kraft Music Hall, The Chesterfield Show, Philco Radio Time* (and other titles)	1930–1956
	Eddie Cantor, *The Chase and Sanborn Hour*	1931–1938
	Arthur Tracy, *The Street Singer*	1931–1942
	Kate Smith, *The Kate Smith Hour*	1931–1952
	(Various hosts), *The Chesterfield Quarter-Hour*	1931–1933
	Whispering Jack Smith, *Whispering Jack Smith*	1932–1935
	Charles Winninger, *The Maxwell House Show Boat*	1932–1937
	(Various hosts), *Manhattan Merry-Go-Round*	1932–1949
	Al Jolson, *Kraft Music Hall, The Lifebuoy Program* (and other titles)	1932–1949
	(Various hosts and formats), *The Camel Caravan*	1933–1954
	Don McNeill, *The Breakfast Club*	1933–1953
	Jimmy Durante, *The Jimmy Durante Show*	1933–1950
	(Various hosts), *The Vicks Open House*	1934–1938

Category	Selected Artists/Performers and Shows	Dates
	Pat Barrett, *Uncle Ezra's Radio Station*	1934–1941
	Phil Spitalny, *The Hour of Charm*	1934–1948
	Edward Bowes, *Major Bowes' Original Amateur Hour*	1934–1948
	Louella Parsons, *Hollywood Hotel*	1934–1938
	Horace Heidt, *The Horace Heidt Show*	1935–1953
	(Various hosts), **Your Hit Parade**	1935–1957
	Martin Block, other disc jockeys, *Make-Believe Ballroom*	1935–1954
	Kay Kyser, *Kay Kyser's Kollege of Musical Knowledge*	1937–1949
	(Various hosts and formats), *The Fitch Bandwagon*	1938–1948
	(Various hosts), *The Texaco Star Theater*	1938–1940
Comedy	Freeman Gosden and Charles Correll, **Amos 'n' Andy**	1928–1955
	Goodman Ace and Jane Ace, *Easy Aces*	1930–1945
	Raymond Knight, *The Cuckoo Hour*	1930–1936
	Will Rogers, *The Will Rogers Program*	1930–1935
	Frederick Chase Taylor and Budd Hulick, *Stoopnagle and Budd*	1930–1938
	Chester Lauck and Norris Goff, *Lum and Abner*	1931–1954
	Art Van Harvey and Bernardine Flynn, *Vic and Sade*	1932–1946
	Ed Wynn, *The Texaco Fire Chief, The Perfect Fool*	1932–1937
	Jack Benny, *The Jack Benny Program*	1932–1958
	Fred Allen, *The Fred Allen Show*	1932–1949
	George Burns and Gracie Allen, *Burns and Allen*	1932–1950
	Jack Pearl, *The Jack Pearl Show*	1932–1937
	Joe Penner, *The Baker's Broadcast*	1933–1937
	Bob Hope, *The Pepsodent Show* (and other titles)	1935–1955
	Jim Jordan and Marian Jordan, *Fibber McGee and Molly*	1935–1959
	Milton Berle, *The Milton Berle Show* (and other titles)	1936–1942
	Edgar Bergen, *Edgar Bergen/Charlie McCarthy Show*	1936–1956
	Fanny Brice, *Baby Snooks*	1936–1951
Drama (Anthology)	*The Collier Hour*	1927–1932
	Grand Hotel	1930–1940
	The First Nighter Program	1930–1953
	Death Valley Days	1930–1945
	Lights Out	1934–1939
	Lux Radio Theater	1934–1955
	The Cavalcade of America	1935–1953
	The Columbia Workshop	1936–1945
	Hollywood Playhouse	1937–1940
	The Campbell Playhouse (originally *Mercury Theater on the Air*)	1938–1940
Crime, Police, and Detective Series	True Detective Mysteries	1929–1930; 1936–1939
	The Shadow	1930–1954

Selected Programming on American Radio during the 1930s (*Continued*)

Category	Selected Artists/Performers and Shows	Dates
	Sherlock Holmes	1930–1936; 1939–1946
	The Eno Crime Club	1931–1936
	Twenty Thousand Years in Sing Sing	1933–1939
	Calling All Cars	1933–1939
	Gang Busters	1935–1957
	Mr. Keen, Tracer of Lost Persons	1937–1955
	Big Town	1937–1951
News, Sports, Public Affairs, and Talk	**Walter Winchell**, *Walter Winchell's Jergens Journal*	1930–1957
	Westbrook Van Voorhis, others, **The March of Time**	1931–1945
	John Howe, *The University of Chicago Round Table*	1931–1955
	Marion Sayle Taylor, *The Voice of Experience*	1932–1939
	Ed Sullivan, *The Ed Sullivan Show*	1932–1946
	Mary Margaret McBride, *Mary Margaret McBride*	1934–1954
	Jimmy Fidler, *The Jimmy Fidler Show*	1934–1950
	America's Town Meeting of the Air	1935–1956
	Bill Stern, *The Colgate Sports Newsreel*	1937–1956
	Hedda Hopper, *The Hedda Hopper Show*	1939–1951
Education	*Betty Crocker*	1924–1953
	Aunt Sammy	1926–1935
	Ida Bailey Allen, *The Radio Homemakers Club*	1926–1936
	Walter Damrosch, *The Music Appreciation Hour*	1928–1942
	Everett Mitchell, *The National Farm and Home Hour*	1928–1958
	Allen Prescott, *The Wife Saver*	1929–1943
	John MacPherson, *The Mystery Chef*	1930–1948
	The American School of the Air	1930–1948

The preceding chart barely begins to list all the programming available on radio. Categories like **soap operas, science fiction**, and **serials** stand as distinctive entries in radio programming and receive separate discussions elsewhere in this encyclopedia. The topics above—music and variety, comedy, and so on—suggest some of the balances of power existing during the period. A series could be created because of an individual's popularity (e.g., Eddie Cantor and *The Chase and Sanborn Hour*, Bing Crosby and *The Kraft Music Hall*, Rudy Vallee and *The Fleischmann Yeast Hour*), but corporate interests and sponsors underwrote the expenses. So Chase and Sanborn Coffee, Kraft Foods, and Fleischmann's Yeast insisted on their product names receiving top billing, not the star. People tuned in for Cantor or Crosby or Vallee, but the sponsors, along with their **advertising** agencies, enjoyed de facto control of any content. Regardless of a show's title, radio entertainers seldom oversaw the productions in which they starred. Radio might exist as a seemingly creative medium, but other interests held the financial reins of power.

The chart also indicates how much early radio featured music and variety in its offerings, an obvious acknowledgment of its roots in vaudeville. By the early 1930s, well over two-thirds of total radio programming consisted of music/variety-based shows, with a large proportion of that figure—about 40 percent—focused on genres other than straight popular selections, such as classical, operetta, ethnic, or regional. Stations also broadcast a great deal of incidental music that served as background or brief features on variety shows, comedy series, and the like. Wherever people turned their radio dials, they could pick up music and, most likely, popular music.

Larger stations often retained studio bands. On call for most of the broadcasting day, they featured lineups that included some of the best instrumentalists in the business. Their job consisted of playing for live commercials, background music for dramatic shows, backing singers and vocal groups, and generally being available whenever someone called for live music. More often than not, what they played could be categorized as mundane; no one considered the studio band the star, who or what they accompanied received the attention. Studio orchestras nonetheless provided stable employment for countless musicians.

As the decade progressed, music programming declined, but only slightly. By 1939, it still constituted 57 percent of all broadcasting, down only about 10 percent from 10 years earlier. The type of music featured, however, changed markedly. Popular music showed a sharp increase at the expense of all other formats. Approximately 75 percent of all the music on the air consisted of popular songs when the 1930s drew to a close.

Classical music, once a staple of early radio, commenced a long, slow decline. To maintain prestige, the networks continued to broadcast programs like *The Voice of Firestone* (NBC, 1928–1954), *General Motors Concerts* (NBC, 1929–1937), and *The Ford Sunday Evening Hour* (CBS, 1934–1942), but they knew such shows drew a limited audience. In the main, classical selections all but disappeared from regular schedules; not until the rise of FM (frequency modulation) in the 1950s would alternative forms of music again be heard with any regularity. The popular song, the "hit," dominated the airwaves.

With the onset of the 1930s, comedy, crime, and dramatic programs grew in number, demonstrating that both the **radio networks** and advertising executives realized the still-new medium could draw audiences and prosper with a broader range of productions. Many "serious" dramatic series, such as *Grand Hotel* and *The First Nighter Program*, also entered programming schedules during the decade. A typical entry in this genre would be *Lux Radio Theater*; its name came from a popular beauty soap. Hosted by Cecil B. DeMille (1881–1959), a celebrated Hollywood director, the series presented one-hour adaptations of leading motion pictures, often using the same performers as had starred in the movie. *Lux Radio Theater* illustrated the close connections between film and radio, an ideal way of publicizing motion pictures while at the same time having a top-ranked radio show.

Although music and variety, comedy, and drama occupied a good part of the broadcasting schedule, radio also emerged in the 1930s as a primary carrier of news and information, and a number of news reporters and journalists rose to prominence. This new breed, weaned on electronic newsgathering instead of newspaper beats, realized radio's potential during the 1930s, and brought a measure of distinction to the networks. Newscasters—itself a relatively new designation that replaced "reporter"—like Elmer

Davis (1890–1958), Gabriel Heatter (1890–1972), H. V. Kaltenborn (1878–1965), Raymond Gram Swing (1887–1968), Lowell Thomas (1892–1981), and Edward R. Murrow (1908–1965) redefined the traditional image of a reporter. They introduced a personal aural style to their scripts, and often added interpretive commentary to ongoing stories. News on the radio, no less colorful than that found in many newspapers, also offered personality.

When World War II loomed, people relied on their radios for late-breaking bulletins about the deteriorating international situation. Entertainment might remain radio's primary function, but listeners sought information along with escapism. Edward R. Murrow, for example, a member of the CBS news team, brought unequalled sincerity and gravity to his reports. In his mournful voice, he described the darkest days of late 1939 after conflict had broken out across Europe. His descriptions of the London Blitz remain classic, a calm voice in the face of disaster, but one foretelling that worse lay ahead.

Another kind of journalist also gained an audience during the Depression era: the electronic gossip columnist. Coming from the newspaper tabloids and fan magazines that had established themselves during the Roaring Twenties, writers like Jimmy Fidler (1900–1988), Hedda Hopper (1885–1966), Louella Parsons (1881–1972), Ed Sullivan (1901–1974), and Walter Winchell (1897–1972) created gossip-oriented shows that audiences loved. Relying on tidbits and innuendo about the most popular (or notorious) celebrities of the day, these rumormongers became celebrities in their own right, often engaging in real and fabricated on-air feuds with one another.

Dr. John Brinkley & Border Radio. As radio increasingly demonstrated its influence in the late twenties and early thirties, a few individuals attempted to take advantage of the power—real or perceived—the medium possessed. In order to sidestep federal restrictions on radio networks imposed by the Federal Radio Commission (FRC), some entrepreneurs built high-powered transmitters in Mexico near the Texas border. They created several stations, all starting with the letters XE; these border broadcasters mushroomed in number by 1930 and, given their power, could saturate North America with a variety of programming. They attracted a widespread rural audience, a group that fundamentalist preachers who had been banned from regular U.S. stations willingly paid a large price to reach.

The move to Mexico gave birth to what some called "border radio." Coupled with advertising from sponsors that included quack medicines and get-rich schemes, this form of broadcasting evolved into a profitable business for all concerned, and it flourished throughout the 1930s. John R. Brinkley of Milford, Kansas, known as the "goat-gland doctor," pioneered the use of radio to such dubious ends. A physician, Brinkley began touting his revolutionary "transplants," along with a special elixir that he claimed would give men renewed sexual potency.

His outrageous promises had, by 1930, made his Kansas station the most popular one in the country, and his profits allowed him to boost its wattage to the point that he could be heard in much of the nation. That same year, however, the FRC denied Brinkley's application for a license renewal, saying he had deceived listeners. Kansas authorities also revoked his medical license, effectively stripping him of any claims of legitimacy. Brinkley appealed the FRC decision, but a state court upheld the agency.

Desperate to regain his influence, Brinkley decided to take advantage of the border stations outside the FRC's jurisdiction. In 1931, he established himself in Del Rio, Texas.

Shortly thereafter he built a huge transmitter for station XERA in Mexico's Ciudad Acuna, just across the Rio Grande. Brinkley contracted with numerous country musicians, such as the **Carter Family**, to attract listeners. Despite the station's power, the goat-gland doctor's star had faded, and he ceased to be a significant force in broadcasting. Briefly, however, this Kansas doctor enjoyed a moment as a radio celebrity, one of the first to use the medium as a means to questionable ends.

Shows directed at selected niche audiences, such as children (*The Children's Hour*, 1927–1934; many others), classical music buffs (*The NBC Symphony*, 1937–1954; *The Metropolitan Opera*, 1931–present; many others), and specific religious groups (*The Catholic Hour*, 1930–1952; others) have been omitted from this article because of space considerations.

See also Jukeboxes; Leisure & Recreation; Recordings; Religion; Streamlining; Swing

SELECTED READING

Barfield, Ray. *Listening to Radio, 1920–1950*. Westport, CT: Praeger, 1996.

Barnouw, Erik. *A History of Broadcasting in the United States*. Vol. 1: *A Tower in Babel*. Vol. 2: *The Golden Web*. New York: Oxford University Press, 1966–1968.

Dunning, John. *On the Air: The Encyclopedia of Old-Time Radio*. New York: Oxford University Press, 1998.

Fowler, Gene, and Bill Crawford. *Border Radio: Quacks, Yodelers, Pitchmen, Psychics, and Other Amazing Broadcasters of the American Airwaves*. Austin: Texas Monthly Press, 1987.

Maltin, Leonard. *The Great American Broadcast: A Celebration of Radio's Golden Age*. New York: New American Library, 2000.

RADIO NETWORKS. In 1919, a consortium of companies, General Electric, American Telephone & Telegraph, Western Electric, and American Marconi, sought to gain control of radio telegraphy and formed the Radio Corporation of America, or RCA. Through a series of intricate maneuvers with several rivals during the 1920s, RCA created a "central broadcasting organization," or network. Consisting of stations linked by land telephone lines leased from AT&T, which had left the original RCA group, it could broadcast, simultaneously, the same signal to many connected stations. The corporate owners of this new network christened it the National Broadcasting Company, or NBC, in 1926. Leading the way for the commercial development of **radio**, NBC started with 19 stations, but that number quickly grew. Henceforth, broadcasting would be driven by network radio, and Americans everywhere would share, via the airwaves, news, **education**, and entertainment.

To fulfill its promise, NBC created two networks under its banner to diversify its programming and attract the maximum number of affiliates. By the beginning of 1927, NBC had a "Red" branch, headquartered at New York City's WEAF, a station originally owned by AT&T but sold to RCA. At the same time, it premiered a "Blue" network, an operation based with WJZ, a neighboring Newark station owned by Westinghouse. Each division offered separate stations, schedules, and shows, with Red stations carrying more **music** and entertainment, while the Blue stations tended to place greater emphasis on news and cultural programming. Not surprisingly, Red usually outstripped Blue in terms of total listeners and sponsor preferences. The sheer size and scope of NBC-Red and NBC-Blue worried lawmakers, who thought that such a concentration of power would impose unfair influence over the airwaves, although parent RCA vowed it would provide impartial news and education, along with quality entertainment, on both the Red and Blue branches of its new network.

In the fall of 1927, envious of the overwhelming success of the NBC venture, a group calling itself United Independent Broadcasters went on the air with 47 affiliate stations and a base in New York City. This second network struggled financially, and in 1928 Columbia Records rescued it by purchasing shares in the operation. Ironically, the network's association with the record manufacturer ended when Columbia Records sold its stock to William S. Paley (1901–1990) in late 1928. He took over the ownership of United Independent Broadcasters, renamed his purchase the Columbia Broadcasting System (CBS radio), and worked to expand and improve the operation.

By 1930, NBC-Red and -Blue could claim 71 affiliates, and CBS boasted 60. Both networks grew dramatically during the 1930s. The success of NBC and CBS captured the attention of those not associated with them, and in time other broadcasters decided to form rival networks. One such competitor, the Mutual Broadcasting System (MBS radio), went on the air in 1934 with four stations. The most successful of a number of attempts to form competing networks, the Mutual effort functioned primarily as a cooperative venture and offered little original programming. Most of its affiliates already had limited associations with NBC or CBS, and they used Mutual to provide further connections among them. In addition, the Mutual shows tended to go to regional or rural markets that attracted small audiences, so it never had the influence or popularity of an NBC or CBS despite an expanding number of associated stations.

By the end of the decade, network radio had emerged as the dominant format in American broadcasting. NBC controlled 182 stations, and CBS stood not too far behind with 112. The Mutual organization claimed 160 affiliated stations. With 765 commercial stations on the air, 454 of them (59 percent) enjoyed affiliation with NBC, CBS, or Mutual; 38 percent, with just NBC and CBS. The numbers can be misleading; of the remaining 300+ stations with no major network connections, most consisted of small, dawn-to-dusk operations that functioned on low power and broadcast to limited local audiences. Like small, rural **newspapers**, they filled the immediate needs of their constituents, such as farming information, market reports, weddings, funerals, and so on; listeners might tune to these stations at times during the day, but could switch over to the stronger network providers for entertainment and drama at other times.

Competition between NBC and CBS remained fierce throughout the 1930s. Both fought to have the biggest names in radio on their rosters. From an entertainment standpoint, NBC leaned more to comedic offerings, such as ***Amos 'n' Andy*** (Charles Correll [1890–1972] and Freeman Gosden [1890–1982]), Fred Allen (1894–1956), Jack Benny (1894–1974), and Edgar Bergen (1903–1978). CBS, on the other hand, sought top-name **musical** personalities like **Bing Crosby** (1903–1977), Al Jolson (1886–1950), and **Kate Smith** (1907–1986). For listeners, the networks' battles meant only that, with a turn of the receiver dial, they could tune into a rich array of shows featuring the best talent money could buy.

The growth of network radio meant the demise of much local, or independent, programming. With growth came increased costs, both for production and for personnel. NBC and CBS signed big-name entertainers to binding but expensive contracts. Smaller local stations without network affiliations soon realized they lacked the financial ability to undertake programming that would attract large numbers of listeners, and so they rushed to join with the networks, recognizing that this form of broadcasting possessed the resources necessary for success.

One show, one dramatic performance, one song, when played over the networks, had the potential to be heard by much of the population. As an acknowledgment of the power and popularity of network radio, Hollywood in 1932 released a motion picture titled *The Big Broadcast*; instead of film stars, it features radio personalities, such as Bing Crosby, George Burns (1896–1996) and Gracie Allen (1895–1964), Kate Smith, and bandleaders Cab Calloway (1907–1994) and Vincent Lopez (1895–1975), among many others. Rather than fighting radio, the film industry courted the new stars of the airwaves, hoping their fame would draw more patrons to theaters. Three similarly titled movies came out—*The Big Broadcast of 1936* (1935), *The Big Broadcast of 1937* (1936), and *The Big Broadcast of 1938* (1938).

The Federal Communications Commission (FCC), a government agency formed in 1934 from the Federal Radio Commission (FRC; 1927–1934), had as its mission to oversee commercial radio operations in the United States. In 1938, the FCC decreed that the National Broadcasting Company, by virtue of its Red and Blue divisions, had grown too big, too powerful, and stifled competition. Charges and countercharges colored the debate, but federal courts in 1939 ordered NBC to divest itself of one of its networks in order to lessen its size and presumed influence. NBC fought the decision, appealed, and lost. As a result, NBC eventually sold off its Blue network to outside radio interests; in 1943 a new network, the American Broadcasting Company (ABC radio), arose as its replacement. Despite the legal wrangles, the 1930s witnessed both the blossoming and the maturation of network broadcasting, along with the unparalleled growth of radio as a mass medium.

SELECTED READING

Barnouw, Erik. *A History of Broadcasting in the United States*. Vol. 1: *A Tower in Babel*. Vol. 2: *The Golden Web*. New York: Oxford University Press, 1966–1968.

Godfrey, Donald C., and Frederic A. Leigh, eds. *Historical Dictionary of American Radio*. Westport, CT: Greenwood Press, 1998.

Sterling, Christopher H., and John M. Kittross. *Stay Tuned: A Concise History of American Broadcasting*. Belmont, CA: Wadsworth, 1990.

READER'S DIGEST. Although it had its beginning in 1922, *Reader's Digest* flourished during the 1930s, when its circulation grew markedly. Founded by DeWitt and Lila Acheson Wallace (1889–1981; 1889–1984), this familiar, purse-size anthology of condensed articles and regular features sold about 250,000 copies a month in 1930, a respectable figure by any standard. By the close of the decade, however, that number had jumped to 4 million monthly copies. Credit for such extraordinary success must be given both to the stewardship provided by the Wallaces, and to the monthly content of the *Digest* itself.

As a young man, DeWitt Wallace showed little promise of ever amounting to much, let alone overseeing a publishing colossus. But he entertained great plans for himself, and began sketching out ideas for a new magazine while serving in France during World

War I. Wallace would take articles he found in popular periodicals of the day and practice condensing them to their basic themes. He wanted to create a sample booklet of
these condensations and take it to editors back in the States for possible publishing.
His notion of reducing previously published materials possessed a certain uniqueness;
other digests had come and gone in years past, but they consisted of reprints, not condensations. Also, Wallace's idea came at a time when other media, especially **radio** and
movies, introduced Americans to the idea of short, brief messages and condensed information. Speed and efficiency increasingly became the norm, and his proposal spoke to
these changing preferences. In addition, growing numbers of readers saw fiction, the staple of most **magazines** of the day, as irrelevant; they demanded factual pieces, informa-
tive and useful, and Wallace's concept avoided fiction writing altogether.

In the midst of polishing his plans for a new magazine, Wallace married Lila Acheson
in 1921, and she encouraged him in his struggling venture. After several futile attempts
to interest publishers in his ideas, he realized he would have to put out his digest himself
if it were to stay true to his dreams, and so the couple began promoting the as-yet
unnamed magazine through mailings and personal appeals for money. Loans, along with
several thousand prepaid subscriptions, finally allowed them to bring out the first edition
in February 1922. They called the new journal *Reader's Digest*. It contained 31 articles,
or roughly one for each day of the month, a number Wallace stayed with for some time.

By 1923, the Wallaces, encouraged that subscriptions continued to pour in, moved
from their cramped quarters in New York City to Pleasantville, an idyllic small New York
town just up the Hudson River. For the rest of the 1920s, the journal grew rapidly, and
the village grew with it, since the magazine quickly became the town's largest employer.
The appropriately named Pleasantville served as the perfect setting for the folksy *Digest*,
and although both the community and the publishing plant have grown enormously over
the years, there the *Digest* has remained. In the midst of this, DeWitt Wallace continued
to assiduously go through other periodicals in search of articles for condensation.

Like the **Saturday Evening Post**, another popular magazine of the era, the *Digest* celebrated trustworthy American values, promoting a conservative, insular view that argued
for hard work, family, and common sense. Liberal in its attitudes toward sex and women's
rights, but doggedly conservative toward immigration, minorities, and race, the somewhat
austere early issues of *Reader's Digest* struck a chord with white, middle-class Americans,
especially women. No one felt particularly challenged, either intellectually or ideologically, when perusing its pages. With easy-to-read nonfiction, coupled with considerable
humor and a dash of self-improvement, the *Digest* entertained, while reinforcing basic
beliefs already present with the vast majority of its audience.

But the real secret to the magazine's popularity lay in a technique Wallace and his
editors perfected, that of expertly condensing materials, stripping them down to their
basic content. Both he and his staffers culled a somewhat narrow range of publications,
hunting for articles appropriate to the *Digest*'s ideology and its multitude of middle-class
readers. For example, the similarly oriented *Saturday Evening Post* occupied a place on
this list, as did such lesser-known publications like the *Century, Forum, McClure's,
North American Review,* and *Scribner's*. When the research teams found a piece they
thought fit the *Digest*, they would rewrite, recasting difficult constructions, and reduce,
excising words, usually descriptive modifiers or unnecessary verbs, along with entire
sentences and paragraphs not essential to the thrust of the writing. The end result

consisted of a boiled-down, simplified synopsis of the original, but one rendered readable and grammatical despite the tinkering and eliminations. *Reader's Digest* did not strive for stylistic excellence, but instead aimed its prose at everyday readers, thereby drawing the disdain of the elite and winning the subscription dollars of everyone else.

The issue of copyright seldom seemed to bother Wallace or his staff. When they found an article they wanted to condense, they rarely went through the niceties of permissions. Most people received *Reader's Digest* through subscription, not a newsstand purchase, and so Wallace did not see his journal as a direct competitor with his sources. Also, the magazine went mainly to the heartland—the Midwest—away from the publishing centers of the East Coast. Circulation figures, although they climbed steadily throughout the 1920s, remained low enough that Wallace thought of his creation as small and not in the big leagues of publishing.

In 1929, however, the *Digest* initiated newsstand sales, a move that heightened its visibility to other publishers, who recognized the newcomer as competition. To be safe, DeWitt Wallace decided, at the urging of others, to pay reprint fees to his primary sources. He had deliberately kept his soaring circulation figures secret, so few people realized how much money the *Digest* made. As the Depression deepened, he drew up exclusive agreements with those magazines he most used, such as *Saturday Evening Post, Collier's, Woman's Home Companion*, and about two dozen other periodicals. This arrangement assured him of a continuous supply of material and little risk of a later copyright battle.

As the *Digest* grew both in importance and circulation, other American magazines increasingly felt the brunt of the Depression and found themselves in financial trouble. Thus, in the early 1930s Wallace conceived the idea of the "planted article." The *Digest* would commission writers to create pieces that matched the magazine's philosophy. These articles would in turn be "planted" in another journal, like *Saturday Review* or *Christian Century*, which would then agree to let the *Digest* reprint it, for a fee. The arrangement worked well and allowed the *Digest* to maintain the facade that it found its material on the open marketplace.

Another innovation that occurred in the early 1930s involved the introduction of anonymous original articles, pieces not taken from other publications, in the *Digest's* contents. This new feature proved so popular with readers that the editors relented and allowed signed pieces beginning in 1933. In a short time, such material occupied fully half the magazine's space. Submitted or commissioned, anything appearing in *Reader's Digest* still had to reinforce the philosophies espoused by the Wallaces. These additions seemed to please subscribers and newsstand buyers alike; by mid-decade, *Reader's Digest* outsold all other American magazines save four—*Saturday Evening Post, Liberty, Collier's,* and *Woman's Home Companion*—and its subscription figures topped 1 million. And the *Digest* achieved this feat without the benefit of **advertising**, fiction, or illustrations.

By 1936, the *Digest* had moved in the direction of condensing entire nonfiction books. Starting with *Man, the Unknown*, a 1935 best seller by the European writer Alexis Carrel (1873–1944), *Reader's Digest* proceeded to publish monthly book condensations, some as brief as 16 pages. A popular feature, it led to Reader's Digest Condensed Books, a separate operation created in the 1940s that offered subscribers bound volumes containing shortened literary works, both fiction and nonfiction.

Despite its obvious commercial success, the *Digest* could hardly be called an elegant or sophisticated magazine. Not until 1939 did the first simple line illustrations appear.

And readers would not see an advertisement in their favorite periodical until 1955; prior to that time, the *Digest* relied on subscriptions and newsstand sales alone, claiming that any advertisements might somehow compromise content and the relationships established with contributing publications. But it did offer chatty, upbeat writing, along with features like "The Most Unforgettable Character I Ever Met," "Toward More Picturesque Speech," and "It Pays to Enrich Your Word Power." After the first few issues, the *Digest* also freely employed humor. It titillated its audience with endless slightly suggestive jokes and puns. In addition, it ran articles that included sex in their focus. Never off-color, *Reader's Digest* nonetheless kept the subject of sex in the forefront, and few complained.

By the end of the 1930s, rich and successful, occasionally liberal and consistently conservative, *Reader's Digest* had become a national institution. It remained ambivalent about aspects of fascism and Nazism; it espoused a fervent anti-Communist bias; and it encouraged American isolationism as World War II approached. The dream of Lila and DeWitt Wallace had reached fruition.

See also Best Sellers; Illustrators; *Life & Fortune*

SELECTED READING

Heidenry, John. *Theirs Was the Kingdom: Lila and DeWitt Wallace and the Story of the* Reader's Digest. New York: W. W. Norton, 1993.

Janello, Amy, and Brennon Jones. *The American Magazine*. New York: Harry N. Abrams, 1991.

Schreiner, Samuel A., Jr. *The Condensed World of the* Reader's Digest. New York: Stein & Day, 1977.

Tebbel, John, and Mary Ellen Zuckerman. *The Magazine in America, 1741–1990*. New York: Oxford University Press, 1991.

RECORDINGS. The history of the American recording industry during the 1930s rivals any drama the most imaginative playwright might create. With a sprawling cast of players, ceaseless warfare among everyone involved, and a byzantine plot almost too complex to follow, the action follows the classic pattern of heady times, disaster, and a long, slow road to recovery.

The mass production of phonographs and recordings commenced in the 1890s; by 1910, records directly challenged traditional **sheet music** as the primary means of reproducing **music** in homes. The Columbia, Victor, and Edison labels dominated the business in the early twentieth century, but names like Brunswick, Gennett, Okeh, Paramount, Perfect, HMV, and Vocalion established themselves as strong competitors, acquainting the public with contemporary dance music, along with popular **jazz** and blues.

The wide introduction of **radio** as a mass medium in the 1920s initially drove record and phonograph sales downward, but the general prosperity of the era had them rising again, and by 1929 the industry had achieved a substantial recovery. For example, in 1921 the recording industry boasted sales in excess of $100 million (roughly $1 billion in contemporary dollars), an historic high. By mid-decade, however, record sales had slumped to $59 million ($683 million). In 1929, income had climbed back to $75 million ($888 million), but in October of that year the stock market collapsed and reversed everything. The following chart shows just how hard the Depression affected the recording industry, and the gradual steps toward a recovery:

American Record Sales during the 1930s

Year	Annual Sales (in millions)	Number of Records Sold (in millions)
1929	$75	about 70
1930	$46	about 40
1931	$18	about 15
1932	$11	about 10
1933	$ 5	about 4
1934	$ 7	about 5
1935	$ 9	about 7
1936	$11	about 8
1937	$13	about 10
1938	$26	about 40
1939	$36	about 55
1940	$52	about 80

The sale of over 350,000 records qualified a song as a popular hit in the early 1920s; by 1930, the figure had fallen to 40,000 records, and showed no signs of improving. In the darkest days of the Depression, 1931–1933, the average sales for a hit record totaled 3,500 copies in the first three months of its release, and an additional 1,500 copies might sell in the remaining three months prior to its disappearance from retailers' inventories. And those figures represent hit records; less popular songs did proportionally worse, to the point that basic recording costs might not even be met by many releases.

The record industry seemed mired in insoluble problems, but radio exhibited ever-growing strength. As evidence, the Radio Corporation of America (better known as RCA) bought the struggling Victor Record Company in 1929. Victor, which had been part of the Victor Talking Machine Company since 1901, lacked financial resources in the weakened economy. RCA, in turn owned by AT&T, General Electric, and Westinghouse, already controlled the successful National Broadcasting Company (NBC radio), and the acquisition of the Victor label gave the broadcasting giant a vast archive of recorded music. In a related move, RCA had also created the RKO (Radio-Keith-Orpheum) film studio, a move that provided the company access to **movies**. In short order, RCA had entrée to all the electronic media of the day, a feat that provided them some insulation from most economic fluctuations and troubles. If recordings faltered, the movies might prosper, and radio seemed impervious to anything.

RCA's acquisitions merely hint at the complex transactions that would occur throughout the American recording industry during the 1930s. For example, Brunswick Records, part of a company that produced pool tables and pianos, came into being shortly after the parent firm began manufacturing phonographs in 1916. Boasting the latest technology, Brunswick also owned a budget line called Melotone. After purchasing the once-prosperous Aeolian and Vocalion catalogs in 1924, Brunswick seemed poised to become a major label. But instead the company witnessed an overall sales decline, despite its new holdings. Warner Brothers Studios, enjoying high profits from their movies, bought Brunswick in 1929. But the filmmakers, like the rest of the nation, fell on hard times after the market crash. Hoping to cut their losses, Warner Brothers in 1931 sold Brunswick to the American Record Company (ARC), an upstart group that had been organized in 1929.

ARC made its money by buying out struggling labels and retailing bargain discs in five-and-dimes and cheap variety stores. Formed in 1929 by the merger of Regal Records, Cameo Records, and the Scranton Button Company, the new firm overnight built an extensive catalog by taking over many smaller, financially straitened recording companies. It acquired the inventories of independent labels like Banner, Conqueror, Medallion, Pathe (U.S. only), and Perfect. Some of these little-known labels also featured subsidiaries of their own. Cameo owned Romeo Records, a brand sold by the S. H. Kress variety stores. It also held the Lincoln brand, a label that featured dance music and jazz.

The 1931 purchase of Brunswick Records from Warner Brothers finally gave ARC a well-known label. Instead of pricing Brunswick selections at their prevailing 25- to 50-cent rates (roughly $3 to $6 in contemporary money), the company made Brunswick their prestige line and retailed the label at a premium 75 cents a disc ($9). This move may have cost ARC some sales, but it gave the company stature in the market.

As these changes reverberated through the recording industry, of the original "big three" labels—Columbia, Victor, and Edison—only Columbia Records, founded in 1888, remained as a major independent label. Victor had been absorbed by RCA, and Edison got out of record and phonograph production entirely. Columbia had grown rich during the Jazz Age boom times; in its heyday, it manufactured not only Columbia discs and phonographs, but also Silvertone and Supertone records for Sears, Roebuck and Company from 1905 to 1931. In addition, from 1925 to 1931 it produced Diva Records for the W. T. Grant chain stores. Okeh Records, a division within Columbia, produced considerable jazz and dance music. The company's wealth even allowed it to assist in the creation of the Columbia Broadcasting System in 1928. What no one foresaw, of course, was how radio would prosper, while the formerly thriving recording industry would stumble.

Change finally came to Columbia in 1931. As a result of mergers, the label survived, first as a part of EMI (for Electric & Music Industries), a British conglomerate. With Columbia continuing to accrue losses, EMI in turn sold the company to Majestic, a firm that nominally manufactured radio receivers. But the economic crisis continued and the label went on the auction block once more. The always-alert American Record Company picked up the once-prestigious label for next to nothing in 1934.

In an ironic turnaround, CBS in 1938 proceeded to acquire the entire American Record Company catalog, a move that once more associated the radio network with its namesake Columbia label. This purchase also gave NBC's primary rival a significant stake in the recording industry. CBS promptly sold one of their acquisitions, the aforementioned Brunswick, to American Decca in 1940. That same year, CBS dropped the remaining ARC listings, retaining only the Columbia imprint.

Before falling on its own hard times, ARC, by virtue of its numerous labels and the practice of discounting records, had become a force in popular music. The company's various discs sold from 25 to 50 cents apiece (roughly $3.50 to $7.00 in contemporary dollars), and often retailed at three for a dollar (or three for $14.00). To achieve these discounts and still turn a profit, ARC sometimes obtained masters from the bigger labels and stamped cheap copies from them. ARC's Banner Records, for example, consisted almost entirely of reissues. To keep manufacturing costs at an absolute minimum, these smaller labels recorded on surfaces like waxed or chemically treated paper, and also on metal or tin foil. As might be expected, they produced minimal fidelity, and the recording seldom lasted much beyond a handful of plays. They also specialized in what the industry disingenuously called "hick discs," performances by little-known rural bands and singers that usually played anonymous songs that required no copyright fees.

While the American Record Company expanded throughout much of the decade, the other surviving record firms slashed prices, dropped artists, cut back on recording sessions, and reduced individual takes on a particular number to just one, provided no obvious defects could be detected. Victor, which had stubbornly held prices to their 1920s levels, created the Bluebird label in 1933 as a response to such policies; the new Bluebirds sold for 35 cents each (roughly $5.50 in contemporary money). Other companies struck deals with large retailers like Woolworth's and Sears, Roebuck and Company to sell miniature records measuring 8 inches in diameter, instead of the traditional 10, for a dime ($1.50 in contemporary money).

Between 1930 and 1932, "Hit of the Week" Records tried selling discs at newsstands. The one-sided records, for the bargain price of 15 cents ($2.00) and made of Durium, a concoction of paper and resin, gave a listener three to five minutes of scratchy music. Aside from presaging radio's *Your Hit Parade* by a few years, "Hit of the Week" fared poorly.

Despite the gloom that pervaded much of the recording industry, a few individuals saw prosperity beckoning and took advantage of it. In 1934, British investors started American Decca, a new label and offshoot of English Decca, a well-established one. Fortunately for American Decca, crooner **Bing Crosby** (1903–1977) came aboard from Brunswick, and the label also acquired the catalog of Gennett Records, an old (1917) firm that had built a rich trove of blues and jazz sides. To battle ARC's low prices, Decca recordings sold for a bargain 35 cents. In a short time, Decca's cheap discs, along with their roster of stars, made them one of the sales leaders for the decade.

As the decade neared its end, the three major labels increased their hold on the industry. In 1938, for example, record sales totaled approximately 40 million discs. A more detailed breakdown would reveal the following figures:

Victor—over 13 million discs
Decca—over 12 million discs
Columbia/ARC—over 9 million discs
Independent labels—about 6 million discs

Although the independents sold a respectable number of recordings, their total came nowhere close to the sales enjoyed by the Big Three.

"Race Records." Although depressions and recessions cannot be considered racially motivated, minority groups have traditionally suffered out of proportion to their numbers during economic upheavals. Black musicians were no exception. In the 1930s, racial prejudice existed as a fact of life in the recording industry. The major labels had long avoided hiring or promoting black artists, forcing black musicians to seek out the small, independent labels for work. But many of these labels failed during the 1930s, which meant the disappearance of job opportunities for uncounted talented people.

Many recording companies carried black artists on their rosters, but in their **advertising** and distribution made little effort to reach mainstream (i.e., white) audiences. Their recordings carried the dubious label "race records," meaning they could usually be obtained only in predominantly black neighborhoods or in small, specialty record shops. Columbia's subsidiary label Okeh, Victor's Bluebird, and Decca's Sepia all included black musicians and singers, but most larger distributors, fearful of a white consumer backlash, refused to carry them.

The dilemma facing black recording artists can be illustrated by Black Swan Records (1921–1924), one of the first labels to feature jazz and blues. Because it specialized in recording black performers, Black Swan found most white markets closed to distribution of their race records. This kind of racial myopia forced Black Swan out of business in 1924, long before swing brought about a renewed interest in jazz and dance bands a few years later. A similar fate awaited any other black-oriented labels, and race records emerged as a metaphor for economic failure from the 1930s onward.

Swing proved the tonic the recording industry as a whole needed. It reinvigorated many struggling companies, and guaranteed the continuing fortunes of the major labels. Although most firms continued to issue purely pop sides and music geared to more specialized tastes, the big swing bands, the most popular performers of the later 1930s, sold in such numbers that they carried everyone with their success.

See also Count Basie; Carter Family; Duke Ellington; Benny Goodman; Woody Guthrie; Fletcher Henderson; Glenn Miller; Race Relations & Stereotyping; Songwriters & Lyricists

SELECTED READING

Chanin, Michael. *Repeated Takes: A Short History of Recording and Its Effects on Music.* New York: Verso, 1995.

Kenney, William Howland. *Recorded Music in American Life: The Phonograph and Popular Memory, 1890–1945.* New York: Oxford University Press, 1999.

Millard, Andre. *America on Record: A History of Recorded Sound.* New York: Cambridge University Press, 1995.

Oliver, Paul. *Songsters and Saints: Vocal Traditions on Race Records.* New York: Cambridge University Press, 1984.

REGIONALISM. In the area of art during the Depression years, two distinct approaches, or "schools," of painting rose to national prominence: Regionalism and **Social Realism**. Of the two, Regionalism attracted the larger popular audience, although Social Realism had its ardent supporters. Regionalists tend toward themes of national identity, and they employ images of the "American scene," especially those of the land itself as a carrier of meaning. Instead of Paris and sidewalk cafes, the Regionalists might paint an American farm and depict the bounteous crops the land provides. A conservative movement, not a radical one, Regionalism celebrates a nostalgia for the past, especially the rural past that artists saw as fast disappearing under the impacts of technology and urban growth.

The Regionalist painters did not limit themselves geographically, and often took American history and mythologized it, elevating the commonplace and giving it heroic status. Unlike their colleagues with ties to Social Realism, Regionalist artists made no attempt to debunk or challenge American institutions and values.

The Regionalist movement had its roots in the 1920s, a time when the arts turned away from Europe and celebrated American culture. The term had originated with a group of Southern writers who wanted to create literary works about the people, places, and activities they knew. Although focused on a particular locale and mainly agrarian in theme, these poets and novelists aimed for a much broader audience, hoping to attract attention to the South and what they saw as its distinctive culture. What began with literary antecedents spread to other areas of American life, and eventually critics applied the term to a number of artists who likewise found their inspiration in the land.

By the 1930s, Americana in all its forms had become fashionable, and scholars and laypeople alike earnestly declaimed on the merits of American **architecture**, art, literature, and **music**. In a short time, supporters of European cultural expression found themselves on the defensive. Critics went out of their way to denigrate much modern European painting, and a form of xenophobia manifested itself in many of the journals that dealt with current trends in the arts. In the field of painting, New York's prestigious Whitney Museum of American Art had its founding in 1931, the first major museum devoted solely to the subject, and numerous American-only exhibitions at other institutions reflected this growing interest that flourished during the decade.

Perhaps in response to the Depression or to the war clouds forming once again over Europe, the arbiters of taste and style threw their support behind any paintings that depicted what many called the "American scene." Those artists who comprised the Regionalist school found themselves the darlings of the intelligentsia, and they enjoyed much praise and little criticism during the 1930s. They also received some modest **New Deal** government patronage after the election of **Franklin D. Roosevelt** (1882–1945) in 1932. The creation of federal arts programs of various kinds encouraged artistic expression that celebrated America and American values; the emphasis the Regionalists placed on just those subjects made their endeavors particularly attractive to government agencies responsible for granting funds.

Although Regionalism may have provided most of the crowd favorites, other schools of art—provided the practitioners themselves were Americans, either by birth or later citizenship—also received critical blessings. But the surest guarantee of success remained a realistic, representational style and the positive treatment of American themes. Nationalism ran deep during the 1930s, and only World War II and its aftermath tempered such jingoistic feelings in the arts, and not completely, even then.

Over the decade, many painters strove to be a part of the popular "Regionalist" category, but with the passage of time, only a few of their number have survived the close examination that always follows any faddish movement. **Thomas Hart Benton** (1889–1975) and **Grant Wood** (1891–1942), two painters who elicited a great deal of popular attention in the 1930s, continue to hold up well. Wood remains the better known of the two, primarily on the basis of his *American Gothic*, a work he first exhibited in 1930, and one of the few paintings from the era that remains instantly recognizable to millions, both in its original form and as the object of countless parodies.

Critics also tended to place John Steuart Curry (1897–1946) in this group, although he never achieved the celebrity of Benton or Wood. Just as Benton claimed Missouri and Wood, Iowa, Curry, too, came from the Midwest—Kansas—and its rural character, its rich fields, and tempestuous weather figure significantly in his works. Examples that display all these themes include *Tornado* (1929) and *Line Storm* (1934). While in his twenties, Curry had worked as an illustrator, and this experience finds reflection in the clear narrative sense, along with a lack of abstraction, characteristic of these works.

Another facet of Curry's painting that places him in the front ranks of the Regionalist movement involves the absence of any social commentary. When farm families live in impoverished surroundings, as in *Kansas Wheat Ranch* (1930) and *The Homesteading* (1939), he attaches no economic or political "messages" to it; rural poverty exists as a fact of Midwestern life in the 1930s, and Curry serves merely as an objective recorder. Instead of a class struggle, he paints the ongoing struggle of man and nature, but often optimistically, in contrast to the more pessimistic and political social realists.

Only in some of his paintings and murals dealing with history does Curry manifest an interest in social injustices, especially in the area of race. His portraits of black Americans may seem stereotypical to some today, but paintings like *The Fugitive* (1933) and *The Mississippi* (1935) possess a real power of their own, especially in light of the times.

Curry went to Wisconsin in 1936. His *Tragic Prelude* for the Kansas State capitol (1938–1939), with its tortured figure of John Brown (1800–1859) urging on his followers, may not be the stuff of bucolic Americana, but it captures a tragic chapter in American history. The background, the Midwestern prairies, carries the threat of natural disasters that could accompany the man-made one of civil war.

It can be argued that a number of American artists made stabs at Regionalist themes in the first 30 to 40 years of the twentieth century. The realistic depiction of the land and its people attracted diverse painters in the 1930s, but seldom if ever would they be considered Regionalist painters. They bring a different artistic sensibility to their work, and use the landscape, particularly the rural landscape, as a means to other ends. The conscious celebration of the American scene remains conspicuously absent from their work, thus divorcing them from the movement itself.

In their own distinctive way, the Regionalists documented American life in the 1930s, arguing for an American art that embraced values and beliefs long held by the majority of citizens. Instead of an art for art's sake, theirs became an art for culture's sake.

See also Edward Hopper; Illustrators; Race Relations & Stereotyping; Reginald Marsh; Charles Sheeler

SELECTED READING

Baigell, Matthew. *The American Scene: American Painting of the 1930s.* New York: Praeger, 1974.

Heller, Nancy, and Julia Williams. *Painters of the American Scene.* New York: Galahad Books, 1976.

Junker, Patricia. *John Steuart Curry: Inventing the Middle West.* New York: Hudson Hill Press, 1998.

RELIGION. The Great Depression took its toll on the American people economically, emotionally, and spiritually. Denominational choice varied but Christianity prevailed virtually everywhere. Contrary to what might be expected, however, few displays of religiosity occurred. Mainstream religious communities for the most part maintained a steady course, presenting a muted response to the times, although some individual churches experienced a drop in income.

Robert and Helen Lynd (1892–1970; 1892–1982), authors of *Middletown* (1931), an influential study of everyday middle-class American life in Muncie, Indiana, returned to that community in 1935 and published *Middletown in Transition* (1937). They found that during the Depression most major religious denominations had small increases in membership, but average weekly church attendance actually dropped. They further learned that women made up the majority of churchgoers, and that few of either sex under the age of 30 attended with any regularity. Even with religion's limited role in American lives, most homes contained some religious decorations and many families paused before a meal to offer a blessing. A 1938 oil painting by the popular illustrator **Norman Rockwell** (1894–1978) titled "Family Saying Grace," lends credence to this 1930s tradition.

Although little changed in most churches and synagogues, the Depression brought with it an interest in religious fundamentalism; energetic evangelistic efforts attracted members of the working class, the unemployed, and the destitute. In many cases, nondenominational Bible schools in major cities trained lay workers and Sunday school leaders, as well as supplying pastors and printed materials. Black Americans moving from the South to northern urban centers brought their religious traditions with them, and created new congregations.

The drop in attendance at mainstream church services possibly can be attributed to two factors. With increased ownership of **automobiles**, many chose to skip church in order to go sightseeing, have a picnic at a scenic spot in the country, enjoy activities at an amusement park, or visit family or friends. Also, the ready availability of radios in most households meant that Americans could stay at home to listen to a broadcast of a weekly church service and other religious programming without getting dressed up or, possibly more important, without having to contribute to the collection plate. With resources short for many families, even a few coins on Sunday assumed great importance.

William Ashley "Billy" Sunday (1862–1935), a rousing, flamboyant evangelist, pioneered in the use of **radio** for religious broadcasting. He became the first of a long line of popular preachers to use the electronic media as a pulpit. A professional **baseball** player for the Chicago White Sox, Sunday gave up the game when he accepted Christ in 1886 and worked briefly for the YMCA before turning to preaching. As a revivalist, he developed a colorful, "fire and brimstone" style that tackled social issues, especially the evils of alcohol. He aired *The Back Home Hour* on the Columbia Broadcasting System (CBS radio) at 11:00 A.M. on Sundays from 1929 until 1931. Ably assisted by Nell Sunday (1868–1957), his wife and business manager, he secured a large, devoted following. Sunday died in 1935, by then a prominent and wealthy evangelist, and the inspiration for many such men of the cloth to come.

Aimee Semple McPherson (1890–1944), a colorful Pentecostal leader, and the most famous woman preacher of her time, in 1927 incorporated the International Church of the Foursquare Gospel, a new, independent denomination of her making. Born in Canada, McPherson had grown up as a member of the Salvation Army; she converted to Pentecostalism in 1908 and shortly thereafter married and worked as a missionary to China. Widowed, she returned to the states in 1911 and continued her preaching. In 1917, she began publishing *Bridal Call*, a monthly magazine that reprinted her sermons. She remarried, but soon divorced in order to continue her evangelistic efforts without constraint. "Sister Aimee," with her good looks and theatrical delivery, drew thousands to her tent revivals and, like Billy Sunday, achieved celebrity status by the 1920s. She also recognized the potential of radio for the new electronic church; throughout the 1930s, in addition to a heavy revival schedule, she could regularly be heard broadcasting, as well as overseeing the collection of donations in order to open soup kitchens and free clinics.

A significant black spiritual leader from around 1907 until his death, the Rev. Major Jealous Divine, better known as "Father Divine" (c. 1877–1965; his birth name remains under debate, but may have been George Baker), in 1914 founded the International Peace Mission Movement. One of the few genuinely integrated organizations of the 1930s, it operated first out of Sayville, New York, before moving to Harlem in 1932. Divine's charismatic messages brought busloads of people to his tent revivals and his organization provided shelter and **food** for those in need. The jobs he obtained for his followers proved especially important during the Depression and its accompanying high unemployment. Recognizing the power of the media, by 1936 Divine could be heard on radio and on **recordings** of his sermons. The International Peace Mission Movement urged high moral standards on its followers but nonetheless attracted thousands to its promise of a better life.

After a colorful career from the 1920s through the 1940s, Divine slowly disappeared from view. His second wife, Mrs. S. A. Divine (for "Sweet Angel"; née Edna Rose Ritchings, b. 1925), or "Mother Divine," has continued as the nominal leader of the organization.

In keeping with individual preachers utilizing radio, various local and independent stations began carrying church services as early as 1921. The National Broadcasting Company (NBC radio), at its inception in 1926, decided to include religious programs, not as commercial offerings, but as a public service. The network made time available to representatives of the mainstream Protestant, Catholic, and Jewish faith communities, a move that ignored the growing religious diversity in the country. NBC instituted three programs, *National Radio Pulpit*, *The Catholic Hour*, and *Message of Israel*, based on a standard that said broadcasters would strive for wide appeal, be nonsectarian, and not advocate strong theological positions.

Some of the radio ministries aroused considerable controversy, much of it nontheological. For example, Father Charles Coughlin (1891–1979), a Roman Catholic priest known as the "Radio Priest," started his religious broadcasting career in Detroit in 1926. Three years later, having achieved national prominence, he spoke weekly at three o'clock on Sunday afternoons to audiences estimated at 10 million on the CBS network. On rival NBC, Fulton J. Sheen (1895–1979), a rising young priest, made his first appearance on *The Catholic Hour* in 1928. Throughout the 1930s, he also gained in popularity and regularity of appearances, but not for the same reasons as Coughlin. Sheen eventually moved to **television** in 1951 and gained his greatest fame in that medium.

While Father Sheen stayed close to church doctrines, Father Coughlin's programs became less spiritual and increasingly political as the Depression worsened. His extreme animosity toward President **Herbert Hoover** (1874–1964) caused CBS not to renew his contract in 1931. Father Coughlin responded by developing his own network of independent radio stations and started a magazine, *Social Justice*. These moves did not hurt his popularity, which peaked after the 1932 election of **Franklin D. Roosevelt** (1882–1945), a man whom he had supported. It is said that Father Coughlin at times received more mail than the president. Coughlin's right-wing, anti-Semitic stance and rhetoric intensified after 1934, and his social protest targets soon included Roosevelt, along with bankers, the wealthy, and individual Jewish leaders and institutions. Times improved and Coughlin's influence began to decline by 1940; he finally left the air in 1942 when he lost listeners, stations, and the support of his Catholic bishop.

Strongly partisan programs such as those broadcast by Father Coughlin and others created public relations difficulties for individual radio stations. In 1932, CBS decided to follow the standard that had been set by NBC and instituted policies stating how airtime would be allotted to religious organizations. They offered representatives of the three major faith communities free time for programs that avoided controversial or theological doctrine matters. In 1934, both NBC and CBS engaged the Federal Council of Churches to provide oversight regarding the content of network Protestant programs.

Troubled by the social and economic inequities that the Great Depression exacerbated, some evangelists and preachers engaged in relief efforts for the jobless and hungry. Dorothy Day (1897–1980), a journalist turned social activist, along with Peter Maurin (1877–1949), in 1931 published a newspaper, the *Catholic Worker*, and founded the Catholic Worker Movement in 1933. This organization regularly condemned capitalism and Communism and urged nonviolent action and hospitality for the impoverished and downtrodden. In the depths of the Depression, Day opened a House of Hospitality in the slums of New York City offering food, clothing, and shelter to the needy. The movement spread and at its peak had established more than 50 houses of hospitality and communal farms.

During the 1930s, media evangelists and others capitalized on the power of radio, with the more charismatic figures gaining widespread popularity and drawing millions to their tent revivals and radio programs. By and large, however, organized religion played a limited role in most Americans' lives. The radio, the automobile, and the rise in leisure time emerged as new competitors for church attendance.

See also Illustrators; Leisure & Recreation; Magazines; Political Parties; Prohibition & Repeal

SELECTED READING

Dunning, John. *On the Air: The Encyclopedia of Old-Time Radio.* New York: Oxford University Press, 1998.

Hangen, Tona J. *Reclaiming the Dial: Radio, Religion, & Popular Culture in America.* Chapel Hill: University of North Carolina Press. 2002.

Kyvig, David E. *Daily Life in the United States, 1920–1940.* Chicago: Ivan R. Dee, 2004.

Lynd, Robert, and Helen Lynd. *Middletown in Transition: A Study in Cultural Conflicts.* New York: Harcourt Brace, 1937.

RESTAURANTS. In the 1920s and 1930s, people who chose to "eat out" faced an array of choices, ranging from the kind of **food** served to the dining atmosphere provided. During those years, American restaurants underwent significant change and growth. The birth of franchises, the proliferation of roadside eateries, along with the expansion of lunch rooms, coffee and sandwich shops, chain restaurants, and diners powered this growth. The names varied—cafeterias, tearooms, hamburger stands, beaneries, delicatessens, greasy spoons, inns, lodges, taverns, soda fountains—but they offered everything from sit-down dinners to a quick bite on the run. Larger cities like New York and Philadelphia also had automats, self-service eating places. Because of the Depression, many Americans initially avoided restaurants to save money, but not for long; even in the days following the crash, people continued to eat out, especially for lunch.

The Prohibition years, 1920–1933, witnessed the closing of the doors to saloons that had traditionally served free lunches, and increasing numbers of workers in urban areas lived too far to go home for a midday meal. With these two factors in mind, Edgar W. Ingram (1880–1966) and Walter L. Anderson (1880–1963) in 1921 opened a small hamburger stand on a public transportation route in Wichita, Kansas. Housed in a concrete building that had been painted white, and featuring a tower at the corner, their establishment offered an affordable, 5-cent (roughly 57 cents in contemporary money) flattened hamburger topped with onions and served in a warm bun. Ingram and Anderson's stand created a winning image for hungry workers—a healthy hamburger in a clean, safe setting. Prior to this time, most hamburger stands, both on the roadside and in urban centers, tended to have the appearance of shacks. Plus they had gained, sometimes rightly, sometimes wrongly, a reputation for serving patties composed mostly of gristle and old beef in a greasy spoon atmosphere.

In a nod to its architectural style, the two entrepreneurs named their venture White Castle. In addition to counter service, they also successfully engaged customers in a takeout business—"Buy a Bagful" and "Buy 'em by the Sack." This innovation allowed them to dispense their burgers from a small shop and that reduced overhead. Open 24 hours a day, the White Castles quickly multiplied to additional sites and burgeoned in the 1930s. Each shop guaranteed no variation in quality or taste of food. Their accomplishment served as a model for urban food stands and restaurant systems for many years thereafter.

Other hamburger stands and restaurants also experienced success, and their owners likewise opened new facilities; a few of these evolved into chains that could span several cities or states. Most chains featured a limited menu and catered to shoppers, workers, and other business people traveling to downtown factories and businesses on bus and trolley routes. Some of the owners did not hesitate to acknowledge their debt to White Castle and offered 5-cent "hamburger sandwiches" served in a spotless facility. Beyond the basic hamburger, the menu varied some from one chain to another, but most included chili, waffles, hotdogs, sandwiches, ham and eggs, along with a limited selection of beverages.

Popular Hamburger Chains That Operated during the 1930s

Date Founded	Chain Name	Location of First Site
1921	White Castle	Wichita, Kansas
1926	White Tower	Milwaukee, Wisconsin
1926	Maid-Rite Hamburgs	Muscatine, Iowa
1929	Toddle House	Houston, Texas
Early 1930s	White Manna	Jersey City, New Jersey
1932	Krystal	Chattanooga, Tennessee
1936	Rockybuilt	Denver, Colorado
1937	Bob's Big Boy	Los Angeles, California
1938	Royal Castle	Miami, Florida

Prefabricated components made construction of new buildings easy and fast and contributed to the success of the chains. It also allowed for buildings to be moved from one site to another in order to adjust to changes in traffic flow or public **transportation** routes. These chains, the precursors to the ubiquitous "fast food" restaurants of today, utilized standardized designs and building materials. Even the financial arrangements for going into such a business fell into identifiable patterns. Yet, each chain boasted its own distinctive architecture, a quality that allowed the buildings themselves to function as billboards, readily identifiable as reliable, clean places to eat.

Fine dining, which traditionally had consisted of elaborate, multicourse meals accompanied by solicitous service, became available only in the fanciest of restaurants. Such places were expensive, something that put off many customers in a difficult economic period. In addition, a growing interest in dieting and a simple, calorie-conscious, purely American menu of meat, potatoes, vegetables, and a light dessert limited their clientele. Haute cuisine faced hard times in the Depression.

While upscale restaurants suffered, new technologies offered assistance to cooks both at home and in cheaper eateries. Refrigeration, which made great strides during the 1930s, guaranteed the safety of a variety of foods. Another benefit manifested itself with Clarence Birdseye's (1886–1956) successful development of a method for quick freezing food in 1923. Inventions like the pop-up toaster (1930), the electric mixer (1930), the electric can opener (1931), improved electric percolators (1930s), the Waring Blendor (1930s), and the electric coffee grinder (1937) made food preparation easier. In addition to these helpful inventions, restaurants readily used canned and other prepackaged items that minimized labor costs.

Although numerous places to eat could be found in factory and business areas, additional food stands and restaurants began to dot the roadside during the 1920s and 1930s. As **automobiles** grew in popularity and highways rapidly improved, choices likewise increased. Americans have always had the wanderlust; they coupled that urge with a love affair with their cars. Twenty-six million vehicles traversed the nation's roads by 1930. Even in the depths of the Great Depression, Americans took to the highway for work, for **travel**, or for a Sunday afternoon family drive. But once on the road, if no one had packed a picnic basket or lunch pail, a place to eat needed to be found.

The diner, a miniature restaurant, served as one source of roadside food and grew in popularity. Initially located near factories and businesses, diners flourished along American highways during the 1930s and attracted a variety of customers looking for fast, inexpensive meals and familiar, friendly service. Distinctive in their appearance, the origins of the buildings housing typical diners varied—they could be obsolete horse-drawn streetcars, decommissioned railroad passenger cars or trolleys, or newly manufactured structures. But all had the cozy, dining car ambiance and provided an alternative to the limited offerings of a hotdog or hamburger stand. Plus they usually offered a full menu, just like more upscale restaurants.

By the 1930s, specially equipped factories mass produced, transported, and erected between 100 and 200 new diners each year. Quickly set up, most of these structures rested on a concrete slab and convinced many people that all diners had once been railroad cars, a mistaken perception that had a negative effect on some potential customers. The automobile was replacing the passenger train as the way to travel and escape, especially from urban areas. Eating in a building reminiscent of a less desirable way to travel did not hold the same enticement for some as stopping at more traditional restaurants. On the other hand, many liked the efficiency and compactness of the diner; they found it less intimidating than a regular sit-down restaurant. In time, the latter group held sway and the diner became a part of the landscape.

Drive-ins provided yet another dining choice. This unique way of eating in the privacy of the car, instead of publicly in a restaurant, first appeared in the fall of 1921 along the road connecting Dallas and Fort Worth, Texas. Jessie G. Kirby and Reuben W. Jackson (both active during the 1930s) opened what they called the Pig Stand and sold hamburgers, sandwiches and a barbeque pork sandwich named the "pig sandwich." Instantly successful, the concept soon expanded throughout Texas and then to other states; by 1934, over 100 drive-ins could be found along busy streets and highways.

Carhops, at first young men and later women, became a fixture at the Pig Stand and other drive-ins. These employees earned their curious name by jumping ("hopping") up onto the running boards then found on most automobiles. A practical means of facilitating entry and exit, the running board proved the perfect way to both take orders and serve food. In good American fashion, the carhops often sported costumes of one sort or another.

In 1931, a Pig Stand in California added the novelty of "drive-through" service. Customers eased their cars to a drive-up window, gave and received their order, and then returned to the highway. This innovative idea quickly caught on, and drive-ins with drive-up, take-out windows added another option to the available dining choices.

Howard Johnson's Restaurants entered the already-crowded field of roadside eating in the mid-1930s. Howard Johnson (1896–1972), a New England businessman, became a part of the food business in 1925 when he bought a small corner drugstore in the Wollaston section of Quincy, Massachusetts. To promote the soda fountain, the busiest part of the store, Johnson replaced the three flavors of commercial **ice cream** (vanilla, chocolate, and strawberry) with his own natural flavored, high-butterfat homemade products. He enjoyed immediate success and gradually increased his selection to 28 flavors. Soon after introducing his own ice cream, Johnson opened a beachfront ice cream stand that he had painted bright orange. Over the next few summers, he added more beachfront stands to his holdings and put high quality hotdogs on his menus. The unique presentation of a tasty hotdog with a slit down the center, placed in a buttered, toasted roll and served in a cardboard holder made it a recognizable Howard Johnson product.

By 1929 Johnson had advanced from ice cream and hotdog stands to a family-style restaurant in Quincy. This establishment served, in addition to hotdogs and 28 flavors of ice cream, typical New England fare consisting of fried clams, chicken pot pies, and baked beans. The stock market crash of 1929 curtailed further expansion until 1935, when Johnson persuaded an acquaintance to become his "agent" and open a Howard Johnson restaurant by the roadside in Orleans on Cape Cod. The two men agreed to a franchise arrangement—Johnson guaranteed uniformity in all aspects of the business and he provided the design, menu, standards, and food products for a fee. The investor-franchisee put up a certain amount of money and got to manage the restaurant and realize a percentage of the profits. A bright orange roof with a cupola on a white, clapboard colonial building ensured immediate recognition and maximum visibility. These first Howard Johnson's enjoyed success, and by the end of 1936 Johnson could claim 56 locations, a total that jumped to 107 sites along East Coast highways by 1939.

Cities, especially the larger ones, also claimed ethnic restaurants that attracted non-ethnic customers. Italian-American restaurants, often decorated with red-and-white checkered tablecloths and sporting a candle stuck in a Chianti bottle, served mine-strone, spaghetti and meatballs, ravioli, and scallopine. Such establishments enjoyed their greatest popularity in cities located in the northeastern section of the country. In order to continue to attract customers, most Italian restaurants relied more on a pasta-and-tomato-sauce theme than on authentic Italian cooking.

Chinese restaurants, frequently called chop suey parlors, also dotted larger American cities throughout the 1920s and 1930s. Their menus featured won ton soup, egg rolls, barbecued spareribs, sweet-and-sour pork, and beef with lobster sauce, a mix that had been created to whet Americans' appetites; it bore little resemblance to authentic Chinese fare.

Greek Americans also realized success in the industry at this time. These entrepreneurs did not usually serve authentic Greek foods, but instead operated American-style restaurants such as coffee shops, steak houses, and family restaurants.

As the number of restaurants grew, people needed guidelines about quality. Duncan Hines (1880–1959), a traveling salesman for a printing firm, usually ate out when on the road. Frequently, his wife accompanied him and over many years the couple had developed a hobby of keeping a list of restaurants and dining rooms that offered exceptional dishes. In 1935, instead of mailing friends Christmas cards, the couple sent out 1,000 copies of a list they had compiled of 167 superior eateries from 30 states and Washington, D.C. Their criteria for "superior" included cleanliness, fresh tablecloths or place mats, neatly dressed staff, no overly fancy décor, no rich sauces, and a good cup of coffee. The response to their listings was overwhelming. Friends requested additional copies, as did strangers who had seen the list. Realizing that their hobby could be turned into a business, in 1936 Hines published his reviews as a book, *Adventures in Good Eating*. It sold so well that two years later he left sales to review restaurants full time. The "Recommended by Duncan Hines" sign became a valuable marketing tool for restaurants around the country.

Prior to the publication of Hines's book, people who ate out had little to rely on for restaurant recommendations. Even when they found a guide, too often an affiliation with the restaurant made the entries read like an advertisement instead of a review. Objectivity and availability arrived with *Adventures in Good Eating* and by 1939 it had became a nationwide best seller. Riding on his success, Hines in 1938 published a hotel guide, *Lodging for a Night*, and in 1939, a cookbook, *Adventures in Good Cooking*.

Throughout the 1930s, and despite the Depression, the restaurant industry grew both in numbers of facilities across the country and in kinds of restaurants and foods available. Americans knew what they wanted—straightforward home cooking, simply prepared and presented, and served quickly. Howard Johnson's, chain restaurants, hamburger stands, drive-ins, diners, and ethnic restaurants experienced success because of understanding and meeting these requirements. In 1937, two brothers, Maurice (1902–1971) and Richard McDonald (1909–1998), opened a hot dog stand, The Airdrome, in Arcadia, California. In an effort to increase sales, they moved the building to San Bernardino. After sizing up the new craze of eating at drive-in restaurants, the McDonalds determined it possessed more potential than had yet been realized. In 1940, the brothers altered their existing restaurant and opened, in May of that year, McDonald's Barbeque (the stress on hamburgers would come later). Always innovating and experimenting, Maurice and Richard McDonald led the way to a bright future for drive-ins.

See also Best Sellers; Buses; Coffee & Tea; Design; Desserts; Frozen Food; Hotels; Prohibition & Repeal; Trains

SELECTED READING

Langdon, Philip. *Orange Roofs, Golden Arches: The Architecture of American Chain Restaurants.* New York: Alfred A. Knopf, 1986.

Levenstein, Harvey A. *Revolution at the Table: The Transformation of the American Diet.* New York: Oxford University Press, 1988.

Mariani, John. *America Eats Out.* New York: William Morrow, 1991.

Pillsbury, Richard. *From Boarding House to Bistro: The American Restaurant Then and Now.* Boston: Unwin Hyman, 1990.

ROBESON, PAUL. A controversial figure throughout much of his life, Paul Robeson (1898–1976) embodied many of the promises and problems faced by prominent American blacks during the twentieth century. Born in Princeton, New Jersey, to a former slave-turned-minister and a Quaker schoolteacher mother, Robeson won admission to Rutgers University in 1915, the third black student to attend the school. While there, he excelled in all that he attempted, earning 15 varsity letters in sports, being selected to the collegiate all-American **football** teams in 1917 and 1918, gaining acceptance to Phi Beta Kappa honor fraternity, and graduating as class valedictorian. From Rutgers, he went to Columbia University Law School, receiving a degree in 1923 and supporting himself by playing professional football on weekends.

In addition to all his other talents, Robeson showed promise as an actor and a singer, especially for his command of black spirituals. While in law school, he appeared in several theatrical productions, and when his legal career faltered because of racial inequities, he turned to performing. A 1925 silent picture, *Body and Soul,* which featured an all-black cast, gave him his introduction to the film world, although his progress would be painfully slow. Not until 1930 did a studio cast him in another movie, *Borderline,* an undistinguished British production. Between *Borderline* and 1942's *Tales of Manhattan,* his final film, he would appear in eight additional pictures, six of them done by English studios.

Robeson said he found a better racial climate in the British Isles than he did the United States, moving there permanently in the late 1920s, after appearing in London stage productions of Eugene O'Neill's (1888–1953) *The Emperor Jones* in 1925 and **Jerome Kern** (1885–1945) and Oscar Hammerstein II's (1895–1960) acclaimed *Show Boat* in 1928. Abroad, he experienced greater freedom, both socially and artistically. Periodically, however, he returned to the United States when opportunities—few and far between—beckoned. Thus in 1933 he repeated his role as Brutus Jones in a film adaptation of *The Emperor Jones.*

The offer of a chance to reprise the *Show Boat* character of Joe in a motion picture retelling of the musical brought Robeson back to his homeland in 1936. His powerful rendition of "Ol' Man River" electrified audiences and continues to be recognized as the definitive interpretation. Strong as his American roles were, they led to little else in the States, and he again traveled to England. Four films—*Jericho* (1937), *Big Fella* (1937), *King Solomon's Mines* (1937), and *Proud Valley* (1940)—marked his return to foreign shores, although none of these **movies** have come down to the present as essential

viewing. His performances at times tee-
ter on the edge of racial stereotyping,
although Robeson never stoops to
embarrassing Uncle Tom caricatures.

In 1939, on a program called *The Pur-
suit of Happiness* that played on the
Columbia Broadcasting System (CBS
radio), Robeson enjoyed one of his finest
moments. Composer Earl Robinson
(1910–1991) had, in collaboration with
lyricist John Latouche (1917–1956),
written an 11-minute cantata called
"Ballad for Americans." Robeson sang
the unabashedly patriotic piece in his
finest baritone. People loved it and
"Ballad for Americans" went on to
become a fixture at the ongoing **New
York World's Fair**, being broadcast several times a day.

A strong advocate of social tolerance
and political liberalism—he refused to
perform before segregated audiences—
Robeson began to speak out against fascism during the later 1930s. He pro-
tested the lack of a united front against
Nazism, and openly embraced the government and policies of the Soviet
Union after a trip there in 1934. These

Actor Paul Robeson (1898–1976). (Courtesy of the Library of Congress)

latter actions brought him under the scrutiny of the **Federal Bureau of Investigation**
(FBI) for possible Communist links, a charge that would haunt him for the rest of his
life. As the likelihood of war grew stronger, so did Robeson's protests; by the early
1940s some saw him as a fervent patriot and others as a Communist sympathizer.

Despite a record-breaking turn in a 1943 Broadway production of *Othello*, the suspi-
cions about his loyalty grew, especially in the Cold War hysteria of the 1940s and 1950s.
He found himself banned from American **television** in 1950, blacklisted by the recording industry in 1953, and generally snubbed by the artistic community. He nonetheless
continued to speak out against racism and intolerance, remaining true to his beliefs and
paying the price of isolation. Only well after his death in 1976 did some of the recognition denied him in life begin to accrue.

See also Musicals; Race Relations & Stereotyping; Radio Networks; Recordings

SELECTED READING
Paul Robeson: Here I Stand. American Masters. Dir. St. Claire Bourne. Public Broadcasting Sys-
    tem. Videocassette. 1999.
Robeson, Paul. http://www.scc.rutgers.edu/njh/paulrobeson/index.htm
Stewart, Jeffrey C., ed. *Paul Robeson: Artist and Citizen.* New Brunswick, NJ: Rutgers University
    Press, 1999.

ROCKEFELLER CENTER (RADIO CITY). Located in the heart of Manhattan and occupying 12 acres of prime real estate, Rockefeller Center represents the hopes and dreams of Depression-era America. One of the largest construction projects of the twentieth century, it involved the talents and skills of tens of thousands of people. By 1940, 14 separate buildings, most of them large, had been erected; that number would continue to grow, and today this massive undertaking comprises over 20 buildings.

The site for Rockefeller Center, three contiguous blocks bounded by 5th and 6th Avenues, and running from 48th Street to 51st Street, could not have looked too promising except to people with a visionary sense. The area had once been the Elgin Botanic Gardens, but this greenery had long since disappeared, replaced by a motley jumble of bars, cheap **hotels**, and rundown shops, sometimes called "the speakeasy belt." Columbia University had obtained possession of the land during the nineteenth century, and the university rather grandly called the deteriorating blocks the Columbia Upper Estate.

In the late 1920s, the Metropolitan Opera, New York City's prestigious musical organization, was searching for a new home, and some thought the Columbia Upper Estate would make a good location. Participants in this search included John D. Rockefeller Jr. (1874–1960), the philanthropist son of the fabulously wealthy family patriarch, John D. Rockefeller Sr. (1839–1937). A patron of the arts, he contacted Columbia University and leased the land for the opera company. But the crash of 1929 forced the Met to back out of the deal, and Rockefeller, lease in hand, looked to other opportunities for his real estate.

Raymond Hood (1881–1934), a prominent and successful architect responsible for such landmarks as the Chicago Tribune Tower (1924), the New York Daily News Building (1930), and the McGraw-Hill Building (1931), proposed that Rockefeller fund a "superblock," a grouping of modern buildings that would interconnect. David Sarnoff (1891–1971), the energetic head of the Radio Corporation of America (RCA), wanted high-quality production facilities for his company's growing **radio** operation, the National Broadcasting Company (NBC radio). From the alliance of Rockefeller, Hood, and Sarnoff, grew the vision for Rockefeller Center. Because of NBC's connection to the enterprise, it promptly got dubbed "Radio City," a name that, even in the age of **television**, has continued to identify the complex.

In order to keep costs down, the planners opted for a plain, stripped-down modernism for the building exteriors. Several architectural firms would collaborate on Rockefeller Center, including Reinhard & Hofmeister; Corbett, Harrison & MacMurray; Godley & Fouihoux; and, of course, Raymond Hood. They agreed that the centerpiece would be a soaring skyscraper surrounded by lower buildings, and Hood's RCA Building, 850 feet and 70 stories tall, fits the bill. For continuity, each building would consist of a steel frame clad in Indiana limestone with aluminum trim. Windows would be assembled almost flush with the surface, providing facades that alternate dark (windows) and light (limestone) vertical lines, an effect that carries the eye upward and emphasizes height. In keeping with New York City's setback regulations, the RCA Building recedes as it rises, but its simplicity of line and form does not suggest **Art Deco** so much as it does the more contemporary **International Style** then beginning to make inroads in architectural thinking. Its spare, slablike **design** looks to the future, and echoes little of the past.

Groundbreaking commenced in 1931, the dark shadows of the Depression notwithstanding. At the end of that year, workmen erected a small, simple Christmas tree amid

Rockefeller Center from the air. (Courtesy of the Library of Congress)

all the construction mud and clutter, and there they received their holiday paychecks. No one knew it then, but a tradition had begun. Each year thereafter a Christmas tree has stood at Rockefeller Center. By 1933, it had gotten more formalized, and lights sparkled on the tree for the first time. Toward the end of the decade, bigger, taller trees came to be the rule, and the decorations grew ever more elaborate. By then, virtually everyone proclaimed Rockefeller Center a rousing success, and the towering Christmas tree bespoke that success.

In December 1932, the sparkling Radio City Music Hall opened its doors. With seats to accommodate almost 6,000 patrons, it boasted an opulent foyer that led audiences to the auditorium. Once seated, they faced the "great stage," a huge, deep-set area that allowed both live performances and movie projection. The interior decoration of the theater displayed the talents of Donald Deskey (1894–1989), a relatively unknown designer, but one destined for success throughout the 1930s. His work at the Radio City Music Hall artfully blends Art Deco, **Streamlining**, and the mechanical precision of industrial design. It all works, and well. The Music Hall has become a beloved American institution, from its 36 high-kicking Rockettes to the latest blockbuster from Hollywood. Everyone who enters the theater for the first time oohs and aahs over the interior decoration, a triumph of modernism and entertainment.

The following year, the RCA Building itself opened. It featured high-speed elevators to whisk visitors to the top floors, and it ensured its tenants' comfort with central air conditioning, a luxury few tall buildings anywhere enjoyed at that time. On the 65th floor, the Rainbow Room, a posh restaurant and lounge, offered superlative views, **food**, and drink, although people would have to wait until the repeal of Prohibition to enjoy anything containing alcohol. That event occurred in late 1933, and it became legal for people in New York to buy and consume **alcoholic beverages** in 1934. The Rainbow Room evinced a hopeful view of the future, and it reinforced a view of New York City as a cosmopolitan town, filled with stylish men and women.

By virtue of his interests in the arts, John D. Rockefeller Jr. saw to it that painting and **sculpture** held an important place in the overall design of the complex. Indoors and out, significant works of art catch the eye. Complementary murals, *Man's Intellectual Mastery of the Material Universe* by the Spanish artist Jose Maria Sert (1874–1945), and *Man's Conquest of the Material World* by the Welsh painter Frank Brangwyn (1867–1956), embellish the lobby of the RCA Building, and Rene Chambellans' (1893–1955) bronze dolphins frolic in the Channel Gardens. Ezra Winter (1886–1949) contributed the mural *The Foundation of Youth* for the Radio City Music Hall, while sculptor Lee Lawrie (1877–1963) created a large outdoor figure of Atlas supporting the earth which, like several other works of art at the center, aroused some controversy. A number of onlookers saw, not Atlas, but the Italian dictator Benito Mussolini (1883–1945) in the heroic rendering, while others claimed the work resembled Christ when viewed from certain angles.

An unseen mural, however, aroused the most attention. In 1932, famed Mexican painter Diego Rivera (1886–1957) received a commission from Nelson Rockefeller (1908–1979), the son of John D. Jr., to paint the commanding mural *Man at the Crossroads* in the main entrance to the RCA Building. Rivera, in addition to his artistic renown, enjoyed considerable notoriety for his left-wing political views, and so the commission from the nominally conservative Rockefellers elicited some surprise. Worked commenced in 1933, and everyone seemed pleased with the progress. But Rivera painted in the recognizable face of the late Russian Communist leader Vladimir Lenin (1870–1924), and to that Nelson Rockefeller objected. Each side offered compromises, but to no avail, so the Rockefellers paid off Rivera's contract and workers destroyed his mural before it ever received a public viewing. In its place, they substituted a less controversial work, *Man's Conquest*, by Jose Maria Sert.

On the other hand, the completion of an ice skating rink in Rockefeller Plaza, an open, public area near the center of the complex, offended no one. Originally this space, a sunken rectangle with plantings and walkways around it, was to be a grand entrance to the New York subways below. But construction on the subway spur got delayed, so the owners tried exclusive, expensive shops, but they proved too isolated, too out of the traffic flow.

A roller skating rink came next, but most people found it too noisy and rowdy. Fortunately, advances in freezing and maintaining ice for outdoor skating came along in 1936 and allowed for the installation of one of the most beloved features of the center. Open during the winter months—an equally popular outdoor café replaces it in warmer weather—the skating rink daily drew overflow crowds. Above the popular sunken rink, the gilded figure of Prometheus gazes benignly down on the people below. Created by Paul Manship (1885–1966), it remains one of the best-known, nongovernmental sculptures in the entire country.

Throughout the decade, Rockefeller Center served as a shining example of civic planning on a grand scale. One compelling reason for its popularity rests in its judicious use of open areas, easily accessible to pedestrians. In fact, the center even boasts its own private street, Rockefeller Plaza, a space happily available to the public. In all, Rockefeller Center displays an enlightened attitude about the role of skyscrapers and the ongoing street life below them.

This huge undertaking, which resulted in the construction of temples of technology and commerce, celebrates American capitalism in all its grandeur. It promises victory over economic disaster, and people of that time agreed. Ira Gershwin (1896–1983), the lyricist brother of composer George Gershwin (1898–1937), penned words to his brother's song "They All Laughed" (1937), a song first heard in the movie musical *Shall We Dance*, starring the inimitable **Fred Astaire** (1899–1987) **and Ginger Rogers** (1911–1995). Art imitating life, it sums up the popularity of Rockefeller Center, suggesting how people laughed about the complex during its construction, and following that with a line about how they fought to get in once it opened its doors.

See also Architecture; Chrysler Building; Empire State Building; George & Ira Gershwin; Movies; Musicals; Prohibition & Repeal; Radio Networks; Restaurants; Songwriters & Lyricists

SELECTED READING
Balfour, Alan. *Rockefeller Center: Architecture as Theater.* New York: McGraw-Hill, 1978.
Hitchcock, Henry-Russell, and Philip Johnson. *The International Style.* New York: W. W. Norton, 1932.
Jordy, William H. *American Buildings and Their Architects: The Impact of European Modernism in the Mid-Twentieth Century.* Garden City, NY: Doubleday [Anchor Press], 1976.
Okrent, Daniel. *Great Fortune: The Epic of Rockefeller Center.* New York: Viking, 2003.

ROCKWELL, NORMAN. No American illustrator has ever enjoyed greater popularity than Norman Rockwell (1894–1978). Born in New York City, he early in life decided on a career in art. As a teenager, he attended the Chase School of Fine and Applied Art, the National Academy of Design, and the Art Students League. In this last institution, he studied under Thomas Fogarty (1873–1938) and learned about the world of commercial art. He also familiarized himself with the work of Howard Pyle (1853–1911), one of the premier **illustrators** of the day.

By age 19, Rockwell had graduated to art director of *Boys Life* magazine, the official journal of the Boy Scouts of America. That ushered in a 64-year affiliation with the Scouts, a relationship that would result in covers, calendars, and many more illustrations for various scouting publications.

In the 1920s he solidified his emerging reputation as a reliable and imaginative freelance illustrator. **Advertising** art for a myriad of products—Edison Mazda Lamps (a trade name for General Electric light bulbs), Fisk Tires, Interwoven Socks, Maxwell House Coffee, Willys-Overland **automobiles**, Jell-O, and a host of other companies—came from Rockwell's studio, and he probably would have been considered a successful commercial artist had he done nothing else.

In 1913 Rockwell moved to New Rochelle, New York, a suburban community that had become something of an artists' haven. Important illustrators like Howard Chandler Christy (1873–1952), John Falter (1910–1982), Joseph Christian Leyendecker (1874–1951) and his brother Frank Xavier Leyendecker (1878–1924), Clare Briggs (1875–1930), Nell Brinkley (1886–1944), and Coles Phillips (1880–1927) resided there,

Artist and illustrator Norman Rockwell (1894–1978). (Courtesy of the Library of Congress)

and Rockwell learned from them all. For 27 years he would call New Rochelle home, and the themes and techniques that characterize his work during the remainder of his career he mastered in this tranquil location. Not until 1930 did he move to Arlington, Vermont (and later to Stockbridge, Massachusetts), the rural villages that appear in so many of the paintings from his mature years.

Three years after his move to New Rochelle, and emboldened by his advertising contracts, Rockwell approached George Horace Lorimer (1867–1937), the famed editor of the **Saturday Evening Post**. Far and away the most popular magazine of the day, it featured cover art done by leading illustrators; a *Post* assignment signaled the pinnacle of commercial success. Lorimer liked Rockwell's samples, and at age 22 the young artist embarked on an affiliation with the magazine that would last through 1963 and result in 322 *Saturday Evening Post* covers and a level of fame unequalled by any other American illustrator. Because of the magazine's high circulation, an average of 4 million people saw each cover, giving him the largest audience ever enjoyed by an artist before or since.

Rockwell did not rely only on the *Saturday Evening Post* once he had become established with the publishing giant. His work also appeared in *Boys' Life, Farm & Fireside, Judge, Ladies' Home Journal, Leslie's, Liberty, Literary Digest, Popular Science*, and *Woman's Home Companion*. A superb technician and stylist, and endowed with a storyteller's imagination, most of Rockwell's pictures are essentially narrative. He knew how to stop action at just the right moment, revealing enough of an ongoing story that viewers find it easy to make sense of the composition.

In reality, Norman Rockwell learned his craft as a classical painter, working in the well-established European tradition of bourgeois story telling. But he complemented that internal talent with exceptional external skills as an artist, a combination that guaranteed success with his public. Throughout his career, he focused on the passing American scene, painting the small towns and their citizens, filling the canvas with anecdotal detail. Despite his penchant for folksy settings, Rockwell can hardly be classified a Regionalist, the school of painting so popular during the 1930s, and even less can he be called a Social Realist. His canvases depict an America that never really existed, a nostalgic exploration of life as people would like it to be. By focusing on the ordinary and the familiar, he casts his subjects in a warm, often humorous, glow. Because of this approach, and because of his technical skills, Norman Rockwell set the standards for American illustration from the 1920s onward into the postwar years.

The Depression never appears in a Rockwell painting. With the onset of the decade, Rockwell's work for the *Saturday Evening Post* does shift slightly from his earlier output. He executed 67 *Post* covers during the 1930s, or about seven a year, and the presence of children, a staple in his earlier covers, undergoes a marked decline. Adults become his focus, perhaps in recognition that the Depression era demanded a more serious—more "adult"—response from artists. At the same time, Rockwell doubtless sensed that most Americans preferred not to be reminded of the economic collapse, particularly on the covers of their favorite **magazines**, or in the illustrations accompanying stories or advertisements. Instead, he provided pictorial reassurances: that social and political rituals had meaning, and that the family and the individual would ultimately triumph. A little laughter and a bit of mischief, he seemed to say, would lighten everyone's spirits.

A few contemporary references nevertheless creep into some of his 1930s work. Hollywood actor Gary Cooper (1901–1961) appears on a 1930 *Post* cover, as does Jean Harlow (1911–1937), the reigning "Blonde Bombshell" of the **movies** in 1936. Two coeds swoon over a photograph of leading man Robert Taylor (1911–1969) two years later. Rockwell also displays a growing appreciation of **fashion** trends during this time. He depicts the slim—but curvaceous—look favored by stylish women, along with their popular permed hair. His men, on the other hand, remain attired in shapeless suits that could come from almost any decade, a wry comment on the lack of distinctive dress for most American males of the period.

In even the most mundane advertisements, Rockwell's carefully lettered signature always appears on his work. A simple device, it helped sustain his growing fame and popularity. And for the innumerable ads, his signature suggests an unspoken endorsement of the product. Over time, Norman Rockwell successfully blurred the line between high and low culture by focusing on popular culture. His work has long appealed to a large, diverse mass of people, and his public acceptance ensconced him as the most beloved—and possibly the most influential—American artist of all time.

See also Regionalism; Social Realism; N. C. Wyeth

SELECTED READING

Buechner, Thomas S. *Norman Rockwell: Artist and Illustrator*. New York: Harry N. Abrams, 1970.

Finch, Christopher. *Norman Rockwell's America*. New York: Harry N. Abrams, 1975.

Hennessey, Maureen Hart, and Anne Knutson. *Norman Rockwell: Pictures for the American People*. New York: Harry N. Abrams, 1999.

Stoltz, Donald Robert, Marshall Louis Stoltz, and William B. Earle. *The Advertising World of Norman Rockwell*. New York: Madison Square Press, 1985.

Stoltz, Donald R., and Marshall L. Stoltz. *Norman Rockwell and the* Saturday Evening Post. Vol. 2, *The Middle Years, 1928–1943*. 3 Vols. Philadelphia, PA: Saturday Evening Post Co., 1976.

RODGERS & HART (RICHARD RODGERS & LORENZ HART). Composer Richard Rodgers (1902–1979) met lyricist Lorenz Hart (1895–1943) when both were still in their teens. Rodgers, born in New York City, had a prosperous childhood and attended Columbia University. Hart, also New York–born, likewise attended

Columbia, and friends introduced the two in 1919. Although dissimilar in personalities—Rodgers prided himself on being steady, reliable, and highly organized; Hart, on the other hand, was disorganized, erratic in his habits, and bordered on being unstable—they found complementary traits in one another and paired up as a songwriting team. By 1925 the two could claim a number of songs, most of them forgotten. But that year also saw their *Garrick Gaieties*, a revue that featured "Manhattan" and "Sentimental Me." The popularity of these numbers and a succession of others put the talented duo on their way to national recognition.

With a new production almost yearly, and sometimes twice a year, Rodgers and Hart ranked among the most prolific of the many **songwriters and lyricists** who found favor in the 1930s. Memorable **music** seemingly flowed from their collective imaginations, and they set new expectations for the American musical theater. Thanks to **movies, radio,** and **recordings**, many of their songs have become standards, those melodies and lyrics known by both the public and a variety of performers over a long period of time.

In 1929, Rodgers and Hart opened *Spring Is Here* on Broadway. It introduced audiences to "With a Song in My Heart." The number became associated with singer Jane Froman (1907–1980) and made her a star; she would perform it frequently, and sang it in First National's 1930 film adaptation of the play. This period also introduced such standards as "A Ship without a Sail" (from *Heads Up*, 1929) and "Ten Cents a Dance" (from *Simple Simon*, 1930). The latter song laments the life of a taxi dancer. This 1920s-era term describes a woman employed by a commercial dance hall who will dance with any man willing to pay a dime (roughly $1.20 in contemporary money). Sung by Ruth Etting (1896–1978), the soulful tune burnished her career, and reminded critics and audiences that Rodgers and Hart could handle just about any subject and make memorable music.

As the Depression worsened, *America's Sweetheart* came to Broadway in early 1931. A superficial musical at best, it nonetheless contained an insouciant response to hard times with "I've Got Five Dollars" (roughly $66 in contemporary dollars). This jaunty piece quickly became a hit with the public, a musical riposte to unemployment, breadlines, and despair.

Later in 1931, the team headed west to join a number of their compatriots in Hollywood. They remained absent from Broadway for four years, instead focusing their energies on movie scores. Their hiatus proved financially profitable, and a number of pictures bore their musical stamp. One of the first of their films released during this period carried the title *Ten Cents a Dance* (1931). Despite the promising use of *Simple Simon*'s familiar song, *Ten Cents a Dance* cannot be considered either a musical or a Rodgers and Hart creation. Instead, the movie functions as a melodrama for actress Barbara Stanwyck (1907–1990), recounting the dreary life of a taxi dancer.

Both Richard Rodgers and Lorenz Hart worked as artists for hire, as did most songwriters and lyricists, both on Broadway and in Hollywood. They provided music appropriate to the project. For example, their collaboration on the film *The Hot Heiress* (1931) forced them to create such forgettable tunes as "Nobody Loves a Riveter" and "You're the Cats." On the other hand, they wrote a sparkling score for *Love Me Tonight* (1932), a lighthearted vehicle for the popular French entertainer Maurice Chevalier (1888–1972), along with Jeanette MacDonald (1903–1965). It features "Mimi," "Isn't It Romantic?" "Lover," and the title song.

An often overlooked film, *The Phantom President* (1932), indulges in some sharp political satire and probably amused people in gloomy 1932. It boasts an all-star cast consisting of George M. Cohan (1978–1942), Jimmy Durante (1893–1980), and Claudette Colbert (1903–1996). The Rodgers and Hart score, although it has no real standouts, does contain the topical "This Country Needs a Man," "Somebody Ought to Wave a Flag," and "Give Her a Kiss."

Topicality continued with *Hallelujah, I'm a Bum!* (1933). An unusual rhymed musical comedy, it features Al Jolson (1886–1950) and captures some of the flavor of the Depression in Ben Hecht's (1894–1964) and S. N. Behrman's (1893–1973) literate script. Unemployment and money worries drive the story, and Rodgers and Hart contributed "You Are Too Beautiful" and "I'll Do It Again," plus a good Depression number, "What Do You Want with Money?" They even have uncredited cameos in the picture.

Evergreen (1934), an original film produced and filmed in England, was also released by theaters in the United States. The somewhat unbelievable story of a young woman masquerading as her mother, the movie contains several outstanding numbers, including "Dancing on the Ceiling" (a tune dropped from Broadway's *Simple Simon* in 1930), "Dear, Dear," and "If I Give In to You."

Bing Crosby (1903–1977) joined with the two songwriters for a light movie musical called *Mississippi* (1935). It proved a good artistic pairing for both, although the major parties did not get along well on the set. Despite much bickering over the music, Rodgers and Hart created "Soon," a tune not to be confused with a 1930 song of the same title from the Gershwin brothers, along with "It's Easy to Remember" and "Down by the River." Crosby enjoyed a hit with "It's Easy to Remember," but because of disagreements would not record anything else by Rodgers and Hart for several years thereafter.

The pair eventually tired of the West Coast, and in 1935 they returned to New York City to score *Jumbo*, an extravaganza mounted by showman Billy Rose (1899–1966). A popular hit, *Jumbo* contained some of the greatest Rodgers and Hart melodies, including "The Most Beautiful Girl in the World," "My Romance," and "Little Girl Blue."

The success of *Jumbo* put the two at the top of their game, and they followed it with another stage hit, *On Your Toes* (1936). This musical allowed Richard Rodgers to compose a more formal, extended work that was contained within the larger play "Slaughter on Tenth Avenue." A ballet, it enlivened the show and eventually took on a musical life of its own, becoming a favorite of classical and "pops" orchestras everywhere. Hart, of course, contributed some fine lyrics for other songs in *On Your Toes*, notably "There's a Small Hotel" and "Glad to Be Unhappy."

The cinematic version of *On Your Toes* did not come out until 1939, and it barely acknowledges the memorable Broadway score. Melodic snippets of the songs remain, but they get relegated to background music instead of production numbers. Nonetheless, "There's a Small Hotel" receives its due, and Hollywood pulls out all the stops—lighting, camera angles, special effects—for Rodgers's foray into ballet, "Slaughter on Tenth Avenue." But film and play remain poles apart.

While *Jumbo* and *On Your Toes* were drawing in Broadway audiences, Rodgers and Hart continued to write scores for the movies. They contributed the music for *Dancing Pirate*, a trifle that played on the nation's screens in 1936. The lilting "When You're Dancing the Waltz" originated with this little-known picture, as did "Are You My Love?" but the film's greatest claim to fame rests with its being the first musical in which the cameras shot the dance sequences in Technicolor.

Continuing their Broadway run of one hit after another, Rodgers and Hart introduced *Babes in Arms* early in 1937, with music that included "Where or When," "I Wish I Were in Love Again," "My Funny Valentine," "Johnny One Note," "Imagine," and "The Lady Is a Tramp," certainly one of the greatest collections of American standards ever written for a single play.

MGM adapted *Babes in Arms* for film in a lavish 1939 production, but one that, like *On Your Toes*, does violence to the original score. The big studios sometimes recognized quality scoring, and with a sympathetic director and producer, everything can come together into a fine picture. Other times, however, too many hands and too many interests muddy up what might have been an outstanding film; *Babes in Arms* serves as a case in point.

Two of the hottest players in MGM's stable at the time were **Judy Garland** (1922–1969) and Mickey Rooney (b. 1920). When MGM obtained the rights to *Babes in Arms*, the studio wanted to promote this pair of popular young actors, but executives felt that much of the original score would be seen as "too adult" for Garland and Rooney, so they hired other songsmiths to create substitutions. Most of the Broadway score disappeared, leaving the title tune and "Where or When" as the survivors. With such a change in credits and music, the theatrical *Babes in Arms* and the screen adaptation become two different vehicles. Both provide audiences good musical comedy; each possesses its own merits; but any attempts to equate them can be linked with the old apples to oranges comparison.

Rodgers and Hart opened a second Broadway show in the fall of 1937, *I'd Rather Be Right*. It included "Have You Met Miss Jones?" and the humorous "We're Going to Balance the Budget," a subject of considerable concern in those post-Depression years. Another of their infrequent forays into topicality, the song exists as a trifle for the pair, but it carries perhaps their most unusual title.

Maintaining their frenetic theatrical pace, in 1938, the duo's *I Married an Angel* gave audiences the title tune plus the haunting "Spring Is Here." In a bow to the success of author Dale Carnegie's (1888–1955) best-selling 1937 book, the show also included "How to Win Friends and Influence People," hardly their best-remembered effort. Later that year Rodgers and Hart collaborated with playwright George Abbott (1887–1995) for a musical version of Shakespeare's *The Comedy of Errors* (1623). Their interpretation, *The Boys from Syracuse*, served as the pair's second offering of the year. A musical romp, the team provided the delightful "Falling in Love with Love," "This Can't Be Love," and "Sing for Your Supper."

On the movie front, 1938 saw *Fools for Scandal*, a comedy designed to feature the talents of star Carole Lombard (1908–1942). It did poorly, both critically and at the box office. The accompanying Rodgers and Hart score, about as light as the movie, includes "How Can You Forget?"

As the decade wound down, the songwriters enjoyed yet another Broadway hit, *Too Many Girls* (1939). The humorous "Give It Back to the Indians," a song about New York and its problems, both real and perceived, brightened the production, as did the tongue-twisting "Potawatomine" and "I Didn't Know What Time It Was," one of their great love songs. In a sly poke at contemporary musical arrangements that frequently buried the melody, they also contributed "I Like to Recognize the Tune."

Too Many Girls became a movie in 1940, the last film adaptation of the decade for Rodgers and Hart. Its move to the screen did little damage, and the score emerged relatively unscathed. Film and **television** buffs might find the casting for the movie of particular interest. On the stage, Marcy Westcott (active 1930s) had the lead, but on the screen a pre–*I Love Lucy* Lucille Ball (1911–1989) takes top honors. Lucy's husband-to-be, Desi Arnaz (1917–1986), also landed roles in both productions.

Lorenz Hart died in 1943, bringing to an end a remarkable pairing. Richard Rodgers would, of course, go on to team up with Oscar Hammerstein II (1895–1960), himself a most successful lyricist from the 1920s and 1930s. The new pairing of Rodgers and Hammerstein would write theatrical history with their great hits like *Oklahoma!* (play, 1943; film, 1955), *Carousel* (play, 1945; film, 1956), *South Pacific* (play, 1949; film, 1958), and many others. But Richard Rodgers and Lorenz Hart also made history in the 1930s, contributing a body of unforgettable songs to American music.

See also Best Sellers; George & Ira Gershwin; Musicals

SELECTED READING

Block, Geoffrey. *Enchanted Evenings: The Broadway Musical from* Show Boat *to* Sondheim. New York: Oxford University Press, 1997.

Hart, Dorothy. *Thou Swell, Thou Witty: The Life and Lyrics of Lorenz Hart.* New York: Harper & Row, 1976.

Marx, Samuel, and Jan Clayton. *Rodgers and Hart: Bewitched, Bothered, and Bewildered.* New York: G. P. Putnam's Sons, 1976.

Zinsser, William. *Easy to Remember: The Great American Songwriters and Their Songs.* Jaffrey, NH: David R. Godine, 2000.

ROLLER SKATING. Primitive roller skates have been traced to seventeenth-century Holland, and roller sports, or "dry land skating," have enjoyed continuous popularity since then. Never a big fad in the 1930s, and limited primarily to children, most roller skates consisted of a metal frame, straps, and four wooden or composite wheels. Clamps, adjusted with a key, locked the skates to the soles of one's shoes. Most youngsters from that period no doubt from time to time experienced a skate coming loose from a shoe.

The Roller Derby came into being with Leo Seltzer (active 1930s) in 1935. An entrepreneur who had staged such events as six-day bicycle races and dance marathons, he conceived of the derby as a mix of racing, **football**, and endurance games. Seltzer's first derby consisted of many competing two-person teams, each trying to skate the equivalent of the distance between New York City and San Francisco. Like the dance marathons of that time, participants had to stay upright and skating, accumulating miles as they raced around an oval track. Spectators cheered them on and waged bets on individual teams.

From this beginning, the sport evolved into nightly exhibitions of roughhousing as teams raced around a track, attempting to best their competitors, bumping and colliding at high speed, and generally trying to create thrills for the onlookers. Most of the time, each team had the same number of men and women skating for it, one of the few athletic contests that allowed both sexes to participate on an equal footing. Real and imagined rivalries among members of competing teams attracted public and press attention, as well as increasing paid admissions, the life blood of the sport.

It would not be until the advent of **television**, however, that the Roller Derby came into its own as a sport. Not much could be done in terms of **radio** descriptions of players

Girls roller-skating in New Orleans. (Courtesy of the Library of Congress)

endlessly going round and around a track, no matter how many collisions they endured, but following the end of World War II the Roller Derby's audience underwent a remarkable expansion.

See also Fads; Leisure & Recreation; Marathon Dancing

SELECTED READING

Brooks, Lou. *Skate Crazy*. Philadelphia: Running Press, 2003.

Phillips, Ann-Victoria. *The Complete Book of Roller Skating*. New York: Workman Publishing, 1979.

ROOSEVELT, ELEANOR. The child of a well-established and wealthy New York family, and the niece of President Theodore Roosevelt (1858–1919), Anna Eleanor Roosevelt (1884–1962) displayed a keen intelligence at an early age. Before she could even speak English, she had learned French from a nurse. After the deaths of both parents during her childhood, she lived with her grandmother and at age 15 enrolled in a boarding school in England. Naturally, everyone hoped the young Eleanor would mature into a conventional society matron. Upon completing her **education**, and seemingly less shy and more willing to engage in social functions, she returned to the United States, made her New York society debut in 1902, and three years later married a distant cousin, **Franklin Delano Roosevelt** (1882–1945), later known to millions as FDR. The couple had six children, five of whom survived infancy.

As was customary for women of her time and social standing, she joined the Junior League of New York. But, unlike many in her class, she felt a deep concern about the less fortunate. Prior to her marriage, she had worked in the East Side slums as a social worker teaching literature, calisthenics, and dance to poor immigrants at a settlement house. She joined the National Consumers' League in order to investigate working conditions in the garment districts.

In 1910, Franklin won election to the New York State Senate; this victory marked the beginning of remarkable careers for both Eleanor and FDR as distinguished public figures. While living in Albany, Eleanor frequented many of the state legislative sessions and attended her first national Democratic Party convention in 1912. Thereafter, she assisted and supported FDR in all his political ambitions and races, a path that culminated in his successful election as the president of the United States, an office he would hold for an unprecedented 12 years, from 1933 until his death in 1945.

First Lady Eleanor Roosevelt (1884–1962). (Courtesy of the Library of Congress)

Eleanor's interest in politics caused her to twice author a piece for the Junior League titled "Why I Am a Democrat"; the first version appeared in 1923, and the second in 1939. She continued to write about politics with "Women Must Learn to Play the Games as Men Do" for *Redbook* magazine in 1928, the year she assumed the position of director for the Bureau of Women's Activities for the National Democratic Party.

A marital crisis occurred in 1918 when Eleanor learned of an affair between Franklin and her social secretary, Lucy Mercer (1891–1948). She considered divorce, but for family, financial, and political reasons decided to remain married; her personal relationship with her husband would never be the same. Feeling alone and betrayed, Eleanor began to engage in more activities outside the home. Since Franklin served as assistant secretary of the navy (1913–1920), the Roosevelts lived in Washington during much of this time. She volunteered at St. Elizabeth Hospital as a visitor to World War I veterans; because of her ability to speak French fluently, she attended the 1919 International Congress of Working Women, a gathering of representatives from 19 nations that met in the capital, to assist with translations and conversations.

Out of an interest in improving working conditions for women, she joined the Women's Trade Union League in 1922. Through that organization, she established significant friendships with Marion Dickerman (1890–1983) and Nancy Cook (1884–1962), two colleagues who held similar interests and concerns. In 1925, the threesome, with Franklin's support and assistance, built Stone Cottage at Val-Kill, a creek that ran two miles from Springwood, the palatial Roosevelt mansion located at Hyde Park, a small community on the Hudson River north of New York City. They next erected a larger structure near Stone Cottage and founded Val-Kill Industries, a nonprofit furniture factory dedicated to providing jobs for unemployed rural workers. After nine years of operation,

Val-Kill Industries closed, and Eleanor had the building remodeled and converted into apartments for herself and guests.

The delegates to the National Democratic Convention in 1920 selected Franklin Roosevelt as the running mate for James M. Cox (1870–1957) in his bid for president. As FDR rose in the political world, newspaperman Louis Howe (1871–1936) became a valued confidante and adviser. Howe had first met the Roosevelts in 1911 and served as chief of staff for Mr. Roosevelt during his tenure as assistant secretary of the navy.

FDR's closest adviser, Howe accurately sensed that Mrs. Roosevelt could make significant contributions as a political partner, and he began to deliberately involve her in a variety of roles. The two discussed drafts of Mr. Roosevelt's speeches, and Howe instructed her in how to gain access to the press. He coached her in speech-making and public appearances and informed her of the issues surrounding the campaign, a practice he would continue in future races. The Cox-Roosevelt ticket suffered a heavy defeat at the hands of Republican Warren Harding (1865–1923), but Eleanor Roosevelt had moved forward in her goal of becoming an activist in many areas of American life. She frequently credited Howe for helping her overcome her natural shyness and reluctance to speak before gatherings.

Shortly after the couple's return to New York in 1921, Franklin contracted infantile paralysis, or polio, and the disease permanently paralyzed his legs, causing him to temporarily withdraw from the public eye and any political endeavors. At the same time, Eleanor expanded her private and public engagements and involvement in social service. She joined the League of Women Voters, chaired its Legislative Affairs Committee, and held the position of vice president for the New York branch. She also actively participated in the women's division of the New York State Democratic Committee. She met and befriended Mary McLeod Bethune (1875–1955), president of Bethune-Cookman College. Along with Marion Dickerman and Nancy Cook, she purchased Todhunter School in 1926, a private school for girls in New York City, and added teacher of history and government to her growing list of accomplishments. Through all of this work, she fought for many controversial issues of the day, such as better working conditions for both men and women, and women's rights in general.

Not only did Mrs. Roosevelt engage in activities pursuant to her own interests, she also served as her husband's eyes and ears, especially during his illness and seclusion, reporting to him the results of her investigations and observations. She remained steadfastly interested in various political efforts, especially those that touched on social conditions. As her husband's stand-in with the Democrats, she kept his name before the public and brought key party officials, public figures, and others to see him.

Mrs. Roosevelt, along with Howe, encouraged FDR to resume his political career. He won a bid for governor of New York in 1928 and repeated it in 1930. At the beginning of his second term, Governor Roosevelt took bold steps to combat the Depression and its effects on New York, actions that gained national attention. With continuing active support and assistance from Mrs. Roosevelt, he began campaigning for the presidency and easily gained the Democratic nomination in 1932. Both he and Mrs. Roosevelt crisscrossed the country on speaking tours that year, and he handily defeated the incumbent **Herbert Hoover** (1874–1964).

Following the election, Mrs. Roosevelt continued to travel extensively across the United States and frequently did so by flying, a means of **transportation** considered unsafe and risky by many. She had first shown an interest in **aviation** by agreeing to fly over the capital city in 1933 with famed aviatrix **Amelia Earhart** (1897–1937). The airlines, always looking for a way to reassure the public about the safety of air **travel**, delighted in the "Flying First Lady" who often allowed herself to be photographed standing next to an airplane. She even wrote an article, "Flying Is Fun," for *Collier's* magazine in 1939.

On March 6, 1933, two days after the presidential inauguration, encouraged by her friend, journalist Lorena Hickok (1893–1968), Eleanor Roosevelt became the first president's wife to hold a press conference for women reporters only, a practice that she continued on a regular basis. Initially, these gatherings helped female journalists keep their jobs as reporters, but they also supplied pertinent information for the reporters to convey to their readers. Mrs. Roosevelt focused her press conference discussions around her activities and the immediate interests of women, not on the president's prerogatives of national and international events.

Throughout her 12 years as First Lady of the United States, Mrs. Roosevelt had much to talk about; in addition to meeting with reporters, she engaged in considerable writing and **radio** work. She had gained some experience in commercial radio before 1933, but ceased this activity with her husband's election. In 1934, however, she decided to resume appearing on sponsored programs in order to reach larger audiences through this growing medium, a decision that exposed her to severe criticism. She won over many of her potential critics by donating any sponsors' money to the American Friends Service Committee, a group that in turn disbursed it to relief efforts recommended by Mrs. Roosevelt. People, especially women, attached importance to her views and her shows enjoyed a wide listenership. Station WNBC dubbed her the "First Lady of Radio" in 1939, and she continued broadcasting beyond the decade.

Before moving to the White House, Mrs. Roosevelt had written a variety of articles for **magazines**. She contributed "What Are the Movies Doing to Us?" in 1932 to *Modern Screen*, and that same year also saw the publication of her first book, *When You Grow Up to Vote*. She followed that with *It's Up to the Women* (1933), a compilation of her articles and speeches that focused on the important role of women in successfully seeing the country through the crisis of the Depression. In this book, Mrs. Roosevelt urged women to be economically wise with household budgets and preparing meals. She offered advice on child rearing, getting along with one's husband and children, and appealed to women to take leadership in issues involving social justice, encouraging them to join and support trade unions, and to enter politics.

When a contract she had with *Woman's Home Companion* ended in 1935, United Features Syndicate immediately offered her a daily 400- to 500-word newspaper column. It appeared in the form of a diary called "My Day." In the first of these, published on December 31, 1935, Mrs. Roosevelt described the White House quarters and activities during the Christmas holidays. The column soon appeared in 62 **newspapers** with a total circulation of a little over 4 million readers. Until shortly before her death in 1962, six days a week she faithfully submitted pieces dealing with current and historical events, social and political issues, and her private and public life. She also continued to write books; in 1937 came *This Is My Story*, and in 1938 both *My Days* and *This Troubled World*.

Upon assuming her responsibilities as First Lady, Eleanor Roosevelt reluctantly resigned her teaching position at Todhunter, but soon found herself on a nationwide lecture circuit, a form of teaching, to explain the **New Deal**. By the end of 1935, she experienced such demand that she signed a contract with the W. Colston Leigh booking agency to do two lecture tours, each two weeks long. Her first audience, almost 2,000 people in Grand Rapids, Michigan, gave her rave reviews and in 1937 she agreed to lengthen her contract to three-week tours. A Leigh brochure advertised five potential speech topics: relationship of the individual to the community; problems of **youth**; the mail of a president's wife; peace; and a typical day at the White House.

With her writings, radio shows, speeches, organizational memberships, and humanitarian efforts during the 1930s, Eleanor Roosevelt was an untiring advocate for improved conditions and opportunities for blacks, youth, the poor, the unemployed, and women. She worked closely with the National Association for the Advancement of Colored People (NAACP) and the National Council of Negro Women. At her urging, President Roosevelt gave a few blacks positions in cabinet-level departments, meeting regularly with them in an informal group known as the "Black Cabinet." She pleaded, unsuccessfully, for the passage of an antilynching bill in 1938.

Perhaps her greatest acts in behalf of the racially discriminated came from two deeply felt personal decisions she made. First, when she attended the Southern Conference for Human Welfare in Birmingham, Alabama, in 1938, she refused to obey a segregation ordinance that required her to sit in the white section of the auditorium, away from her black friends. Just one year later she dropped her membership in the Daughters of the American Revolution (DAR) because they would not allow Marian Anderson (1897– 1993), a world renowned black contralto, to sing at Constitution Hall.

In 1934, she wrote "Youth Facing the Future" for *Woman's Home Companion*. In this article, she worried about the nation's youth as they experienced difficulties in completing a formal education, obtaining occupational training, and securing jobs with adequate compensation. She lobbied hard with her husband and members of his cabinet for the formation of the National Youth Administration (NYA; 1935–1943), a federal program to aid rural and urban young men and women in the areas of education and job training. She also worked closely with the American Youth Congress (AYC), an organization of young people that advocated civil rights, housing, and jobs. In 1939, however, she parted ways with this group when they supported the Nazi-Soviet nonaggression pact.

In addition to speaking out for the unemployed and disadvantaged, Mrs. Roosevelt in 1935 helped create federal agencies that supported the arts, music, theater, and writing. These New Deal projects served jobless artists, musicians, actors, and authors. In addition, she spent time visiting coal mines, slum areas, and relief projects. The construction of Arthurdale, West Virginia, in 1933, a planned New Deal resettlement town, serves as an example of her direct involvement with relief. Mrs. Roosevelt had learned of a plan in West Virginia to move impoverished laborers to newly constructed rural communities. She visited the area and brought it to the attention of FDR; he decided to federalize the project by placing it under the direction of the Department of the Interior. Advocacy such as this for the poor brought her thousands of letters seeking help, a number of which came from children. She answered many of them and always sought ways to offer help, sometimes out of her own pocket.

As First Lady, Mrs. Roosevelt also performed all the traditional duties expected of someone in that role. She oversaw the running of the White House, received special guests visiting the United States, and served as hostess for official receptions and dinners. She also made sure that the family living quarters were comfortably, but modestly, furnished, and she always welcomed visits from her children and many grandchildren.

Eleanor Roosevelt changed the role of the First Lady of the United States, but she should not merely be remembered in this way or simply as the wife of President Franklin D. Roosevelt. Her work as a civil rights activist, humanitarian, social reformer, author, teacher, and lecturer established her as a public figure in her own right and as one of the most important women of the twentieth century.

See also Federal Art Project; Federal Music Project; Federal Theatre Project; Federal Writers' Project; Political Parties; Race Relations & Stereotyping; Radio Networks; Shirley Temple

SELECTED READING
Lash, Joseph P. *Eleanor and Franklin: The Story of Their Relationship Based on Eleanor Roosevelt's Private Papers.* New York: W. W. Norton, 1971.
Roosevelt, Eleanor. *The Autobiography of Eleanor Roosevelt.* New York: Harper & Brothers, 1958.

ROOSEVELT, FRANKLIN DELANO. The 32nd president of the United States, Franklin D. Roosevelt (1882–1945), frequently referred to as FDR, guided the country through the Great Depression, one of its worst domestic crises. In the midst of a debilitating economic collapse, he offered its citizens a **New Deal**, assuring them that they had "nothing to fear but fear itself." His presidency, unparalleled in length and scope, carried into a fourth term and spanned 12 years (1933–1945), making him the only chief executive to serve more than two terms.

Born into a prestigious family of considerable wealth in the Hudson River community of Hyde Park, New York, Franklin was the only child of the elderly James Roosevelt (1828–1900) and domineering Sara Ann Delano Roosevelt (1854–1941). Under his mother's tutelage, he learned to ride, shoot, row, and play **polo** and lawn **tennis** as a young boy, while also gaining an appreciation for public service and active involvement in philanthropic pursuits.

Frequent trips to Europe made him conversant in German and French; at home he received much of his early **education** from private tutors. At age 14 he enrolled at Groton, an elite private preparatory school in Massachusetts. Regarded by his teachers and peers as an amiable young man with an engaging personality, he did not distinguish himself in academics, athletics, or student government. After graduating from Groton, he entered Harvard University and received a BA degree in history in three years (1900–1903).

In 1903, Franklin met Anna **Eleanor Roosevelt** (1884–1962), a distant cousin and niece of President Theodore Roosevelt (1858–1919; president from 1901–1909). They married two years later, despite strong objections from Franklin's mother, and had six children, with five surviving infancy. He entered New York's Columbia University to study law and passed the bar examination in 1907 without taking a degree; he immediately began to practice with Carter, Ledyard, and Milburn, a respected and well-established New York City firm.

After three years, Franklin found he had little interest in law. Emulating his cousin Theodore Roosevelt, whom he admired, he entered public service through politics. He

Franklin D. Roosevelt (1882–1945), the 32nd president of the United States. (Courtesy of the Library of Congress)

ran successfully as a Democrat for the New York State Senate in 1910, and served two terms. A supporter of the presidential candidacy of Woodrow Wilson (1856–1924) in 1912, Roosevelt accepted an appointment as assistant secretary of the navy after Wilson's victory. He held the office from 1913 to 1920. During World War I, he oversaw defense contracts and navy shipyards and bases in New York, which gained him significant state political influence. Louis Howe (1871–1936), a man who would become his trusted friend and confidante, served as his chief of staff.

As assistant secretary of the navy, FDR proved to be an energetic, efficient administrator. His popularity and success in naval affairs brought about his 1920 nomination for vice president on the Democratic ticket beside James M. Cox (1870–1957) of Ohio, the presidential candidate. This experience allowed him to meet Democratic politicians throughout the country, although the Cox-Roosevelt ticket suffered defeat at the polls. Following the election, Franklin and Eleanor returned to private life and maintained a home in New York City as well as spending time at Springwood, Sara Roosevelt's palatial estate at Hyde Park.

In the summer of 1921, while vacationing at the family's summer retreat at Campobello Island, located off the coast of New Brunswick, Canada, Roosevelt contracted infantile paralysis, or polio. He withdrew from politics and public life and in 1924 traveled to Warm Springs, Georgia, in hopes of achieving rehabilitation by swimming in the curative waters. In his determination to get better, which he believed essential to holding public office again, he had heavy iron braces fitted for his hips and legs and taught himself to walk short distances. In private, he utilized a wheelchair, but carefully avoided being seen using the device in public.

Despite his courageous efforts to overcome the crippling disease, Roosevelt never regained the complete use of his legs. He did, however, derive some benefit from the waters at Warm Springs and in 1926 bought an aging spa there and continued to spend considerable time in Georgia. In later years, a cottage that he had built at the springs became known as "the Little White House," where he died in 1945.

During the worst of Roosevelt's illness, Eleanor and Louis Howe strove to preserve his political reputation and encouraged him to again pursue elected positions. They apprised him of social and political conditions both in New York and the country, brought important politicians and other public figures to visit him, and generally kept his name before the public.

Howe, who had become enthralled with the anti–Tammany Hall stands taken by Franklin as a New York senator, headed FDR's state reelection campaign in 1912. Henceforth he assisted Franklin with statements on public issues, wrote magazine articles under FDR's byline, and coordinated his appearance at the 1924 Democratic convention. At this event, Roosevelt dramatically appeared on crutches to nominate fellow New Yorker Alfred E. Smith (1873–1944) as the presidential candidate against

Republican Calvin Coolidge (1871–1933). Although Smith lost, Roosevelt nominated him again in 1928. Smith failed in his second bid, this time at the hands of **Herbert Hoover** (1874–1964). Despite the party's losses, Roosevelt had positioned himself as a rising star of the Democratic Party.

Clearly embarked on a return to the political world, Roosevelt's comeback officially occurred in 1928 when he won the election for governor of New York. Following the stock market crash of 1929, FDR spoke directly to the state's citizens through **radio** broadcasts. He advocated a number of innovative relief and economic recovery initiatives that included low-cost hydroelectric power for rural areas, farm-to-market paved roads, unemployment insurance, and property tax relief for farmers. The New York legislature, controlled by Republicans, either defeated or diluted most of his requests, but Roosevelt had appealed to voters as a liberal reformer and easily won reelection in 1930. His victory in hand, he began to campaign for the presidency. The Depression worsened over the next two years and Roosevelt's bold efforts to combat it in New York enhanced his national reputation. A successful governor with a recognizable name, FDR won the Democratic nomination to run against Herbert Hoover in the 1932 election.

The Roosevelts campaigned energetically throughout the nation. Assisted by the trusted Louis Howe and with friends like party leaders James Farley (1888–1976) and Edward Flynn (1891–1953), FDR won by a landslide with 57 percent of the popular vote and 472 of the 531 electoral college votes. His party also secured large majorities in both houses of Congress, putting the Democrats in charge of the executive and legislative branches of the federal government for the first time in almost 20 years.

Buoyed by his sweeping victory, the new president immediately appointed an administrative staff of people with a wide range of expertise and backgrounds including Farley, a fellow stamp collector, as postmaster general. The highly qualified Frances Perkins (1882–1962) became secretary of labor, the first woman in American history to hold a cabinet post. Other appointees included Henry Morgenthau Jr. (1891–1967), as secretary of the treasury, 1934–1945, and Harry Hopkins (1890–1946). The latter served in a variety of positions, including director, Federal Emergency Relief Administration (FERA), from 1933 until 1934; director, Works Progress Administration (WPA), 1935–1938; secretary of commerce, 1938–1940; and FDR's personal assistant and adviser, 1940–1945. Roosevelt selected a progressive Republican, Harold L. Ickes (1874–1952), as secretary of interior, 1933–1946, and head of the Public Works Administration (PWA), 1933–1938. He also chose Henry Wallace (1888–1965) as secretary of agriculture, 1933–1939. Wallace, a maverick Republican who supported much of the New Deal, in time switched his membership to the Democratic Party. He shared the ticket with Roosevelt as the party's candidate for vice president in the 1940 election.

Prior to FDR's March 4, 1933, inauguration, conditions in the country had deteriorated even more. Factory closings, farm foreclosures, and bank failures increased while unemployment soared. From the vantage point of the campaign trail and concerns brought directly to him by his wife, President-elect Roosevelt grew to better understand the desperation that had crept into public life and relentlessly spoke of the need for action. He frequently said, "Do something. And when you have done that something, if it works, do it some more. And if it does not work, then do something else."

Once in office as president, Roosevelt proceeded to vigorously address the most urgent piece of business, the ongoing banking crisis. Following the 1929 stock market crash, many bank depositors across the country rushed to their banks to withdraw their savings. As a result, between 1930 and 1933, more than 9,000 banks closed their doors because they did not have enough cash on hand to meet this unexpected demand. When banks failed, depositors lost their holdings, and people with money at other banks panicked and, in turn, demanded their cash, creating a vicious cycle.

Roosevelt and his administrative staff proposed, and Congress in a special session in March 1933 immediately passed, the Emergency Banking Relief Act. This legislation called for a four-day shutdown of U.S. banks, referred to as a bank holiday, and gave the executive branch of the government power to reopen banks once they had been examined and declared sound. By April 1, 1933, the situation had stabilized and most of the nation's banks had returned to normal operations. Because of the new backing of the federal government, the people's faith in the banking industry had been restored.

On March 12, 1933, the day before the banks could reopen, FDR initiated on **radio** a remarkable series of evening broadcasts that came to be called "Fireside Chats." Tens of millions of Americans listened at 10:00 P.M. to that first presentation, during which the president took as his topic "On the Bank Crisis." He attempted through this and future chats to give American citizens a sense of hope and security during the difficult times.

Originating directly from the White House, each chat began with a reassuring "My dear friends." Roosevelt chose his words carefully, using a simple vocabulary but never patronizing his audience. He built a sense of intimacy between his listeners and himself. The Fireside Chats built positive public relations for the administration despite the hardships created by the Depression. Critics charged him with unfairly utilizing the airwaves for political purposes, but all reports suggest that the chats had a calming effect and FDR employed the powerful medium of radio throughout his administration.

Between 1933 and 1944, Roosevelt conducted a total of 30 Fireside Chats, with 14 of them occurring during the 1930s. The first chats dealt primarily with economic issues and how New Deal programs would address them. In 1934, he spoke in June and September, first on the subject "review of the achievements of the 73rd Congress," and next "on moving forward to greater freedom and greater security." In September 1936, the topic of the only program for that year bore the title "On Drought Conditions," a reference to the Dust Bowl. The last Fireside Chat for the decade aired on September 3, 1939, immediately following the German invasion of Poland. In it he discussed "the European war." According to estimates, the Fireside Chats drew audiences larger than the top-rated network shows.

Roosevelt also connected with the American public in other "everyday life" ways. For example, he openly pursued his hobby of **stamp collecting** throughout his presidency. An ardent collector since the age of eight, he personally approved the aesthetic composition of every stamp issued by the U.S. Post Office during his terms of office and even had a hand in designing a number of commemorative issues. He willingly posed for endless photographs showing him with his dapper cigarette holder tilted up at a jaunty angle. He reveled in the media attention paid a president, always comfortable in front of a camera or a microphone. He could also be seen in theater newsreels, magazine spreads, and almost daily in the **newspapers**. Franklin D. Roosevelt clearly understood mass media better than any of his predecessors, and he emerged as a popular culture celebrity.

But this notoriety never interfered with his work, and the grueling pace he established during his first hundred days continued unabated throughout his presidency. During those first days and weeks, President Roosevelt and his cabinet formulated, and Congress enacted, sweeping measures to address the economic crisis, to bring relief to the unemployed, and to hasten recovery in business and agriculture. The delivery system designed by the government to carry out these laws consisted of new federal programs, many with long names. These New Deal efforts became known as "alphabet agencies"—CWA, FDIC, FHA, NYA, TVA, and so on.

For example, FERA (the Federal Emergency Relief Administration) operated from 1933 to 1935 and sent $3 billion (roughly $45 billion in contemporary money) to local relief agencies and to fund depleted public work programs, while the **Civilian Conservation Corps** (CCC; 1933–1942) employed young unmarried men to work on tasks that would improve public land and conserve natural resources. This program served as one of the most successful of the New Deal efforts. The PWA (Public Works Administration, 1933–1939) created new infrastructure and community maintenance project jobs. Other agencies assisted business and labor, insured bank deposits, regulated the stock market, and subsidized home and farm mortgage payments.

Two organizations, the NRA (National Recovery Administration, 1933–1935) and the AAA (Agricultural Adjustment Administration, 1933–1945), represented the essence of Roosevelt's New Deal by enforcing controls on prices, wages, trading practices, and production, much to the chagrin of traditionalists more accustomed to a self-regulating economy. The NRA, organized under the terms of the National Industrial Recovery Act (NIRA), worked to stimulate competition and benefit producers by implementing various codes for establishing fair trade, while the AAA provided loans to farmers and subsidies for crop reduction.

Despite the ceaseless activity and remarkable successes during Roosevelt's first years as president, the Depression persisted; jobless workers, along with bankrupt farmers, conservative Republicans, and even some disaffected Democrats, openly expressed strong criticism about the lack of progress and the liberal and far-reaching effects of much of this new legislation. Some voiced concerns about the inequities of relief since white males generally received better benefits than women, blacks, or Mexicans. Politicians, radio personalities, and others spoke of their belief that Roosevelt had given in to big business.

As if the Depression did not create enough problems for the American people and the Roosevelt administration, Mother Nature also conspired against them. In 1930, the rains had stopped falling on the already parched southern Plains, primarily Texas, Oklahoma, Kansas, and Colorado. Four years later, the dry ground had the consistency of a fine powder, or dust; winds created waves of airborne topsoil known as "black blizzards." Roosevelt issued an executive order in 1934 to establish the Shelterbelt Project, which called for large-scale planting of trees across the Great Plains, the so-called Dust Bowl, to protect the land from erosion. Not until 1937 did the project get under way, and disputes over funding sources limited its success, causing FDR to transfer the program to the Works Progress Administration (WPA, 1935–1943; name changed to Work Projects Administration in 1939).

The New Deal measures that directly involved the government in areas of social and economic life also resulted in greatly increased spending and unbalanced budgets, actions that led to fierce criticism of Roosevelt's tactics. The president and his supporters suffered a heavy blow in 1935 and again in 1936 when the conservative Supreme Court found the legislation behind the NRA and AAA to be unconstitutional.

Undaunted, Congress passed another flurry of liberal legislation, referred to as the Second New Deal. More far-reaching than the original New Deal, these measures immediately met opposition. The Wagner Act of 1935 allowed labor unions to organize and bargain collectively. The Social Security Act, passed that same year, provided unemployment compensation and guaranteed pensions to those retiring at age 65. The Works Progress Administration, the most momentous program because it affected so many people's lives, provided work that addressed both the country's infrastructure and cultural activities.

Following the lead of people like Governor Floyd B. Olson (1891–1936) of Minnesota, a handful of citizens declared themselves socialists and tried to build a third party that advocated collective ownership as the best means of production and distribution. During this difficult time, membership in the Communist Party of the United States hit a high in 1935. But these were splinter groups; the nation at large supported Roosevelt and he easily defeated Republican Alfred M. Landon (1887–1987) in 1936, gaining 61 percent of the popular vote and carrying all but two states in the electoral college. The Democrats also continued their dominance in Congress.

With a second overwhelming victory under his belt, Roosevelt took on the critics of the New Deal. The Supreme Court had already declared some of the hundred-day legislation to be unconstitutional and lawsuits challenging many of the major legislative acts of 1935 had been filed. In February 1937, FDR asked Congress for a statute that would allow the president to appoint one additional justice to the Supreme Court, up to a total of six new appointments, for every sitting justice who declined to retire at age seventy. Additionally, he requested authority to name new judges to the federal judiciary.

Critics immediately objected; they insisted that this power would allow him to "pack" the courts and undermine the Constitutional separation of the three branches of government. In response, and in a major setback, Congress defeated his proposal. But in an unexpected turn of events, the "nine old men," as some called them, began to rule more favorably on New Deal legislation, upholding both the Wagner Act and the Social Security Act. Despite his judicial victories, Roosevelt revealed himself to be an unforgiving president. During the 1938 races for Congress, he campaigned against many of those Democrats who had voted against his plans. These heavy-handed attempts at reprisal backfired; most of his opponents won anyway.

On the economic side, and upholding an old campaign promise to balance the budget, Roosevelt introduced some spending cuts in 1936, steps that partially contributed to the 1937–1938 recession. Republicans immediately used what they called "Roosevelt's recession" as proof of the failure of the New Deal. They successfully gained new seats in both the House and the Senate in the 1938 elections, although the Democrats maintained strong majorities in both. After that, however, Congress could no longer pass major New Deal legislation without a fight, and these reversals represented a low point in FDR's career. Although monumental problems remained, the New Deal and Roosevelt's presidency had succeeded in reducing unemployment, poverty, and homelessness. Legal rights for labor unions, a broader distribution of incomes, and a safety net for the poor, unemployed, and elderly now existed.

The 1939 outbreak of war in Europe caused Roosevelt to shift his attention from domestic to foreign affairs. The Neutrality Act of 1937 forbade American commercial dealings with any nations at war. FDR called a special session of Congress in 1939, and at his urging they revised the Neutrality Act to allow arms sales to warring nations so long as they paid in cash and used their own ships for transportation. Roosevelt worked on ways to make foreign aid readily available to Britain, France, and China, the nation's probable allies should the United States get actively involved in the conflict. He also took steps to increase the size of the country's armed forces. President Roosevelt easily defeated Republican Wendall Willkie (1892–1944) in the 1940 presidential election, receiving 27 million popular votes to Willkie's 22 million and 449 out of 531 electoral college votes. After the fall of France in 1940, Congress enacted a conscription program, or draft, for military service. Roosevelt signed a lend-lease bill in March 1941 to enable the nation to furnish aid to those nations at war against Germany and Italy.

New Deal legislation and the various accompanying agencies did much to reshape the United States, while FDR's personal leadership gave Americans hope and confidence. But in the end it took American mobilization for war in the early 1940s to truly bring the country out of its economic problems. Franklin Delano Roosevelt, the champion of the common man, and more central to the life of the country than any previous president, conveyed an infectious self-confidence and steered the country through the darkest and worst days of the Great Depression. He changed the relationship between the federal government and its citizens and also launched the Democratic Party into a position of prolonged political dominance.

See also Federal Art Project; Federal Music Project; Federal Theatre Project; Federal Writers' Project; *The Grapes of Wrath*; Woody Guthrie; Hobbies; Magazines; Photography; Political Parties; Radio Networks; Songwriters & Lyricists; Television; Travel

SELECTED READING

Kennedy, David M. *Freedom from Fear*. New York: Oxford University Press, 1999.

Lash, Joseph P. *Eleanor and Franklin: The Story of Their Relationship Based on Eleanor Roosevelt's Private Papers*. New York: W. W. Norton, 1971.

Leuchtenburg, William E. *Franklin D. Roosevelt and the New Deal*. New York: Harper & Row, 1963.

Molella, Arthur P., and Elsa M. Bruton. *FDR, the Intimate Presidency: Franklin Delano Roosevelt, Communication, and the Mass Media in the 1930s*. Washington, DC: National Museum of American History, 1982.

Schlesinger, Arthur M., Jr. *The Age of Roosevelt*. 3 vols. Vol. 1, *The Crisis of the Old Order, 1919–1933*. Vol. 2, *The Coming of the New Deal, 1933–1935*. Vol. 3, *The Politics of Upheaval, 1935–1936*. New York: Houghton Mifflin, 1957–1960.

S

SATURDAY EVENING POST. Several of the most popular American **magazines** of the 1930s will always be associated with individuals who put their lasting imprints on them: DeWitt and Lila Wallace (1889–1981; 1889–1984), ***Reader's Digest***; Henry R. Luce (1898–1967), ***Life and Fortune***; Bernarr Macfadden (1868–1955), *Liberty*; and last—but hardly least—George Horace Lorimer (1867–1937), the *Saturday Evening Post*.

The history of the *Saturday Evening Post* goes back almost to the beginnings of American magazine publishing. Founded in 1828, this weekly miscellany had fallen on hard times—few subscribers and nonexistent profits—toward the end of the nineteenth century. A nondescript collection of poor fiction and poetry, along with a few mediocre articles, its future looked dim. In 1897, however, Cyrus H. K. Curtis (1850–1933), owner of the Curtis Publishing Company, a growing firm that included the profitable *Ladies' Home Journal* among its properties, bought the struggling *Post*. A year after his purchase, Curtis, in a stroke of marketing cleverness, declared on the *Post*'s masthead that it descended directly from the 1728 *Pennsylvania Gazette*, a journal published by none other than Benjamin Franklin (1706–1790). True or not, this distinguished lineage served as the opening of a lengthy and expensive **advertising** campaign that Curtis orchestrated, coupled with a complete physical makeover of the magazine.

In the midst of all this change, Curtis hired G. H. Lorimer in 1898 as a low-ranking literary editor. A native of Louisville, Kentucky, Lorimer had scattered journalistic experience but few accomplishments, and so he promptly accepted the offer and moved to Philadelphia. A year later, Curtis, mildly impressed with Lorimer's work, promoted him to temporary editor of the magazine, thinking he would find another person to fill the position permanently. But Lorimer in the meantime blossomed as editor in chief, and the "temporary" promotion soon became permanent, enduring until 1936; during those 37 years, Lorimer shaped the *Saturday Evening Post* into a publication that mirrored his beliefs and evolved into the most popular magazine in the country. Following Lorimer's retirement in 1936, veteran journalist Wesley W. Stout (1889–1971) took the helm, doing little to change the successful format established by his illustrious predecessor. The difficult times that would eventually bedevil the high-flying publication did not come until years later.

A meticulous editor, Lorimer allowed nothing to appear on the pages of the *Post* that he himself had not seen and approved. This attention to detail paid off handsomely as circulation for the revised *Saturday Evening Post* rose steadily. Readership soared from 2,000 subscribers when Curtis bought the magazine in 1897 to almost 200,000 at the opening of the twentieth century, a testament to Lorimer's astute leadership. Consistently higher figures would continue to be the rule. By 1920, circulation stood at 2 million copies a week; 10 short years later it stood at almost 3 million. That figure would drop during the early years of the Depression, with 1933 being the low point at 2.7 million, but would rebound later in the decade. It did not earn the title "the national weekly" for no reason.

Depression or not, the *Saturday Evening Post* remained the undisputed leader in the field of mass magazines. Everyone knew about the *Post*. With each big, glossy issue, this large-format weekly offered a sure-fire mix of fact and fiction, lots of photographs and illustrations, many features, and pages and pages of advertising—the lifeblood of any periodical. As a rule, ads occupied more than half of each issue; even during the period 1930 to 1939, the magazine averaged a remarkable 100 or so advertisements an issue.

One of the most popular features found in a typical issue involved the front cover. The country's best **illustrators** eagerly sought to execute them, and **Norman Rockwell** (1894–1978) emerged as the public's favorite. He painted his first *Post* cover in 1916, and proceeded to do 321 more in an association that would last until 1963 and earn him a following unequalled by any American illustrator before or since.

During the 1930s, and at the peak of his long career, Rockwell painted 67 *Post* covers, or about seven a year, a remarkable output. Children, families, pets, humorous situations—these subjects made up the focus of his work, and their warmth and familiarity reassured millions during the Depression. A Rockwell painting, executed in a realistic, traditional narrative style, could be understood by all who saw it, and he reinforced the American virtues of hard work and fair play, spiced with just the slightest bit of harmless mischief. Numerous other illustrators joined the *Post*'s ranks, especially Joseph Christian Leyendecker (1874–1951), who ran a close second to Rockwell in popularity. These artists also achieved some fame as cover artists, but nothing to equal that attained by Rockwell.

In addition to top-rank illustrators, the *Post* also carried the work of the finest writers in the land. Names like William Faulkner (1897–1962), F. Scott Fitzgerald (1896–1940), Bret Harte (1836–1902), Ring Lardner (1885–1933), Jack London (1876–1916), Don Marquis (1878–1937), Mary Roberts Rinehart (1876–1957), Kenneth Roberts (1885–1957), Booth Tarkington (1869–1946), and P. G. Wodehouse (1881–1975) graced its pages. In the 1930s the magazine recognized the ongoing popularity of mysteries and published stories by Agatha Christie (1890–1976), J. P. Marquand (1893–1960), and Rex Stout (1886–1975). In the broad area of fiction, the *Saturday Evening Post* reigned as the leader in the field, running over 200 short stories a year. Unlike today, most large-circulation magazines ran stories and novelettes, with the industry as a whole publishing some 1,000 fictional pieces annually. The *Saturday Evening Post*, however, ran more stories than anyone else.

Politicians, statesmen, scientists, athletes, entertainment figures, and successful businessmen in particular lined up to contribute their ideas in nonfiction. Their messages revolved around the ideas of hard work and common sense, especially the Depression-era essayists. People should not look to government for a dole (or "relief," as most termed it), but should look to their own strengths to see them through any difficulties. Lorimer and his staffers editorialized endlessly that Americans possessed the necessary grit, the

Boys earned money by selling subscriptions to the *Saturday Evening Post*, the most popular magazine in the country. (Courtesy of the Library of Congress)

self-reliance, needed to overcome this economic downturn. Perhaps the most significant acknowledgment of the crisis took place in the early 1930s when the *Post* ran articles giving advice to jobseekers.

Lorimer proved himself a genius when it came to discerning American tastes, and he delivered his interpretations into millions of homes, making believers of countless readers. Many of the offspring of those readers, virtually all boys, had earned a few dollars as *Post* carriers. With canvas sacks over their shoulders, they became a familiar sight as they sought to sell the magazine on the streets, deliver it to homes, and convince people to subscribe. A practice that had commenced in 1899, the small extra income the carriers earned, a penny or so an issue (or roughly 15 cents an issue in contemporary money), proved important during the Depression years. Weekly ads in the back pages of the magazine promised boys additional cash prizes for increasing sales and subscriptions, and the incentives worked. The carriers may not have realized it, but the *Post* and Lorimer were presenting them with the American dream of success, that good salesmanship and pluck would bring them well-deserved rewards.

When President **Franklin D. Roosevelt** (1882–1945) and his **New Deal** swept into power in 1933, Lorimer made no secret of his opposition to their liberal policies in one editorial after another, but his stance obviously had little impact on subscribers. In an apparent contradiction, *Post* readers purchased the conservative, probusiness magazine and simultaneously voted for Roosevelt and his New Deal. The nostalgic picture painted by the magazine of an America that possibly never was perhaps provided a kind of stability and familiarity lacking in day-to-day life; at the same time, readers' electoral choices reflected a desire for security that demanded embracing change in the form of a new administration and leadership. For his part, Lorimer continued to inveigh against anything connected with the New Deal, making it his editorial mission until his 1936 retirement.

Politics aside, advertisers eyed the *Post*'s subscription numbers happily; anything in the low millions meant a true mass audience. The magazine enjoyed national distribution and so served as a marketplace for products available everywhere. It took a pioneering role in standardizing consumer wants, and much of the ad copy reflects this unification of the buying public. City dweller, suburbanite, or farmer, they all had wants and needs. An ad in the *Post* suggested that everyone desired the product or service. Even in the depths of the Depression, advertisers boldly displayed nationally known products on the pages of the *Saturday Evening Post*, a tacit rejection of any economic collapse.

Throughout the first four decades of the twentieth century, the *Saturday Evening Post* stood as the unchallenged carrier of American values. From the perspective of the *Post*, the 1929 stock market debacle did little to dim this view, and George Horace Lorimer and his associates worked tirelessly to continue providing readers an endless, uplifting variety of historical romances, sports yarns, Westerns, and urban tales with businessman heroes, along with nonfiction success stories. That combination, along with the legions of youthful carriers, would have made Horatio Alger (1832–1899) proud.

See also Best Sellers; Photography; Youth

SELECTED READING

Cohn, Jan. *Creating America: George Horace Lorimer and the* Saturday Evening Post. Pittsburgh: University of Pittsburgh Press, 1989.

Moline, Mary. *Norman Rockwell Encyclopedia: A Chronological Catalog of the Artist's Work, 1910–1978.* Indianapolis, IN: Curtis Publishing Co., 1979.

Stoltz, Donald R., and Marshall L. Stoltz. *Norman Rockwell and the* Saturday Evening Post. Vol. 2, *The Middle Years, 1928–1943.* 3 Vols. Philadelphia: Saturday Evening Post Co., 1976.

Tebbel, John. *George Horace Lorimer and the* Saturday Evening Post. New York: Doubleday, 1948.

SCIENCE FICTION (MAGAZINES & BOOKS, COMIC STRIPS, MOVIES, & RADIO).

Throughout the twentieth century, science fiction has teetered on the fringes of American popular culture, and the 1930s proved no exception, although a few flurries of interest did develop, especially in the realm of **pulp magazines, comic strips,** and movie **serials**. In 1911, inventor, author, and publisher Hugo Gernsback (1884–1967) had penned *Ralph 124C 41+*, a pioneering novel that helped usher in modern science fiction writing. That event, coupled with a rash of cheap fantasy **magazines** during the 1920s, laid the groundwork for much that would happen in the genre, at least for the first half of the century.

Gernsback not only led the way for longer works but also founded the first American magazine dedicated wholly to science fiction in 1926 with *Amazing Stories*. He closely monitored what other writers were doing in the nascent field, and he correctly sensed that some readers would enjoy a publication that focused more on science and less on fantasy, the direction most authors seemed to be taking at the time. A few years earlier, *Weird Tales* had made its debut, an anthology of fantasy fiction that emphasized BEMs (*bug-eyed monsters*) on its garish covers, along with other repellent creatures. They could usually be seen threatening a helpless woman while her male comrade struggles to overcome these otherworldly adversaries. Fiction, but hardly science, *Weird Tales* made a niche for itself in the then-growing pulp magazine market.

At first, *Amazing Stories* contained its share of fantasy, running reprints of material by the likes of Edgar Allan Poe (1809–1849), Jules Verne (1828–1905), and H. G. Wells (1866–1946). The magazine nonetheless attracted a sizable audience and soon branched out into publishing stories by more contemporary writers. As sales climbed, Gernsback followed *Amazing Stories* with *Wonder Stories* in 1930. Other publishers recognized a trend in the making, and soon a host of rival publications, all with sensational covers featuring distant planets and galaxies, along with rockets and ray guns, competed for newsstand space.

By the mid-1930s, the height of their popularity, periodicals bearing such similar titles as *Astounding Stories, Dynamic Science Stories, Marvel Tales, Planet Stories, Science Wonder Stories, Startling Stories, Super Science Stories,* and *Thrilling Wonder Stories* collectively sold more than 1.5 million issues a year. These futuristic compilations effectively recorded the aspirations of the present, both visually and in their texts, and the future became but an extension of the present. Many of the writers who would later make names for themselves in the field during the 1940s and 1950s, the so-called golden years of science fiction, first saw publication in these pulp magazines.

For the Depression decade, the pulps featuring science fiction outsold anything in more traditional bindings, including like-minded books. With the advent of the inexpensive paperback at the end of the decade, many types of literature, such as Westerns, **aviation** tales, war stories, mysteries, exotic adventures, and fantasy found an inexpensive format that made them accessible to most readers. Most science fiction novels appeared primarily in paper, often serialized in magazines. Although this format might please fans, it relegated such writing more to newsstands than to traditional bookshops and libraries, reinforcing some people's view that science fiction somehow lacks literary quality.

Despite its perceived absence of credentials, several outstanding novels saw publication during the 1930s: John W. Campbell's (1910–1971) *Black Star Passes* came out in 1930, and *The Mightiest Machine* appeared in 1935. The veteran H. G. Wells published *The Shape of Things to Come* in 1933, later to become a distinguished 1936 film. Perhaps not science fiction in the truest sense, but a classic in its own right, *Brave New World*, by Aldous Huxley (1894–1963), shocked readers in 1932 with its descriptions of human engineering. Jack Williamson (b. 1908), the "dean of science fiction," wrote *After World's End* in 1939, and Philip Wylie (1902–1971) created *Gladiator* in 1930, which usually receives credit for the genesis of **Superman** later in the decade.

Science fiction moved to newspaper comic pages in 1929 with the premiere of *Buck Rogers in the 25th Century*. Written by Phil Nowlan (1888–1940) and drawn by Dick Calkins (1895–1962), the strip gave readers something new and different, and quickly developed a devoted following. Based on a serialized 1928 story by Nowlan called *Armageddon 2419 AD*, it first ran in *Amazing Stories* and featured a young man named Anthony "Buck" Rogers. The model for many subsequent space heroes, Rogers comes out of a 500-year state of suspended animation after a mysterious gas rendered him unconscious in 1919. Nowlan's tale quickly transferred to the comics, went to **radio** in 1932, and appeared as a movie serial in 1939. Looking back at *Buck Rogers*, the images of space adventure come across as crude and dated, and the dialogue ranks as among the most wooden of any series, even by the standards of the early 1930s.

Although *Buck Rogers* may have had some shortcomings as comic art, its success inspired others to try their luck with science fiction strips. *Brick Bradford* premiered in 1933; William Ritt (1902–1972) penned the stories, Clarence Gray (1902–1957) drew the accompanying frames. After a slow start, *Brick Bradford* established itself as a more scientifically knowledgeable counterpart to the fantastic adventures enjoyed by Buck Rogers. Never a blockbuster strip, it nevertheless carved out a comfortable niche for itself on the crowded comic pages of the 1930s. Eventually adapted to **comic books, Big Little Books**, and a 1947 movie serial, *Brick Bradford* stayed in circulation until 1987, long after Ritt and Gray had left it.

In 1934, Alex Raymond's (1909–1956) stylish **Flash Gordon**, recognized as one of the greatest of all science fiction strips, made its newspaper debut. Raymond brought an artistic sensibility to his creation that sets it apart from any rivals. He exhibited particular drafting skills when it came to depicting **Streamlining** for mechanical devices. This made *Flash Gordon* a reflector of the style's popularity in the later 1930s. No doubt the comic strip influenced the way generations of Americans would imagine futuristic technology and **design**. Sleek rocket ships cruise to gleaming curvilinear cities, although Flash himself more often resembles a medieval warrior than he does a citizen of the future, since swords and cloaks replace ray guns and space suits when combat occurs.

Buck Rogers and *Flash Gordon* may have been the leaders in presenting science fiction on the comic pages, but other media also tested time **travel**, alien life forms, and all the other standbys of the genre. Science fiction **movies**, closely tied to **horror and fantasy films**—such as **Dracula** (1931), **Frankenstein** (1931), **King Kong** (1933), and a host of others—in their use of special effects, also diverged from them by emphasizing science and the depiction of possible inventions and changed modes of living.

In the Depression decade, American audiences had their first introduction to what the future might hold with *Just Imagine*, a 1930 musical supposedly set in 1980. Largely forgotten today, *Just Imagine* distinguishes itself for its view of the later twentieth century. Looking more like a polished version of the 1930s, strong **Art Deco** and incipient Streamlined details abound. In many ways, this pioneering movie suggests the modernistic milieu featured in most of the **musicals** with **Fred Astaire** (1899–1987) **and Ginger Rogers** (1911–1995) that would achieve such popular acclaim just a few years later.

More serious ventures into the realm of science fiction include *Deluge* (1933), a well-done spectacle that features a tidal wave hitting New York City. Director James Whale (1889–1957) released *The Invisible Man* (1933), a cinematic adaptation of an 1897 H. G. Wells novel, and the movie marks the debut of actor Claude Rains (1889–1967) in the title role. *Transatlantic Tunnel*, a 1935 British import, boasts futuristic sets as engineers bore beneath the Atlantic Ocean, and *Things to Come* (1936), another English offering, adapts H. G. Wells's 1933 novel, *The Shape of Things to Come*. Both the movie and the book have the distinction of eerily foreshadowing World War II, although they take place over the period 1940–2036.

A recurring image in much 1930s movie science fiction involves a mad scientist, a theme that mirrored public uneasiness toward science and technology. In an adaptation of H. G. Wells's *The Island of Dr. Moreau* (1896), filmmakers created *Island of Lost Souls* (1932). Actor Charles Laughton (1899–1962) portrays the evil Dr. Moreau, master of an island where horrific experiments take place. In a pair of similar efforts, Lionel Atwill (1885–1946) plays two crazed men of science, Dr. Von Niemann in *The Vampire Bat* (1932) and Dr. Xavier in *Doctor X* (1932). Boris Karloff (1887–1969) similarly takes on the role of Dr. Janos Rukh in *The Invisible Ray* (1936), and Albert Dekker (1905–1968) adopts the persona of Dr. Thorkel in *Dr. Cyclops* (1940). In all of these movies, science gets distorted when evil humans use it to their advantage.

The comics' *Flash Gordon* made the transition to film in three serial tales that feature the space hero fighting cartoonish evildoers and employing outlandish—but imaginative— renderings of what space ships and ray guns might look like in some distant future. Deranged scientists and their henchmen may supply material for a number of frightening movies, but this trio of serials brought an element of good spirits to Saturday matinees. Although the villains still play villainous roles, they come across as bizarre creations, not figures of horror.

Flash Gordon: Space Soldiers, in 13 parts, led the way in 1936. Enthusiastic audience responses caused the studio to condense the serial into a regular feature, *Flash Gordon: Rocketship*, that same year. In 1938, *Flash Gordon's Trip to Mars*, this time with 15 episodes, played movie screens. *Flash Gordon Conquers the Universe* came out in 1940; it consists of 12 parts. In all three serials, Larry "Buster" Crabbe (1907–1983) plays the stalwart space voyager. Popular then, the series eventually took on cult status for a new generation of audiences possibly unfamiliar with the comic roots of the movies.

Because of the popularity enjoyed by the *Flash Gordon* serials, Hollywood attempted a similar set of adventures taken from the *Buck Rogers* strip. In fact, Buster Crabbe even received the title role in a case of unusual (or uninspired) casting. Looking just like Flash Gordon, Crabbe undertakes heroic deeds in *Buck Rogers in the 25th Century* (1939), a 12-part serial shot in the period between the production of the second and third *Flash Gordon* efforts. By most estimates, the *Buck Rogers* serial does not measure up to the flair of the *Flash Gordon* trilogy.

Science fiction did not fare well on radio during the 1930s. Networks seemed reluctant to create shows built around outer space or futuristic technologies. They displayed no such hesitation toward **crime** or suspense series, the exotic adventures of a character like **Tarzan**, or even the remarkable exploits of a high school student in *Jack Armstrong, the All-American Boy*, but only a handful of science fiction productions made it on the air.

One of the very first shows in this vein borrowed directly from the comic strips: *Buck Rogers in the 25th Century*. First broadcast from 1932 until 1936, it reappeared sporadically after that, in 1939, 1940, and made its last appearance in the 1946–1947 season. *Flash Gordon* proved less successful. Despite its success in the comics, it found few takers in the radio medium. A handful of stations on the West Coast and later in the East carried it as a syndicated (nonnetwork) offering. At the conclusion of the decade, *The Adventures of Superman*, already garnering considerable attention in comic books, could be heard, first as a syndicated show, and then as a Mutual Network offering in the early 1940s. By that time, however, the curtain had fallen on the 1930s, and the Man of Steel had to contend with World War II.

Lest anyone at the various **radio networks** think that science fiction themed shows lacked the power to thrill, Halloween night in October 1938 dispelled that idea completely. **Orson Welles** (1915–1985), an energetic new presence in both radio and theater, had organized a repertory company called the Mercury Theater. In the summer of 1938, the Columbia Broadcasting System (CBS radio) began carrying *The Mercury Theater on the Air*. Each week, the players presented a new drama. For Halloween, they decided to do H. G. Wells's *The War of the Worlds*, a radio adaptation of his 1898 classic about a Martian invasion of Earth.

Using a style that resembled newscasts of the day, Welles and his troupe galvanized listeners with reports of Martians wreaking havoc in the swamps of New Jersey. Despite many disclaimers throughout the show that the broadcast was a dramatic production, a number of people panicked, telephone lines were jammed, and confusion ensued. Probably the best piece of science fiction ever broadcast, it demonstrated beyond the slightest doubt that radio could successfully carry the genre. Unfortunately, it proved too realistic for some officials, and the Federal Communications Commission (FCC) clamped down restrictions on what could and could not be broadcast for public consumption.

The 1930s witnessed a modest amount of science fiction being created in a variety of media. Overshadowed by other popular genres, such as mysteries and big historical **best sellers**, science fiction nurtured a small, but devoted, audience. Following World War II, it would blossom, but the 1930s have to be seen as a decade of building.

See also Mysteries & Hard-Boiled Detectives; Newspapers; Toys

SELECTED READING

Bleiler, Everett F., and Richard J. Bleiler. *Science-Fiction: The Gernsback Years*. Kent, OH: Kent State University Press, 1998.

Clute, John, and Peter Nicolls. *The Encyclopedia of Science Fiction*. New York: St. Martin's Press, 1993.

Corn, Joseph J., and Brian Horrigan. *Yesterday's Tomorrows: Past Visions of the American Future*. New York: Summit Books, 1984.

Science Fiction. http://www.magicdragon.com/UltimateSF/SF-Index.html

SCREWBALL COMEDIES. Throughout the Great Depression, American **movies** provided a wonderful escapist outlet. The gangster violence of **Little Caesar** (1930), the horror of **Dracula** (1931), the fantasy of **King Kong** (1933), and the bubbly music of **42nd Street** (1933) offered respite from the real world. On the humorous side, the film industry served up ample helpings of looniness, absurdity, and wackiness in a long series of pictures called "screwball comedies." Physical comedy and slapstick have always been a major part of motion pictures, but the so-called screwball comedies brought a wholly new kind of comedy to the screen. Aptly named, these popular movies set up ridiculous plot situations and then resolve them in equally ridiculous ways.

The word "screwball" traces its origins back to the mid-nineteenth century, meaning something eccentric or whimsical. It also gained popularity during the 1930s with **baseball**, especially pitching. In that context, it means a carefully controlled and delivered pitch that seems erratic, at least to the batter. For the movies, the word has become part of a larger vocabulary, suggesting a plot and characters that lack predictability or reason. A fitting term, since irrationality lay at the core of most screwball comedies.

Virtually all the movie comedies that fall into the "screwball" category revolve around romance, but romance from a nontraditional point of view. In these stories, the lovers— for lack of a better term—usually aggravate one another, and their love gets expressed in playful conflict and sometimes mock combat. Lovers' spats and lovers' quarrels escalate into outright comic fights. Abrasive dialogue characterizes screwball comedy, although no one, speaker, target, or audience, takes the words seriously. The distorting mirror of screwball humor makes sure that everyone sees just how skewed romance can be.

Sex drives much of the action in this genre, but since these films were made at the height of the restrictions imposed by the **Hollywood Production Code**, nothing overtly sexual can be shown on screen. Undaunted, the screenwriters and directors worked overtime to lace their scripts with innuendo and suggestiveness, but never at the expense of good taste or respectability. They sublimated passion into slapstick and pratfalls, making comedy that passed the censors without fooling anybody. In fact, among the popular themes of screwball comedies are bigamy, divorce, and adultery, but presented with such lightness and grace that no one can be offended, particularly the official arbiters of the code.

Another important motif involves money. Most of the characters in a screwball comedy have both wealth and class, although their wealth often makes them act like nitwits. Otherwise sensible males become amazingly entangled with poor little rich girls, and together they stumble through one misadventure after another, but money cushions all blows. Sometimes the situation gets reversed, and one or the other is suddenly without funds, but the moment passes, and they continue on their madcap adventures. For Depression audiences, this constant reminder of how money greases all wheels seemed to have little effect on the popularity of these movies, and any attempts to read larger meaning into this aspect of screwball comedies will probably bear little reward. First and foremost, they were, and they remain, among the funniest pictures ever produced by Hollywood, and their sociological underpinnings have little connection with their success.

The following list presents a chronological sampling of some of the best titles in the genre, but should not be thought exhaustive or complete:

Representative Screwball Comedies of the 1930s

Title & Date	Director	Stars	Comment
It Happened One Night, 1934	Frank Capra (1897–1991)	Clark Gable (1901–1960) & Claudette Colbert (1903–1996)	One of the first, and still one of the best, it defined the genre and made Capra one of the leading directors of the decade. Won a sweep in the Academy Awards—Best Picture, Best Director, and Best Actor and Actress.
The Thin Man, 1934	W. S. Van Dyke (1889–1943)	Myrna Loy (1905–1993) & William Powell (1892–1984) as amateur sleuths	Loosely based on a novel by Dashiell Hammett (1894–1961), and one of many screwball mysteries that played upon both genres. The first in a series of six films, 1934–1947.
Twentieth Century, 1934	Howard Hawks (1896–1977)	Carole Lombard (1908–1942) & John Barrymore (1882–1942)	Lombard's stellar performance made her the virtual "queen of the screwballs."

459

Title & Date	Director	Stars	Comment
After the Thin Man, 1936	W. S. Van Dyke	William Powell & Myrna Loy	The second in the *Thin Man* series; a sequel, but a good comedy in its own right.
The Ex-Mrs. Bradford, 1936	Stephen Roberts (1895–1936)	William Powell & Jean Arthur (1900–1991)	Another mystery, but this time the investigating couple is divorced.
Mr. Deeds Goes to Town, 1936	Frank Capra	Gary Cooper (1901–1961) & Jean Arthur	A man inherits millions and proceeds to give the money away. Frank Capra won his second Oscar for Best Director with this movie.
My Man Godfrey, 1936	Gregory La Cava (1892–1952)	William Powell & Carole Lombard	Powell shines as a man of wealth turned butler.
The Awful Truth, 1937	Leo McCarey (1898–1969)	Cary Grant (1904–1986) & Irene Dunne (1898–1990)	This picture made both Grant and Dunne major players in the screwball genre.
Easy Living, 1937	Mitchell Leisen (1898–1972)	Jean Arthur & Ray Milland (1905–1986)	A reversal: a working girl finds herself in the lap of luxury.
Nothing Sacred, 1937	William A. Wellman (1896–1975)	Carole Lombard & Fredric March (1897–1975)	A harsh, abrasive comedy, laced with racism and misogyny.
Topper, 1937	Norman Z. McLeod, (1898–1964)	Cary Grant & Constance Bennett (1904–1965)	Two ghosts return to the world of the living.
True Confession, 1937	Wesley Ruggles (1889–1972)	Carole Lombard & Fred MacMurray (1908–1991)	A woman cannot stop telling fibs.
Bluebeard's Eighth Wife, 1938	Ernst Lubitsch (1892–1947)	Claudette Colbert & Gary Cooper	An heiress versus a millionaire and the wacky situations that their wealth creates.
Bringing Up Baby, 1938	Howard Hawks	Cary Grant & Katharine Hepburn (1907–2003)	Certainly one of the most hilarious films in the entire grouping.
You Can't Take It with You, 1938	Frank Capra	James Stewart (1908–1997) & Jean Arthur	An eccentric family teaches others about happiness. This film earned Frank Capra his third Academy Award as Best Director, and his second for Best Picture.
Mr. Smith Goes to Washington, 1939	Frank Capra	James Stewart & Jean Arthur	Not really a screwball comedy at all, but more a populist lesson in how faith can overcome cynicism. The movie is included in this listing because Capra directed it, it stars two actors (Stewart and Arthur) who had made a mark just a year earlier in *You Can't Take It with You*, and it contains enough Capraesque touches to be close, in spirit if not in actual plotting, to his previous work.

Title & Date	Director	Stars	Comment
His Girl Friday, 1940	Howard Hawks	Cary Grant & Rosalind Russell (1907–1976)	A screwball remake of the classic *Front Page* (1931), but the hardboiled reporters have comedic romantic twists added.
My Favorite Wife, 1940	Garson Kanin (1912–1999)	Cary Grant & Irene Dunne	This movie reunites Grant & Dunne after their success with *The Awful Truth*.

Screwball comedies continued to be box office favorites well into the 1940s. Although they rely on stereotypes (wealthy people lacking in common sense, thwarted lovers, jealous spouses, etc.) to a degree, they do so by turning them around. But they also rely on tradition; in the end, the theme of reconciliation overcomes the last obstacles: love conquers all. Their success signaled a return to a more positive kind of movie in the mid-1930s and thereafter, and they replaced the grim, negative images found in the early years of the decade with an affirming vision, albeit a zany one.

See also Mysteries & Hard-Boiled Detectives; Newspapers; Social Consciousness Films

SELECTED READING

Capra, Frank. *The Name above the Title: An Autobiography*. New York: Macmillan, 1971.
Kendall, Elizabeth. *The Runaway Bride: Hollywood Romantic Comedy of the 1930s*. New York: Alfred A. Knopf, 1990.
Poague, Leland A. *The Cinema of Frank Capra: An Approach to Film Comedy*. New York: A. S. Barnes and Co., 1975.
Sikov, Ed. *Screwball: Hollywood's Madcap Romantic Comedies*. New York: Crown Publishers, 1985.

SCULPTURE. Traditional, realistic, heroic, and monumental: these terms would lead any listing of the qualities possessed by American sculpture during the 1930s. And yet, despite these attributes, the art form lacked a large popular following at that time. Unless people lived in a large city with access to major museums or attended an event such as a world's fair, they had little access to sculpture, especially contemporary pieces. Two 1930s federal government projects supported the work of sculptors and increased the opportunity for Americans to view and enjoy their work. First came the U.S. Treasury Department Section of Painting and Sculpture (1934–1938), followed by the **Federal Art Project** (FAP; 1935–1943), the latter a part of the Works Progress Administration (WPA; 1935–1943; name changed to Work Projects Administration in 1939). In the nation's capital, these programs contributed immeasurably to a construction boom that transformed the federal presence in Washington, but they also enlivened similar projects across the country.

Edward Bruce (1879–1943) headed the Treasury Department Section and directed the decoration of federal buildings. He assigned jurisdiction for this project to Louis A. Simon (1867–1958), charging him with embellishing new and recent structures with art of all kinds. Under Simon's leadership, approximately 300 pieces of sculpture came to grace many of the capital's buildings. Works by Robert Aitken (1878–1949) at the National Archives Building (1933–1935), Albert Stewart (1900–1965) at the U.S. Customs Building

(1935), Elliot Means (1904–1962) at the Government Printing Office (1937), Charles R. Knight (1874–1953) at the National Zoological Park (1937), and Heinz Warneke (1895–1983) at the Department of Interior building (1939) figured among Simon's choices. Sculpture also embellished the construction of post offices and courthouses throughout the country, allowing Americans to experience fine examples of the carver's art.

With its **architecture** by Cass Gilbert (1859–1934), the capital's 1935 Supreme Court Building stands as one of the best and last large neoclassical federal structures from the era, and statuary plays a major part in its overall presentation. John Donnelly Jr. (active 1920s & 1930s); provided carvings for the entrance doors, and sculpture groups by Robert Aitken and Herman A. McNeil (active 1920s and 1930s) can be found on pediments above the entrances. Sculptor James Earle Fraser (1876–1953) contributed two 45-ton allegorical seated marble figures that flank each side of the main steps to the building. On the left sits a female, the Contemplation of Justice, and on the right her male counterpart, the Guardian or Authority of Law.

Best known for his earlier works, the Indian head, or Buffalo, nickel (1913), and a seated horseman that symbolizes the passing of the American Indian's way of life, *End of the Trail* (1915), Fraser became a prolific creator of large-scale public monuments. In addition to the huge Supreme Court statues, his work during the 1930s included *Heritage* and *Guardianship* (1933–1935) for the National Archives Building and two statues of Abraham Lincoln (1930) in Jersey City, New Jersey, and Syracuse, New York. In 1938, for the Franklin Institute in Philadelphia, he executed a 30-ton marble memorial to Benjamin Franklin (1706–1790) that rests on a 92-ton pedestal. He closed the decade with a 60-foot-tall George Washington (1731–1799) for the 1939–1940 **New York World's Fair**. Fraser placed the father of the country facing the iconic sculptural symbols of the fair, the Trylon and Perisphere, designed by the architectural firm of Harrison and Foulihoux; this juxtaposition made it appear that Washington looked to the future.

The New York fair was not alone in providing statues for public view; statuary played an important part in all of the major U.S. **fairs and expositions** of the 1930s. The decade saw Chicago's **Century of Progress Exposition** (1933–1934), the California Pacific International Exposition (1935–1936), the Texas Centennial Central Exposition (1936), the Greater Texas and Pan American Exposition (1937), the Great Lakes Exposition (1936–1937), and the Golden Gate International Exposition (1939–1940). All of them presented fountain sculptures, along with animal and human figures, as major components of gardens and walkways. American heroes, placed at strategic points on the various fair grounds, reminded citizens of their heritage or, in the case of the siting of Fraser's Washington statue in New York, some also encouraged contemplation of both the past and future. Other statues conveyed information about current happenings and efforts being made to overcome the hardships of the Depression. For example, at the California Pacific Exposition in San Diego, a heroic, 10-foot-high plaster **youth** coated in bronze celebrated the **Civilian Conservation Corps** (CCC; 1933–1942) and heightened the awareness of fairgoers about this important **New Deal** program.

While the Treasury Department Section contributed sculpture and other decorations for public buildings, the Federal Art Project focused on providing jobs to unemployed artists who in turn would create works of art for other public facilities. Under the direction of Girolamo Piccoli (active 1930s), the FAP sculpture division created over 13,000 pieces, ranging in size from small ceramic figures to huge stone monuments. Carved animals enhanced the grounds at the Brookfield Zoo in Chicago, indestructible cement storybook characters found homes in housing project playgrounds, traditional statues of local heroes appeared on the lawns of city buildings and in town squares. Hospitals, parks, and botanical gardens likewise became the proud owners of stone fountains.

Artist Lenore Thomas (Straus) (1909–1988) found employment working for the federal government's Resettlement Administration (RA, 1935–1937; renamed the Farm Security Administration [FSA], 1937–1943); she sculpted large pieces for newly built planned communities. A 12×4×4-foot limestone figure of a mother and child in Greenbelt, Maryland, stands as an example of Thomas's work, and it suggests the monumental quality possessed by much sculpture executed during the Depression.

Like many sculptors, Anna Hyatt Huntington (1876–1973) had studied at the Art Students League in New York City with the renowned Gutzon Borglum (1867–1941). One of the most prolific sculptors of the twentieth century, Hyatt produced hundreds of models of wild and domestic animals as well as heroic monuments. In 1923, she married Archer Milton Huntington (c. 1871–1955), a wealthy philanthropist and collector who generously supported her skills in this art form, as well as the efforts of many of her counterparts. With the onset of the Great Depression, the couple recognized the financial difficulties experienced by numerous artists and through the National Sculpture Society they offered loans to provide relief for those temporarily in need of assistance.

In 1930, the Huntingtons purchased four former South Carolina indigo and rice plantations totaling nearly 10,000 acres at Murrells Inlet, intending to build a winter home and studio. Instead, in 1931 they founded a nonprofit institution with the mission of providing a showplace for American figurative sculpture within a refuge for native plants. A year later the venture opened to the public as Brookgreen Gardens; there the couple placed the works of many American sculptors throughout the gardens and around pools and fountains. Among others, the artists initially included Mrs. Huntington herself, James Earle Fraser, Jo Davidson (1883–1952), Paul Howard Manship (1885–1966), Wheeler Williams (1897–1972), and Joseph Kiselewski (1901–1986).

Elsewhere in the country, another contemporary project of unusually large proportions brought sculpture to the attention of many Americans. Gutzon Borglum in 1924 grew enthusiastic about a proposal to carve historic figures into the granite sides of Mount Rushmore in South Dakota. If undertaken, it would represent one of the largest sculptural projects on earth. The following year he accepted the challenge and in 1927 commenced work on the face of George Washington. Carving continued until October 1941, although actual work took place for only about six and a half years. Delays, caused by weather, lack of funding, and technical problems, accounted for the remaining seven and a half years. Borglum followed Washington with Abraham Lincoln (1809–1865), Thomas Jefferson (1743–1826), and Theodore Roosevelt (1858–1919). Each bust measures some 60 feet high, with noses 20 feet long and mouths 18 feet wide. The four presidents gaze out across the Black Hills.

Borglum's son, Lincoln (1912–1986), while still a boy, accompanied his father on the project and officially joined the crew in 1933. That same year the National Park Service started managing the memorial. As delays kept mounting, the Mount Rushmore Commission in 1937 appointed Lincoln Borglum to function as the project's chief sculptor in his father's absence; he would eventually spend more time at Mount Rushmore than did Gutzon Borglum. Workmen finished the mammoth undertaking just before the outbreak of World War II.

Paul Howard Manship, one of the most important figures in American sculpture during the first half of the twentieth century, created, during the 1930s, the Paul J. Rainey Memorial Gateway for the Bronx Zoo (1934). He also did the popular gilded *Prometheus* (1934) that overlooks the ice skating rink at **Rockefeller Center** in New York City, as well as the *Time and Fates of Man* sundial and *Moods of Time* fountain installed in front of the Trylon and Perisphere at the 1939–1940 New York World's Fair. Towering 80 feet into the air, the sundial ranked as the biggest one in the world at the time.

Another prominent sculptor, Jo Davidson, received many commissions for portrait busts of world leaders. In the United States, his works include a 1934 creation of the then-mayor of New York City, Fiorello LaGuardia (1882–1947), and two 1939 full-body bronze renderings: one of humorist Will Rogers (1879–1935), commissioned for the U.S. Capitol Building National Statuary Hall, and the other of poet Walt Whitman (1819–1892), placed at the edge of the grounds of the Perylon Court at the New York World's Fair. The Whitman statue, among the few nonplaster sculptures at the fair, bore the name *The Open Road*, or *Afoot and Lighthearted*.

While most sculptors of the 1930s created traditional representational statues, Alexander Calder (1898–1976) dared to experiment. He had gained recognition and some financial success with his *Calder Circus*, a miniature reproduction of an actual circus made from wire, cork, wood, cloth, and other easily found materials. In 1932, he began making small moving sculptures and produced his first "stabiles," motorized, free-standing pieces. They worked by manipulating cranks and pulleys. Just two years later, he had completed a number of more delicate, wind-propelled "mobiles." Calder soon concentrated only on these forms, seemingly floating contrivances that relied on motion generated naturally by air currents. Beginning in the 1940s, his mobiles would grow significantly in size.

Sculpture, certainly not the most popular form of artistic expression in the eyes of the general public, nonetheless found official support during the Great Depression, especially through federal programs. Mostly monumental, sculpture by the end of the decade graced many buildings and gardens and could be seen by all who passed by. Brookgreen Gardens became the country's first public sculpture garden and today continues as a National Historic Landmark.

See also Circuses; Ice Skating & Hockey

SELECTED READING
Aspinwall, Margaret, ed. *200 Years of American Sculpture*. New York: Whitney Museum of American Art, 1976.
Craven, Wayne. *Sculpture in America*. New York: Thomas Y. Crowell, 1968.
McKinzie, Richard D. *The New Deal for Artists*. Princeton, NJ: Princeton University Press, 1973.
Mount Rushmore. http://www.pbs.org/wgbh/amex/rushmore/peopleevents/p_lborglum.html
Rawls, Walton, ed. *A Century of American Sculpture: Treasures from Brookgreen Gardens*. New York: Abbeville Press, 1988.

SEABISCUIT. Born on the West Coast, Seabiscuit (1933–1947) did not appear to have a promising future as a racehorse. He lost his first 17 contests, and most owners would have given up on him. But then he won several small-time events, and trainers and jockeys saw something, holding out hope that Seabiscuit would eventually discover his own inner strengths. He went on to endear himself to millions during the later 1930s.

Charles Howard (1877–1950), a wealthy California car dealer, expressed a fondness for the bay colt and purchased him in the summer of 1936. Seabiscuit repaid him by winning the Governor's Handicap in September. October had him winning the Scarsdale Handicap, November the Bay Bridge Handicap, and December the World's Fair Handicap. People began to take notice, especially in California. Seabiscuit traveled east, continuing his winning ways, developing a cadre of devoted fans, and receiving mention in sportswriters' columns.

In June 1937, War Admiral, another impressive horse of the era, won the Triple Crown of Thoroughbred Racing, the sport's premier accomplishment. In a single season, he took the Kentucky Derby, the Preakness, and the Belmont Stakes. For the remainder of 1937, controversy raged over the merits of Seabiscuit and War Admiral and talk of an eventual matchup grew in intensity. Both horses were close in size and weight, although Seabiscuit's supporters tried to paint him as a hopelessly outclassed underdog, while War Admiral's people portrayed their horse as unbeatable. It seemed an ideal contest, making them rivals long before they ever met on a track.

After a seemingly endless series of delays, and an equally endless publicity buildup, the long-awaited match took place on November 1, 1938. At Maryland's Pimlico track, site of the Preakness, and before a crowd in excess of 40,000 spectators, the two horses met for their one and only contest. Broadcast around the country to an estimated 40 million **radio** listeners, the famous racing announcer Clem McCarthy (1882–1962) breathlessly described the race as Seabiscuit demonstrated his authority and set a track record, winning by four lengths over War Admiral. They would never meet again.

That impressive victory won Seabiscuit "Horse of the Year" for 1938, propelling him to the peak of his fame and popularity. Merchandisers had by this time already begun to capitalize on his ardent following. Books, articles, hats, scarves, and a host of gewgaws emblazoned with Seabiscuit's name and picture already flooded the market, and more would come. Unfortunately, Seabiscuit developed several injuries in 1939 and did little racing after that. But he came back in March 1940, winning impressively at the Santa Anita Handicap, a race that had previously eluded him. A month later, Howard announced Seabiscuit's retirement. The celebrity horse, the world's leading money winner and the first to pass $400,000 in winnings (roughly $6 million in contemporary dollars), would live on until 1947, dying at age 14. Shortly thereafter, a mediocre movie starring **Shirley Temple** (b. 1928) titled *The Story of Seabiscuit* (1949) came out, but attracted little attention.

Despite the outpouring of affection for Thompson's horse during the 1930s and early 1940s, Seabiscuit somehow disappeared from most recountings about **horse racing** and **fads** of the time. Since he accomplished most of his victories in lesser-known West Coast races and never won the Triple Crown or a number of other prestigious Eastern events, many record books downplayed or overlooked him. The publication of Laura Hillenbrand's (b. 1967) best-selling *Seabiscuit: An American Legend* (2001), along with a follow-up 2002 Public Broadcasting System (PBS) **television** documentary about the colt and a 2003 Hollywood feature film adaptation of the book (not to be confused with the 1949 movie), introduced a whole new generation of fans to Seabiscuit and secured his place in sports history.

SELECTED READING
Hillenbrand, Laura. *Seabiscuit: An American Legend*. New York: Ballantine Books, 2001.
Seabiscuit. Dir. Gary Ross. Universal Pictures, 2003.
"Seabiscuit." On *The American Experience*. Dir. Stephen Ives. PBS Home Video. DVD. WGBH Educational Foundation, 2002.
The True Story of Seabiscuit. Dir. David Butler. Warner Brothers, 1949.

SERIALS (RADIO & MOVIES). On any given weekday afternoon, kids across America tuned their radios to increasing numbers of continuing stories guaranteed to leave their listeners hanging at the conclusion of each thrilling episode. Come Saturday, that same audience marched to the neighborhood movie house, usually to attend a matinee and see a double feature, along with a newsreel, shorts, and a cartoon or two—and of course, the latest episode of a motion picture serial. These rip-roaring stories ended with the same cliff-hanging excitement that made their **radio** counterparts so popular, and an entire generation of young people breathlessly followed them throughout the decade.

It did not take long for the major networks to block off their late afternoon schedules for this kind of **youth**-oriented programming, although countless adults no doubt got caught up in the stories, too. From roughly 4:00 until 6:30, the romance-centered **soap operas** of the earlier afternoon gave way to the adventure serials aimed at the after-school crowd. Continuing 15-minute miniplots that stressed action over everything else, and filled with patriotism and heroics, the plotting could, like the soaps, be interminable. But they seldom disappointed. In essence, they filled the airwaves with soap operas for kids, especially boys.

Typical radio serials involved a young man and his pals. "Pals" could be male or female, but usually did not include adults, although a friendly uncle might find a supporting role. As the decade progressed the young males tended to mature, and popular figures from the **comic strips**, or superheroes from **comic books**, replaced many of the earlier characters. All manner of media crossovers occurred in the realm of these radio series. Popularity meant, possibly, a film serial—or even a feature-length movie—based on a radio serial, or vice versa.

As a rule, the radio series pitted good against evil, and good always triumphed, although every conceivable obstacle would be thrown in the way of that triumph. Morality tales in quarter-hour segments, the serials attracted dedicated audiences. With good planning, listeners could hear five episodes each of their favorite shows during the week and then see the latest movie serial involving similar characters at a Saturday matinee. And toward the end of the 1930s, in a perfect week, those same listeners could go to the corner newsstand and devour the latest issues of comic books that also chronicled the exploits of similar heroes. Parents and teachers might bemoan the younger generation's listening, viewing, and reading tastes, but for the school-age crowd, the decade offered a cornucopia of exciting riches.

The credit for possibly the very first adventure-oriented radio serial goes to **Little Orphan Annie**. Based on the popular comic strip of the same name by Harold Gray (1894–1968), the newspaper series had first appeared in 1924; an instant success with readers, imaginative producers at Chicago's station WGN decided to try *Annie* as a continuing radio series. The program premiered in 1930, and the station wisely scheduled it at 5:45, creating the precedent for children's broadcasting in the late afternoon. Positive listener responses prompted the National Broadcasting Company (NBC radio) to pick it up in 1931, and the network carried it until 1940.

Unlike most adventure heroes then in vogue, Annie is neither male nor born with any great physical prowess. But she possesses grit, a toughness in the face of adversity, a desirable quality in Depression-era America. With a colorful cast of characters straight from the newspaper strip—"Daddy" Warbucks, the Asp, Punjab, and of course her irreplaceable dog, Sandy—Annie makes her independent way. Her adventures charmed children and adolescents who saw in her the freedom to do almost anything, and adults appreciated her ability to endure the worst the Depression could throw at her.

Sponsored by Ovaltine, a popular chocolate-flavored beverage, the serial also established the time-honored custom of offering premiums to listeners. **Toys** and novelties featuring both Annie and Sandy, along with wristwatches, pop-up books, and mugs, could be obtained for proofs of purchase throughout the 1930s. The sponsor's most popular premium, however, turned out to be a "decoder ring" that held secret messages that could not be deciphered without knowledge of the code, available only through Ovaltine. In the midst of this kind of promotion, Hollywood made two feature films about the orphaned heroine, one in 1932 and another in 1939, but neither did well at the box office.

Since paid **advertising** financed most radio broadcasting, these afternoon serials had many different sponsors. The soap operas might have their detergents and cleansers, the evening variety shows cigarettes and **automobiles**, but the late afternoon serials had **food**. The majority of these sponsors had no problems getting their characters to regularly plug the products, and they tied their gifts and premiums in with the series, an approach that proved irresistible for most youngsters. It usually took box tops or other proofs of purchase in order to obtain these treasures, and that provided sponsors an easy way to track listenership.

In 1932, three new entries, also taken from the newspaper comics, came along to challenge *Little Orphan Annie*. First came *Skippy* from 1932 until 1935; based on the long-running strip of that name by Percy Crosby (1891–1964), and also a popular 1931 movie, this afternoon serial tended more toward childish high jinks than it did adventure or suspense. *Buck Rogers in the 25th Century*, the second challenger, provided thrills, **science fiction**, and many radio special effects. It made its debut in 1932, just three years after the futuristic adventures first appeared in **newspapers**. Originally scheduled for 7:15 P.M., from 1933 onward it could be heard at 6:00 P.M. *Buck Rogers* so captivated its print and radio fans that a movie serial featuring the intrepid hero came along in 1939. **Tarzan**, the third offering, already in books, **movies**, and comic strips, ran for four years, 1932–1936, on syndicated radio.

If *Little Orphan Annie* got the incipient boom in radio serials started, *Jack Armstrong, the All-American Boy* serves as the quintessential example of the genre. Making its debut on the Columbia Broadcasting System (CBS radio) in 1933 at 5:30 P.M., this long-running series touted loyalty, friendship, obedience, service, perseverance, clean living, sportsmanship—certainly the qualities American youth should ideally possess, and all couched in one thrill adventure after another. Jack attends Hudson High School, and has as his faithful friends Billy and Betty, along with his fabulously wealthy Uncle Jim. This group follows Jack wherever he may go, few questions asked. Betty and Jack are pals and excite no sexual tensions, since sex did not exist in 1930s-era radio, and Uncle Jim has his uses, since Jack frequently needs access to expensive technology. In the fantasy world of *Jack Armstrong*, no adventure can be too exotic, no villain too villainous, and no scientific gadgetry too advanced for this remarkable young man. Jack's mix of pep, a popular term denoting enthusiasm, and curiosity played well, making for a serial that endured until 1950 and went far in defining the genre.

A big star in **Western films** for many years prior to the 1930s, Tom Mix (1880–1940) seemed a natural to make the transfer to radio. Capitalizing on his name, NBC offered a new serial, *The Tom Mix Ralston Straight Shooters* in 1933; it would run until 1950 and the death of most dramatic programming on radio. But the popular actor never actually appeared on the 5:15 P.M. show. Instead, numerous stand-ins played the cowboy, and the action took place at the equally fictitious "T-M Bar Ranch." Wonder horse Tony (or his stand-in) even had a recurring role. Ralston products offered numerous premiums, along with a memorable theme song that reminded everyone that "Shredded Ralston can't be beat."

As the decade progressed, and movies in particular celebrated **crime** as a topic, radio again turned to the comic pages for inspiration. **Dick Tracy**, a strip created by cartoonist Chester Gould (1900–1985) in 1931, came to the airwaves as a late afternoon serial in 1935. The popularity of Tracy soon carried over into all kinds of commercial tie-ins, such as toy guns, **games**, badges, and the like. The hawk-nosed detective also appeared in four separate movie serials between 1937 and 1941. If America ever harbored vigilante fantasies, *Dick Tracy* was there to act them out, and the radio version lasted until 1948.

Another transfer from the comics involved an explorer named Jungle Jim. Created by Alex Raymond (1909–1956), who also originated **Flash Gordon**, *Jungle Jim* premiered on syndicated radio in 1935. Accompanied by a native sidekick named Kolu, Jim prowled unexplored tropical regions, finding adventure and villains at every turn. It all made for good listening and stayed on the air until 1954.

The later years of the decade saw more and more afternoon adventure serials crowding onto the already-jammed network schedules. For example, *Renfrew of the Mounted* (1936–1940) took its audience into the frozen northwest. The series found competition from *Challenge of the Yukon* (aka *Sergeant Preston of the Yukon*; 1938–1955), another syndicated show. In these tales of the Canadian Mounties, Sergeant Preston has as his helper a faithful dog, Yukon King, a Husky ready for any situation involving his master.

The jump from the tranquil campus of Hudson High to the exotic Far East took no effort at all on afternoon radio. **Terry and the Pirates** (1937–1948) came on at 5:15 P.M. and took its listeners on a tour of new and different locales. Adapted from the popular newspaper comic strip drawn by Milton Caniff (1907–1988), *Terry and the Pirates* succeeded immediately when its cartoon original premiered in 1934. With a likable young hero and countless colorful supporting players, it matched up well with the radio serials of the day. Since some of the clouds presaging World War II had already gathered in Asia, it also brought a dash of realism to afternoon programming.

With international events increasingly dominating the news, many of the newer characters appearing in radio serials bore a military look. Clearly, they stood ready to fight any enemies of the United States. This reflection of the real world presented young listeners with exciting ways to cope with it. For example, *Don Winslow of the Navy* (1937–1943) provided a traditional story line about an evil conspiracy and Winslow's attempts to combat it. After 1941 and Pearl Harbor, the serial turned into a rousing

America versus the Axis yarn. The roots of the show came from Frank Martinek's (1895–c. 1960) strip of the same name that had appeared in papers since 1934.

With war almost a certainty, *Captain Midnight* (1939–1949) provided the requisite thrills and eventually joined in battle against the country's enemies. Captain Midnight, in reality Jim "Red" Albright, differed little from other adventure heroes, but the show offered listeners a chance to join a "secret squadron," yet another premium designed to attract audiences. A reflection of the popularity of anything dealing with **aviation**, *Captain Midnight* grew out of several earlier sources. The Model Airplane Club of the Air came into being in 1933. It offered hints and advice about constructing models and underwrote a regionally syndicated radio serial, *The Air Adventures of Jimmie Allen*. This show followed the exploits of "Jimmie Allen," the pseudonym of Dudley Steele (active 1930s), a real-life pilot. The Jimmie Allen Club published a newsletter, along with a cartoon strip that advocated flying for all. Youthful Hollywood stars like Mickey Rooney (b. 1920) and **Shirley Temple** (b. 1928) proudly displayed their Jimmie Allen membership badges, which at the time was high endorsement indeed. From this connection came the new serial with Captain Midnight and the "secret squadron" that supplanted the Jimmie Allen Club.

Virtually all of these radio series took their cue from the innumerable movie serials that had been cranked out from the early silent days of film and on into the sound era. Beginning in 1912 with the Edison Company's silent *What Happened to Mary?* a 12-reeler divided into one episode per reel, producers knew they were onto a popular new format for movies. Actress Pearl White (1889–1938) emerged as the early queen of the serials with fare such as *The Perils of Pauline* (1914), one of the best known of the early serials.

With the onset of sound in the late 1920s, the emphasis changed from heroines in distress to heroes in command, no matter what the dangers. Tarzan, the ape-man creation of writer Edgar Rice Burroughs (1875–1950), had already made his debut in feature movies with *The Adventures of Tarzan* in 1921, followed by *Tarzan the Mighty* in 1928. Thus it came as no surprise that the serialized *Tarzan the Fearless* (1933) and *The New Adventures of Tarzan* (1935) thrilled audiences on Saturday afternoons. The first stars Larry "Buster" Crabbe (1907–1983), an actor destined to make a number of other serials; *The New Adventures of Tarzan* features Herman Brix (b. 1909), one of the lesser-known Tarzans.

Westerns, both books and full-length films, also provided fertile ground for weekly installments of action and adventure. *The Indians Are Coming* (1930) and *The Phantom of the West* (1931) typify the genre. Gene Autry (1907–1998), himself the cowboy star of many a "B" Western feature, appears in *The Phantom Empire* (1935), a curious mix of science fiction and conventional Western storytelling. Buck Jones (1889–1942), another veteran cowboy actor, kept busy throughout the 1930s appearing in regular features and serials such as *The Red Rider* (1934), *The Roaring West* (1935), and *The Phantom Rider* (1936), among others. Even a later big-name Western star like John Wayne (1907–1979) labored in serials early in his career, with roles in *The Hurricane Express* (1932) and *The Three Musketeers* (1933), though neither qualifies as a Western. Instead, they offer audiences straight adventure fare.

Always a source of exciting visual effects, aviation entertained young and old at the movies, and proved adaptable to the serial format. *Mystery Squadron* (1933) has the heroes hunting for the "Black Ace," an unscrupulous pilot who commands a squadron of vintage airplanes up to no good. In 1934, *Tailspin Tommy*, a series lifted from the newspaper comic pages, proved popular. The strip, drawn by Hal Forrest (1892–1959), had originated in 1928 and quickly attracted readers. Straightforward in its exposition, it easily transferred to the cinematic medium, and many serial fans consider its 12 installments among the best in an increasingly crowded field.

The success of *Tailspin Tommy* led producers to release *Ace Drummond* (1936), another character borrowed from newspaper comics. Originally the joint creation of Clayton Knight (1891–1969) and famed World War I ace Eddie Rickenbacker (1890–1973), the strip features a number of youthful characters, a device that made it popular among children and teenagers, and that in turn caused it to attract the attention of Universal Pictures. The resultant 13-part aviation thriller has a mysterious villain called "The Dragon" (shades of "The Black Ace") and lots of aerial action. The crossover from comic strips would continue unabated during the 1930s and 1940s, a period when the comics flourished as never before.

A number of futuristic science fiction serials rivaled their aviation counterparts in popularity, and they frequently came from comic strips as well. Buster Crabbe, 1933's incarnation of Tarzan, made much more of a name for himself in the role of Flash Gordon. In 1934, cartoonist Alex Raymond, who had created *Jungle Jim*, inaugurated *Flash Gordon*, one of the best of a spate of science fiction series. A public favorite, and exquisitely drawn, Universal Pictures wasted no time in bringing it to the screen. The first serial, *Flash Gordon: Space Soldiers*, could be seen in 1936. Crabbe's blond good looks overcome his wooden acting, and two years later *Flash Gordon's Trip to Mars* played theaters for 15 episodes. Lots of gadgets and evil villains fill the screen, and the action, cheap and unrealistic by today's standards, seldom lets up. Audiences did not seem to object, however, and in 1940 came *Flash Gordon Conquers the Universe*, the last of the group. A fitting finale, it has Flash battling his nemesis, Ming the Merciless, a continuing villain from previous adventures.

Buster Crabbe also landed the role of Buck Rogers, another space pioneer from the newspaper comic pages. Writer Phil Nowlan (1888–1940) and artist Dick Calkins (1895–1962) introduced *Buck Rogers in the 25th Century* just before the Great Depression commenced. One of the very first science fiction strips, it immediately caught the public eye, but not until 1939, would Hollywood create a serial around Rogers' intergalactic adventures. Buoyed by the success of *Flash Gordon*, Universal Studios purchased film rights to the characters in the strip and released the 12-part *Buck Rogers* in 1939, in between the second and third *Flash Gordon* serials. Virtually interchangeable with *Flash Gordon*, including leading man, the various episodes even share gadgetry and props from one another, but enthusiastic audiences seemed not to mind.

Some have labeled the 1930s the golden age of serials, and the term fits well. Whether broadcast in the afternoon or playing at a neighborhood theater, serials provided a healthy dose of escapism throughout the decade and continued to do so well into the 1940s.

See also Hobbies; Radio Networks; Singing Cowboys; Soft Drinks

SELECTED READING

Cline, William C. *In the Nick of Time: Motion Picture Sound Serials.* Jefferson, NC: McFarland & Co., 1984.

Dunning, John. *On the Air: The Encyclopedia of Old-Time Radio.* New York: Oxford University Press, 1998.

Lackmann, Ron. *The Encyclopedia of American Radio*. New York: Checkmark Books, 2000.

Lahue, Kalton C. *Continued Next Week: A History of the Moving Picture Serial*. Norman: University of Oklahoma Press, 1964.

Nachman, Gerald. *Raised on Radio*. Berkeley: University of California Press, 1998.

Stedman, Raymond William. *The Serials: Suspense and Drama by Installment*. Norman: University of Oklahoma Press, 1971.

SHEELER, CHARLES. A native of Pennsylvania, artist Charles Sheeler (1883–1965) had decided, after his 1900 graduation from secondary school, to be a painter. He entered Philadelphia's School of Industrial Art to study **design** and then enrolled at the Pennsylvania Academy. Under the auspices of the academy, he traveled to Paris in 1904. Once back in the United States, he found himself on his own as a painter.

Sheeler worked long and hard to achieve recognition as an artist. A second trip to Europe exposed the young painter to the currents of change then exciting many artists abroad. To supplement his income, Sheeler took up commercial **photography** around 1912, usually taking pictures of local architects' commissions. By 1917, he had begun to use his camera expressively and exhibited a number of his prints.

During these formative years, Sheeler came to appreciate **architecture**, especially the lean unadorned lines of Shaker and Amish buildings found scattered throughout southeastern Pennsylvania. At the same time, he saw in the growing factories, and in the great machines housed within them, a new architecture, one based on speed, efficiency, and power. This interest manifested itself in a series of photographs he took of the Ford Motor Company's vast River Rouge manufacturing plant in Michigan. He also produced a painting titled *Upper Deck* (1929), a detailed view of the mechanical trappings of a modern vessel; this notable oil suggested the direction his work would take.

By the time of the Great Depression, Sheeler's artistry as painter and photographer had already reached maturity. He produced many of his finest works during the 1930s, and the themes he pursued in his paintings and photographs caused some to place him among the Social Realists. But such an attempt at categorization does him an injustice, since Sheeler, a product of the machine age, had already charted his own, individualistic course years earlier. Because of his meticulous attention to detail, a larger percentage of critics and art historians have chosen to label him a Precisionist, and certainly a more convincing argument can be made for his leanings in that direction.

Given his interest in vernacular buildings, it might come as a surprise that Sheeler displays little of the fondness for nostalgic scenes in rural settings that often characterize the efforts of the Regionalists at that time. Much of his output, however, revolves around urban subject matter, a trait that becomes particularly evident with those works executed in the 1930s, such as *City Interior* (1936). This painting presents, not a city at all, but the complex inner workings of a large factory. Sheeler chose for his own artistic territory the industrial landscape, a place of factories and smokestacks, and he then proceeded to suck any remaining life out of it, as in two of his best-known paintings, *American Landscape* (1930) and *Classic Landscape* (1931). Painted with technological clarity and exactitude, his industrial portraits tend, like the street scenes done by his contemporary, **Edward Hopper** (1882–1967), to be eerily quiet, with an overriding feeling of loneliness permeating them. When people do appear, they seemingly cannot connect with one another. Instead, a sense of detachment dominates his pictures and he places the viewer outside the canvas, looking at the subject from a considerable distance.

Sheeler's photographs of machines exist as a mediating force between his paintings and real life. Filled with minute detail, and capable of sharp contrasts between light and dark, photographs served Sheeler as guides into his paintings. Geometrically ordered, both his photographs and paintings heighten the isolation inherent in his compositions. The two approaches allow viewers to contemplate technological America without intrusion.

Although Sheeler's unsullied factory landscapes and depictions of technology convey the power of industrial America, he shows no workers prepared to run the machines he so lovingly details. The manufacturing potential might be there, but it has not been unleashed. With great factories standing idle in the Depression, Sheeler's paintings provide mute comment on the unrealized force of American industry. In this quiet, unmoving environment, he perhaps reflects the Depression economy, likewise frozen and silent, unable to move.

Not all of his work involved great engines or vast factories. Sheeler could also paint warm, personal scenes, such as *Bucks County Barn* (1932) and *American Interior* (1934). Even with these subjects, however, the attention to detail and precise, geometric arrangement of all elements within the pictures take precedence.

Sheeler never achieved the popular following enjoyed by some of his colleagues, but he had earned great respect from leading museums and galleries. In 1939, in a fitting close to the decade, he produced another classic, *Rolling Power*, an intimate study of the great steel wheels and piston rods of a steam locomotive. That same year he also enjoyed recognition and a rare honor, a one-man show at New York's Museum of Modern Art. He would continue to paint and practice photography until a stroke in 1959 made these activities impossible.

See also Thomas Hart Benton; Reginald Marsh; Regionalism; Social Realism; Grant Wood

SELECTED READING

Brock, Charles. *Charles Sheeler: Across Media.* Berkeley: University of California Press, 2006.

Friedman, Martin. *Charles Sheeler.* New York: Watson-Guptill Publications, 1975.

Friedman, Martin, Bartlett Hayes, and Charles Millard. *Charles Sheeler.* Washington, DC: Smithsonian Institution Press, 1968.

SHEET MUSIC. A print medium that predates **recordings**, **radio**, tapes, CDs, and all other electronic forms of preserving **music**, sheet music could be found in the United States from the earliest colonial times. By the opening of the twentieth century, cheap printed music stood as an important component of American popular culture. Publishing houses that produced only sheet music thrived, and the success or failure of a song could be measured in its sheet music sales. With the Great Depression, coupled with the availability of alternative sources of music, those prosperous days came to an end.

Instead of turning on a radio or playing a recording, people used to listen to live performances of a particular song, performances that often occurred in the home. Many households acquired a piano or a parlor organ, or sometimes a guitar, and young and old mastered the instruments and learned to read music. Sheet music, relatively inexpensive and accessible, provided the necessary notation and assured performers reasonably accurate reproduction. It took technology, in the form of phonographs, recordings, and radio, to challenge the long-standing dominance of this old and trusted medium.

Until the mid-1920s, however, these new technologies coexisted with sheet music, with no one format dominant. Although sheet music sales showed some decline, many Americans continued to enjoy the pleasures of playing an instrument and reading music. Publishers nonetheless took moves to stabilize their industry. In order to compete with the growing popularity of the new electronic media, they lowered the prices on printed popular songs, establishing a set price of 30 cents a copy (roughly $3.50 in contemporary money) for most titles. An arbitrary figure, they felt 30 cents would be competitive with the prices for recordings, which ranged from less than 50 cents a disc (or $5.75) for some imports to well over a dollar ($11.50) for certain classical discs. Since a single recording yielded two sides and two songs, cost-conscious consumers immediately noted that records provided a considerable per-song saving over sheet music, which usually contained just one number.

In addition, recordings and radio permitted listeners to hear their favorites performed by professional artists, instead of a home-style version done by friends gathered around a piano. The nuances of a particular singer or orchestra could be captured on discs, something printed musical notation might never convey. During the 1930s, recordings of popular tunes established a permanent lead over sheet music in total sales, although both formats suffered sharp drops as the Depression worsened. Only radio, perceived as free entertainment, flourished, an advantage it never relinquished.

In the face of plummeting sales induced by the economic crisis, music publishers, along with the record companies, slashed their prices. Twenty-five cents (roughly $3.75 in contemporary money), sometimes less, became the common price for sheet music for most of the decade, although that figure reverted to pre-Depression levels around 1938–1939. The industry considered any song that boasted sales of over 200,000 copies in a year a real success, and such tunes came along infrequently. The Woolworth's chain of five-and-dimes, discouraged by this declining market, closed its once-bustling sheet music departments in the late 1930s, and rival Kresge's emerged as the main outlet.

Despite shrinking popularity, sheet music did possess one significant advantage over recordings: longevity. Provided it remained in print and available for a sufficiently long time, a song could sell 500,000 or more sheet music copies, but it might take years to accomplish this. A phonograph recording, on the other hand, experienced a much more limited shelf life; the average availability of a record ranged from a few weeks to a few months before wholesalers replaced it with a new release. But if sheet music publishers boasted an advantage in longer availability, the various record labels countered by releasing many more titles. Buyers had far more choices in recordings than they did with sheet music, an important factor for most consumers, one that led to the further decline of music publishing.

The longer life of sheet music also led to discrepancies about how the music industry interpreted popularity with the public. Since record companies tracked their sales closely, they knew within a couple of weeks what records sold well and what releases moved more slowly. In the sheet music business, however, a time lag of 10 weeks or more often existed. People generally did not rush to purchase new sheet music as readily as they might new recordings, and publishers therefore had to allow printed music to remain with outlets much longer. A song declared a hit by record manufacturers might barely have made a dent in sheet music sales. Most retailers, however, were reluctant to carry sheet music titles for months or years at a time, and so many titles disappeared before they had a chance to become established favorites.

A recording ban that occurred during the 1940s brought about a temporary surge in sheet music sales during World War II, but when the ban ended sales again dropped off. With radios and phonographs in virtually every home by the end of the 1930s, sheet music would never again be a major part of the popular music business.

See also Songwriters & Lyricists; *Your Hit Parade*

SELECTED READING

MacDougald, Duncan, Jr. "The Popular Music Industry." In *Radio Research 1941*, ed. Paul F. Lazarsfeld and Frank N. Stanton. New York: Duell, Sloan & Pearce, 1941, 65–109.

Sanjek, Russell. *Pennies from Heaven: The American Popular Music Business in the Twentieth Century*. New York: Da Capo Press, 1996.

SINATRA, FRANK. A native of Hoboken, New Jersey, Francis Albert Sinatra (1915–1998) would in time become the leading male vocalist in American popular **music**. Most of that journey to fame and fortune would occur in the 1940s and the decades following, but Frank Sinatra's extraordinary career began in the 1930s.

During his later teenage years, Sinatra listened to many singers, especially **Bing Crosby** (1903–1977) and Billie Holiday (1915–1959), on records and **radio**; this exposure to other soloists encouraged him to emulate aspects of their styles and apply them to his renditions of contemporary songs. Possessed of a tenor voice as an adolescent, he could reach lower ranges comfortably. Sinatra dropped out of high school at 15 and focused on pursuing a career in music.

In 1935, along with three friends, he entered a radio talent contest, *The Original Amateur Hour*. Calling themselves the Hoboken Four, they hoped for instant fame. The show, which had just premiered Sundays of that year on the National Broadcasting Company's (NBC radio) Red network and enjoyed national sponsorship with Chase and Sanborn Coffee, offered performers the opportunity to be heard by a large audience. The program originated in New York City and Major Edward Bowes (1874–1946) presided over the activities on stage. A genial, easygoing personality on the air, Bowes found himself an overnight celebrity, and thousands of people, young and old, flocked to New York for auditions to be on the wildly successful show. Only 20 musicians, singers, actors, mimics, comedians, and so on would make the final cut for each night's performance, but hopes sprang eternal in those Depression-wracked years. The selected contestants got to do their acts, and listeners voted for their favorites. Only a tiny percentage of winners ever advanced much beyond their moment on *The Original Amateur Hour*, but the Hoboken Four proved to be one of the lucky ones, with Sinatra giving a rendition of Cole Porter's (1891–1964) "Night and Day" (1932), a song destined to be a regular part of his future repertoire.

Soon thereafter, he broke with the quartet and branched out on his own. Good looks and obvious talent got him bookings in small New Jersey nightclubs during the later 1930s. His voice remained somewhat high, and only later would it drop into the baritone range.

He demonstrated a knack for musical phrasing, which allowed him to become an extension of the band rather than just a vocalist in front of it. On romantic ballads he seemingly caressed the lyrics, creating an intimacy between him and the listener. The crooners of the early 1930s—**Rudy Vallee** (1901–1986), **Russ Columbo** (1908–1934), and of course Crosby—had also exploited this gift of creating a romantic atmosphere within the confines of a three-minute popular song, the playing time of most 78 rpm records.

Scrabbling for jobs in the late 1930s, Sinatra became a singing waiter at the Rustic Cabin, a well-known Englewood, New Jersey, club that boasted radio remotes. Thanks to widespread broadcasting from the nightspot, people from beyond the confines of the Rustic Cabin heard Sinatra's interpretations of popular songs. Harry James (1916–1983), a virtuoso trumpeter and leader of a newly formed **swing** orchestra, listened to the young waiter in the spring of 1939 and soon thereafter offered him a contract to perform with his band.

Sinatra came on board the James aggregation in midyear as the lead singer in a vocal group called the Music Makers. Within a short time, the band cut its first **recordings**, and Sinatra had the honors on two sides, "From the Bottom of My Heart" (music and lyrics by Harry James, Andy Gibson [1913–1961], Morty Beck, and Billy Hayes [both active 1930s]) and "Melancholy Mood" (music by Walter Schumann [1913–1958], lyrics by Vick Knight [1908–1984]). Since the swing era was in full flower and James's band a popular one, the records enjoyed respectable sales, but nothing sensational. He also recorded "All or Nothing at All" (words and music by Jack Lawrence [b. 1912] and Arthur Altman [1910–1994]), but it too did little at the time. Rereleased in 1943, when Sinatra had emerged as a full-fledged star, "All or Nothing at All" became an enormous hit, another song long associated with the singer.

After about six months with James, Sinatra moved on to the Tommy Dorsey (1905–1956) orchestra, another top-flight swing ensemble. As the 1930s drew to a close, this new association would mean great things for the vocalist. Lush arrangements, fine musicians, and a chance to sing some of the best tunes of the day made everything jell, and in the first months of 1940 Frank Sinatra found himself the hottest property in the band. Audiences, especially teenage girls, could not get enough of the "skinny kid from Hoboken," and his career skyrocketed.

One of his first recording sessions with Dorsey included "I'll Never Smile Again" (1939; words and music by Ruth Lowe [1915–1981]); it rapidly climbed the charts to the number 3 position, his first real hit. The overnight popularity of Sinatra presaged a groundswell of change that would alter the face of popular music as the 1940s progressed. Vocalists, male and female, and vocal groups as well, had begun to upstage the bands. The instrumental remained important, but audiences also expected singers to take the stage. In time, the vocalists themselves would begin to front many of the bands, and they often received top billing on record labels.

But that seismic shift occurred after the 1930s officially ended. The Voice, the Chairman of the Board, Ol' Blue Eyes—those familiar nicknames for Frank Sinatra came later, after Harry James, after Tommy Dorsey. The foundations for future acclaim, however, had been established in the 1930s, when Frank Sinatra stood poised to embark on a phenomenal show business career that most other entertainers could only envy.

See also Jukeboxes; Radio Networks; Songwriters & Lyricists; *Your Hit Parade*; Youth

SELECTED READING

Freedland, Michael. *All the Way: A Biography of Frank Sinatra*. New York: St. Martin's Press, 1998.

Mustazza, Leonard. *Frank Sinatra and Popular Culture*. Westport, CT: Greenwood Press, 1999.

———. *Ol' Blue Eyes: A Frank Sinatra Encyclopedia*. Westport, CT: Greenwood Press, 1999.

O'Brien, Ed, and Scott Savers. *Sinatra: The Man and His Music: The Recording Artistry of Francis Albert Sinatra, 1939–1992*. Austin, TX: TSD Press, 1992.

SINGING COWBOYS. Western films, always a popular genre in American **movies**, continued to attract a steady audience during the 1930s. With the addition of sound in 1927, Westerns could go beyond their traditional visual aspects of shoot-outs, cattle drives, and the endless conflicts between cowboys and Indians. Some of the more cheaply produced films—the B movies of second features and Saturday matinees—added **music** to their screenplays, creating a new category of hero, the singing cowboy.

Throughout the settling of the West and thousands of cattle drives, legend has it that cowboys sang to their cows to calm them and to fill the long lonely hours of work. Relaxing around the campfire at night, the cowhands would pass these songs along to one another, making them part of the oral tradition of folk music. John Lomax (1867–1948), an important American folklorist, published an anthology of these tunes, *Cowboy Songs and Other Frontier Ballads* (1910), one of the first such collections that attempted to preserve this unique part of American musical culture.

In the mid- to late 1920s, two authentic working ranch hands, Carl T. Sprague (1895–1978) and Jules Verne Allen (1883–1945), recorded cowboy songs for RCA Victor Records. Sprague achieved a degree of individual success with a 1925 disc titled "When the Work's All Done This Fall." **Radio** entered the picture in 1930 when John I. White (1902–1992) of Washington, D.C., used the moniker "the Lonesome Cowboy," and from 1930–1936 played his guitar and sang on the National Broadcasting Company (NBC radio) show *Death Valley Days*, a program that ultimately ran from 1930 until 1951. It then went on to more years on **television**.

The credit for the first person to sing cowboy tunes in a sound movie probably belongs to Ken Maynard (1895–1973). A famous trick rider for stunts that he did with his horse Tarzan, Maynard worked with the Buffalo Bill Wild West Show and later with Ringling Brothers Circus. He entered films in 1923 as a stuntman and actor and easily made the transition from silent to sound movies with his performance in *The Wagon Master* (1929), a film in which he sang. Maynard went on to make dozens more Westerns, singing in some, but not all, of them.

Once the ice had been broken, many more musically oriented Westerns made their way to local movie houses. Most have been forgotten, perhaps mercifully so. A young John Wayne (1907–1979), playing himself in *The Hollywood Handicap* (1932), seems to strum a guitar and sing in this 20-minute short, but the technique of dubbing allowed someone off-camera to actually play and sing for him. Wayne wisely declined to appear again in a singing role, either real or simulated.

By the mid-1930s, the newly formed Republic Studio, a creation resulting from a 1935 merger bringing together three small production companies, Monogram Pictures, Liberty Films, and Mascot Pictures, used the singing cowboy formula advantageously. Since these

Westerns could be shot outdoors on simple sets, the process usually proceeded quickly and cheaply. They met any standards regarding presentations of sex and violence by the **Hollywood Production Code,** and it all seemed easier with films located in the old West instead of contemporary cities. Also, any cowboy who sang and played for dances capitalized on the ongoing popularity of movie **musicals.**

Soon, auditions for aspiring cowpokes with musical talent had them sitting astride a horse, strumming a guitar, and singing. Finding anyone with this mix of skills, as well as a modicum of acting ability, proved difficult. Gene Autry (1907–1998), a successful radio and recording personality, had already issued a songbook and performed on *The National Barn Dance* when he made his 1934 film debut as a guest vocalist in Mascot Picture's *In Old Santa Fe,* also known as *Down in Old Santa Fe.* Both the motion picture and Autry's appearance received enthusiastic approval, especially from youthful fans in small towns. Despite some obvious deficiencies in acting, along with limited riding experience, Autry found himself Republic's hope for success. The studio billed him as "the Screen's New Singing Cowboy Star" in a 1935 production called *Tumbling Tumbleweeds,* a movie that also featured his horse, Champion, destined to appear with him in most of his subsequent pictures.

Autry quickly became the hottest singing cowboy in Hollywood; between 1934 and 1939 he starred in 36 films. A 1936 effort, appropriately titled *The Singing Cowboy,* even showcased the still-experimental medium of **television.** Autry and the ranch hands appear on screen as if guests on a television show. In 1937, the movie industry voted Autry as its top Western star, and in 1939 his box office appeal rivaled that of veteran actors like Clark Gable (1901–1960), **Bing Crosby** (1903–1977), and Gary Cooper (1901–1961). That same year, he made more money from product endorsements, such as toy cap pistols bearing his name, than from his movies and records combined.

Smiley Burnette (1911–1967), a friend of Autry's and a musician who had worked with him on *The National Barn Dance,* also made his debut in 1934's *In Old Santa Fe.* The next year, he signed on with Republic and became well known as Autry's plump comic sidekick. He appears with Autry in all of his 1930s films and provided considerable music as a songwriter. Over the course of his career, in addition to working with Autry in over 80 Westerns, Burnette also managed to play the comic relief for other cowboy stars at Republic.

When Autry's contract for renewal with Republic came up in 1938, he asked for more money. The studio executives refused. Because of this contractual dispute, Autry failed to report for his next movie. But Republic had expected this move and had already scouted for a replacement. They selected Leonard Slye (1911–1998), a member of a western singing group called the Sons of the Pioneers. Slye, no newcomer to motion pictures, had appeared in minor, uncredited film roles since 1935. He changed his name to Dick Weston in 1937–1938, and because of his prior work, had a strong musical résumé.

When Republic approached Slye, the Sons of the Pioneers had just signed a contract with Columbia Pictures. In order to work for Republic, Slye/Weston withdrew from the group and assumed the name Roy Rogers. With this new billing, he took the lead in *Under Western Stars* (1938), and Republic boasted that "a new Western star is born." Rogers starred in 12 more pictures by the end of the decade. He always appeared with his horse, Trigger, and acquired the nickname "King of the Cowboys." Although Rogers's career did not blossom as early as Gene Autry's, he quickly became Autry's primary rival. In the 1940s, singer Dale Evans (1912–2001) became Rogers's steady onscreen companion as well as his offscreen wife, and the couple often shared top billing.

In 1938, another fairly new and struggling studio, Grand National Pictures, signed Dorothy Page (1904–1961) to star in a series of Westerns featuring a singing cowgirl. Page had a strong background in radio, had sung with several name bands, and appeared in three lackluster movies. For her first singing cowgirl movie, *Water Rustlers* (1939), Grand National billed her as "the new songbird of the range in a Western picture that's different." Unfortunately for both Dorothy Page and the studio, the picture did not prove different enough to be successful. Two more attempts in the series, *Ride 'Em Cowgirl* and *The Singing Cowgirl*, came out in 1939, but also did poorly at the box office. Page retired from acting and Grand National Pictures eventually went out of business.

Before its collapse, Grand National tried to compete with Republic Pictures by producing singing cowboy films that featured Tex Ritter (1905–1974) and his horse, White Flash. The studio hoped that Ritter's lankiness and persona of a "true" Westerner would give him an advantage over the other, more manicured, cowboy crooners. He started with *Song of the Gringo* in 1936 and followed that with 20 more B productions during the 1930s, including *Sing, Cowboy, Sing* (1937) and *Song of the Buckeroo* (1938), almost always playing a character nicknamed "Tex." For a brief time his popularity did challenge Autry's reign, but his solo starring career ended in 1941.

On other musical fronts, the **swing** era had begun to move into high gear in the mid-1930s. In an attempt to capitalize on both the popularity of swing music and singing cowboys, Paramount Pictures brought out *Rhythm on the Range* in 1936. As possibly the least likely cowboy in movie history, the picture stars Bing Crosby, the most popular crooner of the day. In the course of the story, he sings "I'm an Old Cowhand," a cheerful little hit that features music and lyrics by Johnny Mercer (1909–1976), an up-and-coming **songwriter and lyricist**. Roy Rogers, in an uncredited cameo, makes an appearance in this spin-off of the singing cowboy phenomenon.

The singing cowboy movies offered audiences a nostalgic vision of the American West and continued as a popular movie genre through the 1940s. Never claiming to be realistic, their simple plots generally consisted of the good guy catching the bad guys. Usually, a lovely young woman finds herself in a predicament, and a singing cowboy, surrounded by a group of fellow musicians, calms her with a soothing song. In the end, however, the cowboy rides off into the sunset without the girl but with his guitar and his best friend, his horse.

See also Circuses; Radio Networks; Recordings; Serials; Songwriters & Lyricists; Toys; Youth

SELECTED READING

Green, Douglas B. *Singing in the Saddle: The History of the Singing Cowboy*. Nashville, TN: Vanderbilt University Press, 2002.

Peterson, Richard A. *Creating Country Music: Fabricating Authenticity*. Chicago: University of Chicago Press, 1997.

Stanfield, Peter. *Horse Opera: The Strange History of the 1930s Singing Cowboy*. Urbana: University of Illinois Press, 2002.

SKIING. Lake Placid, a small town in upstate New York, served as the site of the 1932 Winter **Olympic Games**; until that time, the majority of Americans had never attempted skiing. Unless a person resided in a mountainous region with snowy winters, the opportunity simply did not present itself; skiing required more promotion. And, despite the Depression, the Olympics provided a healthy dose of the necessary promotion. The games failed to generate as much interest as had been hoped—a lack of snow contributed to this situation—but the various events convinced uncounted numbers of people to attempt schussing down a snow-covered hill. Nonetheless skiing remained an activity with a low level of national participation. Depending on whose estimates were quoted, the end of the decade placed the total number of American skiers at approximately 1 to 3 million. Out of a population of 131 million, that translates as anywhere from less than 1 percent to perhaps 2.5 percent—a low percentage in any case.

Not that promoters did not try. In the winter of 1931, the first ski train left Boston, headed for the New Hampshire slopes. It consisted of a Boston and Maine passenger train that carried members of an urban ski club for a weekend outing. By the time of the Lake Placid Games, a number of railroad lines had begun running special **trains** to nearby New England towns. For most of the 1930s, and fueled by the success of railroad excursions, the Northeast enjoyed the lion's share of publicity about skiing and resultant commercialization. Although places like Wisconsin and Colorado inaugurated ski trains of their own, the expansion of the sport in the North Central and Western states would not gain significant momentum until after World War II.

The **Civilian Conservation Corps** (CCC; 1933–1942), one of the many offspring of the **New Deal**'s Works Progress Administration (WPA, 1935–1943; name changed to Works Projects Administration in 1939), labored in the Rockies and other mountainous areas to blaze new ski trails and erect shelters. Their efforts, often executed under primitive conditions, helped prepare many federal lands for the growing popularity of skiing and provided jobs to young men who might otherwise have been unemployed.

In those simpler days, enthusiasts required little; hickory skis, wooden poles, boots, and stout leather bindings sufficed. Both boots and bindings grew progressively more sophisticated as the 1930s progressed, but most skiers voiced no objections to these costlier improvements. Entrepreneurs in 1931 introduced the first tows, simple rope affairs that required considerable strength and dexterity on the part of the person being pulled. Soon the majority of ski areas advertised them. The lodges themselves tended to be rustic and cheap. All the fanciness, **fashion**, and expense now associated with the activity came later, although a glimpse of the future occurred in 1936 when the Union Pacific Railroad opened its posh Sun Valley resort in Idaho. Among other things, it offered the first chairlift, a feature that other ski centers promptly imitated.

Several ski-oriented **magazines** sprang up during the later 1930s, with names like the *Ski Bulletin, Skiing, Ski West, Ski-Week,* and the like. A number of books and manuals, such as *Modern Ski Technique* (1932; went through eight editions) and *Skiing: The International Sport* (1937), were published. **Newspapers** regularly noted skiing conditions in nearby locales, and **radio** stations provided regional ski reports.

Hollywood at first missed the cinematic potential in skiing, limiting most of its output to newsreels with short clips of jumpers or spectacular falls. United Artists finally cranked out *Winter Carnival* in 1939, a frothy Ann Sheridan (1915–1967) movie, and it proved to be a harbinger: after 1940, a number of motion pictures employed winter **leisure and recreation** as part of their plots. In the meantime, the public got ahead of the studios; by 1940, skiing had become a multimillion-dollar enterprise and only the demands of World War II slowed the growth of the sport.

See also Advertising; Movies; Travel

SELECTED READING

Allen, E. John B. *From Skisport to Skiing: One Hundred Years of an American Sport, 1840–1940.* Amherst: University of Massachusetts Press, 1993.

Engen, Alan K. *For the Love of Skiing: A Visual History.* Salt Lake City, UT: Gibbs-Smith, 1998.

SMITH, KATE. Fondly remembered by many as "America's songbird" and "the songbird of the South," singer Kate Smith (1907–1986) first began to attract attention in the mid-1920s; she would remain a musical favorite for the next 50 years. A native of Greenville, Virginia, a small town near Staunton, she spent her early years in Washington, D.C. While still a child, she sang for American troops based in the capital area during World War I.

Smith broke into professional show business with a 1926 Broadway play, *Honeymoon Lane.* Her strong contralto voice impressed promoters, and she gained billing as a stage comedienne, subsequently appearing in *Hit the Deck* (1927–1928) and *Flying High* (1930). She also cut some records during this period, but they gained no notice. In 1930, a talent agent named Ted Collins (d. 1964) witnessed her stage singing. Through his efforts, Columbia Records signed Smith, an important breakthrough for the young vocalist. Following her recording contract, Collins agreed to become her manager, a position he would hold until his death. In 1931, she enjoyed her first recorded hit with "River, Stay Away from My Door" (music by Harry Woods [1896–1970], lyrics by Mort Dixon [1892–1956]). The success of this recording, along with Collins' continuing astute direction, brought her to network **radio** and increasing fame.

In 1931, Kate Smith began a long relationship with the Columbia Broadcasting System (CBS radio) and quickly rose to become a star of the first rank. Her work with CBS commenced with *Kate Smith Sings*, a 15-minute show destined to survive until 1952, despite changing titles, shifting timeslots, and different networks. Syndicated variations remained on the air until 1960. Although she already had one show under way, Smith added *The Kate Smith Hour* (aka *The Kate Smith A&P Bandwagon*), a guest-filled variety offering in 1936; it ran until 1945.

Smith introduced *Speaking Her Mind* and *Kate Smith's Column* in 1938. Daytime talk shows filled with folksy wisdom and practical advice, they coalesced into *Kate Smith Speaks* the following year. Her talk format proved popular and endured until 1951. A deeply conservative woman, Smith espoused homespun American values, wholesomeness, and patriotism, themes that gave her a solid following over the years.

As a performer, both on radio and live, Smith opened her shows with a hearty "Hello, everybody!" This signature greeting she accompanied with a farewell "thanks for listenin'." In her early *Kate Smith Sings* broadcasts, she introduced "When the Moon Comes Over the Mountain" (1931; music by Harry Woods, lyrics by Howard Johnson [1887–1941]) as her theme. The song quickly became associated with the singer, and until her death in 1986, it "belonged" to her. Radio exposure led Smith to Hollywood; she broke into the **movies** with *The Big Broadcast* (1932), a celebrity-filled picture in which she does a cameo singing none other than "When the Moon Comes Over the Mountain." Smith then starred in a first-run feature called *Hello, Everybody!* Despite her presence,

Hello, Everybody! performed poorly at the box office, and it finished Smith's short-lived venture into the movies, at least for the 1930s.

Kate Smith's recording career, as far as hit singles go, fared little better than her film efforts. Not until 1940 and "The Woodpecker Song" (music by Eldo di Lazzaro [b. 1912], English lyrics by Harold Adamson [1906–1980]) did she next have a hit. But her numerous records sold steadily through the decade, and producers showed little reluctance to employ her, given her immense popularity on radio.

One other Kate Smith recording merits attention. In 1918, at the close of World I, composer **Irving Berlin** (1888–1989) wrote a song for an army camp musical, *Yip Yip Yaphank.* Dropped from the final score, the tune languished in a trunk until Berlin exhumed it in 1938. He saw the signs of World War II gathering, wanted to give the nation an unabashedly patriotic song in those dark days, and knew exactly who should perform it. Recognizing her considerable fame and talent, Berlin granted Kate Smith exclusive rights to the words and music to "God Bless America." She first sang it, on radio, in November 1938. Her strong, optimistic rendition of the lyrics lifted people's spirits whenever they heard it, and "God Bless America" evolved into a kind of second, unofficial national anthem. She would cut a recording of "God Bless America" in 1939. Both Smith and Berlin turned over their considerable royalties from the song to the Boy and Girl Scouts of America.

By the end of the 1930s, Kate Smith found herself ranked among the most influential women of the era. "The first lady of radio" had received numerous honors; her music and talk shows had audiences in the millions; and she had attained, at age 33, the status of a national treasure. World War II would only serve to burnish her reputation, and "God Bless America," like "When the Moon Comes Over the Mountain" before it, would always be associated with her.

See also Musicals; Radio Networks; Recordings; Songwriters & Lyricists

SELECTED READING

Dunning, John. *On the Air: The Encyclopedia of Old-Time Radio.* New York: Oxford University Press, 1998.

Hayes, Richard K. *Kate Smith: A Biography, with a Discography, Filmography, and List of Stage Appearances.* Jefferson, NC: McFarland & Co., 1995.

SNOW WHITE AND THE SEVEN DWARFS. Amid considerable publicity, RKO Radio Pictures released a movie version of *Snow White and the Seven Dwarfs* just before Christmas 1937. Nominally directed by David Hand (1900–1986), but overseen in every detail by producer **Walt Disney** (1901–1966), the plot comes from a freely adapted fairy tale by the Brothers Grimm. For children of all ages, the film stands, almost 70 years after its initial release, as one of the greatest animated features ever made. When it premiered, promoters proudly proclaimed it the first full-length (83 minutes), all-color cartoon feature.

Disney and his staff had been discussing the project since 1933. The actual creation of *Snow White* took over three years and cost a then-astronomical $1.75 million (about $24 million in today's dollars). RKO had been fearful of losing money on a feature-length cartoon, and as production costs rose, studio hands nicknamed *Snow White* "Disney's folly." They need not have worried; the picture garnered over $8 million (or

$108 million) in its 1937–1938 release, and has continued to show enormous profits ever since. Only 1939's **Gone with the Wind** earned more during the era.

In order to generate interest in the film, King Features gained rights to run a serialized *Snow White* comic strip on Sundays. Drawn by Hank Porter (1905–1951) and written by Merrill deMaris (active 1930s), the series commenced two weeks before the December premiere of the movie, and about two months prior to the picture's general release. Porter worked from the film's original drawings, so that the strip would serve as a print replica of the motion picture. Additional merchandising included dolls, figurines, **Big Little Books**, and other reminders of the ongoing movie.

Snow White deserves its early publicity. From the first days of animation, artists had meticulously drawn by hand each frame of film. Disney, always a pioneer in the field, made the decision that every frame should not only be hand-drawn but also contain action. He saw to it that his artists depict characters moving, that flowers, even in the background, wave in the breeze, that birds swoop about in the sky. He also filled his **movies** with sound: those same characters speak and sing, the flowers and birds likewise contribute songs and happy chirps. *Snow White* bursts with action, both visual and aural.

Using what has come to be called a multiplane camera effect, Disney created the illusion of depth on the flat screen. He placed several layers of different drawings, done on glass, on top of one another, allowing each to move independent of the other. Thus stars could orbit the heavens, seemingly in the distance and behind objects in the foreground. Or a forest could consist of many trees, some in the immediate foreground, others at a midpoint behind them, with yet more distant trees in the background. As a character passes these woods, each row, or layer, of forest shifts, allowing the camera to see these various trees at differing angles, just as in real life. Developed in the mid-1930s, the multiplane camera made its first public appearance in "The Old Mill," a 1937 short cartoon in the long-running (1929–1939) *Silly Symphony* series. The success of "The Old Mill" encouraged the studio to utilize the technology in *Snow White*, its first extended use.

Although *Snow White* lacks some of the smooth, effortless movement, or fluidity, seen in later Disney movies like *Pinocchio* and *Fantasia* (both 1940), every frame manages to stand as a masterpiece of color and composition. In addition, the **music**, while memorable, sometimes seems stilted or operatic in its presentation. Action comes to a halt while a number gets performed; at its completion, the picture returns to the storyline. Nevertheless, the movie provides a delightful score, with melodic music by Frank Churchill (1901–1942) and lyrics by Larry Morey (active 1930s). Songs like "Some Day My Prince Will Come," "Whistle While You Work," and "Heigh-Ho" received considerable airplay. They climbed the charts to become hits in 1938 and remain as standards today.

Snow White, as a character, lacks a strong personality; cynics might say she comes across as cloyingly sweet. Even the handsome prince speaks and acts in a wooden manner. But those are quibbles; the evil witch, the mirror on the wall, the seven dwarfs, and all the animals burst with personality, giving the picture its interest and zest. Whenever any or all of the colorful dwarfs—Bashful, Doc, Dopey, Grumpy, Happy, Sleepy, and Sneezy—come on screen, they usually steal the show. Each dwarf possesses a distinct personality and physical characteristics, a major step forward in cartoon creation. Until *Snow White*, most animated films focused on one character. In 1933, Disney had broken that barrier with *The Three Little Pigs*, a short cartoon that served as something of a model for *Snow White*. Clearly, the three pigs provided invaluable instruction for creating the seven dwarfs.

Walt Disney had won several Academy Awards for his short cartoons in the early part of the decade, and in 1939 he received an Honorary Academy Award for Screen Innovation. **Shirley Temple** (b. 1928), the popular child star, presented him an unusual Oscar: the normal gold statuette along with seven miniatures, one for each of the dwarfs.

See also Architecture; Children's Films; Songwriters & Lyricists; Toys

SELECTED READING
Behlmer, Rudy. *America's Favorite Movies: Behind the Scenes.* New York: Frederick Ungar, 1982.
Dirks, Tim. Synopsis of *Snow White and the Seven Dwarfs.* http://www.filmsite.org/snow3.html
Ebert, Roger. *The Great Movies.* New York: Broadway Books, 2002.
Finch, Christopher. *The Art of Walt Disney: From Mickey Mouse to the Magic Kingdoms.* New York: Harry N. Abrams, 1975.
Maltin, Leonard. *The Disney Films.* New York: Disney Editions, 2000.

SOAP OPERAS. Variety, laughter, and **music** may have dominated American **radio** programming during the 1930s, but pathos, with an occasional dash of bathos, also found a large audience. Continuing, serialized stories that introduce vividly emotional characters and plotting became a major part of the typical radio day. These dramas soon gained the name "soap operas," so called because soap companies—Procter and Gamble, Lever Brothers, Colgate-Palmolive, and others—sponsored most of them, working on the supposition that women constituted most of the listening audience. Broadcasters positioned the shows in the late morning and early afternoon hours, with the idea that housewives, presumably at home with idle time on their hands, would tune in. These sponsors and programmers also assumed—rightly or wrongly—that men would be neither interested nor available, so the "soaps" emerged as a small but significant area of radio created for women in an essentially male-oriented medium.

Several individuals, especially Irna Phillips (1901–1973) and the team of Anne and Frank Hummert (1905–1996; 1882–1966), became the leading names in soap opera production during that era. Together, they wrote and oversaw some 30 different daytime **serials**. Phillips, often called "the mother of the soap opera," developed *Painted Dreams* for Chicago's WGN in 1930. This show, generally considered to be the first true soap opera, had, in fact, a detergent manufacturer as its sponsor. Phillips based the series on the success of melodramatic love stories then appearing in women's **magazines**, as well as some romantic film antecedents. Her scripts touched a nerve in her listening audience. *Painted Dreams*, which ran until 1940, led to a succession of similar serials penned by Phillips, who also took speaking roles in some productions of her material. *Today's Children* (1933–1937, 1943–1950), *The Guiding Light* (1937–1956), *The Road of Life* (1937–1958), *Woman in White* (1938–1948), and *The Right to Happiness* (1939–1960) rank among her more memorable creations.

Unlike Phillips, Anne and Frank Hummert did not write soaps but instead created an agency devoted to their production. From all reports, the couple demanded much of their writers and performers, but their high standards assured quality production values. Sponsors agreed; the Hummerts accounted for over half of the **advertising** revenue generated by soap operas. At times, their agency had as many as 18 different serials going simultaneously, including such popular titles as *Betty and Bob* (1932–1940, considered the first network soap opera), *Just Plain Bill* (1932–1955), *Ma Perkins* (1933–1960), *The Romance of Helen Trent* (1933–1960), and *Our Gal Sunday* (1937–1959). The Phillips and Hummert names did not die out with the decline of radio in the 1950s; a number of their series went on to new lives on **television**.

For housewives and anyone else—clearly soap opera audiences went beyond the stereotype—the daily stories dished up a bit of escapism. They featured molasses-like pacing, a deliberate touch on the part of writers; if a listener missed an episode or two, it required little or no catching up, and their simple plotting and black-and-white characterizations required minimal audience attention. These shows emphasized women—their love lives, their families, and the trials and tribulations of contemporary domestic life. Most serials stood guilty of gender stereotyping, but the followers apparently loved it and maintained a high level of enthusiasm and loyalty.

Like many **movies** of the period, soap operas affirm tradition: marriage, family, and friends. Often set in rural locales, the stories feature simple folk placed in dramatic situations. Good, solid American values eventually win the day, although it takes a seeming eternity to reach resolution. When a story finally winds down, the main characters resolutely march on to the next problem, reassured by the verities expressed in the previous episode. No problem is too great, no crisis too complex for their simplistic solutions. But listeners enjoyed knowing that when an episode eventually reached its conclusion, a new calamity awaited.

Rural or urban, the soaps usually have their characters return, over and over, to lessons learned at mother's knee, or better yet, have mother herself appear to remind them of what they should know. Moralistic and conservative, the writing and plotting function as guideposts for the 1930s.

Popular Radio Soap Operas of the 1930s (alphabetical & by network)

Mutual	CBS	NBC
Backstage Wife (Mutual, 1935–1936; NBC, 1936–1955; CBS, 1955–1968)	*Arnold Grimm's Daughter* (CBS, 1937–1938; NBC, 1938–1942)	*Against the Storm* (NBC, 1939–1942; ABC, 1951–1952)
Kitty Keene, Incorporated (1937–1941)	*Aunt Jenny's True Life Stories* (1937–1956)	*Betty and Bob* (NBC, 1932–1936; CBS, 1936–1938; NBC, 1938–1940)
The Life of Mary Sothern (Mutual, 1934–1937; CBS, 1937–1938)	*Bachelor's Children* (CBS, 1936–1941; NBC, 1941–1942; CBS, 1942–1946)	*Dan Harding's Wife* (1936–1939)
The O'Neills (Mutual, 1934–1935; CBS, 1935–1941; NBC, 1942–1943)	*Big Sister* (1936–1952)	*David Harum* (NBC, 1936–1947; CBS, 1947–1950; NBC, 1950–1951)
	The Couple Next Door (1937–1960)	*Girl Alone* (1935–1941)
	Hilltop House (CBS, 1937–1941, 1948–1955; NBC, 1956–1957)	*The Guiding Light* (originally NBC, 1937–1946; CBS, 1947–1956)
	Joyce Jordan, M.D. (CBS, 1938–1945; NBC, 1945–1948; ABC, 1951–1952; NBC, 1955)	*John's Other Wife* (1936–1942)

Mutual	CBS	NBC
	Just Plain Bill (CBS, 1932–1936; NBC, 1936–1955)	*Life Can Be Beautiful* (NBC, 1938; CBS, 1938–1946; NBC, 1946–1954)
	Marie, the Little French Princess (1933–1935)	*The Light of the World* (1940–1950)
	Myrt and Marge (1931–1942)	*Lone Journey* (NBC, 1940–1943, 1946–1947; ABC, 1951–1952)
	Our Gal Sunday (1937–1959)	*Lorenzo Jones* (1937–1955)
	Painted Dreams (Independent, 1930–1933; CBS, 1933–1934; Mutual, 1935–1936; independent, 1936–1940; NBC, 1940)	*Ma Perkins* (NBC, 1933–1949; ran concurrently with CBS, 1942–1949; CBS, 1949–1960)
	Portia Faces Life (CBS, 1940–1941; NBC, 1941–1951)	*Midstream* (1938–1941)
	Pretty Kitty Kelly (1937–1940)	*Moonshine and Honeysuckle* (1930–1933)
	The Romance of Helen Trent (1933–1960)	*One Man's Family* (1932–1959; an evening show instead of daytime)
	Valiant Lady (CBS, 1938; NBC, 1938–1942; CBS, 1942–1946; ABC, 1951–1952)	*Pepper Young's Family* (1936–1959)
	When a Girl Marries (CBS, 1939–1941; NBC, 1941–1951; ABC, 1951–1957)	*The Right to Happiness* (NBC, 1939–1940; CBS, 1940–1941; NBC, 1941–1956; CBS, 1956–1960)
	Woman of Courage (1939–1942)	*The Road of Life* (NBC, 1937–1954; ran concurrently with CBS, 1938–1942, 1945–1947, & 1952–1954; CBS, 1954–1958)
		Second Husband (NBC, 1937; CBS, 1937–1946)
		Stella Dallas (1938–1955)
		The Story of Mary Marlin (NBC, but often CBS, 1935–1945; ABC, 1951–1952)
		Today's Children (1933–1937, 1943–1950)
		Woman in White (NBC, 1938–1940; CBS, 1940–1942; NBC, 1944–1948)
		Young Dr. Malone (NBC, 1939–1940; CBS, 1940–1960)
		Young Widder Brown (1938–1956)

The chart gives only a partial listing; many other series existed during the decade. Some lasted for only a few episodes; others lingered on but achieved little fame. A handful bypassed the networks and went into syndication; for a fee, stations could subscribe to them. Few series involved big-name actors; cheaply produced and with small budgets, the soap opera world worked on the proverbial shoestring. Players would breathlessly rush from stage to stage, studio to studio, in order to act out their assigned roles in multiple dramas. For their rapt audiences, the radio soap opera provided a 15-minute breather in a busy day, a dash of escapism in the midst of troubled times.

See also Advertising; Radio Networks

SELECTED READING

Cantor, Muriel G., and Suzanne Pingree. *The Soap Opera*. Beverly Hills, CA: Sage Publications, 1983.

Dunning, John. *On the Air: The Encyclopedia of Old-Time Radio*. New York: Oxford University Press, 1998.

Higby, Mary Jane. *Tune in Tomorrow*. New York: Cowles Education Corp., 1968.

Hilmes, Michele. *Radio Voices: American Broadcasting, 1922–1952*. Minneapolis: University of Minnesota Press, 1997.

Lackmann, Ron. *The Encyclopedia of American Radio*. New York: Checkmark Books, 2000.

SOCIAL CONSCIOUSNESS FILMS. Generally speaking, most Hollywood studios avoided making pictures about social issues in the 1930s, working on the dubious premise that anything topical would turn away much of the audience. In reality, the handful that did get produced attracted reasonable crowds, rebutting the idea that people did not want such reminders of the times.

The outstanding film in this category has to be *I Am a Fugitive from a Chain Gang* (1932). Released by Warner Brothers, and directed by Mervyn LeRoy (1900–1987), until then most noted for the gangster film **Little Caesar** (1930), it stars Paul Muni (1895–1967), an actor made famous by his title role in *Scarface: Shame of the Nation* (1932). *I Am a Fugitive from a Chain Gang* marked a new direction for everyone involved.

The story, a true one, originated with Robert C. Burns (1891–1955), who in 1932 published a book titled *I Am a Fugitive from a Georgia Chain Gang*. It proved a sensation, exposing as it did the inhumane conditions then allowed in Georgia prisons. Burns had returned from World War I a penniless veteran and in 1922 got involved in a bungled Atlanta robbery. Justice, swift and harsh, sentenced him to a notorious "chain gang," which physically (and painfully) linked prisoners with chains, making the chances of escape most unlikely. But escape Burns did, fleeing north to Chicago. State authorities tracked him down, and in 1929 they returned him to the horrors of Georgia prison life.

Burns escaped once more and shortly thereafter published his exposé. The book outraged Georgia authorities, but some legal maneuvers—along with considerable public sympathy—allowed him to remain a free man. In the movie, his second escape thrusts him into Depression America, a place where no opportunities exist, and so he will always be on the run, the fugitive of the title.

Americans had already witnessed several film treatments of the nation's prisons, most notably *Big House* (1930), *The Criminal Code* (1931), and another chain gang movie, *Hell's Highway* (1932). But the honesty of *I Am a Fugitive from a Chain Gang* struck a chord; the picture received several Academy Award nominations and emboldened studios, particularly Warner Brothers, to undertake other motion pictures that investigated social ills.

In 1933, the darkest year of the Depression, director William A. Wellman (1896–1975) undertook two movies for Warner Brothers, *Heroes for Sale* and *Wild Boys of the Road*. Both fit the category of socially conscious filmmaking. *Heroes for Sale* focuses on

Tom Holmes, played by Richard Barthelmess (1895–1963), a leading actor from silent pictures who had successfully made the transition to sound. A story of hardships brought on by the economic crisis, the movie deals with drugs, **crime**, Communism, unemployment, and hunger, the last through images of breadlines and soup kitchens. A populist film, it argues for hard work, fair pay, and sharing the wealth. Didactic in its treatment of these themes, *Heroes for Sale* paints a grim picture of the country at that time.

Wild Boys of the Road could easily fit into the **teenage and juvenile delinquency** genre of films. It deals with homeless **youth**, wandering from one "sewer pipe city" to another. Cast largely with unknowns, the picture has a gritty reality to it, and depicts the plight of thousands of young people who cannot find work and often resort to petty crime to survive. A predecessor to the popular Dead End Kids movies of the later 1930s, but more attuned to the Depression and its ripple effects in the lives of families, an overly optimistic ending mars its otherwise harsh realism.

Two similarly titled pictures, *Black Fury* (1935) and *Black Legion* (1937), come later in the decade, but continue the economic themes explored in *I Am a Fugitive from a Chain Gang, Heroes for Sale*, and *Wild Boys of the Road*. By the mid-1930s, employment had begun a slow rebound, and attention had shifted from national problems to more localized ones. *Black Fury*, directed by Michael Curtiz (1886–1962), brings back Paul Muni, a multitalented actor. Now playing a Polish coalminer in Pennsylvania, he must endure venal unions, crooked bosses, and a vicious strike. Effective imagery depicts the harsh conditions imposed on miners and gives the film a documentary feel, but it lacks the underlying despair of *I Am a Fugitive from a Chain Gang*.

Black Legion, on the other hand, offers a more involved plot, using vigilantism and hate groups as its villains. The Black Legion, a variation on the Ku Klux Klan, but clad in black, spreads unrest by playing on prejudice and ignorance. Humphrey Bogart (1899–1957), in one of his early leading roles prior to full-fledged stardom, plays a man who falls into the clutches of such a group. The legion also resembles the Black Shirts and Brown Shirts of fascist organizations then becoming increasingly visible in Europe. Their appeals to patriotism and nationalism provide, in retrospect, a chilling glimpse of things to come with World War II. As with *Black Fury*, however, the themes of *Black Legion* concern themselves less with the Depression and more with bigotry and intolerance. By 1937, the Great Depression, while fresh in everyone's memory, had become history, and the gathering clouds of war had captured people's attention.

Not every movie that dealt with social issues clothed itself in grim reality. A handful of clever comedies also took on contemporary problems, but in a much more lighthearted way. Director Frank Capra (1897–1991), one of the great innovators of the 1930s, practically wrote the book on **screwball comedies**, those wacky, irreverent mixes of slapstick and sophistication that took moviegoers' minds off the problems of the day. He also created a group of pictures that addressed those very problems, but in a comedic way. In movies like *Mr. Deeds Goes to Town* (1936) and *Mr. Smith Goes to Washington* (1939), Capra combines corruption and politics, and completes a populist trilogy of sorts with *Meet John Doe* (1941). His masterpiece, **It Happened One Night** (1934), looks unblinkingly at Depression hardships, as well as the gap between rich and poor, and all in the context of one of the funniest films of the decade.

Capra was not alone in blending humor with the Depression. Directors like Leo McCarey (1898–1969), Howard Hawks (1896–1977), George Cukor (1899–1983), and

W. S. Van Dyke (1889–1943) created a number of gems that likewise used the Depression and its problems as parts of their plots. More often than not, the foibles of the rich and the schemes of the poor collide, usually with hilarious results, but in a way that brings out the social and economic inequities so apparent in the 1930s.

See also Gangster Films; Propaganda & Anti-Axis Films; Social Realism

SELECTED READING

Bergman, Andrew. *We're in the Money: Depression America and Its Films.* New York: Harper & Row [Colophon], 1971.

Kendall, Elizabeth. *The Runaway Bride: Hollywood Romantic Comedy of the 1930s.* New York: Alfred A. Knopf, 1990.

Roffman, Peter, and Jim Purdy. *The Hollywood Social Problem Film: Madness, Despair, and Politics from the Depression to the Fifties.* Bloomington: Indiana University Press, 1981.

Sikov, Ed. *Screwball: Hollywood's Madcap Romantic Comedies.* New York: Crown Publishers, 1985.

SOCIAL REALISM. In the area of art during the Depression years, two distinct approaches, or schools, of painting rose to national prominence: **Regionalism** and Social Realism. Of the two, the Regionalists and their primarily rural pictures elicited more popular attention, but the Social Realists, students of the urban scene, also achieved a measure of recognition. More often than not, these latter painters depicted the poor, the dispossessed, and the jobless that dwelt in the nation's cities. Urban centers have both inspired and repelled American artists since the early nineteenth century and the beginnings of industrialization, so that the unemployment and despair seen in too many towns and cities during the Depression brought about a new wave of interest in depicting this dark side of urban life. Whereas the Regionalists usually embraced an optimistic vision of the United States, the Social Realists saw a need for change; their art carries more of a political or sociological message than does that of the Regionalists.

Although it can be argued that artists like **Edward Hopper** (1882–1967) and **Charles Sheeler** (1883–1965) do not fit comfortably into the Social Realist classification, their depictions of the city as an essentially cheerless, drab, and even ugly place at times put them in league with their Social Realist counterparts. On the other hand, a painter like **Reginald Marsh** (1898–1954), who usually receives the Social Realist brand, imbues the city with a syncopated, raucous life. He examines, often in satirical detail, the big, crowded milieu familiar to millions of Americans. Hopper and Sheeler make the onlooker ponder, but Marsh provides a more celebratory air.

As a rule, the Social Realists found most of their fame limited to museums, galleries, and public displays, such as murals. For example, Ben Shahn (1898–1969) first attracted attention with a series of 23 paintings he called *The Passion of Sacco and Vanzetti* (1932). Shahn dedicated the works to two Italian anarchists, Nicola Sacco (1891–1927) and Bartolomeo Vanzetti (1888–1927), executed in Massachusetts on charges of murder. Their deaths became a rallying cry for the American Left for many years thereafter, immortalized in story and song, as well as art.

Shahn, Lithuanian-born and thus something of an outsider, brings to his Sacco-Vanzetti series a searing sense of injustice, and the paintings earned him a reputation as a left-wing radical, a painter of "causes." In a large 1937 mural executed for the Jersey

Homesteads community center, Shahn depicts the path to the American Dream as an attainable one, but strewn with many obstacles. Unlike the sweeping vistas and patriotic themes explored by the Regionalists, his works challenge cherished beliefs, a stance also undertaken by many of his Social Realist colleagues.

Trained as a typographer and fascinated with lettering, Shahn frequently incorporates bits of text in his paintings. A case in point would be *The Bowery Clothing Store* (1936), where names, numbers, and quotations often aid the viewer in interpreting the work and make his paintings more pointed and precise.

Also a photographer of some note, Shahn traveled under government auspices through the Midwest. His pictures from that journey document some of the wrenching problems faced by Depression-era America, and they gave him materials for his subsequent painting. Works like *Dust* (1936) and *Steel Mill* (1938) capture a portion of that imagery. As the decade wound down, Shahn continued to create socially significant works, but his vision became increasingly personal and less political. Some of the fire from his Sacco-Vanzetti days had waned, replaced by the artist's interest in religious and spiritual questions.

Many other artists, for both ideological and aesthetic reasons, found themselves drawn to Social Realism during the 1930s. In addition to Reginald Marsh and Ben Shahn, any listing of Social Realist artists might include the following names: Philip Evergood (1901–1973), Moses Soyer (1899–1974), and Raphael Soyer (1899–1987). Others, of course, also participated, and this listing should not be thought conclusive.

Evergood received a splendid European education, and his comfortable family background hardly matched the experiences suffered by the economic groups he chose to portray. It took a conscious effort on his part to bridge the gaps that existed between himself and his subjects, and so he developed a distinctive personal vision of the troubled times, often employing grotesque, surreal details as a way of making his point. Like many of his counterparts, Evergood created a number of large-scale murals, such as *The Story of Richmond Hill* (1937), a painting for a library in Queens, and *Cotton from Field to Mill* (1938), a picture for a post office in Jackson, Georgia. One of his most famous works bears the title *Lily and the Sparrows* (1939). On the one hand it depicts a tenement, but it also suggests that tenement life creates an urban prison. Its strange primary figure looks out from her window as sparrows flock around her.

Like Evergood, Moses Soyer (1899–1974) hardly qualified as a member of the proletariat. But in his paintings he displays a heightened social consciousness. He articulates some of the dehumanizing aspects of city life, such as the need for social services, in *Employment Agency* (1935) and *Artists on WPA* (1936).

In a similar vein, Raphael Soyer (1899–1987), Moses Soyer's twin brother, illustrates urban problems with paintings like *Under the Bridge* (1932), *In the City Park* (1934), *Office Girls* (1936), and *Transients* (1936). Neither he nor his brother held any strong political beliefs, but they displayed a tenacious humanitarian spirit. In their art, they show a leftist militancy, a trait shared with a number of other Social Realists.

Because its themes often troubled onlookers, Social Realism never achieved the popularity of Regionalism. Art with a conscience, it challenged the status quo and raised questions many did not want to consider. Although Social Realism lives on, especially in the works of editorial cartoonists, its audience remains a small one.

See also Federal Art Project; New Deal; Photography; Political Parties; Social Consciousness Films

SELECTED READING
Baigell, Matthew. *The American Scene: American Painting of the 1930s*. New York: Praeger, 1974.
Hughes, Robert. *American Visions: The Epic History of Art in America*. New York: Alfred A. Knopf, 1997.

SOFTBALL. The game of softball, first played at indoor facilities, originated in 1887; enthusiasts had a variety of names for the new sport, including "indoor baseball," "mush ball," "playground ball," "ladies' baseball," and "kitten ball." Not until 1926 did the term "softball" officially supplant the others.

Perhaps the most obvious difference between **baseball** and softball concerns the ball itself: a baseball (or hardball) measures 9 inches in circumference, whereas a softball has a circumference of 12 inches (some players favor a 16-inch ball). The outer surface of a softball has a slightly mushy feel, as opposed to the unyielding firmness of a baseball. The dimensions of a softball field also differ: 60-foot base paths versus 90-foot base paths for baseball, and the pitcher stands 20 feet closer to the batter in softball (40 feet vs. 60). A softball bat tends to be smaller and lighter than its baseball cousin; games last seven innings instead of nine; and teams can field 10 players rather than the traditional 9, with the extra player usually having the title of rover. Some of the preceding measurements can be further altered, depending on age, gender, and whether the game involves slow or fast pitching. In short, softball accommodates its players.

Many dismissed softball in its formative years as an inferior version of baseball. By the early 1930s, however, the sport had achieved a new level of play and respect, although it continued to be ideally suited for an informal game by players of differing abilities. Leagues had been formed, it enjoyed an official organizing association, and the sport stood poised to attract more players than ever before in its history.

The onset of the Depression caused softball to bloom—a cheap, entertaining, outdoor diversion for everyone, regardless of abilities. Teams flourished, as factories, offices, schools, churches, unions, and even neighborhoods put their 10 players on the field. The rise of identifiable teams led to leagues, and leagues led to rankings and contests, just like baseball. By 1932, various championships attracted sizable crowds, which in turn focused more national attention on the game. Chicago's **Century of Progress Exposition** of 1933–1934 sponsored a softball tournament with designated slow- and fast-pitch categories. These events garnered considerable publicity, and over 350,000 people watched the tournament at one time or another. With that success, by 1936 as many as 1 million Americans participated in softball in some capacity.

Both the Columbia Broadcasting System (CBS radio) and the National Broadcasting Company (NBC radio) networks covered national championships, and the number of players just kept growing; 1 million grew to 5 million, and by the end of the decade, 11 million Americans played softball, with women constituting almost one-quarter of that figure. Millions more—men, women, and children—came to the games as avid fans, and entrepreneurs even attempted, unsuccessfully, to create professional softball teams and leagues. The game, true to its roots, stubbornly remained an amateur diversion, open to all.

As part of the national recovery effort, various government agencies constructed thousands of parks and recreational areas around the country, and many included fields that fit the official dimensions of a softball diamond. In addition, the National Youth

Administration (NYA, 1935–1943) also assisted in building fields on private property, allowing churches and fraternal organizations to have proper playing areas. The Federal Rural Electrification Administration (REA, 1935–1994), another government agency, introduced night lighting to hundreds of fields long before the major league baseball teams enjoyed such play. Softball became so widespread and so popular that many sporting goods manufacturers witnessed an upturn in business despite the economic hard times.

It did not hurt the game that President **Franklin D. Roosevelt** (1882–1945) himself sponsored a team, the White House Purgers. In fact innumerable celebrities of the day— newscasters Edward R. Murrow (1908–1965) and Lowell Thomas (1892–1981), writers Franklin P. Adams (1881–1960) and Dale Carnegie (1888–1955), to name but a few— played the game. Softball, not baseball, in many ways served as the national pastime during the Depression, one of the most open and democratic sports ever to achieve such remarkable popularity.

A softball game. (Courtesy of the Library of Congress)

See also Leisure & Recreation; Radio Networks

SELECTED READING

Bealle, Morris A. *The Softball Story.* Washington, D.C.: Columbia Publishing Co., 1957.

Dickson, Paul. *The Worth Book of Softball: A Celebration of America's True National Pastime.* New York: Facts on File, 1994.

SOFT DRINKS. Called "soda," "soda pop," "pop," "dope," or "tonic" depending on the region, soft drinks contain two basic ingredients: sugar, or another acceptable sweetener, and carbonated water, or "soda water." The "soft" comes from the absence of alcohol; people refer to intoxicating drinks as "hard" beverages. Originally sold for medicinal purposes, as well as for personal enjoyment, soft drinks evolved quickly. They went from beverages with naturally carbonated mineral water to manufactured products using artificially carbonated water. An additional step involved adding flavors—lemon, strawberry, vanilla, ginger, cherry, peach and so on, along with flavors found in nature like root beer and sarsaparilla.

During the first 10 years of Prohibition, 1919–1929, annual American per capita consumption of bottled soft drinks increased from 38.4 bottles to 53.1, and nationally the number of manufacturing and bottling plants grew from 5,194 to 8,220. With the stock market crash, however, the numbers began to drop. In 1932, consumption had fallen to its lowest point since before Prohibition, 27.1 bottles per person. The number of plants also declined because small operations merged into larger regional facilities. The industry rebounded as the country commenced its long recovery from the Depression; by the end of 1939 per capita consumption had passed pre-Depression numbers. Statistics showed the figures standing at 88.6 bottles per person, with 6,155 plants supplying that demand.

Soda fountains date back to the early 1800s, and those located in drugstores could dispense medicinal drinks as well. Pharmacists naturally became involved in the creation of drinks sold at their fountains. The more enterprising ones hoped to find a mix of ingredients that attracted customers and increased sales.

One such pharmacist, John Pemberton (1831–1888), in 1886 made a syrup from kola nuts, the leaves of the coca plant, and cinnamon. He called his concoction "my temperance drink," and saw it as a cure for hangovers, headaches, and depression. After several trial runs that involved serving this elixir to customers at Jacob's Pharmacy in Atlanta, Georgia, Dr. Pemberton expressed his satisfaction with the formula; he began selling the drink on May 8, 1886.

Frank M. Robinson (active late 1800s), Pemberton's bookkeeper and partner in this venture, suggested the name of Coca-Cola—a catchy phrase that described the two principal ingredients. Robinson trademarked the name in 1893 after creating the distinctive Coca-Cola script in 1886. It first appeared in an advertisement in the *Atlanta Journal* on May 29 of that year. Coca-Cola became the first widely available drink that qualified both as a patent medicine and a soda fountain beverage.

Soon after the syrup's introduction, soda water joined the list of ingredients. Its inclusion changed a medicinal potion into a refreshing soft drink. The name went through an unofficial shift, when patrons began to call it "Coke." In 1887, another pharmacist, Asa Candler (1851–1929), bought the rights to Pemberton's syrup. Through two timely strategies—organizing the company to sell the syrup to franchised bottling operations for the final addition of the soda water and initiating a massive **advertising** campaign first in **newspapers** and later on **radio** to raise public awareness of the product—Candler expanded the consumption of Coca-Cola from Atlanta and its environs to much of the South and then to every part of the nation.

Robert W. Woodruff (1889–1985), president of Coca-Cola from 1923 to 1939, standardized the product by training salesmen in the proper mixing of the syrup with soda water; they in turn trained soda fountain jerks in these procedures. Woodruff also continued the company's extensive advertising. During the 1930s, in a unique selling strategy, the company hired women to go door to door offering to install, free of charge, wall-mounted bottle openers in the kitchen. These salespeople also left coupons for six-packs of Coke.

With Repeal in 1933, Coca-Cola sales dropped temporarily, but Woodruff's leadership prevented any drastic economic disasters during the Depression. His successes at that time culminated with an exclusive contract for distribution rights at the 1939–1940 **New York World's Fair**. Prior to the fair, Coca-Cola had enjoyed a series of "firsts": countless service stations acquired official Coca-Cola coolers, electrically chilled units with sliding lids; standardized coin-operated vending machines that dispensed Coke could be found everywhere; the Piggly Wiggly and A&P grocery store chains sold Coca-Cola in six-pack cartons; two airlines, Eastern and Delta, served free, cold Coke during their flights; and billboard and print advertisements featured **food** along with the ubiquitous Coke bottle, suggesting a natural partnership with good things to eat.

Along with all the advertising and bottle openers, the company gave away millions of copies of a booklet, *When You Entertain: What to Do, and How* (c. 1932), by Ida Bailey Allen (1885–1973), a popular cookbook author and hostess on the network radio show, *The Radio Home-Makers Club* (1928–1936). At several places in her booklet she mentions Coca-Cola by name. For example, Allen suggests Coke as an appropriate sipping drink while eating canapés. Considered an expert on the etiquette of entertaining at home, Allen's recommendations were a coup for the Coca-Cola Company.

Marketing strategies and advertisements employed during the 1930s relentlessly focused more on the product's image than on the product itself. Men, women, and teenagers could be seen enjoying a prominently displayed Coke at work and at play. Movie stars regularly appeared in Coke ads, and the obliging company supplied cases of Coke to major stars and all current Hollywood productions. Leading man Spencer Tracy (1900–1967), in a 1939 movie called *Test Pilot*, asks on screen for "two Coca-Colas, please," and Dizzy Dean (1910–1974), the colorful St. Louis Cardinals pitcher and sportscaster, gulps a Coke in 1934's *Dizzy and Daffy*.

As the Depression dragged on, Coca-Cola came up with a slogan" "Everyone can find a nickel to 'bounce back to normal.'" In its make-believe world of advertising, a Coke offered a pleasant, inexpensive time-out from an increasingly difficult reality. With its wide availability, Coca-Cola, and soft drinks in general, made the neighborhood soda fountain a popular gathering place. In many ways, during Prohibition, it displaced the corner saloon.

The company also gave the country a classic image of Santa Claus: a jolly fat man, with pink nose and flowing white beard, dressed in red with a shiny black belt and boots, receiving a refreshing reward of Coca-Cola for a hard night's work of toy delivery. Haddon Sundblom (1899–1976), an illustrator with the D'Arcy ad agency, created that icon of Christmas in 1931. Prior to Sundblom's widely distributed paintings, Santa had appeared wearing blue, yellow, green, or red, and usually looked more mischievous than jolly. Coca-Cola's seasonal ads, which first appeared in the 1930s, have run annually ever since. They directly shaped the way Americans think of this happy, bigger-than-life figure attired in a Coca-Cola red suit.

Coca-Cola, a master in the art of product promotion and successful sales, cannot be thought the only soft drink success story. Back in 1893, Coca-Cola was registered as a trademark. Another pharmacist, Caleb Bradham (1867–1966), of New Bern, North Carolina, developed a similar syrup mixture to serve at his drugstore soda fountain. Called Brad's Drink, it contained water, sugar, vanilla, rare oils, pepsin, and cola nuts. In 1898, Brad's Drink became known as Pepsi-Cola, after the pepsin and cola nuts. Registered as a trademark in 1903, the company unveiled its scripted logo in 1906.

Like the management of Coca-Cola, the leadership of Pepsi-Cola developed aggressive marketing strategies and engaged in extensive mass advertising. Despite some financial difficulties at the beginning of the 1930s, the company emerged as a serious competitor for Coca-Cola. Those financial woes included two bankruptcies and continuing legal battles with its rival over accusations of Pepsi being substituted for Coke at soda fountains. In 1934, Pepsi's Baltimore plant began bottling a 12-ounce drink, using beer bottles as the containers. They still charged just a nickel (roughly 75 cents in contemporary money), the same price Coke got for six ounces. For Depression-era consumers, buying twice the drink for the same price made Pepsi a wise choice, and this ingenious scheme took the struggling soft drink company from the edge of bankruptcy to the welcome problem of trying to meet demand.

From 1936 through 1939, Pepsi used a variety of advertising approaches and, for the first time since the early days of the company, turned a substantial profit. One approach, skywriting, had been developed during World War I as a way for airplanes to communicate with ground troops by trailing smoke and maneuvering to form letters or symbols that floated in the air. It had not, however, been widely used for commercial purposes. Since Coca-Cola had a stranglehold on soft drinks at the New York World's Fair, Pepsi countered in 1939 with a spectacular aerial advertising display in the skies over Chicago. Planes wrote out, in script, "Drink PEPSI-Cola." Each letter measured about a mile in height and width; the name Pepsi-Cola could stretch for many miles in the sky. Pleased with the publicity event, Pepsi continued to use skywriting throughout the 1940s.

Another ad strategy involved cartoon characters. Pepsi and Pete, or the Pepsi-Cola Cops, premiered in 1939. These two humorous figures, modeled after the Mack Sennett (1880–1960) Keystone Kops from the days of silent **movies**, came into being after an aborted attempt to buy the rights to Popeye, another cartoon hero. Walter Mack (1897–1990), Pepsi-Cola's president from 1939 until 1950, had wanted to change the popular spinach-eating sailor into a recognizable Pepsi-drinking sailor. Undeterred, Mack instructed the advertising department to create a new comic strip and use characters that would appeal to the entire family. As policemen, Pepsi and Pete symbolically guaranteed the protection of the good name and quality of Pepsi-Cola. Featured in the Sunday newspaper cartoon pages, in magazine ads, and on various display materials, by the end of two years Pepsi and Pete ranked among the most identifiable advertising characters in America.

In addition to the 1939 Pepsi and Pete campaign, the company aired its most effective advertising tool on radio. Two songwriters, Alan B. Kent (active 1930s) and Austen H. Croom-Johnson (1910–1964), had been commissioned to write a singing jingle to replace the dry copy previously used for Pepsi radio ads. They came up with a catchy tune that extolled the refreshing qualities of Pepsi-Cola, and continued to stress that consumers got "twelve full ounces" for their nickel, as opposed to the familiar, but smaller, six-ounce bottles marketed by archrival Coca-Cola. Starting in 1939, their ditty aired on radio for 10 years, to the point that everyone knew it. In fact, it even became a jukebox selection, and years later the jingle continues to be recognized by listeners with good memories.

As the two cola giants slugged it out for sales supremacy, other smaller companies worked to develop their own distinctive soft drinks. C. L. Grigg (active 1920s and 1930s) spent more than two years experimenting with formulas for lemon-flavored drinks before finalizing on Bib-Label Lithiated Lemon-Lime Soda. Manufactured by Grigg's Howdy Corporation (the "Howdy" referred to an orange-flavored beverage the company manufactured), this soft drink first appeared for sale in the fall of 1929 in St. Louis, Missouri, just two weeks before the great stock market crash.

Initially available only in St. Louis and successful despite the poor timing, the name soon changed to 7-Up. No one knows why the company chose 7-Up, but theories abound. The most popular says that Grigg renamed the drink after seeing a cattle brand with the number 7 and the letter *u* in its composition. Others suggest that the name reflects the seven ingredients and carbonation employed in 7-Up's formulation. Still others claim that Grigg came up with the name playing dice. Whatever the reason—and certainly 7-Up comes more trippingly off the tongue than Big-Label Lithiated Lemon-Lime Soda—the drink proved a success. In 1936, Grigg renamed his bottling operation the Seven-Up Company.

Turning a local or regional product into a nationally known one is no easy feat even in the best of times; Grigg wanted 7-Up to go national in the midst of an economic depression. The company did manage, while Prohibition remained in force, to capitalize on selling 7-Up to speakeasies. The beverage, like ginger ale, became a popular mixer for **alcoholic beverages**. Following Repeal in 1933, Grigg openly advertised 7-Up as a mixer. Other ads for 7-Up emphasize its refreshing and thirst-quenching qualities, in contrast to the heavy sweet taste of its major cola competitors. By the 1940s, 7-Up had successfully moved to the number three sales position among soft drinks; only Coca-Cola and Pepsi-Cola outranked it.

The Nehi Corporation of Columbus, Georgia, a major soft drink manufacturer in the South, in 1934 introduced into the ongoing competition a new beverage, Royal Crown Cola. Since it carried a heavy debt at the time, the company decided that to stay in business it needed a different, improved cola product. Within six months, market testing had verified for Nehi the potential of its new beverage. The company named the cola after its original Royal Crown ginger ale; like Pepsi-Cola, Nehi bottled the drink in 12-ounce bottles and sold them for a nickel. All over the South, people drank Royal Crown, and quickly shortened the name to RC.

In 1939, Royal Crown Cola became a sponsor for the ongoing radio show *Believe It or Not!* subtitled *See America First with Bob Ripley* (1930–1948; various times and formats). An aural version of the popular newspaper feature, *Ripley's Believe It or Not!* introduced the relatively new cola to a huge audience, and by 1940 Nehi had experienced fast growth and big profits.

Many other American soft drinks that had been around for years also survived the Depression and experienced renewed popularity during the later 1930s. Names like Dr. Pepper, Orange Crush, Canada Dry, Kist, Cheer Up, A&W Root Beer, and Moxie, to mention only a few, continued to entice a public that clearly enjoyed sweet carbonated drinks. Colored labels, applied directly to the bottle, came along in 1934, giving the industry a visual boost. Owens-Illinois Glass Company of Toledo, Ohio, led the way in the production of these fused labels. The decade also witnessed experimentation with steel soda cans. In 1935, the American Can Company and Kreuger Brewing Distribution introduced the metal beer can. It met with immediate success, and so the can companies next considered similar containers for soft drinks. Clicquot Club Ginger Ale in a can first appeared in 1938, but the citric acid present in ginger ale proved too much for the lining to handle; soft drinks in cans would have to wait until the 1940s and improved liners.

The decade ended with two major soft drink manufacturers—Coca-Cola and Pepsi-Cola—leading the field. Rapidly gaining ground, 7-Up proved a feisty competitor, and another, Nehi's Royal Crown Cola, stayed close behind. Despite Repeal, the soft drink industry had come to occupy an important place in American culture.

See also Aviation; Baseball; Comic Strips; Gas Stations; Grocery Stores & Supermarkets; Illustrators; Jukeboxes; Magazines; Prohibition & Repeal; Radio Networks; Toys

SELECTED READING

Levenstein, Harvey A. *Revolution at the Table: The Transformation of the American Diet.* New York: Oxford University Press, 1988.

Lovegren, Sylvia. *Fashionable Food: Seven Decades of Food Fads.* New York: Macmillan, 1995.

Mariani, John F. *The Dictionary of American Food and Drink.* New York: Ticknor & Fields, 1983.

Pendergrast, Mark. *For God, Country and Coca-Cola.* New York: Charles Scribner's Sons, 1993.

7-Up. http://www.brandspeoplelove.com/csab/Brands/7UP/7UPFullHistory/tabid/148/Default.aspx

Soft drinks. http://www.bottlebooks.com/ACL%201937/Soda%20in%201937.htm

Stoddard, Bob. *Pepsi: 100 Years.* Santa Monica, CA: General Publishing Group, 1997.

SONGWRITERS & LYRICISTS. The world of commercially popular **music** encompasses several genres, ranging from hard-charging **jazz** to the most delicate and romantic ballads. Successful songwriters and lyricists ply their trade by writing for the market, that is, they work on commission, responding to specific wants and needs. Plays and **movies** require scores; the record industry demands an unending supply of new music; and performing groups—orchestras, bands, combos, vocalists—have distinct requests. The most successful songwriters and lyricists of the 1930s personified Tin Pan Alley; they could work in virtually any format and composed for the theater, the movies, and general popular consumption.

Although thousands of songs get written each year, only a handful ever sees publication, and an even smaller percentage achieves any kind of popular acceptance. Throughout the twentieth century, songwriting could, at best, be called a tough business, with failures far exceeding those rare compositions that became hits. In this regard, the 1930s were no exception to such a generalization.

Despite the obstacles inherent in a songwriting career, countless individuals have chosen to follow its call. The most successful, the Berlins, the Gershwins, the Kerns, the Porters, and so on, achieved fame and the accompanying financial rewards, but they constitute a distinct minority. Most songwriters and lyricists enjoy only occasional success, and many labor in relative anonymity. A brief alphabetical listing follows, identifying some of those people who composed the melodies, words, or both to American popular music of the decade. As a rule, these individuals worked behind the scenes; the public seldom knew their names, but it took pleasure in their music.

Harold Arlen (1905–1986; b. Hyman Arluck). During the 1920s, Harold Arlen made his initial appearance on the American musical scene; by 1929 he had enjoyed his first hit, "Get Happy," with lyrics by Ted Koehler (1894–1973). The collaboration with Koehler would carry over into the early 1930s, producing such standards as "I Gotta Right to Sing the Blues" (*Earl Carroll's Vanities*, 1932) and two from 1933's *Cotton Club Parade*, "I've Got the World on a String" and the classic "Stormy Weather."

Equally at home with theater songs or movie scores, Arlen found another good pairing with lyricist E. Y. "Yip" Harburg (1896–1981 [see below]). The two joined talents for "It's Only a Paper Moon" (film, *If You Believe in Me*, 1933) and "Last Night When We Were Young" (film, *Metropolitan*, 1936). His greatest renown came—again with Harburg's words—in 1939 with the release of MGM's **The Wizard of Oz**. The score included many favorites, but "Over the Rainbow," especially as sung by **Judy Garland** (1922–1969), entered the pantheon of immortal pop songs.

As proof of its staying power, in 2001, the Recording Industry Association of America (RIAA) chose "Over the Rainbow" as the number one "song of the century" (out of a list of 365 twentieth-century songs). Three years later, the American Film Institute placed it on top of its list, *One Hundred Years, One Hundred Songs*, a survey of music associated with motion pictures.

Irving Berlin (1888–1889; b. Israel Baline). See his entry elsewhere in this encyclopedia.

Sammy Cahn (1913–1993). A lyricist much admired by his peers, but not a familiar name to most listeners, Sammy Cahn rose to professional prominence in Hollywood during the mid-1930s. His best-known work, however, would not gain public notice until the 1940s. As the craze for **swing** in all its forms reached a peak in the last years of the decade, Cahn worked on the scores for films like *52nd Street* (1937), with music by Walter Bullock (1907–1953) and the title song for *Manhattan Merry-Go-Round* (1938), music by Saul Chaplin (1912–1997).

Cahn's breakthrough occurred in 1937 when he, along with Chaplin, wrote the English words for a song titled "Bei Mir Bist Du Schoen," a number composed by Sholom Secunda (1893–1974) in 1932 for a Yiddish operetta. For whatever reasons, "Bei Mir Bist Du Schoen" (the title translates as "To Me You Are Beautiful," although Cahn and Chaplin say in their lyric that it means "to me you are grand") achieved great popularity when the Andrews Sisters, a trio of siblings, introduced the English version on a 1937 recording. It sparked their careers, and three 1938 feature films (*Love, Honor, and Behave*; *Holiday*; and *Swing!*) featured it on their soundtracks. Thanks to this combination, Cahn found himself in demand and had no scarcity of work. Soon thereafter, he teamed up with composer Jule Styne (1905–1994) and the two created many memorable songs during the 1940s.

Hoagy Carmichael (1899–1981; b. Howard Hoagland Carmichael). A composer, pianist, singer, and occasional actor, the Indiana-born Carmichael became a popular figure during the 1930s. His good looks and laconic manner gained him roles as a Hollywood character actor, and he appeared in 14 films. But Hoagy Carmichael is probably best remembered for "Star Dust," a 1927 composition, and one of the most recorded and performed songs of the twentieth century. In 1929, lyricist Mitchell Parish (1900–1993 [see below]) added words to Carmichael's melody and also slowed the tempo. The resulting meditative ballad promptly became an outstanding entry in the American popular song repertory.

Carmichael composed over 600 songs. He wrote the music and lyrics for "Rockin' Chair" (1930); "Georgia on My Mind" (1930), with words by Stuart Gorrell (1901–1963); and "Lazy River" (1931), featuring lyrics by Sidney Arodin (1901–1948). In the early years of the decade, Carmichael began what would be a long-lasting association with lyricist Johnny Mercer (1909–1976 [see below]). "Lazybones" (1933), one of their first collaborative efforts, soon became a standard, and one of their greatest successes, "Skylark," released in 1941, affirmed the affinity they had for one another musically. The two continued, off and on, to work together until the early 1970s.

Carmichael also created other lasting songs; "The Nearness of You" came along in 1938. With lyrics by Ned Washington (1901–1976 [see below]), it had been scheduled for a film never produced. The tune languished for two years, and then resurfaced in 1940, became a hit, and took its rightful place among American standards. In addition,

"I Get Along without You Very Well" and "Hong Kong Blues," with words and music by Carmichael himself, were released in 1938 and 1939, respectively.

Walter Donaldson (1893–1947). During the 1920s, Donaldson established himself as skillful songwriter, with compositions such as "Yes, Sir, That's My Baby" (1925), with lyrics by Gus Kahn (1886–1941), and the best-selling "My Blue Heaven" (1927), lyrics by George Whiting (1892–1968). In 1930, he wrote two big hits for bandleader Guy Lombardo (1902–1977), "Little White Lies" and "You're Driving Me Crazy! (What Did I Do?)." With these successes, Donaldson moved to Hollywood and began composing for the movies. He and Kahn had written a Broadway score for a 1928 musical titled *Whoopie!*; after moving to California, he adapted *Whoopie!* for film, and three hit songs—"Makin' Whoopee," "Love Me or Leave Me," and "My Baby Just Cares for Me"—entertained audiences in 1930. A succession of motion picture scores followed, including *The Prizefighter and the Lady* (1933), and the tune "Dancing in the Moonlight" (lyrics by Gus Kahn). In 1936, Donaldson and lyricist Harold Adamson (1906–1980) earned an Academy Award nomination for Best Song with "Did I Remember?" from the movie *Suzy*. He continued to write film music on into the 1940s.

Al Dubin (1891–1945). An outstanding lyricist of the era, the Swiss-born Dubin came to Hollywood in the early 1930s. His long association with composer Harry Warren (1893–1981 [see below]) resulted in the joint creation of a remarkable series of standards during the decade, a partnership that actually commenced in the 1920s with some miscellaneous tunes and lasted until the later years of the decade. In all, Dubin and Warren collaborated on over 160 songs, as well as working with many other composers and lyricists.

Their efforts moved into high gear with the score for the musical hit **42nd Street** (1933). That pioneering picture featured such enduring songs as the title song, along with "Shuffle Off to Buffalo," and "You're Getting to Be a Habit with Me." Almost immediately thereafter the duo put together the music for *Gold Diggers of 1933*, the first of four "Gold Digger" pictures. The 1933 edition includes the powerful "Remember My Forgotten Man," a song that showed Dubin could write timely, meaningful lyrics, as well as the usual fluff required in most **musicals**. That same film can also claim "We're in the Money," a spirited number that helped launch the career of Ginger Rogers (1911–1995), who sings and dances it in the motion picture. Dubin's other work with Warren includes "Boulevard of Broken Dreams" (*Moulin Rouge*, 1933), "I Only Have Eyes for You" (*Dames*, 1934), "Lullaby of Broadway" (*Gold Diggers of 1935*, 1934) "About a Quarter to Nine" (*Go into Your Dance*, 1935), and "September in the Rain" (*Stars over Broadway*, 1935).

In 1939, Dubin adapted a melody by composer Victor Herbert (1859–1924) and set lyrics to it. Herbert's music had been called "An American Idyll"; Dubin changed that title to "Indian Summer." The following year, the popular band led by Tommy Dorsey (1905–1956) made a recording of "Indian Summer" that featured vocalist **Frank Sinatra** (1915–1998); it soon ranked as a number one hit and the song has gone on to become a standard for many singers and orchestras.

Vernon Duke (1903–1969; b. Vladimir Dukelsky). Russian-born, Duke pursued both popular music and classical composition, retaining his birth name of Dukelsky until 1955 for his ballets, concertos, and oratorios. At the suggestion of his friend George Gershwin (1898–1937), he began, in the early 1920s, to use "Vernon Duke" for his more commercially oriented compositions. Gershwin also urged him to continue his explorations in popular music, and many of those compositions have turned out to be his most significant musical accomplishments.

He first achieved both critical and popular success in 1932 with his music for *Walk a Little Faster*, a Broadway revue. Teamed with lyricist E. Y. "Yip" Harburg (1896–1981 [see below]) for that show, they created the haunting "April in Paris," among other numbers. Harburg and Duke also worked on the score for the *Ziegfeld Follies of 1934*, contributing "I Like the Likes of You" and "What Is There to Say?" That same year, Duke penned both the music and lyrics for "Autumn in New York," another song destined to become an American standard, a perennial favorite of vocalists and jazz artists for decades. It first appeared in a little-noticed revue called *Thumbs Up*. Duke collaborated with lyricist Ira Gershwin (1896–1983) for "I Can't Get Started," a number featured in the *Ziegfeld Follies of 1936*. President **Franklin D. Roosevelt** (1882–1945), actress Greta Garbo (1905–1990), the Spanish Civil War, and the 1929 stock market crash all receive mention in this highly topical number. Noted for his harmonic complexities in both his classical and popular compositions, Vernon Duke/ Vladimir Dukelsky maintained dual careers until his death in 1969.

Duke Ellington (1899–1974; b. Edward Kennedy Ellington). See his entry elsewhere in this encyclopedia.

Dorothy Fields (1905–1974). See her entry elsewhere in this encyclopedia.

Rudolf Friml (1879–1972). Early in the twentieth century, the Czechoslovakia-born Friml settled in the United States. With a background in European musical styles, he strove to acquaint American audiences with these unfamiliar forms, especially the operetta. A variation on the traditional opera, the operetta, or "little opera," tends to be light and amusing instead of serious or tragic. Theater lovers were then discovering **operettas** through the compositions of Victor Herbert (1859–1924), an American composer. Herbert had attained considerable popularity, and so Friml turned out to be the right person at the right time.

In 1912, Friml inherited an incomplete Herbert operetta, *The Firefly*, when out of artistic pique Herbert refused any further association with the production. Friml finished the composition and thereby launched himself on a successful new career. A number of Friml operettas—*High Jinks* (1913), *You're in Love* (1917), *Rose-Marie* (1924), *The Vagabond King* (1925), numerous others—came along to enthusiastic responses. Their success laid the groundwork for the genre's greatest popularity, a phenomenon that occurred during the 1930s through the medium of motion pictures.

Friml's *The Vagabond King* became a movie with the same name in 1930. It stars Jeanette MacDonald (1903–1965), a singer who built a career around musicals, especially operettas. She played the lead in *Rose-Marie*, which went to celluloid in 1936. The film costars Nelson Eddy (1901–1967), the second pairing by the two actors in what turned out to be a long-running series. *The Firefly*, another MacDonald vehicle, enjoyed a slick Hollywood production in 1937, but with Allan Jones (1907–1992) in the male lead. The movie adaptation includes in its score "The Donkey Serenade," a Friml tune that had the assistance of Herbert Stothart (1885–1949). This popular favorite evolved from a song in the original stage version that he called "Chansonette."

George & Ira Gershwin (1898–1937; 1896–1983). See their entry elsewhere in this encyclopedia.

Oscar Hammerstein II (1895–1960). Best known by modern audiences for his longtime (1943–1960) association with composer Richard Rodgers (1902–1979 [see **Rodgers & Hart**]), lyricist Oscar Hammerstein II had years earlier established a significant reputation on Broadway. Working with composer **Jerome Kern** (1885–1945), the pair virtually defined the modern stage musical in 1927 with *Show Boat*. Their collaboration continued sporadically with hits like "I've Told Ev'ry Little Star" and "The Song Is You" (both from *Music in the Air*, 1932), and "All the Things You Are" (*Very Warm for May*, 1939). When not working with Kern, Hammerstein teamed with composer Rudolf Friml (1879–1972 [see above] for the operetta *Rose-Marie*, a show that first appeared on stage in 1924 and then went to film in 1936. Hammerstein's clever words embellish such well-known songs as "The Mounties," Rose Marie," and "Indian Love Call."

Given the popularity of operettas in the 1930s, he also worked with Sigmund Romberg (1887–1951 [see below]) for *May Wine*, a 1935 Broadway effort, by contributing the words for "Once Around the Clock." He even provided lyrics for the zany Olsen & Johnson comedy revue, *Hellzapoppin'* (1938). As far as movies went, Hammerstein spent much of the decade overseeing film adaptations of his earlier stage work. Kern's *Roberta* became a motion picture hit in 1935, as did *Showboat* in 1936. He set words to music by Johann Strauss II for *The Great Waltz* (1938), and he worked on a handful of other pictures, but by and large, Hammerstein's career coasted during much of the 1930s; not until he and Richard Rodgers teamed up in 1943 for *Oklahoma!* would he write the lyrics for which he has become most famous.

E. Y. "Yip" Harburg (1896–1981; b. Isidore Hochberg). A popular lyricist, Harburg crafted the words for 1932's **"Brother, Can You Spare a Dime?"** Jay Gorney (1906–1990) contributed the music. No other song captures as strongly the despair felt by many during the Depression, and the lyrics, more so than the melody, carry this message. But "Yip" Harburg, a true Tin Pan Alley professional, could fashion lines to fit almost any mood.

After Harburg failed in a business venture, Ira Gershwin (1896–1983), an old friend and mentor, convinced him to try his hand at music. He began writing with Gorney and the two completed several small, short-lived Broadway shows. In 1932, one of the worst Depression years, they shared credit for a revue called *Americana*. That production introduced "Brother, Can You Spare a Dime?" and subsequent **recordings** by **Rudy Vallee** (1901–1986) and **Bing Crosby** (1903–1977) alerted millions to the song; it soon became an anthem for the times. *Americana* also marked a new chapter in Harburg's life. He moved on to Hollywood to sample the endless opportunities offered by the movie industry.

Once settled on the West Coast, Harburg worked with a number of songwriters, but his association with Harold Arlen (see above) and Vernon Duke (see above) merits special mention. "It's Only a Paper Moon" (1933), one of the first Arlen/Harburg songs, appeared in *Take a Chance*, an otherwise lackluster movie. Their "Let's Take a Walk around the Block" appeared in *Life Begins at 8:40*, a 1934 Broadway show. "April in Paris" marks an early (1932) collaboration with Vernon Duke in the musical *Walk a Little Faster*, as does "What Is There to Say?" in the *Ziegfeld Follies of 1934*.

The Singing Kid, a 1938 vehicle for entertainer Al Jolson (1886–1950), brought Arlen and Harburg together again. "Here's Looking at You," among others, came from this picture, and the hilarious "Lydia, the Tattooed Lady" had a prominent place in *A Day at the Circus*, a 1939 **Marx Brothers** comedy. But it was all just a prelude to their greatest accomplishment, the music for the 1939 film of *The Wizard of Oz*. One of the finest scores to accompany any movie from any era, everything—story, music, and Harburg's lyrics—fit together seamlessly. E. Y. Harburg continued an active career on into the following decades and wrote many a memorable lyric, but nothing surpassed his work in *The Wizard of Oz*.

Lorenz Hart (1895–1943). See the entry for Rodgers and Hart elsewhere in this encyclopedia.

Jerome Kern (1885–1945). See his entry elsewhere in this encyclopedia.

Jimmy McHugh (1895–1969). Composer McHugh entered the music business as a song plugger, a salesman who goes from office to office, trying to convince music publishers to buy particular tunes written by others. In time, he realized his own talent, left plugging and turned to composition. After the usual misses, McHugh enjoyed his first hit with "When My Sugar Walks Down the Street" (1924). Vocalist and lyricist Gene Austin (1900–1972) provided the words. In the mid-1920s, McHugh began a long association with Dorothy Fields. Their first effort, "I'm a Broken-Hearted Blackbird" (1926) went nowhere, but the two soon found their musical niche. "I Can't Give You Anything But Love" and "I Must Have That Man" came from their score for *Lew Leslie's Blackbirds of 1928*, a Broadway revue featuring black performers. After that, McHugh and Fields became Broadway regulars, with a string of hits—"Exactly Like You" and "On the Sunny Side of the Street" (1930; *The International Revue*), "Don't Blame Me" (1933; *Clowns in Clover*), "I Feel a Song Comin' On" and "I'm in the Mood for Love" (1935; *Every Night at Eight*)—in both movies and shows.

His reputation in the profession firmly established, McHugh worked with numerous other lyricists in the latter half of the decade. In 1937, he teamed with Harold Adamson, an auspicious union. They promptly created "You're a Sweetheart" in the movie of the same name, and "Where Are You?" in *Top of the Town*. The Adamson/McHugh combination would continue writing on into the 1940s, but the composer also worked with other lyricists in the years to come.

Johnny Mercer (1909–1976). Barely out of his teens when he decided on the music business as his vocation, Johnny Mercer would write the words to over 600 published songs before his death in 1976. Also an accomplished composer, a born entertainer, and by the end of the 1930s a singer of some renown, he rose to modest fame during the decade. Unlike so many of his counterparts, Mercer had no struggling boyhood in New York City; he enjoyed a comfortable upbringing in Savannah, Georgia, but he nonetheless found his way to New York and the bustling music scene. With his ingratiating manner, he soon knew many people in Tin Pan Alley and found employment working on revues for Broadway.

His breakthrough came when he and composer Hoagy Carmichael (see above) wrote "Lazybones" in 1933. An immediate hit, he followed that with a string of songs, including 1934's "If I Had a Million," a piece he did with Matty Malneck (1904–1981) for the movie *Transatlantic Merry-Go-Round*. With credentials on both Broadway and in Hollywood, the young Mercer was on his way. He displayed a flair for vernacular, idiomatic language yet never patronized his audience. Composers were usually delighted to have him as their lyricist because he almost always enhanced their music. Versatile, he wrote words and music for "I'm an Old Cowhand," a popular song from *Rhythm on the Range* (1936). The picture stars Bing Crosby (1903–1977), and when he recorded it, "I'm an Old Cowhand" found a huge public. Mercer even appears in bit parts in several films from the era, usually singing something he himself composed.

Mercer next penned "Too Marvelous for Words" for *Ready, Willing, and Able*, a 1937 movie musical starring dancer Ruby Keeler (1909–1993). Richard Whiting (1891–1938 [see below]) provided the music. By the latter half of the decade, he could be found working on **radio**, singing on records, and appearing occasionally in nightclubs and other public venues. In the midst of all this activity, he teamed up with composer Harry Warren (see below) for "Jeepers, Creepers," a clever tune that Louis Armstrong (1901–1971) sings to a horse in *Going Places* (1938). The swing classic "And the Angels Sing" came from Mercer and trumpeter Ziggy Elman (1914–1968) in 1939. A hit recording, artists as diverse as Bing Crosby, **Count Basie** (1904–1984), and **Benny Goodman** (1909–1986) all had a go at it, and it quickly rose to number one.

With the advent of the 1940s, Mercer's snowballing career showed no letup. He cofounded Capitol Records, a major label, in 1942; continued to put words—and occasionally music—to hit after hit; vocalized in his distinctive, easygoing manner; and generally remained a force in the popular music world.

Mitchell Parish (b. Michael Hyman Pashelinsky). In a popular song, the words do not exist alone, they depend on a melody. As poetry, when read by themselves, the lyrics usually do not stand up particularly well. Instrumentalists, on the other hand, can frequently play just the music of a pop tune and it succeeds admirably. The challenge facing the lyricist is how to wed the words to the song, to make them an inextricable part of the composition. Mitchell Parish rose to this challenge and created a body of work exceptional in its lyrical quality.

The best example of his skills rests with "Star Dust," a melody Hoagy Carmichael (see above) composed in 1927. When first written, "Star Dust" got lost among a plethora of similar medium-tempo songs. Two years later, Parish wrote the words that made it one of the all-time great standards. At the same time, he slowed the tempo to fit his meditative lyrics, giving the composition its dreamy, ethereal quality. In 1933, Carmichael and Parish collaborated for the delightful "One Morning in May," and again in 1939 for "Riverboat Shuffle." Parish's successes with Hoagy Carmichael tunes illustrate his consummate writing abilities, and he put these talents to work by creating narratives to accompany the music of some of the era's finest composers.

In 1931, Parish added words to "Mood Indigo," a lovely ballad composed the previous year by Duke Ellington and released as an instrumental with the title "Dreamy Blues." Initially uncredited for his work with the song, Parish's participation marked one of the few times someone outside the tight circle maintained by Ellington and his musicians had a hand in the musical process. In this case it worked, and "Dreamy Blues" became "Mood Indigo." Parish took on another Ellington melody, "Sophisticated Lady," in 1933. An instrumental classic that Ellington wrote in 1932, "Sophisticated Lady" takes on added depth with the overlay of Parish's lyrics.

A little-known American composer, Frank Perkins (1908–1988), in 1934 wrote "Stars Fell on Alabama." A nice enough melody, but the Mitchell Parish lyrics make it memorable. Thanks to the blending of words and music, "Stars Fell on Alabama" has become a standard, one of those songs that transcends time. Two years later, Parish participated in the composition of an up-tempo swing song written by clarinetist Benny Goodman and arranger Edgar Sampson (1907–1973). Called "Don't Be that Way," it could be a jazzy instrumental favorite for jitterbugs, or it could be a romantic plea with the addition of Parish's lyrics. Either way, "Don't Be That Way" proved to be a big hit in the early days of the swing era for dancers and listeners alike.

Parish enjoyed a banner year in 1939. He wrote lyrics for "Stairway to the Stars," a 1935 instrumental composed by Matty Malneck and Frank Signorelli (1901–1975). **Glenn Miller** (1904–1944), one of the most popular bandleaders of the day, had as his theme song "Moonlight Serenade," a melody he composed and to which Parish contributed the words. Finally, he took "Deep Purple," a 1934 song composed by Peter De Rose (1900–1953), and added lyrics that resulted in a popular hit for several bands that year, especially the one led by Larry Clinton (1909–1985). In all, Mitchell Parish played a significant role in American music during the 1930s; the decade would be the poorer without his memorable words to so many songs.

Cole Porter (1893–1964). See his entry elsewhere in this encyclopedia.

Andy Razaf (1895–1973; b. Andreamentania Paul Razafkeriefo). Usually thought of as the lyricist partner of pianist Fats Waller (1904–1943), Andy Razaf's career encompassed considerably more. By the onset of the 1930s, he had created a memorable body of work, and would continue to do so for years afterward. For a time, however, much of his writing revolved around compositions by Waller. One of the few successful black lyricists in the music business during that segregated era, he had already put words to such classics as "Willow Tree" (1928; music by Waller) and "Black and Blue," "Honeysuckle Rose," and "Ain't Misbehavin" (all 1929; all with music by Waller).

In 1930, Razaf teamed with the legendary pianist Eubie Blake (1887–1983) to create "Memories of You" for the Broadway show *Lew Leslie's Blackbirds of 1930*. The revue also included another standard by them, "You're Lucky to Me." Waller and Razaf continued their winning ways in 1932 with "Keeping Out of Mischief Now," although Waller increasingly turned to singing instead of writing. "A Porter's Love Song to a Chambermaid" (1934) found Razaf providing lyrics for the music of pianist James P. Johnson (1891–1955). Saxophonist Leon "Chu" Berry (1908–1941) wrote a jazz riff as swing grew in popularity that bore the unlikely title "Christopher Columbus." Razaf, comfortable in this element, provided lyrics and it became a minor hit in 1936. That same year, bandleaders Benny Goodman and Chick Webb (1902–1939), along with arranger Edgar Sampson, created an up-tempo delight with "Stompin' at the Savoy" ("Savoy" refers to a popular Harlem ballroom of the 1930s; Webb led the house band). Andy Razaf provided the lyrics. Eventually a number of top-name swing orchestras and vocalists made recordings of this dancers' favorite.

The end of the decade saw Razaf still working in the swing idiom. In 1939, he shared credits with composer Joe Garland (1903–1977) for another up-tempo number, "In the Mood." This particular collaboration produced one of the best-selling songs of 1939–1940, and certainly one of the biggest hits for Glenn Miller and his orchestra. Its popularity has continued unabated into the present.

Richard Rodgers (1902–1979). See the entry for Rodgers and Hart elsewhere in this encyclopedia.

Sigmund Romberg (1887–1951). Hungarian by birth, composer Sigmund Romberg spent some of his youth in Vienna, an exposure that would influence his artistic development. He came to the United States in 1909, but it took several years in his new home before he met with any musical recognition. At this time, the operetta format had assumed considerable popularity, and Romberg, given his European background, chose to work in this area, as had his fellow émigré, Rudolf Friml (see above). In 1917, Romberg wrote *Maytime*, following it with another show, *Blossom Time*, in 1921. Both enjoyed acclaim, and helped mark the heyday of the operetta in the United States.

The early 1930s found Romberg settled in Hollywood, busily transcribing his stage operettas into movie musicals. *The New Moon*, which he wrote for Broadway in 1928, went to film twice; first in 1931 with singers Lawrence Tibbett (1896–1960) and Grace Moore (1898–1947), and again in 1940 with the popular vocal team of Jeanette Mac-Donald and Nelson Eddy. It includes the popular "Stout-Hearted Men," with lyrics by Oscar Hammerstein II (see above). Romberg's trail-blazing *Maytime* finally reached the screen in 1937, 20 years after its initial composition. MacDonald and Eddy lead an all-star cast, and it helped reinforce their standing as the most popular interpreters of the operetta format.

Romberg's successful work in movies allowed him to score, along with Hammerstein, an original screenplay, *The Night Is Young* (1935). The picture features "When I Grow Too Old to Dream," and it gave Nelson Eddy, who does not appear in the film, a hit song. Although the operetta faded in popularity as the 1930s waned, Romberg kept busy in Hollywood, and he remained firmly ensconced there in the 1940s, working on countless film scores.

Arthur Schwartz (1900–1984). Instead of a Tin Pan Alley background, composer Arthur Schwartz studied law. He became a practicing attorney in the early 1920s, but indulged a passion for theater and music in his free time. Schwartz finally gave in to his avocation of songwriting and switched careers in 1929. He brought to his music a quiet elegance, something often ignored by other composers during the Jazz Age. Fortunately, he found in lyricist Howard Dietz (1896–1983), a friend and frequent collaborator, a kindred spirit. The two contributed a small but distinguished body of work to American popular music.

In 1930, Schwartz and Dietz could claim their first hit, *The Little Show*, a revue. It ran over 300 performances and introduced "I'll Guess I'll Have to Change My Plan." *The Second Little Show* followed in 1930, and then a succession of other Broadway musicals that featured such standards as "Dancing in the Dark" (1931; *The Band Wagon*), "Alone Together" (1932; *Flying Colors*), "You and the Night and the Music" (1934; *Revenge with Music*), "By Myself" (1938; *Between the Devil*), plus a host of others.

Toward the end of the decade, Schwartz worked with a number of other lyricists and enjoyed success with compositions like "Seal It with a Kiss" (1937; movie, *That Girl from Paris*), with words by Edward Heyman (1907–1981), and the folksy "Tennessee Fish Fry" (1940) that he wrote with Oscar Hammerstein II (see above) for *American Jubilee*. Schwartz's enduring work, however, will be those sophisticated show tunes that he and Howard Dietz turned out in remarkable quantity during the 1930s.

Harry Warren (b. Salvatore Guaragna, 1893–1981). Most discussions of composer Harry Warren mention his long association with lyricist Al Dubin (see above) during the 1930s. Although the two made an outstanding team, creating one memorable song after another, Warren also worked with others, including some of the finest lyricists of the day. Unlike many of his counterparts who labored on Broadway, Tin Pan Alley, and Hollywood, he devoted most of his career to motion picture music. A prolific songwriter with hundreds of songs to his credit, Warren seldom wandered far from the film capital.

Despite his connections to film scores, Warren started out in New York City, as did so many composers during the early years of the twentieth century. His first successes came in the early 1920s, and in 1930 he wrote "Cheerful Little Earful," with lyrics by the renowned Ira Gershwin and Billy Rose (1899–1966) for a Broadway revue called *Sweet and Low*. From there, Warren headed west to work in movie musicals. Although he and Al Dubin had met in the 1920s, it took the runaway acclaim for *42nd Street* to establish their credentials as the hottest team in the business. For the next several years, the two churned out one score after another, ranging from all four of the "Gold Digger" movies—*Gold Diggers of 1933* (1933), *Gold Diggers of 1935* (1935), *Gold Diggers of 1937* (1936), and *Gold Diggers in Paris* (1938)—to such gems as *Moulin Rouge* (1934), *Dames* (1934), *Broadway Gondolier* (1935), and *Stars Over Broadway* (1935). "Lullaby of Broadway," from *Gold Diggers of 1935*, earned Warren his first of three Academy Awards for Best Song.

Midway through the decade, Warren and up-and-coming lyricist Johnny Mercer (see above) discovered some mutual musical interests; a number of good songs resulted. In 1936, "I'm an Old Cowhand" (from *Rhythm on the Range*) cemented their friendship. "Jeepers Creepers" (from 1938's *Going Places*) became a hit, as did "You Must Have Been a Beautiful Baby" (1938; *Hard to Get*). "Hooray for Spinach," another Warren/Mercer collaboration for the 1938 movie *Naughty but Nice*, carries perhaps the oddest title. The pair continued to work together on a number of pictures during the 1940s.

Ned Washington (1901–1976). Yet another talented lyricist, Washington worked with some of the era's best songwriters; he enjoyed an especially rewarding association with composer Victor Young (1900–1956). Together, the two wrote many standards, including "Can't We Talk It Over?" (1932), "A Ghost of a Chance," and "A Hundred Years from Today" (both 1933). He provided words for "I'm Getting Sentimental Over You" (1932), the popular theme song of the Tommy Dorsey Orchestra. George Bassman (1914–1997) wrote the music. Washington likewise took "Smoke Rings," the theme created by Gene Gifford (1908–1970) for the Casa Loma Orchestra, and supplied lyrics in 1933.

Washington often worked uncredited in motion pictures, as did many of his counterparts, a standard practice of the day. Not until years later did every conceivable job in a movie receive onscreen credit. Thus pictures like *Lilies of the Field* (1930), *Straight Is the Way* (1934), *Frankie and Johnnie* (1936), and *Everybody Sing* (1938) had musical contributions from Ned Washington, but audiences had no knowledge of the fact. "The Nearness of You," an American classic that Washington wrote to the music of Hoagy Carmichael (see above), had been scheduled for a 1937 Paramount release, but for whatever reason, the studio chose not to produce it. The tune gathered dust for several years, and then finally got published in 1940 and quickly established itself as a favorite for vocalists.

At the end of the decade, **Walt Disney** (1901–1966) released *Pinocchio*, an animated film. Leigh Harline (1907–1969) composed the music, and Washington wrote the lyrics. "When You Wish upon a Star," one of the hits from the score, won a 1940 Academy

Award for Best Song. In this case, Harline and Washington did not labor in anonymity, but received full credit, a fitting close to a productive decade.

Richard Whiting (1891–1938). Composer Richard Whiting spent most of his brief career in Hollywood. He had the good fortune to work with some of the best lyricists in the business, and in the 1930s wrote the music for melodies like "Beyond the Blue Horizon," a tune that appeared in *Monte Carlo* (1930) with lyrics by Leo Robin (1900–1984), a frequent collaborator. "On the Good Ship Lollipop," the 1934 **Shirley Temple** (b. 1928) classic from *Bright Eyes*, has lyrics by Sidney Clare (1892–1972). His "Too Marvelous for Words" enjoyed a prominent place in 1937's *Ready, Willing, and Able* and boasts words by Johnny Mercer (see above).

Whiting also holds the distinction of being the composer for possibly the first popular song to feature the term "rock and roll" in its title. In 1934, he and Sidney Clare shared the labor on "Rock and Roll," a tune destined for a movie musical titled *Transatlantic Merry-Go-Round*. On the soundtrack, the popular Boswell Sisters perform a rousing rendition of "Rock and Roll," but hardly in the way the phrase would later be used. He also composed the unofficial anthem of the film industry, "Hooray for Hollywood" (lyrics by Johnny Mercer) in 1937. It highlights the movie *Hollywood Hotel* (1937).

Vincent Youmans (1898–1946). At the onset of the 1930s, Youmans had already established himself as a successful Broadway composer. He and lyricist Irving Caesar (1895–1996) wrote "Tea for Two" for inclusion in the 1925 Broadway show *No, No, Nanette*, and it had become a hit. Others followed, such as "More Than You Know," created with Billy Rose and Edward Eliscu (1902–1998), and "Time On My Hands" (1930), which he composed with lyricists Harold Adamson and Mack Gordon (1904–1959).

The advent of sound for movies lured Youmans, like so many others, to Hollywood. He found immediate success with "Sometimes I'm Happy," a tune he and Irving Caesar wrote for *Hit the Deck* in 1930. Three years later he scored the music for *Flying Down to Rio*, the picture that made **Fred Astaire** (1899–1987) **and Ginger Rogers** the hottest song and dance team in Hollywood. Youmans, Eliscu, and Gus Kahn penned "The Carioca" for this peppy musical, and it stole the show.

In 1940, RKO Radio Pictures finally brought *No, No, Nanette* to the screen. The original score survived the transition, including "Tea for Two" and "I Want to Be Happy," another hit from the show that Youmans had penned with Irving Caesar.

This list of lyricists and composers merely scratches the surface. A survey this brief cannot begin to cover all the talented people who contributed to the musical riches of the 1930s. But it does establish the fact that, despite the economic hardships of the decade and the looming threat of war, popular music flourished and left as its legacy a treasure trove of songs that have endured and become part of the nation's cultural heritage.

See also Children's Films; Jitterbug; Race Relations & Stereotyping

SELECTED READING

Hischak, Thomas S. *Through the Screen Door: What Happened to the Broadway Musical When It Went to Hollywood*. Lanham, MD: Scarecrow Press, 2004.

Hyland, William G. *The Song Is Ended: Songwriters and American Music*. New York: Oxford University Press, 1995.

Suskin, Steven. *Show Tunes: The Songs, Shows, and Careers of Broadway's Major Composers*. 3rd ed. New York: Oxford University Press, 2000.

Zinsser, William. *Easy to Remember: The Great American Songwriters and Their Songs.* Jaffrey, NH: David R. Godine, 2000.

SPECTACLE & COSTUME DRAMA FILMS. For purely mercenary reasons, Hollywood has always loved spectacle and dressing up. Filling the screen with action and actors, thrilling the audience with special effects and death-defying stunts—crowds, costumes, noise, excitement—these have been the basic elements of the big film, those moving pictures that brought, and continue to bring, droves of people into theaters for a couple of hours of escapism.

The Depression had a strong negative effect on the movie industry; distributors saw attendance drop and studios faced tight budgets. Theaters wanted their lost audiences to come back, and big, expensive pictures usually drew crowds. But most studios could not afford a succession of costly productions, and so Hollywood faced a dilemma that had its foundations in financial reality. The early 1930s witnessed a distinct fall-off in the number of new, extravagant films, although the industry did a quick turnaround when economic conditions improved after 1933–1934.

Despite the economic constraints, one of the best **movies** in the "spectacle" genre had its release during these difficult years. *All Quiet on the Western Front* (1930), under the direction of Lewis Milestone (1895–1980), tells the grim story of soldiers in World War I. It stars Lew Ayres (1908–1996) and bases its plot on the best-selling 1929 novel of the same name by German author Erich Maria Remarque (1898–1970). Playwright Maxwell Anderson (1888–1959) did the adaptation, and it remains a searing indictment of the senselessness of war.

Universal Studios, with little money to spare, spent it wisely on the action sequences, as terrifying today as they were in 1930. Soldiers scrambling out of trenches get mowed down by machine guns, or blown up by artillery, and yet they keep going "over the top" into almost certain death or wounding. *All Quiet on the Western Front* won Best Picture and Best Director in the Academy Awards that year, despite the small-minded complaints of some that it favored the "enemy" by having Ayres depict a young German soldier instead of an American doughboy.

That same year, Vitaphone/First National released *The Dawn Patrol*, with direction by Howard Hawks (1896–1977). Richard Barthelmess (1895–1963) and Douglas Fairbanks Jr. (1909–2000) portray World War I pilots in this **aviation** epic. Although it features some good aerial sequences, it hardly measures up to the spectacular effects achieved in *All Quiet on the Western Front.* Box office success, however, led to many an imitator during the decade, such as *The Lost Squadron* (1932), *West Point of the Air* (1935), *Devil Dogs of the Air* (1935), and *Test Pilot* (1938). Trying to recapture some of the excitement generated by the original *Dawn Patrol,* Warner Brothers in 1938 remade the picture, this time with direction by Edmund Goulding (1891–1959). Pulling out most, but not all the stops, the studio cast Errol Flynn (1909–1959) and David Niven (1910–1983) as the pilots, employed some of the combat footage from the 1930 original, and yet did little to improve on it. Even with all the airplanes and dogfights, few of these Depression-era films ever really rose to a true spectacle.

Hollywood truly excelled with the ornate costume drama. Since the movies exist primarily as a visual medium, dressing up actors in period dress or the most fanciful outfits

A lobby card for *Hell's Angels* (1930), a spectacular aviation film. (Courtesy of Photofest)

imaginable has usually served to bring patrons to the box office as much as special effects, wide screens, color, and all the other devices the studios employ to ensure attendance. More examples of the costumer's art went to movie theaters than any other type of expensive, prestige picture.

As an illustration, *The Private Life of Henry VIII*, a 1933 epic, features Charles Laughton (1899–1962) as the colorful monarch. His portrayal won him Best Actor honors, and the lavishly costumed cast gives a vivid feel for the sixteenth-century royal court. That same year, theaters announced *Cavalcade* on their marquees. Winner of the Academy Award for Best Picture and directed by Frank Lloyd (1886–1960), it features a huge cast of mainly British actors. An adaptation of a popular 1931 stage play by Noel Coward (1899–1973), the movie chronicles the lives of two English families from New Year's Eve in 1899 to New Year's Eve in 1932.

Since *Cavalcade* covers then-recent history, it brings an ironic tone to the events, ending with a wish for peace just as Hitler began gathering the reins of power in Germany. Sumptuous in their production values, both *The Private Life of Henry VIII* and *Cavalcade* presented audiences with a welcome dose of escapism. Pictures such as these led to a continuing succession of similar films.

In 1934 came *The Scarlet Empress*, a visually ornate retelling of the life of Catherine the Great or Russia. Perfect for the role of the colorful ruler, Marlene Dietrich

(1901–1992) imbues her character with an eroticism that would not have made it past the increasingly rigorous **Hollywood Production Code** in years to come; how it received wide distribution without criticism remains a mystery. Graced with elaborate sets, shadowy lighting, and bizarre characterizations, *The Scarlet Empress* stands as one-of-a-kind among movie spectacles.

Paramount Pictures and director Cecil B. DeMille (1881–1959) greeted 1934 audiences with *Cleopatra*, an opulent production starring Claudette Colbert (1896–1993). Already done as a silent motion picture four times previously, DeMille decided that instead of Egyptian artifacts he would have his set designers create a world of **Art Deco** grandeur, a device that gave the ancient story contemporary appeal. *Cleopatra* won an Academy Award for Best Cinematography, but Colbert herself steals the show, generally playing the vamp to the hilt and slinking about in outlandish costumes that have little to do with historical authenticity but everything to do with sex appeal.

An equally unusual film came out in 1935. *Mutiny on the Bounty*, based on the best-selling 1932 novel by Charles Nordhoff (1887–1947) and James Norman Hall (1887–1951) about a real mutiny on the HMS *Bounty* in the late 1780s, once more features Charles Laughton in a rich role, this time as the cruel Captain Bligh. He directs those cruelties toward the handsome young Fletcher Christian, played by a dashing Clark Gable (1901–1960). Mainly filmed on location on Tahiti by MGM, its $2+ million price tag (roughly $30+ million in contemporary dollars) made it the most expensive production for its time, although the studio more than recouped the costs at the box office. Audiences loved its mix of costumes, nautical adventures, and a dramatic story.

Victorian novelist Charles Dickens (1812–1870) achieved cinematic recognition with two big 1935 productions of his popular books: *David Copperfield* (1850) and *A Tale of Two Cities* (1859). Both films boasted large casts (advertisements for *A Tale of Two Cities* claimed a "cast of 49,000") and utilized extensive sets and period costumes. The relative commercial success of both urged Hollywood on to ever more costly endeavors.

Advances in special effects allowed two otherwise forgettable pictures to reach new heights. In 1936, MGM, by this time a leader in star-laden, spectacular productions, released *San Francisco*. A story of the great 1906 earthquake, it pairs Clark Gable and Spencer Tracy (1900–1967) in a fairly mundane tale of good (Tracy) and bad (Gable—but with a last-minute change of heart). What audiences got for their money, and their patience, occurs in the last 20 minutes of the picture: the earthquake itself. The destruction of the city comes across effectively and thrillingly, a tour de force for studio technicians who labored to create and destroy San Francisco in a matter of minutes. The movie served as the first, but hardly the last, really big-budget disaster film.

Shortly after *San Francisco* came *The Hurricane* (1937). Another natural calamity epic, this picture, directed by John Ford (1894–1973), spends most of its time with a humdrum romantic story of thwarted love. Then, like its earthquake counterpart, United Artists unleashed everything with a 20-minute hurricane (typhoon) that mixes miniaturization with full-scale mock-ups. Certainly not one of Ford's great films, but a great spectacle just for the storm sequence.

Anthony Adverse (1933), one of the biggest **best sellers** of the decade, came to the screen in 1936. Fredric March (1897–1975) plays the titular hero of Hervey Allen's (1889–1949) sprawling tale. Warner Brothers, mounting their biggest-ever production, claimed the movie required 130 sets and 98 different speaking parts. Filmed in black-and-white instead of Technicolor, and compressed into a running time of just over two hours, the picture nevertheless attempts manfully to capture the scope of the much longer, much more complex novel.

Pearl S. Buck's (1892–1973) *The Good Earth*, published in 1931 and another best seller, likewise showed up in theaters a year later, 1937. Paul Muni (1895–1967) and Luise Rainer (b. 1910) play two farmers, heavily made up to look Chinese. Perhaps incongruous today in an age of international filmmaking, such racial and ethnic disguising was commonplace in an earlier, less sensitive time. British and American actors (i.e., white actors, both male and female) frequently took roles that required them to appear to be of another racial or ethnic group, and makeup artists responded accordingly, often with ludicrous results. Neither of the leads in *The Good Earth* looks particularly "authentic."

The movie itself, however, captures much of Buck's love for the land that makes up China, although most of it was shot in the San Fernando Valley in California, another bit of "make up." MGM spent more on this exotic picture than it did on *Mutiny on the Bounty*, and the studio hired several thousand extras for a tumultuous mob scene. A big hit, it earned Rainer an Academy Award for Best Acting.

An older novel, 1894's *Prisoner of Zenda*, by Anthony Hope (1863–1933), received a film adaptation in 1937. It had been previously filmed in 1914 and 1922 in silent versions, but this rendering boasted sound. Another extravagant production, it features Ronald Colman (1891–1958) in a dual role, that of king and commoner. Filled with flamboyant costumes and equally flamboyant action, *The Prisoner of Zenda* quickly attracted a popular following. The mythical country of Ruritania in which the action occurs, lent its name to a new adjective, "ruritanian," meaning anything small, romantic, and make-believe.

The end of the decade saw several more costume dramas done on a grand scale. In 1939, *Drums along the Mohawk*, based on Walter D. Edmunds's (1903–1998) best-selling 1936 novel of the same name, drew an appreciative audience, as did that same year's *Hunchback of Notre Dame*, taken from Victor Hugo's (1802–1885) memorable 1831 story. The latter also gave Charles Laughton yet another meaty role as Quasimodo, the hunchback of the title. Finally, *Northwest Passage* in 1940 transferred one more popular novel to the screen, in this case a 1937 effort by Kenneth Roberts (1885–1957). With a "cast of thousands," this tale of the French and Indian Wars moves briskly, and in the shadows of World War II, saluted fighting men and the idea that war justifies almost any means.

Within the overall spectacle genre, the so-called swashbuckling movies merit attention. Derived from a sixteenth-century term to identify swordsmen and adventurers, these pictures have always had a modicum of popularity, but that surged in the 1930s, primarily because of the influence of actor Errol Flynn.

Already established as a handsome bit player, Flynn took the starring role in *Captain Blood*, a 1935 action-adventure tale filled with swordplay. Directed by Michael Curtiz (1886–1962), it costars Olivia de Havilland (b. 1916) and Basil Rathbone (1892–1967), two actors who would reappear with him in a number of subsequent films. Based, loosely, on a novel by Rafael Sabatini (1875–1950), *Captain Blood* served as Flynn's first starring role, and both he and the movie enjoyed overnight success. The story of a man wrongfully accused of treason, it depends on hairbreadth escapes, rousing swordfights, and colorful buccaneers—just the recipe for boundless adventure.

Warner Brothers recognized the appeal of *Captain Blood* and promptly lined up several similar pictures. In 1936, the studio released *The Charge of the Light Brigade*, again with the team of Curtiz, Flynn, and de Havilland (Rathbone was unavailable). Taken—with considerable liberties—from Alfred, Lord Tennyson's (1809–1892) stirring 1854 poem, the movie tells a romantic story for most of its length, saving the famous charge until the end. At last the moment arrives, and countless horses and men go sweeping across the California desert—on-location shooting was still the exception at that time. Gorgeously photographed, even in black-and-white, and extremely realistic, it cost the lives of over 200 horses. Their stunning falls, so thrilling to audiences, brought about much-needed legislation to protect animals during filming.

After a two-year wait, Warner Brothers brought out *The Adventures of Robin Hood* in 1938. With Curtiz, Flynn, de Havilland, and Rathbone all together once more, for many fans this remains the best of the many retellings of the Robin Hood legends. A swashbuckler from start to finish, it served as the first Warner Brothers movie to be done in what studio scribes called "glorious Technicolor," and color does make a welcome addition to these action-packed pictures. Sherwood Forest never looked greener.

In 1940 (planning and production actually occurred in 1939), Warner Brothers, Curtiz, and Flynn got together once more with *The Sea Hawk*. This film marked the 11th time the two worked together, a collaboration that dated back to 1935 and *The Case of the Curious Bride*, a picture in which Flynn had a bit part. *The Sea Hawk* again has Flynn playing a pirate, a role that allows for plenty of thrills and physical action, by now the formula for these swashbuckling pictures. Remotely based on a 1915 story by Rafael Sabatini, the source for 1935's *Captain Blood*, the studio reversed itself and filmed *The Sea Hawk* in black-and-white. Perhaps an economy move, given high production costs; it did release some prints in "Sepiatone," a cheap substitute for color.

Paramount Pictures, witnessing the success enjoyed by rival studios, early on made the decision to produce action-packed films of its own. In 1935, the company brought out *The Lives of a Bengal Lancer*, which, despite its supposed locale in India, was in reality filmed in its entirety in California. Deceptions aside, the picture has much in common with films like *Captain Blood, Charge of the Light Brigade*, and so on. Directed by Henry Hathaway (1898–1985), it stars Gary Cooper (1901–1961) as one of his majesty's lancers; the role further burnished the actor's image as a good character ready to stand against all odds.

This characterization, along with a swashbuckling plot, brought Cooper back to the screen in 1939's *Beau Geste*, another winner for Paramount and a classic action picture of the era. The title, which means a "fine or noble gesture," also happens to be the name of Cooper's character, a nice touch, since he too possesses gallant, noble qualities. Set in North Africa (southern California, yet again), the fast-moving plot has Foreign Legionnaires stranded at Fort Zinderneuf battling ferocious Arab bandits.

Finally, 1939 also saw RKO Radio Pictures' *Gunga Din*, yet another exotic swashbuckler, but with Cary Grant (1904–1986) taking on the role of the brave, athletic hero usually played by Errol Flynn or Gary Cooper. Adapted and expanded from Rudyard

Kipling's (1865–1936) famous 1892 poem of that name, "Gunga Din" refers to an Indian water boy, a role played with zest by character actor Sam Jaffe (1891–1984). Shot in California in black-and-white, *Gunga Din*, with its battles and heroics, rounds out the decade's generous selection of rousing, swashbuckling features.

As far as "Spectacle and Costume Drama Films" goes, three of the greatest pictures of the 1930s fit this category perfectly. **Snow White and the Seven Dwarfs** (1937), **The Wizard of Oz**, and **Gone with the Wind** (both 1939) receive discussion under their individual titles. In addition, many **musicals** of the 1930s, in themselves another form of spectacle, are discussed elsewhere.

See also Advertising; Book Clubs; Design; Walt Disney; Fashion; Race Relations & Stereotyping

SELECTED READING

Baxter, John. *Hollywood in the Thirties*. New York: A. S. Barnes & Co., 1968.

Quigley, Martin, Jr., and Richard Gertner. *Films in America, 1929–1969*. New York: Golden Press, 1970.

Sweeney, Russell C. *Coming Next Week: A Pictorial History of Film Advertising*. New York: Castle Books, 1973.

Trent, Paul. *Those Fabulous Movie Years: The Thirties*. Barre, MA: Barre Publishing, 1975.

STAGE PRODUCTIONS (DRAMA). The theater world, especially New York's Broadway, felt immediate and long-term effects from 1929's stock market crash. *Variety*, the show business weekly, reported 187 openings in 1930 compared to 233 in 1929 (the *New York Times* gave slightly higher figures). These numbers represent a decrease of approximately 20 percent fewer productions following the onset of the Depression. With the exception of a small increase for the 1931–1932 season, the trend established in 1930 continued for the rest of the decade. By the 1939–1940 season, only about 60 new productions opened in New York's theaters; it had been a difficult decade for serious drama.

Legitimate theater raises not just the problem of levels of activity; it also poses the question of how much a role it plays in popular culture. Then, as now, professional stage productions occurred primarily in urban centers such as New York, Boston, Cleveland, Chicago, and San Francisco. Tickets—especially when compared to other popular entertainments—carried a hefty price of several dollars: a $5 ticket in the early 1930s would cost about $60 in contemporary dollars. A person could see a double feature at a movie theater for 25 cents (about $2.50 in current money) or less. Along with the prohibitive admission fee, theater before and throughout the 1930s had the reputation of being an elaborate social event, with glamorous opening nights attended by women in the latest fashionable gowns and escorted by tuxedoed men, hardly a typical event for a representative cross section of the population. Traditional dramatic stage productions received little exposure; they usually played in urban settings, and more often than not experienced poor box office receipts.

Despite these strictures, plays that did make a name for themselves quickly found their way to Hollywood and film adaptations. For example, impresario Florenz Ziegfeld (1867–1932), famed for his Ziegfeld Follies, suffered heavy losses with the market crash. In an attempt to recoup, he closed *Whoopee!* (1928–1929), one of his successful New

York plays, and sold the film rights to the Samuel Goldwyn Company, a major movie studio. Eddie Cantor (1892–1964), the Broadway lead in *Whoopee!*, went to Hollywood and performed the same role on the screen. For this and many other productions, what might have been an art form with a small audience became a part of popular culture through this media crossover.

Although the number of new Broadway shows declined during the Depression and put many theater people out of work, the crisis caused an unusual surge of creativity. The formation of several theater companies during this time offered support and encouragement to actors and writers. The Theatre Guild, begun in 1919 by a small group of people interested in drama, stated that they wanted to improve theater in America by producing better plays. In 1931, the guild formed the Group Theatre with the intent of offering works containing elements of social protest. The economic upheavals occurring then seemed to inspire established playwrights and newcomers alike to write plays that expressed more concern with contemporary events in America than previously.

Winterset (1935), Maxwell Anderson's (1888–1959) prize-winning drama, reflects some of these concerns. Anderson, a member of the Playwrights' Company, based his play on the Sacco-Vanzetti case, a sensitive political issue from the 1920s. Nicola Sacco (1891–1927) and Bartolomio Vanzetti (1888–1927), two Italian immigrants, were executed in 1927 on charges of murder, a hotly contested verdict then and for many years after. Anderson addressed the theme of injustice by presenting this trial and its ramifications in dramatic form.

In a daring move, he wrote the dialogue in blank verse—which as a rule does not do well on the American stage. *Winterset*, however, was an exception. The play won the first New York Drama Critics Circle Award, and in 1936 RKO Radio Pictures released a film adaptation that remained close to the Broadway original. The movie brought Burgess Meredith (1907–1997) from his stage role of Mio to the **movies** and the beginning of a lengthy film career. Not only did Hollywood reach much larger audiences; it also provided far more secure and lucrative employment for actors.

Like *Winterset*, Robert E. Sherwood's (1896–1955) *Idiot's Delight* first appeared on Broadway in 1935, a time when a new world war seemed far from people's minds. But World War II already loomed when the play became a movie in 1939. Both the drama and its screen version carry a strong message of pacifism, that war truly serves as an "idiot's delight." By the picture's release, its antifascist stand had taken on new meaning and the film spoke directly to current events. It drew large audiences, offering them the chance to see Clark Gable (1901–1960) play an out-of-character role; he even performs a song-and-dance routine to *"Puttin' on the Ritz"* (1930; words and music by **Irving Berlin** [1888–1989]).

Playwright Clifford Odets (1906–1963), who had joined the American Communist Party in 1934, had his first work, *Waiting for Lefty*, produced by the Group Theatre the following year. The story concerns the revolt of the members of a taxi union against its corrupt officials, and unlike *Winterset*, concludes with a call to action—to strike in order to resolve the problem. Immediately successful, this production, along with two others staged by the Group Theatre in 1935—*Awake and Sing* and *Till the Day I Die*—meant the busy author had an unprecedented three plays running simultaneously, and they established him as a champion of the underdog. After the premiere of *Paradise Lost*, his fourth drama during 1935, Odets moved to Hollywood to try his hand at screenwriting; his scripts continued to vividly communicate the experiences of the times.

Despite Odets's flurry of creativity and subsequent residency in Hollywood, many of his social themes frightened off the movie studios and only one of his plays made it to the screen during the decade. In 1937, he wrote *Golden Boy*, and its Broadway production earned him his greatest commercial success. It came to movie houses in 1939 and stars William Holden (1918–1981) in his film debut. Less propagandistic than his previous writing, both the play and picture focus more on the human condition than they do on politics. A young man, yearning to break free from his meager existence, lives a bleak working-class life and struggles between prize fighting and playing the violin. **Boxing**, faster and more direct, seems promising, but the main character breaks his hand in the ring and thus loses both opportunities. Hardly a cheerful story, *Golden Boy* provides one of those rare moments when Hollywood took off its rose-colored glasses.

Another successful playwright, Lillian Hellman (1905–1984), wrote only 12 plays over her lengthy career. Despite her relatively meager output, 3 of Hellman's works received Broadway productions during the 1930s and she emerged as a strong voice in the American theater. From the mid-1930s on, she became involved, as did many of her colleagues, with liberal and leftist activities and organizations, although social issues did not dominate her creative approaches. Her first Broadway success, *The Children's Hour* (1934), tells the story of a spoiled child who attacks her teachers through destructive gossip. Another play, *Days to Come* (1936), deals with a labor strike in a Midwestern town, but it failed to connect with audiences. *The Little Foxes*, staged in 1939 and one of her best-known works, comes from Hellman's memories of the South and chronicles hatred and greed among the members of the Hubbard family. In New York, it starred Tallulah Bankhead (1902–1968). Made into a distinguished movie in 1941, it featured Bette Davis (1908–1989) in the Bankhead role; the film received nine Academy Award nominations, but no Oscars.

Usually thought of as a novelist and not a playwright, John Steinbeck (1902–1968) in 1937 wrote a novella called *Of Mice and Men*; it examines the lives of working-class and migrant workers in California during the Great Depression. The tale almost immediately went to stage and had a successful run from November 1937 to May 1938. Broderick Crawford (1911–1986) played a dim-witted but physically powerful itinerant farmhand, Lennie, with Wallace Ford (1898–1966) as Lennie's companion, George. Two years later, *Of Mice and Men*, adapted for film under the direction of Lewis Milestone (1895–1980), with music by Aaron Copeland (1900–1950), received an Academy Award nomination for Best Picture. Lon Chaney Jr. (1906–1973) portrays Lennie and Burgess Meredith plays George.

President **Franklin D. Roosevelt** (1882–1945), along with First Lady **Eleanor Roosevelt** (1884–1962), encouraged the inclusion of the arts in **New Deal** work relief and employment programs. The **Federal Theatre Project** (FTP; 1935–1939), a part of the Works Progress Administration (WPA; 1935–1943; name changed to Work Projects Administration in 1939), employed an average of 10,000 theatrical artists and workers annually. In addition, these New Deal programs opened theatrical doors previously closed to black Americans. Although minorities had been making small gains in dramatic productions, the FTP gave them a major boost. Black units worked in cities such as Atlanta, Birmingham, Boston, Durham, Greensboro, Hartford, Oklahoma City, Philadelphia, San Francisco, Seattle, and Tulsa. Those in New York and Chicago experienced the greatest success, especially with adaptations of classical plays such as a voodoo *Macbeth* (1936) and *Swing Mikado* (1938).

The FTP program created a phenomenal variety and number of high-quality productions as well as educational experiences, both in New York City and in 31 states across the country. Perhaps best known for its component called the Living Newspaper, the FTP provided a satirical look at social and political topics in the guise of newspaper copy. Eventually, Congress challenged the thrust of certain FTP productions, calling them subversive propaganda, and in 1939, legislators cut off FTP funding.

Of course, not all drama produced in the 1930s focused on social and political issues. In 1932, author **Erskine Caldwell** (1903–1987) aroused a flurry of controversy when he published *Tobacco Road*. Many critics condemned its gritty realism and open descriptions of sex, but a majority of readers loved it. While the arguments raged, playwright Jack Kirkland (1901–1969) sensed that the book had some dramatic potential, and its lurid reputation would doubtless attract the curious. He gained rights to the book and wrote a stage version of *Tobacco Road* that went to Broadway, opening in December 1933.

Despite cries of outrage at putting such a scandalous work on the legitimate stage, the play's unparalleled box office success placed the nay-sayers in the minority. *Tobacco Road* ran for an unprecedented 3,182 performances, which translates as seven and a half years, closing in May 1941. A record for Broadway at the time, the show held an appeal for Depression-era audiences, perhaps because it depicted, often humorously, a way of life immeasurably harder than anything they might be experiencing.

While Caldwell and Kirkland dealt with the trials of dirt farmers in rural Georgia, playwright Eugene O'Neill (1888–1953) strove for mightier themes. Most of his plots embrace human tragedy, but in 1933, O'Neill, long a successful dramatist, wrote his only comedy, *Ah, Wilderness!* A nostalgic retelling of his own youth as O'Neill wished it might have been, the play takes place in 1906 around the Fourth of July and brought entertainer George M. Cohan (1878–1942) back to the stage from Hollywood to portray the father. *Ah, Wilderness!* came out as a movie in 1935 starring Lionel Barrymore (1878–1954) in Cohan's role and Mickey Rooney (b. 1920) as a younger brother. In 1936, O'Neill became the first American playwright to win the Nobel Prize for Literature, an international honor awarded annually for an author's total body of work.

Another prestigious award, the Pulitzer Prize, originated in 1918. Established in the name of Joseph Pulitzer (1847–1911), an outstanding and successful newspaper publisher, it recognizes excellence in several literary areas, including journalism, fiction writing, histories of the United States, and original American plays. The Pulitzer prizes for drama cover the fall–spring season; the following chart lists the winners from 1929–1930 to 1939–1940. It provides a summary of what many considered the cream of the dramatic crop for the decade. Recipients often saw their works adapted for the movies, and five enjoyed this honor during the 1930s. Three additional Pulitzer Prize–winning plays from the 1930s had movie versions made during the 1940s.

Pulitzer Prize Recipients, Drama: 1929–1940

Season	Play	Number of Stage Performances	Playwright	Year Movie Released	Plot
1929–1930	*The Green Pastures*, a musical drama and one of the most popular Broadway plays of the decade	640 (71 for a 1935 revival; 44 for a 1951 revival)	Marc Connelly (1890–1980). Hall Johnson (1888–1970), a composer, conductor, and arranger of spirituals, was the play's musical director.	1936. Directed by Marc Connelly. Eddie Anderson (1905–1977), who played "Rochester" in radio's *Jack Benny Show*, appears in the movie.	Both the play and movie of this black folk fable had an all-black cast; it presented several Old Testament stories, as well as depictions of God and heaven.
1930–1931	*Alison's House*, a drama	41	Susan Glaspell (1882–1948), a founding member of the Provincetown Players and Provincetown Playhouse.	Not made into a movie.	The story, which dramatizes the life of American poet Emily Dickinson (1830–1886), has a feminist perspective.
1931–1932	*Of Thee I Sing*, a musical comedy; the first musical to be awarded a Pulitzer Prize for drama	441 (32 for a 1933 revival; 72 for a 1952 revival)	Book by George Kaufman (1889–1961) & Morrie Ryskind (1895–1985), music by **George Gershwin** (1898–1937); Lyrics: **Ira Gershwin** (1896–1983).	Not made into a movie during the 1930s or 1940s; adapted for **television** in 1976.	A satire on politics and government, it poked fun at a political system that appeared to be helping banks, not people.
1932–1933	*Both Your Houses*, a drama	120	Maxwell Anderson, a founding member of the Playwright's Company. Written during **Herbert Hoover**'s (1874–1964) administration, this play opened two days after Franklin Roosevelt's (1882–1945) inauguration.	Not made into a movie.	This political satire, set in the Depression, blasts the dishonesty of government. It presents the assumption that bribes and compromises serve as the primary way to accomplish anything in the political arena.

Year	Title		Author note	Film note	Description
1933–1934	Men in White, a drama	351	Sidney S. Kingsley (1906–1995). This play marked Kingsley's dramatic debut and was the first Broadway hit for the newly formed Group Theatre.	1934. Stars Clark Gable, Myrna Loy (1905–1993), and Jean Hersholt (1886–1956).	The entire play, which takes place within the walls of a hospital, deals with moral and social issues such as abortion.
1934–1935	The Old Maid, a drama	305	Zoe Akins (1886–1958). The stage play starred Judith Anderson (1898–1992).	1939. Stars Bette Davis (1908–1989) and Miriam Hopkins (1902–1972).	Based on a best-selling 1924 novella by Edith Wharton (1862–1937), the story takes place during the American Civil War.
1935–1936	Idiot's Delight, an anti-war story with music and comedy	300	Robert E. Sherwood, a founding member of the Playwrights' Company. The play starred the husband-wife team of Alfred Lunt (1892–1977) & Lynn Fontanne (1887–1983).	1939. Stars Norma Shearer (1902–1983) and Clark Gable.	Set in an alpine resort hotel where a group of people talk and rediscover associations, the play describes a fictional beginning of World War II and concludes with bombs bursting offstage.
1936–1937	You Can't Take It with You, a comedy	837 (239 for a 1965–1966 revival; 16 for a 1967 revival; 312 for a 1983–1984 revival)	Moss Hart (1904–1961) & George Kaufman (1889–1961).	1938. Directed by Frank Capra (1897–1991), it stars Jean Arthur (1900–1991), Lionel Barrymore, and James Stewart (1908–1997).	The story revolves around the unlikely romance of a boy and girl from two families who are poles apart in virtually everything.

Pulitzer Prize Recipients, Drama: 1929–1940 (*Continued*)

Season	Play	Number of Stage Performances	Playwright	Year Movie Released	Plot
1937–1938	*Our Town*, a drama	336 (36 for a 1969 revival; 136 for a 1988–1989 revival; 59 for a 2002–2003 revival)	Thornton Wilder (1897–1975).	1940. Screenplay by Wilder; stars William Holden, Martha Scott (1912–2003), and Frank Craven (1875–1945). Also adapted for TV in 1959, 1977, 1989, and 2003.	A classic American story about everyday life in Grover's Corners, New Hampshire, from 1901–1913. People grow up, marry, live, and die.
1938–1939	*Abe Lincoln in Illinois*, a drama	472 (40 for a 1993–1994 revival)	Robert E. Sherwood.	1940. Stars Raymond Massey (1896–1983) re-creating his stage role as Lincoln (1809–1865); also features Gene Lockhart (1891–1957) and Ruth Gordon (1896–1985).	The story tells of Lincoln's life from his early days as a woodsman until his election to the presidency in 1860, and takes place in New Salem and Springfield, Illinois.
1939–1940	*The Time of your Life*, a comedy	217 (52 for a 1969 revival; 7 for a 1975 revival)	William Saroyan (1908–1981), who declined to accept the prize.	1948. Stars James Cagney (1899–1986) and William Bendix (1906–1964).	Set in 1939 in Nick's Pacific Street Saloon, Restaurant, & Entertainment Palace, located at the foot of the Embarcadero in San Francisco, where a colorful cast parades through the bar.

In addition to being adapted into movies, much American drama during the 1930s also attracted a diverse audience through **radio**. Programs included *The First Nighter Program* (1930–1953), carried over the course of its long run by the National Broadcasting System (NBC radio, 1930–1936; 1952–1953) and the Columbia Broadcasting System (CBS radio, 1937–1949), and *The Mercury Theater on the Air* (1938–1946) on CBS. *The First Nighter* offered Americans across the country the opportunity to be transported to "the little theater off Times Square," where **Orson Welles** (1915–1985) and his newly organized Broadway Mercury Theatre Acting Company provided radio adaptations of original drama.

An experimental radio show called *The Columbia Workshop* aired on CBS radio from 1936 through 1947. It offered established and aspiring playwrights an opportunity to try new ideas and techniques over the air. Soon after the show's inauguration, the network annually received thousands of plays to consider. These broadcasts seldom provided straight readings of Broadway offerings, featuring instead original scripts that better fit the limitations of radio. They gave many Broadway writers and stage actors an opportunity to supplement their incomes. In 1937, *The Columbia Workshop* presented perhaps its most famous production, *The Fall of the City*, by Archibald MacLeish (1892–1982). A timely work, it highlighted the growth of fascism in Europe.

In other parts of the country, regional and local theater groups struggled to survive. Given the economic realities of the day, the majority of such efforts failed. Funding proved all but nonexistent, and the rights to the more popular contemporary plays cost so much that small theatrical troupes could not afford them. Many groups attempted to make do with older plays or with new, original material. Audiences, however, usually stayed away, and so there existed no solid financial basis to support local theater.

The Barter Theatre, founded by Robert Porterfield (1905–1971), a Broadway actor, proved an exception. Also known as Robert Porterfield's Barter Theatre of Abingdon, Virginia, the State Theatre of Virginia, and the World Famous Barter Theatre, this organization's initial performance, John Golden's (1874–1955) Broadway play *After Tomorrow* (written in 1931), opened to a full house at the Town Hall/Opera House in Abingdon on June 10, 1933. The Barter Theatre operated throughout the 1930s, helped greatly by financial and professional support in 1934 from actor Hume Cronyn (1911–2003) and his first wife, Emily Woodruff (active 1930s). Still in business today, the Barter Theatre limits its productions to its Abingdon playhouse. Over the years it has seen the start of many successful theatrical careers.

Overall, traditional theater played a minor role in the popular culture arena. Despite efforts to make drama more attractive to larger audiences, the production of new plays declined along with the number of performances. Sporadic attendance did not help matters. The Theatre Union, organized in 1933, deliberately set prices low—30 cents to $1.50 (about $4.50 to $23.00 in contemporary dollars)—and took the bold step of desegregating seating at a time when blacks usually sat in the balcony. Exposure to drama across the country did increase during the years of the Federal Theatre Project and radio also provided an opportunity for the mass distribution of plays. But Hollywood accomplished the most by adapting many Broadway productions for film. These versions might differ markedly from the stage original, but millions of people could say they "saw the movie of the play."

See also Fashions; *The Grapes of Wrath; Life & Fortune;* Musicals; Newspapers; Race Relations & Stereotyping; Radio Networks; Teenage & Juvenile Delinquency Films

SELECTED READING

Atkinson, Brooks, and Albert Hirschfeld. *The Lively Years, 1920–1973*. New York: Association Press, 1973.

Bordman, Gerald. *American Theatre: A Chronicle of Comedy and Drama, 1930–1969*. New York: Oxford University Press, 1996.

Dunning, John. *On the Air: The Encyclopedia of Old-Time Radio*. New York: Oxford University Press, 1998.

Durham, Weldon B., ed. *American Theatre Companies, 1931–1986*. Westport, CT: Greenwood Press, 1989.

Reynolds, R. C. *Stage Left: The Development of the American Social Drama in the Thirties*. Troy, NY: Whitson Publishing Co., 1986.

STAMP COLLECTING. As a leisure activity, stamp collecting during the 1930s crossed all economic and social lines, from Boy Scouts working on a hobby badge to **Franklin D. Roosevelt** (1882–1945), the most prominent collector of all. Dating back to the nineteenth century, philately (its official name, which comes circuitously from French and Greek and loosely means "a love of stamps") consists of collecting and studying postage stamps and related items in all their infinite variations.

The United States issued its first postage stamp in 1847, and the federal government gained a monopoly on mailing rights in 1863. In just a short time, people began collecting these symbols of commerce and taxation, an activity that quickly evolved into a popular hobby. Enthusiasts had founded the American Philatelic Society (APS) by 1886, an organization that still thrives today. Membership in APS soared in the 1920s and 1930s, and the society's annual National Stamp Show received considerable publicity and welcomed record crowds. The 1934 event, held at **Rockefeller Center** in New York City, drew 100,000 enthusiasts in nine days.

Estimates placed the number of active collectors for the 1930s in the millions—9 million for 1934 alone—and stamp collecting received support from many areas. Educators in particular encouraged the hobby and employed it as a teaching device; through stamps a teacher could tell the story of the settling of America or instruct students about the countries of the world. Sociologists, psychologists, and religious leaders labeled stamp collecting as a "good" activity because of the knowledge gained from the endeavor along with the productive use of spare time. Articles on the pleasures of stamp collecting and suggestions about how to create a valuable collection appeared in leading popular **magazines** of the period such as *Scientific American* and *Popular Science*. The National Broadcasting Company (NBC radio) even ran a successful show, *The Ivory Soap Stamp Club of the Air*. Host Tim Healy (active 1930s) told collectors "the story behind the stamp," and the sponsor invited listeners to send in an Ivory soap wrapper in order to receive a free album along with stamps to place in it.

President Roosevelt, an ardent collector since the age of eight, proudly displayed and talked about his collection of over 25,000 specimens; his enthusiasm clearly endorsed philately as a worthwhile activity. During his tenure (1933–1945), Roosevelt personally approved the composition of every stamp issued by the U.S. Postal Service—over 200 issues in all. He rejected some proposals, suggested some ideas of his own, and had a hand in designing a number of commemorative stamps, special stamps honoring a person, place, or event. Three examples include the 1933 Little America issue celebrating Antarctic exploration, the 1934 Mother's Day commemorative, and the 1936 Susan B.

Anthony stamp. Each of the final designs grew from sketches provided by Roosevelt. Some of the public interest in the hobby doubtless grew from his celebrity status and the frequent media coverage of his philatelic pursuits.

Roosevelt's selection of his close friend and political associate James A. Farley (1888–1976) as postmaster general of the United States from 1933 to 1940 had considerable impact on stamp collecting. Although he knew little about stamps when he accepted the position, Farley soon realized that commemorative issues could be both popular with hobbyists and profitable for the federal government. In years past, the U.S. had issued only a few commemoratives annually; Farley authorized an immediate increase: six to nine new commemorative stamps came out each year, along with additional new regular series, stamped envelopes, and air mails. All this activity delighted collectors.

The practice continued throughout the decade, and Farley also ordered the printing of special uncut, ungummed sheets and blocks in various denominations. At first, Farley had these issues, called "Farleys," created for his political cronies, a practice that outraged philatelists. They rightly labeled it favoritism and demanded equal access to any new issues. The tempest grew, gaining the title of "Farley's Follies," and the postmaster general finally acknowledged the protests; soon all new U.S. stamps of any kind had to be made immediately available to the general public, a remarkable show of strength and numbers by the stamp collecting community.

In 1921, some years before Farley's arrival on the scene, the Post Office Department had established a Philatelic Agency to assist collectors. With the flurry of new issues under Farley's leadership, the agency began to realize sizable profits. Stamps bought by collectors ended up in their albums, not on envelopes destined to be mailed, and during the four fiscal periods from June 30, 1935, to June 30, 1938, sales at the agency exceeded $7.8 million (roughly $110 million in contemporary dollars), or more than twice the combined total sales during the preceding 12 fiscal years. Financial analyses have suggested that at least 85 percent of the Philatelic Agency's money consisted of straight profits, and that does not include the millions of additional dollars spent by collectors and dealers at conventional post offices.

During the decade, postal authorities honored everything from **fairs and expositions** (the **Century of Progress Exposition**, 1933–1934; the California-Pacific Exposition, 1935; the Golden Gate Exposition, 1939; the **New York World's Fair**, 1939–1940) to holidays (Mother's Day, 1934) to famous people (Admiral Richard E. Byrd, 1933) to the land itself (the National Parks System, 1934) to sports (**baseball**, 1939). The issuance of new stamps received substantial publicity; for example, 2 million copies of the 1933 Century of Progress Exposition stamps were specially flown to Chicago for their first day of sale at the fair's post office. Some of the new issues carried political overtones: the 1933 National Recovery Act (NRA) stamp celebrated a **New Deal** endeavor that the courts would eventually rule against. With the NRA's defeat, the post office in 1935 had to hurriedly destroy its remaining inventory of that particular issue.

Most collectors consider the U.S. stamps of the 1930s particularly handsome; all were meticulously engraved and many rose rapidly in value. Philatelists stockpiled unused, or "mint," copies with the hope of selling them for a sizable profit after a few years' time. So many engaged in this practice, however, that the pot of gold never materialized and stamps from the era turned out to be a glut on the market. The 1930s nevertheless proved to be a bonanza for collectors and dealers, and the sales of albums and related paraphernalia reflected the ever-increasing numbers of people participating in this popular hobby.

See also Airships; Design; Education; Hobbies; Leisure & Recreation; Radio Networks; Religion

SELECTED READING
Baur, Brian C. *Franklin D. Roosevelt and the Stamps of the United States, 1933–1945.* Sidney, OH: Amos Press, 1993.
Smith, Hal H. "Special Stamp Issues Yield Profit to Nation." *New York Times,* 10 June 1934. *Historic New York Times.* Proquest, Lynchburg College Library, Lynchburg, VA.
———. "Stamp Show Closes; Crowds Set Record." *New York Times,* 19 February 1934. *Historic New York Times.* Proquest, Lynchburg College Library, Lynchburg, VA.
Stiles, Bent B. "Sales Vast Every Year." *New York Times,* 17 July 1938. *Historic New York Times.* Proquest, Lynchburg College Library, Lynchburg, VA.

STREAMLINING. In myriad ways, the 1930s can be called the Streamlined Decade. The primary **design** idiom of the era, Streamlining appeared in cars, **trains**, planes, and ships, and then carried over into more prosaic products, such as appliances, tools, electronics, and household decoration. Streamlining took an engineering concept and made it into a form of aesthetic expressionism.

A lack of ornament stands as the chief characteristic of most modern product design during the 1930s. Lines—both straight and curving, but always uncluttered—dominate. In many ways, the architects and designers of the period continued to be in rebellion against the ornamentation of the Victorian and Edwardian eras, periods that carried applied decoration to excess. They even dismissed many of the motifs found in the **Art Deco** of the 1920s, such as the familiar chevrons and jagged, zigzag lightning bolts, calling them mere indulgences. The Streamline ethic, a smooth surface seemingly devoid of any adornments, could be summed up in the ovoid, or teardrop, shape; that simple, idealized form served as the essence of Streamlining, an image of speed, efficient motion with a minimum of friction, the essence of modernism.

Whereas Art Deco tended to be steeped in classical traditions, the Streamlining movement came close to a clean break with the past. Moderne, Modern, Modernism, Modernistic, Machine Art, functionalist, organic, International—the terms attempting to identify and define the trends that succeeded Art Deco in the 1930s have proliferated and defy easy categorization. Streamlining and Art Deco share an affinity for geometric form, which helps to explain why many people confuse one with the other. So "modern" in the 1920s, Art Deco does not present a radical approach to design as much as it serves to substitute machinelike ornament for classical motifs. Eventually, however, Streamlining replaced the zigzags and chevrons. The geometry of Streamlining generally stands as more abstract and less representational than that found in Art Deco.

Streamlining, with its background in modern mass production methods, brought about the rise of the industrial designer. With sales dwindling in the 1930s because of the depressed economy, manufacturers turned to designers to make their products both more attractive and more salable. Since most firms once considered the role of the designer secondary to the parts played by engineers and other more technically specialized personnel, designers traditionally found themselves consigned to the background in any promotional efforts. As consumers began to find sleek, Streamlined products attractive, however, names like Norman Bel Geddes (1893–1958), Donald Deskey (1894–1989), Henry Dreyfuss (1904–1972), Paul Frankl (1887–1958), Raymond Loewy (1893–1986), Walter Dorwin Teague (1883–1960), Harold Van Doren (1895–1957), and Russel Wright (1904–1976), industrial designers all, moved to the forefront in corporate advertising and publicity.

In the United States, designers achieved early success with Streamlined trains. In 1934, during the second year of Chicago's **Century of Progress Exposition**, both the Union Pacific and the Burlington Railroads exhibited sleek new concepts of how a train should look. The Union Pacific's City of Salina and the Burlington's Pioneer Zephyr excited audiences with tubular seats, stainless steel panels, strip lighting, pastel colors, and an absolute lack of extraneous decoration. New York Central's Mercury (1936) and 20th Century Limited (1938) carried these ideas further, as did the Milwaukee Road's Hiawatha (1938). All achieved a design unity never before seen in American industrial products, and they suggested to passengers speed and luxury, the saving of time and energy.

In the field of aircraft, engineers had long recognized that a bulky shape created drag, and drag diminished performance. By the late 1920s, a number of experimental airplanes began to show elements of Streamlining—a smoother, sleeker fuselage, fewer struts and other obtrusions, retractable landing gear—but the greatest advances occurred in the early 1930s in commercial **aviation**. Streamlining rendered obsolete the veteran Ford Trimotor, with its squarish body and awkward angles, and also the Curtiss Condor, a curious mix of modernity and biplane tradition. In the winter of 1933, the Boeing Company introduced its 247 airliner, arguably the first Streamlined passenger plane. The company manufactured about 75 of these craft, but in July of that year the Douglas Aircraft Corporation displayed its first DC-1. An improvement over Boeing's model, it quickly evolved into the DC-2 in 1934 and made aviation history as the DC-3 late in 1935. The Streamlined **Douglas DC-3** would prove to be the most successful airliner of all time, with some 11,000 being built; it would remain in production until 1946.

American automobile manufacturers likewise showed an interest in Streamlining, but approached any design changes gingerly. With the Depression, they were loath to introduce new vehicles with no guarantees of public acceptance. In a daring move, the Chrysler Corporation in 1934 unveiled its Airflow model line. The Airflow's headlights appeared to blend in smoothly with the flow of the fenders and chassis. A roundly sloping hood and a sweptback windshield, along with some chrome detailing, sweeping, unbroken surfaces, and rounded contours completed the emphasis on Streamlined design. Industrial designers had touted, on paper, futuristic **automobiles** manufactured in teardrop shapes, and these ideas found echoes in the Airflow, a vehicle ahead of its time.

Thanks to an almost unlimited **advertising** budget, wide brand recognition, a far-flung chain of dealerships, and a relatively low sticker price, the new Chrysler line generated considerable interest, but it failed to be a rousing commercial success. Beneath the modernistic sheet metal, unfortunately, resided a rather staid passenger car that had undergone few mechanical changes. After an initial flurry of interest and sales, the public looked elsewhere. Chrysler may have prepared consumers for the direction automotive design would take, but 1934 and ongoing economic conditions hampered any rapid transition to Streamlining. By the late 1930s, however, most mainstream American automobiles displayed, in varying degrees, Streamlined elements—fenders, chassis, headlight mountings, and so on—that had seemed so revolutionary in 1934.

Some of the hallmarks of Streamlining include horizontal bands, or raised fluting—often called "speed lines"—reproduced in stainless steel or chrome, and usually grouped in threes. The use of curving metal tubing for furniture and railings gained popularity, as did rounded exterior corners on the most modern buildings of the day. With an implied emphasis on speed and apparent airflow, the Streamlined motifs announced a move from the applied stylistics of Art Deco to a truly functional, stripped-down modernity. The 1930s thus witnessed the rise of a machine aesthetic, an acceptance of the machine itself as art and desirable in that way.

But manufacturers knew they were creating products for mass consumption, not works of art for display in a museum, and so they promoted their wares with an eye both to style and ease of production. Most consumer-oriented industries rejected one-of-a-kind crafts and specialized works of art and instead aimed at larger markets. For instance, mass-produced Streamlined salt and pepper shakers, each a perfect teardrop, reproduced in a shiny chrome finish, pay homage to an elite tradition, that of the silversmith working expensively by hand. At the same time, those humble table items acknowledge the popularization of that tradition by their very numbers and resultant low price. The use of such modernistic tableware in a traditional, or period, house (i.e., nonmodern, non-Streamlined, such as Queen Anne, colonial, Georgian, etc.) reinforces how popular culture cuts across all lines of tradition and class.

On November 7, 1929, the Museum of Modern Art (MoMA) opened its doors in New York City. Under the astute leadership of Alfred H. Barr Jr. (1902–1981), MoMA emerged as a leader in the promotion and exhibition of modern design, as well as documenting movements in modern art and **sculpture**. By maintaining close relationships with the leading department stores and interior design venues around the country, the museum kept abreast of trends in furniture, decoration, appliances, and other household items. In so doing, it heightened American awareness of industrial design, especially with its 1934 show, Machine Art, that proposed a marriage among aesthetics, technology, and consumption. Designs featuring a Streamlined motif figured prominently in the show. The exhibition proved so popular that a traveling version toured the country for the next 10 years.

Modernism attained fashionability in the 1930s, and Americans eagerly accepted Streamlined designs in appliances, electronics, cameras, automobiles, public **transportation**, and commercial buildings, although they seemed less inclined to accept them in personal housing and government structures. In those areas, they leaned toward tradition, but they nonetheless accepted Streamlining as a middle path between nostalgia (tradition) and the future (modernism). It was industrial and it was neutral.

See also Fred Astaire & Ginger Rogers; Comic Strips; *Flash Gordon*; Musicals; Science Fiction

SELECTED READING

Bush, Donald J. *The Streamlined Decade*. New York: George Braziller, 1975.

Greif, Martin. *Depression Modern: The Thirties Style in America*. New York: Universe Books, 1975.

Hanks, David A., and Anne H. Hoy. *American Streamlined Design: The World of Tomorrow.* Paris: Flammarion, 2005.

Johnson, J. Stewart. *American Modern, 1925–1940: Design for a New Age.* New York: Harry N. Abrams, 2000.

Wilson, Richard Guy, Dianne H. Pilgrim, and Dickran Tashjian. *The Machine Age in America: 1918–1941.* New York: Harry N. Abrams, 1986.

SUPERMAN. At the mention of **comic books,** many people immediately think of *Superman.* The Man of Steel made his debut in the spring of 1938, the joint creation of writer Jerry Siegel (1914–1996) and artist Joe Shuster (1914–1992), in *Action Comics.* Although the comics industry had been moving away from newspaper reprints and more toward original stories featuring action-adventure, no one envisioned the success of *Superman.*

Characters possessing unusual abilities or traits had been a staple of the pulp magazine market for many years, larger-than-life heroes able to oppose even the worst evil doers. *Doc Savage,* the creation of Lester Dent (1904–1959; writing under the pen name Kenneth Robeson), thrilled readers in the 1930s with one pulp novel after another. Savage, "the Man of Bronze," relies on physical prowess and an array of futuristic weapons to get out of one jam after another. More sinister, perhaps, but just as exciting, *The Shadow* stories of Walter B. Gibson (1897–1985; writing as Maxwell Grant) involves the adventures of a mysterious playboy named Lamont Cranston. Instead of amazing athletic abilities, Cranston can "cloud men's minds" and thus make himself invisible to society's enemies, easily penetrating their lairs in order to bring them to justice.

Both the **radio** networks and Hollywood, always alert to trends that might attract audiences, strove to duplicate these pulp successes. *The Shadow* premiered on radio in 1932 and became a staple of the airwaves. An invisible **crime** fighter presented no problems for the aural medium, and the series would continue until 1954. Introduced by the strains of Rimsky-Korsakov's "Flight of the Bumblebee," radio's *Green Hornet* likewise gave listeners a disguised hero who protected the innocent. Motion picture **serials** involving all kinds of heroes—The Green Hornet, The Shadow, **Flash Gordon,** Buck Rogers, Zorro, "Crash" Corrigan—brought droves of youngsters into theaters for Saturday matinees. By the end of the decade, the concept of a superhero, a person able to overcome any and all obstacles, had taken hold, and it only remained for Superman to embody the idea.

So it was that the firm of Detective Comics, better known as DC, gave *Superman* some space in its first issue of *Action Comics* (June 1938). Two young men, writer Jerry Siegel and artist Joe Shuster, had been trying to interest publishers in a character they called "Superman" since 1934, sustaining themselves with forgotten strips like *Doctor Occult* and *Slam Bradley.* DC, emboldened by the success of action and adventure **comic strips,** decided to take a chance with this muscular man dressed in a skintight blue outfit complete with a billowing cape. Siegel and Shuster's Superman even graces the cover of the new *Action Comics,* but anonymously. The drawing shows him single-handedly lifting a smashed automobile overhead, while frightened citizens scatter.

The story included in the comic book reveals Superman's origins on the planet Krypton and his escape to Earth. Readers learn he can leap (flying would come later) "an eighth of a mile," and outrun speeding **trains.** In the course of a few pages, he takes on the identity of the innocuous Clark Kent, stops a lynching, saves an innocent

The cover of a 1939 *Superman* comic book. (Courtesy of Photofest)

woman from the electric chair, captures the guilty parties, meets Lois Lane, and lands a job as a reporter on the *Daily Planet*.

In 1939, flushed with success, DC launched a comic book devoted exclusively to Superman. Soon they were selling over 1 million copies per issue, a new industry record. In a clever reversal, a daily newspaper strip based on the comic book came out early that same year, and a radio serial, destined to run for over 11 years, followed close behind. Almost immediately, other publishers readied their own superheroes. *The Crimson Avenger* hit newsstands soon after *Superman*, and the Arrow brought his deadly archery skills to the comics within months. A more enduring superhero was The

Batman (the article would be dropped shortly). The first issue of *The Batman* came along in 1939, and he too attracted an enthusiastic following, although he possessed no actual superhuman qualities. With these and other entries, the stage had been set; one superhero after another entered what would soon become a crowded field.

By and large, however, the reign of the superheroes did not commence until the early 1940s and the growth of concerns about World War II. For the late 1930s, *Superman* dominated this new genre of comic book. His public persona of Clark Kent doubtless fit the adolescent daydreams of many readers. Superman could move from the mild-mannered and ineffectual Kent to someone capable of the most incredible deeds. Who wouldn't want such powers? But because Superman evolved so late in the decade, it would be rash to suggest that the Man of Steel in some way serves as a reflector of the 1930s.

See also Automobiles; Movies; Newspapers; Pulp Magazines; Radio Networks; Science Fiction; Youth

SELECTED READING
Bridwell, E. Nelson. *Superman: From the Thirties to the Seventies*. New York: Bonanza Books, 1971.
Dooley, Dennis, and Gary Engle, eds. *Superman at Fifty: The Persistence of a Legend!* Cleveland: Octavia, 1987.
Goulart, Ron. *Over 50 Years of American Comic Books*. Lincolnwood, IL: Mallard Press, 1991.

SWIMMING. Americans have long loved going to a beach or pool for a swim, making it one of summer's favorite activities. The 1930s proved no exception for those fortunate enough to live near water. Swimming provided cheap, healthy fun, and millions flocked, any way they could, to public and private facilities. With fewer rules and regulations than almost any other form of recreation, swimming allowed men and women to mingle and play freely, often in abbreviated dress. Throughout the decade, the last remaining taboos about modesty tumbled down as bathing suits for both sexes became briefer and more revealing.

Synchronized swimming, a feature of the 1933–1934 **Century of Progress Exposition** in Chicago, generated modest interest, but it had to wait until after World War II before it became something that would draw significant crowds. American swimmers developed the butterfly stroke in the 1930s, eventually adding it to international competition. Despite these modest advances, most water sports received scant public attention.

Long-distance swims and competitive diving attracted a few dedicated onlookers, and Hollywood tried to capitalize by making **movies** that included segments with these activities. Comedian Joe E. Brown (1892–1973), always alert for any subject that might provide a laugh, took on distance swimming in 1932's *You Said a Mouthful*. As usual for his pictures, everything that can go awry does so. The film provides some shots of the Catalina marathon swim, an event where the hardy try to make it from the island to the California mainland. As for diving, the momentary excitement of the jump off a board and the subsequent plunge into the water carried more interest than the repeated strokes of swimmers. In 1934, Regis Toomey (1898–1991) starred in *Big Time or Bust*, a so-so drama that features several diving sequences. By and large, however, the motion picture industry seldom employed swimming as any context for releases during the 1930s.

Spectators watch swimmers at Columbia Country Club, Washington, D.C. (Courtesy of the Library of Congress)

Larry "Buster" Crabbe (1908–1983) and Johnny Weissmuller (1904–1984), two busy actors from the period, may not have used swimming as the primary content of their movies, but they nonetheless took advantage of the film medium to display their mastery of the sport. Both Crabbe and Weissmuller had been outstanding Olympic swimmers, and they parlayed their amateur exploits into profitable movie careers. Weismuller had swum in the 1924 and 1928 games, and Crabbe had made his mark in the 1932 events. Young and attractive, they received considerable attention, and Hollywood recognized both with movie contracts.

In 1932 Weissmuller starred in **Tarzan** the Ape Man, becoming, in the process, the definitive Lord of the Jungle for many. Then in 1933, Crabbe made *Tarzan the Fearless*, plus a Tarzan look-alike film titled *King of the Jungle*, in which he played Kaspa the Lion Man. Weissmuller came right back in 1934 with *Tarzan and His Mate*, and his audience appeal led MGM to contract with him for 10 more Tarzan films between then and 1948. For his part, Crabbe shifted to **science fiction**, playing both Buck Rogers and Flash Gordon in several popular **serials**. Although both actors had to frequently plunge into the water and display their aquatic expertise, along with their attractive physiques, especially in the Tarzan films, swimming served as a secondary component in their pictures.

Both Weissmuller and Crabbe donned bathing suits for the 1939–1940 **New York World's Fair**, where they appeared as featured performers in Billy Rose's Aquacade, a water spectacle that consistently drew large crowds and helped further popularize professional swimming. Despite these exceptions, however, swimming remained on the periphery of American sports events throughout the 1930s.

See also Fairs & Expositions; Fashion; *Flash Gordon*; Leisure & Recreation; Olympic Games

SELECTED READING

Dulles, Foster Rhea. *A History of Recreation: America Learns to Play.* Englewood Cliffs, NJ: Prentice-Hall, 1965.

Grimsley, Will, ed. *A Century of Sports by the Associated Press Sports Staff.* New York: Associated Press, 1971.

SWING. For a brief period, roughly 1935 to 1945, swing dominated American popular **music**. An inclusive term, swing incorporates numerous areas of musical expression. Its most direct roots include **jazz** and dance music, but pop songs, standards, country music, light classics, and other influences also enter any definition. Not jazz, at least not jazz in any academic or historical sense, swing exists as an amalgam, a mix, of many styles and formats. In a toe-tapping, finger-snapping sense, swing enjoys a rhythmic emphasis that causes music to possess a propulsive energy; it "swings."

A manifestation of popular culture, swing grew on its own, not because of its links to other music. It represented a cultural event that swept aside virtually everything before it, but by the mid-1940s the craze had run its course. **Radio**, which rose to unprecedented prominence during the 1930s, played a significant role in popularizing swing since it provided the means by which most Americans heard the latest trends in music. What stations chose to program—and what they did not—illustrates how commercial interests, once they decide something can be profitable, have the power to shape public taste.

The two major **radio networks**, the National Broadcasting Company (NBC radio) and the Columbia Broadcasting System (CBS radio), early on sensed the widespread appeal of this new musical phenomenon and gave swing-oriented orchestras the spotlight for numerous popular shows. For example, *The Chesterfield Quarter-Hour* (1931–1933), *The Camel Caravan* (1933–1954), *The Old Gold Show* (1934), *Let's Dance* (1934–1935), *Kay Kyser's Kollege of Musical Knowledge* (1937–1949), and *The Fitch Bandwagon* (1938–1948) constitute but a sampling of the many shows that revolved around swing orchestras and popular tunes.

In contrast to contemporary American radio, which relies almost entirely on **recordings**, many of these programs came to audiences in the form of live broadcasts. Stations also employed recordings in their programming, but in the swing era many aggregations traveled directly to the studio to perform. If a band could not conveniently make the trip, stations frequently dispatched crews, along with portable equipment, to clubs or concert halls to capture the live sound of the group in performance. These broadcasts went under the name of "remotes." As a result, many bands relied on radio for exposure, a time when they could play selected numbers from their "book" (a collection of scores a particular group might perform) and allow the unseen audience to sample more than a single song.

Broadcasters found band remotes an inexpensive way to present live music over the air. Wherever orchestras might play—dance halls, pavilions, auditoriums—the station could transmit the shows to its affiliated network (NBC or CBS) for national distribution. In addition, this allowed music to be preserved by making transcriptions, recorded discs or wire recordings, of the proceedings. Swing and the big bands, in fact, served as a primary catalyst for the sagging recording industry, which had fallen on hard times with the Great Depression. If people liked what they heard on their radios, they usually could

The swing era was also a time for dancing; when the band played, everyone took to the floor. (Courtesy of the Library of Congress)

find the music in their neighborhood record shops. By the end of the 1930s, the record business—in large part thanks to radio exposure—again enjoyed flush times.

Swing benefited everyone connected with the music. Not only did millions of fans purchase recordings by their favorite bands, they also bought tickets to hear them in person, and an impressive number of people took to the many dance floors that proliferated during the decade. Swing could be lush and romantic, but it could also be hard-driving and up-tempo; it emphasized melody, so it could be hummed, whistled, sung, and, for a whole generation of devotees, danced to. Much American popular music, from the 1920s onward, proved attractive for dancing, and that attraction translated, for most people, into the fox trot, a combination of slow and quick steps. But tastes in dancing change over the years, and in addition to the relatively staid fox-trot, the 1930s witnessed the rise of many up-tempo dances that broke with convention.

Following trends that had commenced in the 1920s with dances like the Charleston, traditional ballroom dancing evolved into a more individualistic style, one that involved the partners putting on a performance, or "cutting a rug," as the slang of the day would have it, that is, the couple's dance steps are so good—so "sharp"—that they destroy the rug or carpeting beneath their feet. These new steps eventually could be summed up in one word: **jitterbug**.

If swing served as the musical manifestation of the era, the jitterbug—fast, rhythmic, individualistic—existed as its physical expression. This step (or steps, since few people jitterbugged exactly alike) brought a new freedom to the dance floor, and fans, especially those in their teens and early 20s, loved it. Their elders might occasionally bemoan these new, uninhibited dances, but their complaints fell on deaf ears. The jitterbug and all its variants changed American popular dancing, evolving, as did the music, into rhythm 'n' blues and, later, rock 'n' roll.

Much of what constitutes swing grew out of black American musical expression. A number of pioneering black bands, unheard, for the most part, by the larger white audience, began experimenting with new musical formats that grew directly from jazz. Groups like those led by **Fletcher Henderson** (1898–1952), Andy Kirk (1898–1992), Jimmie Lunceford (1902–1947), William McKinney (1895–1969), Lucky Millinder (1900–1966), Bennie Moten (1894–1935), Noble Sissle (1889–1975), and Chick Webb (1902–1939) labored in relative obscurity, polishing their approaches to what would eventually be called swing. Only a few black bandleaders attracted much widespread public attention, with **Duke Ellington** (1899–1974) and Cab Calloway (1907–1994) serving as two outstanding exceptions. Their success opened previously closed doors—film, stage, and radio—for other black performers, even if the opening amounted to little more than a crack.

For the most part, the music business remained rigorously segregated. Seldom did black bands enjoy significant air time; the choice shows went to white aggregations; and major record labels continued to push their white stars. As in the larger society, black artists found themselves relegated to second-class citizenship. But swing's appeal transcended race; its audience, young and more socially liberal, represented changing values, not traditional ones. By the end of the decade, an increasing number of black musicians, buttressed by a large and enthusiastic youthful following, finally began receiving their due.

What these bands played involved a synthesis of two strands of American music, popular dance numbers and jazz. Paul Whiteman (1890–1967), a successful white bandleader and the self-styled "King of Jazz," had searched for this synthesis in the 1920s, but seldom achieved it. This wave of mostly black orchestra leaders discovered an approach that found receptive audiences who were tired of the blandness offered by most of the so-called sweet bands then ruling the American popular music roost. The phrasemakers, anxious to differentiate this new music from older styles, called them "swing bands," and they lived up to the name. As more people became aware of these orchestras, interest grew and other musicians came aboard. A quiet shift had, by the mid-1930s, become a stampede. The swing era had arrived.

The odyssey of bandleader **Benny Goodman** (1909–1986) illustrates how swing emerged as the dominant popular music of the 1930s. A white, Chicago-born clarinetist, Goodman had begun his professional career as a teenager in the 1920s, playing with a variety of jazz-oriented groups. He eventually formed his own group and won a spot on NBC's *Let's Dance* in 1934 with the premiere of the show. This radio exposure gained him enough recognition that by 1935 he embarked on a cross-country tour that culminated with a riotously successful concert in Los Angeles. From there, the recording and radio offers poured in, and Goodman emerged as "the King of Swing," a title he held throughout the remainder of the 1930s.

Goodman moved to CBS in 1936, starring on *The Camel Caravan* (also called *Benny Goodman's Swing School*) until 1939. He also switched from RCA Victor's Bluebird label to Columbia for recordings, and a steady stream of best-selling records followed. The climax of all this activity occurred in January 1938, when Goodman and his band, along with a host of invited musicians, performed at New York's prestigious Carnegie Hall for a jazz concert. More accurately a swing concert, it bestowed a certain legitimacy on this hybrid musical form and assured increased public and commercial support for swing.

Overnight it seemed, orchestras as diverse as those led by brothers Jimmy and Tommy Dorsey (1904–1957; 1905–1956), Charlie Barnet (1913–1991), **Count Basie** (1904–1984), Larry Clinton (1909–1985), Glen Gray (1906–1963), Earl Hines (1903–1983), Harry James (1916–1983), Kay Kyser (1906–1985), **Glenn Miller** (1904–1944), Artie Shaw (1910–2004), along with dozens of others, sprang up. By 1940, over 200 dance bands of one kind and another were crisscrossing the land, playing concerts, dances, and making recordings. Many enjoyed stints on radio and some even found themselves cast in **movies** that usually served as vehicles for presenting more swing. The overwhelming majority of leaders and sidemen tended to be white, although a few black bands—Basie, Calloway, Ellington, and Hines stand out—managed to achieve a modicum of commercial success. At the same time, a handful of white leaders dared to integrate their ranks in the later 1930s. Led by popular stars like Benny Goodman and Charlie Barnet, the inclusion of black musicians caused no backlash among audiences, although truly mixed bands would not be the rule until well after World War II.

Other events also changed the face of the music business. The overwhelming success of swing in the latter half of the decade meant that much new popular music originated with the bands themselves, not with old-fashioned **songwriters and lyricists** as in the past. As the sheer number of orchestras grew and competition stiffened, arrangers, those individuals who took the compositions of others and organized (i.e., arranged) them in a distinctive manner, achieved a new importance. They had the responsibility of creating music to fit the qualities, the "sound," of a particular orchestra or group. As their importance grew, arrangers moved into actual composition, often contributing charts (arrangements scored for the band as a whole) that consisted of original work, rather than arrangements of the work of others. Thus arrangers like Gene Gifford (1908–1970), Jerry Gray (1915–1976), Jimmy Mundy (1907–1983), Sy Oliver (1910–1988), Don Redman (1900–1964), and Edgar Sampson (1907–1973), hardly household names, helped mightily to define the sound of swing throughout the decade, and frequently emerged as important as the songwriters themselves.

When Hollywood realized that swing had all the trappings of a new national craze, the studios wasted no time in capitalizing on it. Bands big and small, black and white, band leaders known and unknown, along with vocalists and singing groups, were snatched up and thrust into movies. Most of the musical roles consist of bit parts or extended cameos; Hollywood's regular roster of nonmusical stars took the leads, only allowing the musicians to perform their latest hits and contribute occasional bits of dialogue. But their mere presence signified a growing awareness of swing and those who played it.

The quality of the films mattered little in the haste to have a swing number or two in the course of the story. That attitude resulted in several flops (*The Big Broadcast of 1937* [1936]), some mediocrities (*Second Chorus* [1940]), and a small group of pictures that accurately captured the flavor of this new phenomenon (*Hollywood Hotel* [1937]). These movies also gave a visual presence to a number of black artists, such as Duke Ellington and Cab Calloway, previously invisible to their audiences and heard only on radio and recordings.

By 1938, swing could be found just about anywhere. That summer in New York, a Swing Festival on Randall's Island drew 24,000 people. The mammoth event featured

25 bands and lasted some six hours. That same year, bandleader Tommy Dorsey cut "Boogie Woogie," a big-band instrumental version of a piano composition previously written and recorded by Clarence "Pinetop" Smith (1904–1929) in 1928 as "Pinetop's Boogie Woogie." Up to that time, most white listeners viewed boogie-woogie, an instrumental approach to rhythm that stresses a repeated bass figure, as a kind of low-class black music and paid it little heed. Although collectors had sought Smith's record over the years, it made little impression on the mass audience. Dorsey's version quickly changed all that, selling a million copies and making boogie-woogie a part of the expanding world of swing and a prominent part of white popular culture. Within the next couple of years, bands and pianists of every description performed boogie-woogie tunes to enthusiastic applause, and white groups scored most of the hits. At the height of the swing phenomenon, a new musical fad had been born.

This appropriation of an essentially black musical format by white performers had occurred before in American culture. Ragtime and New Orleans jazz (renamed Dixieland) had witnessed the same thing. For example, Count Basie's theme, the up-tempo "One O'Clock Jump" (1937; music by William "Count" Basie), had first been recorded by his band in 1937, but a majority of record buyers ignored it. Benny Goodman cut the tune in 1938, and his version enjoyed modest success. Then Harry James and his band released yet another interpretation of "One O'Clock Jump" later in 1938; the number promptly climbed the charts, took on hit status, and proved so successful that the trumpeter four years later garnered a second big seller with "Two O'Clock Jump" (1942; music by Harry James, Count Basie, and Benny Goodman), a not-too-subtle variation on the original.

Big bands and small groups, instrumentalists and vocalists, originals and variations—it mattered little to swing enthusiasts. Record sales kept pace with all the live performances, reaching $26 million (roughly $373 million in contemporary dollars) in 1938. Singles sold at the rate of 700,000 discs a month, their highest rate ever. In 1939, Columbia Records, a perennial third against leaders Decca and RCA Victor, introduced a new, laminated disc that advertised much better sound quality and longer life than the shellac records of the competition. It retailed for 50 cents (roughly $7.00 in contemporary dollars), a few pennies above the usual price of 39 cents (or about $5.50), but no one seemed to mind. By that time, eager buyers were snatching up 140 million recordings a year. **Jukeboxes**, once relegated to bars and cheesy dance halls, became ubiquitous, and deeply influenced record sales. Anything that received wide jukebox play could be expected to sell well in record stores.

Two national **magazines** closely monitored swing, chronicling both its meteoric rise and eventual fall. Chicago-based *Down Beat*, which had been founded in 1934, and New York–based *Metronome*, founded in 1932, an outgrowth of two previous publications of the same name that dated back to the 1880s, quickly established large circulations and their readership showed no hesitancy about voicing opinions. Other magazines, among them *Jazz Hot*, *Swing*, and *Tempo*, also had their followers, but they seldom rivaled the influence enjoyed by *Down Beat* and *Metronome*. The journals remained fiercely competitive, but they quickly took to task anyone who voiced opposition to jazz or swing. Trade publications like *Variety* and *Billboard* also covered swing, but more objectively, tracking record sales, song rankings, and business matters connected with the music industry.

In 1936, *Down Beat* inaugurated an annual readers' poll; *Metronome* followed suit a short time later. Hardly scientific, these polls served primarily as popularity contests instead of indicators of true merit, but they nonetheless provided information about readers' tastes at a given time. Cries of dishonesty and racism sometimes accompanied these votes, since the magazines included the ballots within their pages and zealous fans could send in multiple copies by buying extra issues. No accurate statistics exist on the racial breakdown of the two periodicals' readership, but some people felt white musicians received favoritism at the expense of their black counterparts. A few black publications ran polls of their own, and then critics reversed the charge. Despite the scattered complaints, readers eagerly anticipated the yearly polls, which doubtless had an effect on resultant jukebox play and record sales.

As the decade closed, countless bands and musicians could be found in the swing ranks. Good or mediocre, they catered to an insatiable public. Virtually every community boasted at least a few dance bands or combos that provided nightly or weekend music. Department stores and specialty shops reveled in skyrocketing record sales, and everyone talked about his or her favorites. A heady time, the swing era gave Americans a mutually shared music unlike anything before or since.

See also Musicals; Race Relations & Stereotyping; *Your Hit Parade*; Youth

SELECTED READING

Oliphant, Dave. *The Early Swing Era, 1930 to 1941*. Westport, CT: Greenwood Press, 2002.

Schuller, Gunther. *The Swing Era: The Development of Jazz, 1930–1945*. New York: Oxford University Press, 1989.

Swing That Music! The Big Bands, the Soloists, and the Singers. 4 CDs. Smithsonian Collection of Recordings. RD 102, 1993.

Yanow, Scott. *Swing*. San Francisco: Miller Freeman Books, 2000.

T

TARZAN. In 1912, author Edgar Rice Burroughs (1875–1950) created a story about a man raised in the jungle by apes, a man free of the restraints of civilization. That character, of course, turned out to be Tarzan, the most famous adventure-fantasy hero of modern times. *Tarzan of the Apes* first appeared in a pulp magazine called *All-Story*; the tale's immediate success prompted a full-length book version in 1914. Over the years, Burroughs wrote 25 more novels about this lord of the jungle, the last appearing in 1964; since then, other writers have carried on the saga.

The 1930s alone witnessed the publication of nine different Tarzan stories by the prolific Burroughs: *Tarzan at the Earth's Core* (1930), *Tarzan the Invincible* (1931), *Tarzan the Triumphant* (1932), *Tarzan and the City of Gold* (1932), *Tarzan and the Lion Man* (1934), *Tarzan and the Leopard Man* (1935), *Tarzan's Quest* (1936), *Tarzan the Magnificent* (1936), and *Tarzan and the Forbidden City* (1938). These novels, along with the many other titles in the series, represent examples of mass-market fiction. From the onset, Tarzan struck a nerve with the public, and Burroughs, like all popular artists, responded to his public's perceived wants and needs. Many libraries and "respectable" book stores expressed a reluctance to carry such "trashy" fiction, but eager readers bought the titles by the millions, making Burroughs one of the biggest-selling writers of the twentieth century.

The success of the Tarzan saga did not go unnoticed by the growing movie industry. Three silent films about the ape man appeared in 1918; the best-known, *Tarzan of the Apes*, starred a muscular actor named Elmo Lincoln (1889–1952) and established many of the traditions found in subsequent Tarzan motion pictures. With the advent of sound, Hollywood released the most famous of them all, *Tarzan, the Ape Man* (1932). This classic film features Johnny Weissmuller (1904–1984), a former Olympic **swimming** champion turned actor. Weissmuller developed the famous "Tarzan yell," a call he uttered before plunging into a jungle pool or swinging on a handy vine. It immediately became a permanent part of the character, almost an icon in its own right.

Tarzan, the Ape Man did spectacularly at the box office, prompting MGM to rush into production more features about Burroughs's hero. Weissmuller completed three additional Tarzan **movies** during the decade, *Tarzan and His Mate* (1934), *Tarzan Escapes* (1936), and *Tarzan Finds a Son!* (1939). In all four of these outings, Maureen O'Sullivan (1904–1984) costars as Jane, Tarzan's civilized mate. She proved a valuable addition, lending an element of femininity to Weissmuller's more primitive persona.

The definitive Tarzan and Jane, Johnny Weissmuller (1904–1984) and Maureen O'Sullivan (1911–1998). (Courtesy of Photofest)

In the meantime, Larry "Buster" Crabbe (1907–1983), an actor who would strike gold playing Flash Gordon, an adventure hero from the **comic strips**, donned a loin cloth for *Tarzan the Fearless* (1933), a feature made by a small studio, Principal Productions. The same group employed Herman Brix (b. 1909; later known as Bruce Bennett) as the ape man for two additional features, *The New Adventures of Tarzan* (1935) and *Tarzan and the Green Goddess* (1938). Principal Productions also released *Tarzan's Revenge* with Glenn Morris (1912–1974) in 1938. In all, eight different *Tarzan* movies played theaters during the 1930s, and every one found receptive audiences. Cinematic Tarzans did not disappear with the end of the decade; a steady stream of features continued to come out, so that today over 40 Tarzan pictures have been made, with no indication that moviegoers have seen the last of the ape man.

Burroughs had always envisioned Tarzan not just on the screen but on the comic pages as well, and the first such strip finally appeared at the beginning of 1929. An **advertising** illustrator named Harold C. Foster (1892–1982) agreed to try the cartoonist's trade, albeit reluctantly. He excelled at draftsmanship and completed about 10 weeks' worth of dailies, all to high praise. Despite the compliments, Foster returned to his more lucrative advertising accounts, and Rex Maxon (1892–1973) took over as the lead artist on *Tarzan*. Although Maxon worked competently, his drawing did not match the caliber of Foster's. United Features Syndicate added a Sunday page in 1931, and Maxon found himself overwhelmed with both duties. Foster, now suffering the financial effects of the Depression, came back to do Sundays only. In those days, a Sunday strip could occupy a full page, and Foster's work blossomed. He became so admired in the industry that in 1937 King Features, the biggest of the syndicates, lured him away with the promise he could both write and draw a strip of his own. That strip turned out to be **Prince Valiant**, probably the most realistically drawn adventure series of the decade.

With Foster's departure, the *Tarzan* Sunday page then became the property of Burne Hogarth (1911–1996), another talented cartoonist. He dropped some of Foster's realism, replacing it with a flowing, sensual style that emphasized muscles and movement over detail. People liked this new look and Hogarth continued with the series until the 1940s. Maxon, meanwhile, labored on the dailies throughout the decade and, like Hogarth, stayed on board until 1947. A succession of artists drew the strip for the remainder of the century.

Early **comic books**, which consisted of reprints of existing newspaper strips, began using recycled *Tarzan* material in the early 1930s with black-and-white collections. A full-color anthology of the Sunday panels, *Tip-Top Comics*, hit newsstands in 1936. As the sale of comic books burgeoned, *Tarzan* also appeared in several new collections.

In addition to comic strips and comic books, the *Tarzan* imprint could also be found on such items as **Big Little Books**, clothing, **toys**, **jigsaw puzzles**, and even some foods. Starting in 1932, a serialized **radio** version of *Tarzan of the Apes* entertained listeners three times a week; when it ended in 1934, stations commenced broadcasting additional **serials** about the ape man, programming that would carry into 1936.

Clearly, the 1930s was the heyday for Tarzan in all its many formats. Edgar Rice Burroughs had incorporated himself in 1923 to save on taxes and see that users honored his copyrights. As his ventures expanded, the writer exerted strict control over all manifestations of Tarzan and created Burroughs-Tarzan Enterprises in 1934 to protect his holdings. The idea of dropping out of civilization and living in a jungle paradise, even as fantasy, must have held a certain appeal in the turbulent 1930s. In addition, the pure escapism of all the various books, movies, radio serials, and comics provided a momentary respite from reality. Whatever the reasoning, the entire *Tarzan* franchise thrived, far beyond anyone's initial expectations.

See also Best Sellers; *Flash Gordon*; Food; Illustrators; New York World's Fair; Newspapers; Olympic Games; Pulp Magazines

SELECTED READING

Couperie, Pierre, and Maurice C. Horn. *A History of the Comic Strip*. New York: Crown Publishers, 1968.

Holtsmark, Erling B. *Edgar Rice Burroughs*. New York: Twayne, 1986.

Porges, Irwin. *Edgar Rice Burroughs: The Man Who Created Tarzan.* Provo, UT: Brigham Young University Press, 1975.

Robinson, Jerry. *The Comics: An Illustrated History of Comic Strip Art.* New York: G. P. Putnam's Sons, 1974.

TEENAGE & JUVENILE DELINQUENCY FILMS. The owners of movie theaters reported that significant numbers of teenagers came to their establishments during the Depression years. The local movie house functioned as a meeting place away from home, a hangout, a place to go to and kill some empty hours. With opportunities for employment almost nil, teens had unheard-of leisure time. A double feature, short subjects, and a couple of cartoons could take care of another dull afternoon or evening, plus a darkened auditorium proved ideal for some impromptu courtship. The Hollywood studios, always alert to audience trends, often played to this audience after discovering that teenagers and the subject of the adolescent years could be a marketable commodity, and so a new kind of film came into its own.

Movies with young actors have always been popular—many of the silent stars in the early days of the industry fell into the 16 to 21 age bracket. The sound era continued this tradition, capitalizing on the fact of a performer's **youth** and the generational concerns associated with adolescence. In the second half of the decade, Metro-Goldwyn-Mayer (MGM) began to release the Andy Hardy movies, certainly one of the most popular film series of all time, running from 1937 to 1946.

The Hardy saga began with *A Family Affair* (1937), a lighthearted look at small-town America starring Mickey Rooney (b. 1920) as Andy Hardy, the typical American teen, and Lionel Barrymore (1878–1954) as his father, the wise Judge Hardy. This first title proved so unexpectedly successful that the studio quickly followed with *You're Only Young Once* (also 1937), a short titled *Andy Hardy's Dilemma: A Lesson in Mathematics . . . and Other Things* (1938), along with three full-length features in 1938: *Judge Hardy's Children, Love Finds Andy Hardy,* and *Out West with the Hardys.* The pace did not slacken in 1939, and another three tales graced American screens: *The Hardys Ride High, Andy Hardy Gets Spring Fever,* and *Judge Hardy and Son.* Seven more Andy Hardy adventures came out between 1940 and 1946, and it all ended in 1958 with the release of *Andy Hardy Comes Home.*

In 1937's *You're Only Young Once,* veteran actor Lewis Stone (1879–1953) replaced Barrymore, a role he would repeat for the next 14 Andy Hardy stories. The series made Stone one of Hollywood's most beloved Hollywood character players, a fountain of sage advice, a father always there for his naive son. Spring Byington (1886–1971) initially played Hardy's mother, but Fay Holden (1893–1973) took over the role with the second feature and kept it thereafter. In an unusual gesture, the Academy of Motion Picture Arts and Sciences in 1942 awarded a special Academy Award to MGM for the series and how it "furthered the American way of life."

Dated for today's audiences, the Hardy films portray a nation that probably never was, but one that people longed for just the same. The series relentlessly reinforces a small-town mythic America and ignores any unsettling contemporary events. Audiences flocked to these simplistic homilies; they might sugarcoat both past and present, but people did not seem to tire of them.

Mickey Rooney, by virtue of his role as Andy Hardy, came to symbolize the American male teenager, or at least the way millions of anxious parents and politicians wanted to perceive him. But Rooney served to fill only part of the picture; if he epitomized the adolescent boy, then **Judy Garland** (1922–1969), another stock player from the MGM studios, emerged as the model teenage girl. The two made just three films together prior to 1940, *Thoroughbreds Don't Cry* (1937), *Love Finds Andy Hardy* (1938), and *Babes in Arms* (1939), but the chemistry was such that they would be teamed up numerous times in subsequent years. *Babes in Arms*, only loosely based on the Broadway musical of the same name by **Richard Rodgers** (1902–1979) **and Lorenz Hart** (1895–1943), was a big hit, and its success made Rooney the top male box-office star for 1939, something he would repeat in 1940 and 1941.

For her part, Judy Garland went on to portray Dorothy in the smash **Wizard of Oz** (1939), a role that allowed her to exude a healthy innocence that doubtlessly reassured the parents of teenage daughters across the land. Actually, the role of Dorothy called for someone younger than Garland, by then a 17-year-old who looked it. MGM had previously offered the part to **Shirley Temple** (b. 1928), who fit the age requirements, but her studio, 20th Century Fox, would not allow it. Thus Garland got her star turn and made the most of it.

With attendance at movies starring adolescent actors soaring, Hollywood quickly brought new releases to the screen with new, fresh young faces in the leads. Performers such as the Pollyanna-like Deanna Durbin (b. 1921; *Three Smart Girls*, 1936; *One Hundred Men and a Girl*, 1937; *That Certain Age*, 1938; *It's a Date*, 1939; *Three Smart Girls Grow Up*, 1939; and others) soon had top billing in one feature after another. Such was Durbin's regard in Hollywood, the Motion Picture Academy of Arts and Sciences gave her a special Academy Award, along with Mickey Rooney, for their "personification of **youth**" in 1938.

But teenagers did not attract attention only in movies. In 1930, the Stratemeyer Syndicate, a publishing phenomenon created by Edward Stratemeyer (1862–1930), a pioneer in the production and promotion of series fiction for adolescents, released a novel called *The Secret of the Old Clock*. A young woman named Nancy Drew serves as the main character, and the book became a classic for adolescent girls around the country. That title would turn out to be but the first in one of the longest-lasting, best-selling series in American literature. Mildred Wirt Benson (1905–2002) anonymously penned most of the early stories, writing under the pseudonym of Carolyn Keene, the same name that all successive Nancy Drew ghost authors would employ.

Hollywood attempted to adapt the enormously successful tales for film, although it took almost a decade for them to make the transition. In four pictures in two years, 1938–1939, director William Clemens (1905–1980) chronicled the adventures of the teenage detective. Bonita Granville (1923–1988), a veteran of over a dozen **children's films**, portrayed the fictional Nancy Drew in all four, starting with *Nancy Drew—Detective* (1938) and concluding with *Nancy Drew and the Hidden Staircase* (1939). Her spunky character solves crimes, appears independent of adult authority, can do much as she pleases, and depicts a modern, self-reliant young woman. With that combination, she appealed to countless girls who would have liked to emulate her if they could. And, with teenage films riding high at the time, the Nancy Drew stories proved a success.

By the end of the decade, the major studios had stables of promising players who acted out the trials and tribulations of teenage love and romance in one forgettable film after another that nonetheless demonstrated the strength and profitability of the youth market. Along with the good teenagers, however, Hollywood also occasionally portrayed a "bad" variety, ranging from misunderstood young people who occasionally ran afoul of society's mores to reprehensible no-goods—losers—lacking in any conscience.

In order to describe a young person gone wrong, the twentieth century invented the term "juvenile delinquent." In earlier times, the age of a lawbreaker mattered little; a **crime** begot punishment. Reform schools for wayward youth came into being during the nineteenth century, but their existence hardly served as an acknowledgment of juvenile delinquency. In the 1920s, a handful of movies came out that depicted "roaring youth"—smoking, drinking, dancing—but most crime pictures focused on adults, not teenagers. *Our Dancing Daughters* (1928) helped pave the way to stardom for Joan Crawford (1904–1977), and it depicted flappers in all their glory, but it focuses on youthful high jinks, not on criminal activities

With the onset of the 1930s, however, several up-and-coming actors built careers depicting lives of crime. James Cagney (1899–1986) stunned audiences with his performance in *Public Enemy* (1931), in which he portrays an amoral gangster. Not a teenager in 1931, he nonetheless brought a youthful vitality to his role, and much of the picture shows him as a younger character. Cagney personified many of the fears people felt about the lawlessness then gaining headlines. With his cock-of-the-walk air, he made the ideal Depression antihero, somebody who thumbs his nose at all authority. Since the period marked the heyday of **gangster films**, Cagney would reprise his role many times (*Blonde Crazy* [1931], *Hard to Handle* [1933], *The Mayor of Hell* [1933], others), always the wiseacre, always scheming.

More often than not, the bad eggs either died, often violently, or were sent off to prison or reform school. Some of those who got into trouble found redemption with an understanding adult male or the love of a good teenage girl—a "good woman" would be too sexually threatening in those strict **Hollywood Production Code** days. *Wild Boys of the Road* (1933) serves as an example of the evolving genre of films about young men in trouble. It stars Frankie Darro (1917–1976), an actor, forgotten today, who made his name in this kind of picture. Using the worst conditions spawned by the Depression, it tells of homeless gangs living in utter poverty. The movie raises the question, if things don't get better, what will happen?

What happened, in the movie industry, at least, was a succession of pictures that purport to show juvenile delinquency as a new national concern. Virtually all these films take place in slums, the inner city, and they equate crime with poverty. The "good" young people, the Mickey Rooneys and Judy Garlands, live in more affluent surroundings. Seldom do the scripts employ the words "teenager" or "teen"; those terms did not come into common parlance until after World War II.

For many people, one picture in particular gives the best dramatization of the questions about environment and juvenile delinquency: *Dead End* (1937). Both a box office and critical success, the movie adapts playwright Sidney Kingsley's (1906–1995) theatrical hit, a play that ran for 700 Broadway performances between 1935 and 1937. The film version stars Humphrey Bogart (1899–1957) as an adult gangster who has returned to his old slum neighborhood; it costars Joel McCrea (1905–1990) as Bogart's good brother who wants positive change. The plot argues for the primacy of environment in shaping the lives of young people. As an added bonus, *Dead End* marks the cinematic debut of the so-called Dead End Kids, a group of six young actors, Leo Gorcey (1917–1969), Huntz Hall (1919–1999), Billy Halop (1920–1976), Bobby Jordan (1923–1965), Bernard Punsly (1923–2004), and Gabriel Dell (1919–1988), who had appeared in the stage version. They portray every shade of youthful hoodlum.

With success under their belts, the Dead End Kids left Broadway behind, changed studios, and became stars in their own right, cranking out a series of features—*Angels with Dirty Faces* (1938; it costars James Cagney and Humphrey Bogart), *Crime School* (1938; Bogart returns to this feature), *Hell's Kitchen* (1939; it costars a young actor named Ronald Reagan [1911–2004]), *Angels Wash Their Faces* (1939; Reagan makes an encore appearance), *They Made Me a Criminal* (1939), and *The Dead End Kids on Dress Parade* (1939). The group then moved over to Monogram Studios in 1939 and became the East Side Kids. Later on, they would become the Bowery Boys, but the slapstick and wisecracks changed little. Their pictures depicted crime and despair at first, but quickly degenerated into physical comedy, with the implicit message that audiences should not take them seriously.

The late 1930s mark the heyday of the juvenile delinquency film. The chronological list below suggests some of the many other titles coming out of Hollywood during this period:

Boys Town (1938)
Reformatory (1938)
Rebellious Daughters (1938)
Delinquent Parents (1938)
Little Tough Guy (1938)
This Day and Age (1938)
Juvenile Court (1938)
Girls on Probation (1939)
You Can't Get Away with Murder (1939)
Boy's Reformatory (1939)

The threat of war and the lessening of the worst aspects of the Depression turned people's attention away from this genre of picture. The "good" teen who would soon be marching off to war, coupled with increasing prosperity, made the gritty realism of many such pictures less relevant, although the theme of juvenile delinquency has resurfaced periodically on movie screens, especially during the 1950s. Cinematically, the 1930s mark the discovery of the American teenager as a profitable category of film. The Hollywood studios rushed into production countless movies that displayed "that awkward age" and in the process helped define teenage behavior for audiences around the country. For good or for ill, this influx of pictures influenced both young and old.

See also Best Sellers; Federal Bureau of Investigation; Leisure & Recreation; Musicals; Social Consciousness Films; Stage Productions

SELECTED READING
Elder, Glen H., Jr. *Children of the Great Depression*. Chicago: University of Chicago Press, 1974.
Jackson, Kathy Merlock. *Images of Children in American Film*. Metuchen, NJ: Scarecrow Press, 1986.

McGee, Mark Thomas, and R. J. Robertson. *The J.D. Films: Juvenile Delinquency in the Movies.* Jefferson, NC: McFarland & Co., 1982.

Palladino, Grace. *Teenagers: An American History.* New York: Basic Books, 1996.

TELEVISION. Scientists and engineers had long dreamed of transmitting electronic pictures directly into residences or businesses years before concept became reality. What had been the province of **science fiction** writers shifted as wireless communication evolved into **radio**. By the late 1920s, with radio receivers already in many homes, people knew that in a matter of time images would be added to sound.

Although crude pictures had been transmitted over telegraph lines in the nineteenth century, it took twentieth-century inventors and technicians, laboring in laboratories large and small, to refine those first steps and eliminate the need for connecting wires. In the United States, Philo Farnsworth (1906–1971) and Vladimir Zworykin (1889–1982), working independently of one another, developed much of the technology that made modern television possible. In England, John Logie Baird (1888–1946), a Scottish electrical engineer, transmitted the first discernable moving image in 1925; the following year, crowds in a London department store saw similar images in a display that Baird had put together. Not to be outdone, American engineers sent wireless pictures from Washington, D.C., to New York City in 1927, and the General Electric Company devised a home television receiver with a 3-inch screen in 1928. The company's radio station, WGY in Schenectady, New York, agreed to transmit television signals and commenced doing so in the spring of 1928. The only recipients of these pioneering broadcasts consisted of General Electric engineers who had company receivers on loan, but the stage had been set.

In 1929, the Bell Telephone Company gave a demonstration of color television—still images, but color nonetheless. The stock market crash in October put many developments on hold, but some research continued. Throughout the 1930s, engineers strove mightily to make television a reality for American consumers. Everyone knew the technical problems associated with the medium would eventually be ironed out; it just became a question of when.

David Sarnoff (1891–1971), the general manager of the Radio Corporation of America (RCA), and his team of scientists led the move to get television into American homes—and to do so profitably for the firm. He had distinguished himself with RCA by establishing the first radio network, the National Broadcasting Company (NBC radio), and he helped popularize the word "television"—the ability to meld sound and image and transmit the result over great distances.

The continuing popularity and profitability of radio dissuaded sustained efforts at any commercial exploitation of television during the Depression era. Despite the obstacles, in 1930 NBC gained permission to operate W2XBS (the predecessor of today's WNBC) in New York City; the following year found the rival Columbia Broadcasting System (CBS radio) operating W2XAB (today's WCBS), also out of New York. The two rivals used movie theaters as venues and hired popular radio and vaudeville personalities as hosts to promote their new technologies, presaging the entertainment function that television would eventually fill so well.

In the summer of 1936, employing space atop the **Empire State Building**, with a handful of bulky receiving sets and an invitation-only group of about 200 people as witnesses, NBC television went on the air. A pretty limited affair—David Sarnoff appeared on screen, as did some radio personalities, along with a few models and other entertainers—but those in attendance sensed the importance of this event.

In 1937, NBC equipped a truck with a mobile television transmitter; it cruised the streets of New York and broadcast signals of things the crew found interesting. The following year saw the live television performance of *Susan and Gold*, an ongoing Broadway play. Although only a few thousand receivers existed, with virtually all of them concentrated in metropolitan New York, these events presaged things to come.

Allen B. DuMont (1901–1965), another radio pioneer, developed an interest in television in the late 1920s. A supporter of the concept of home television reception, as opposed to theatrical presentation, he demonstrated his ideas in 1930 by broadcasting images to specially equipped New York offices and hotel rooms. His efforts drew little attention, but they prompted him to create a small manufacturing firm with the express aim of providing television sets to the consumer market. His company's Model 180, the Clifton, went on sale in 1938, making it the first commercially available television set. It featured a huge—for its time—14-inch screen and its release compelled RCA to bring out sets of its own in order to compete. Had World War II not intervened, DuMont might have become more of a force in this new market; as it was, he created the DuMont Television Network at the war's end and battled the established networks for a decade before throwing in the towel.

The leading name in television at the end of the 1930s, however, remained NBC. The network telecast shows from the stage of Radio City Music Hall, and mobile units covered several sporting events in the New York area, including the first-ever televised **baseball** game. At a May 1939 contest between Columbia University and Princeton, announcer Bill Stern (1907–1971) gave the play-by-play. They televised the annual Macy's Thanksgiving Parade for the first time in 1939.

NBC made its biggest public splash at the **New York World's Fair**, which opened in April 1939. There the network introduced television to a mass audience. Using the RCA Pavilion, one of the exposition's most popular exhibits, NBC featured continuous telecasting of proceedings at the fair that played on banks of receivers with 5-inch, 9-inch, and 12-inch screens. People flocked to see these early sets, and RCA promoted their sale. Prices ranged from $199.50 (roughly $2,800 in contemporary dollars) for a basic receiver to $600 (about $8,400 today) for a deluxe model. During the 1939–1940 run of the fair, historians estimate that consumers bought slightly over 120 of RCA's model TRK 660 receiver.

President **Franklin D. Roosevelt** (1882–1945) attended the dedication ceremony of the RCA Pavilion. Naturally, television crews included him in their telecasts, the first head of state ever seen on the new medium. Shortly thereafter, the king and queen of England also appeared at the fair, both in person and on screen. Wherever a visitor turned, he or she probably encountered television. In addition to RCA and NBC, Ford, Westinghouse, and General Electric also sponsored displays of working receivers. Allan DuMont, also in attendance, used the smaller Crosley Appliance building to show off his sets. The future of television seemed clear: it would emerge as a new entertainment medium. Only the outbreak of World War II prevented its immediate, widespread adoption.

See also Radio Networks; Rockefeller Center; Soap Operas; Western Films

SELECTED READING

Barnouw, Erik. *Tube of Plenty: The Evolution of American Television*. New York: Oxford University Press, 1982.

Fisher, David E., and Marshall J. Fisher. *Tube: The Invention of Television*. Washington, DC: Counterpoint, 1996.

Settel, Irving, and William Laas. *A Pictorial History of Television*. New York: Grosset & Dunlap, 1969.

TEMPLE, SHIRLEY. The most famous child star in movie history and one of the youngest people ever to grace the cover of *Time* magazine (April 27, 1936), Shirley Temple (b. 1928) set records throughout her early years. When only three, she appeared in "Baby Burlesks," low-budget short movies that featured children parodying adults. By age five she had advanced to legitimate acting and attained fame with a featured role in *Stand Up and Cheer* (1934). In quick succession, she starred in *Little Miss Marker* (1934), *Now and Forever* (1934), and *Bright Eyes* (1934), in which she sang "On the Good Ship Lollipop," featuring music by Richard A. Whiting (1891–1938) and lyrics by Sidney Clare (1892–1972). The tune has since then been associated with her.

Between 1934 and 1939, Temple took top billing in 13 films, with four of her most memorable roles occurring in 1935—*The Little Colonel, Our Little Girl, Curly Top*, and *The Littlest Rebel*. In *The Little Colonel*, a civil war drama with **music**, she broke racial barriers by appearing with Bill "Bojangles" Robinson (1878–1949), a famous black entertainer. Temple proved herself an accomplished dancer and a spunky one as well. When the studio would allow it, she preferred to do her own stunts. Immensely talented, she quickly became the most popular movie star of the era. In 1938, Shirley Temple, nicknamed both "Dimples" and "Curly Head," reigned as the biggest box office draw for the year. Her fan mail averaged 60,000 letters a month.

As a popular, busy performer, she met and worked with famous Hollywood celebrities. She costarred with Carole Lombard (1908–1942) and Gary Cooper (1901–1961) in *Now and Forever*, Cesar Romero (1907–1994) in *Wee Willie Winkie* (1937), and Randolph Scott (1898–1987) in *Rebecca of Sunnybrook Farm* (1938). She claimed **Amelia Earhart** (1897–1937) and **Eleanor Roosevelt** (1884–1962) as her heroines, and the first lady even visited her on a film set. As did all visitors, she departed sporting a Shirley Temple police badge.

Along with her film career, Temple also served as the inspiration for a wide range of mass-produced records, books, watches, playthings, and clothes. Shirley Temple dolls, a particularly popular item, had sales of 1.5 million miniature Shirleys in 1933 alone. The dolls came in many sizes, costumes, and prices; collectors even considered the boxes holding them valuable artifacts. Her income from endorsing these items soon exceeded anything that 20th Century Fox paid her.

This remarkable child influenced contemporary **fashion**, film, and beverage preferences. In 1935, the Sears, Roebuck and Company catalog presented a complete Shirley Temple wardrobe of hats, dresses, snow suits, and hair bows for children. The most elaborate little girl's hairstyle in the 1930s came from an image of Shirley Temple. Her ringlets served as the norm not only for her dolls but also for any little girl's dress-up style as well. Both children and adults, when eating out, might order a Shirley Temple, a sweet,

Shirley Temple (b. 1928) with entertainer Eddie Cantor (1892–1964) at a March of Dimes fund-raiser. (Courtesy of the Library of Congress)

nonalcoholic drink invented in 1936 by the bartender at Hollywood's Chasen's Restaurant (1936–1995), a favorite ribs and chili bar of the stars.

It has been reported that photographers took more pictures of Shirley Temple than they did of President **Franklin D. Roosevelt**. He publicly praised her infectious optimism, a persona perfect for the Depression years, and one that she sustained in her films. On screen, filled with a mix of self-reliance and innocence, she guides adults through a threatening world while at the same time relying on their love and wisdom. She usually plays an orphan, but sometimes an heiress; either way, she always comes across as honest and fair in all her dealings and offers both hope and entertainment to the audience. Her character radiates wholesomeness and—most importantly—shows how to right a world gone askew. Shirley Temple's angelic looks and good humor uplifted millions, young and old, throughout the 1930s.

See also Children's Films; Magazines; Musicals; Photography; Race Relations & Stereotyping; Soft Drinks; Toys

SELECTED READING
Elder, Glen H., Jr. *Children of the Great Depression*. Chicago: University of Chicago Press, 1974.
Jackson, Kathy Merlock. *Images of Children in American Film*. Metuchen, NJ: Scarecrow Press, 1986.
Zierold, Jack J. *The Child Stars*. New York: Coward-McCann, 1965.

TENNIS. Like **horse racing** and **golf**, tennis suffered from a problem of perception. Although estimates have some 3 or 4 million Americans playing the game during the 1930s, many nonparticipants saw it as an activity for a wealthy, leisured class. Most urban areas nonetheless provided courts at parks and school grounds, and the **New Deal**, working through agencies like the Works Progress Administration (WPA, 1935–1943; name changed to Work Projects Administration in 1939), assisted in the construction of new facilities.

Not only did the activity want for large numbers of participants, it also lacked much of a following as a spectator sport. Helen Wills Moody (1905–1998), a favorite with those few fans devoted to the game, dominated women's tennis, particularly during the 1930s. Nicknamed "Little Miss Poker Face" for her nonemotional court style, she retired from tournament play in 1938. "Big" Bill Tilden (1893–1953), the leading male player of the later 1920s, gave up his amateur standing in 1931 and turned professional, a move that took him out of the public eye. In those days, as far as the public and tennis officialdom were concerned, amateurs dominated the sport. All the major tournaments barred professional players, making them virtually invisible. Given its aristocratic background, many people felt tennis carried a gentlemanly mantle with it; from dress to court behavior, they expected a certain level of decorum. Playing for pay detracted from that aura and therefore should be avoided.

Moody's retirement dampened interest in women's tennis, and Tilden's departure from the amateur ranks relegated the game to the back pages of the sports sections of **newspapers**. Not until 1938 did men's tennis enjoy any real revival. That marked the year amateur Don Budge (1915–2000) achieved the grand slam of tennis by winning the Australian, French, Wimbledon, and U.S. Open tournaments. As the first player ever to do it, the sports media rewarded him with a torrent of publicity. Ever so briefly, tennis reappeared on the front pages. But Budge turned pro shortly thereafter, and, like Tilden before him, disappeared from public view. It would be many years before tennis—professional or amateur, women's or men's—again attracted a large following.

Tennis club. (Courtesy of the Library of Congress)

Even the **movies** ignored the game. Cameramen found tennis difficult to film effectively, and so the list of titles is disappointingly small. *Love, Honor, and Behave* (1938) has a tennis player, portrayed by actor Wayne Morris (1914–1959), as the lead, but the game itself gets lost in the romantic aspects of the story. Beyond that, most references to tennis involve people carrying rackets and sipping drinks, usually at some posh country club, a reinforcement of the perception of wealth that surrounded the game.

See also Fashion

SELECTED READING
Grimsley, Will. *Tennis: Its History, People, and Events.* Englewood Cliffs, NJ: Prentice-Hall, 1971.
Rader, Benjamin G. *American Sports: From the Age of Folk Games to the Age of Televised Sports.* 3rd ed. Englewood Cliffs, NJ: Prentice-Hall, 1996.

TERRY AND THE PIRATES. A popular adventure comic strip, *Terry and the Pirates* attracted a wide audience with its youthful hero and fast-paced stories. Conceived, drawn, and written by Milton Caniff (1907–1988), the series began in the fall of 1934; despite a crowded field, it quickly set itself apart from the competition. After a change of artists in 1946, the strip would run until 1973.

Caniff entered the world of **comic strips**, as did many of his colleagues, first by drawing panel cartoons and then graduating to series work. He could count the now-forgotten *Puffy the Pig* and *The Gay Thirties*, both drawn in the period 1932–1934, as part of that apprenticeship. In the summer of 1933, while working for the Associated Press, he created *Dickie Dare*, the prototype for the later *Terry*. Awkward in its drawing and pedestrian in its plotting, *Dickie Dare* first told the story of a boy, about 12 or 13 years old, dreamily enjoying adventures out of storybooks he had read. Seeing that such an approach went nowhere, Caniff introduced "Dynamite" Dan Flynn, a handsome, 30-ish male who gets Dickie into and out of dangerous situations. He still had not arrived at his desired formula, but the revised version held potential for greater success.

As Caniff struggled with *Dickie Dare*, his work caught the eye of Captain James Medill Patterson (1879–1946), owner of the News-Tribune Syndicate, and a man who helped many comic strips achieve success. He urged the cartoonist to leave the Associated Press and create a new series for the News-Tribune group. Caniff submitted a proposal for *Tommy Tucker*, essentially an extension of *Dickie Dare*; Patterson responded by suggesting a new title—*Terry and the Pirates*— and a more exotic locale, the Far East.

Those changes in place, *Terry and the Pirates* debuted in October 1934. At first, the drawings themselves still looked like frames from *Dickie Dare*, but Caniff evolved into a far more sophisticated illustrator. He shared studio space with another cartoonist, Noel Sickles (1910–1982). At that time, Sickles drew an **aviation** strip called *Scorchy Smith* that he had taken over late in 1933. The two artists jointly experimented with aesthetic approaches to the cartoon medium. From simple line drawings, they moved toward the freer use of brushed-in ink areas, blocks of black that gave their work a distinctive chiaroscuro effect. This use of shadow added to suspense and heightened story lines, and within a short time *Terry* began to separate itself from most other action-adventure series of the era.

Terry Lee, who had started his cartoon life looking remarkably like Dickie Dare, takes on his own traits, and by the end of the decade has grown into a young man capable of independent action. Initially he has Jack Ryan, who stands in for and resembles Dan Flynn, as an adult sidekick, but Ryan's role diminishes as Terry's increases. For comic relief, George Webster "Connie" Confucius plays a stereotypical Chinese, dressing oddly, speaking in strange aphorisms, and butchering the language. In the mid-1930s, however, such demeaning characterizations of racial minorities, especially Asians, appeared in many comic strips and no one voiced complaints. The old image of "the Yellow Peril" had not died out, and variants abounded, from the good detective Charlie Chan to the villainous Fu Manchu.

Terry and the Pirates broke new ground for newspaper comics in a variety of ways. Milton Caniff discovered he had a gift for rapid-fire, snappy dialogue, which allowed him to place wisecracks and one-liners throughout the speech balloons. No matter how desperate the situation, someone will utter a flippant remark at the height of the tension. *Terry* never ceases being an action strip, but one with a humorous edge, as a rule. Caniff also found he had a flair for drawing beautiful, sensuous women, and never more so than in his seductive Dragon Lady. This reappearing character plays a femme fatale, and she plays it to the hilt. Readers might never be sure whose side this temptress takes, but they know she will lead most of the male characters to no good. Even innocent Terry occasionally falls into her clutches, but she usually takes sympathy on him, even going so far as to teach him to dance in one episode. With her presence, sex entered the usually sexless comics.

Other media soon became aware of this innovative strip. The late afternoon **serials** on **radio** already had *Jack Armstrong, the All-American Boy* (1933–1951), featuring the adventures of a precocious high school teen and his pals. The National Broadcasting Company (NBC radio) network brought *Terry and the Pirates* to the airwaves in his own afternoon show; it would survive, off and on, until 1948. But the adult dialogue and plot lines of the strip never transferred successfully over to radio, and Terry Lee seemed more an imitation of Jack Armstrong. A subpar movie serial came off the Hollywood back lots in 1940. Made on the cheap, it shared little more than its title with the comic strip. The innumerable **Big Little Books** also borrowed episodes, but these usually consisted of newspaper reprints, so little violence occurred to any of the basic concepts.

As the 1930s progressed, the Far Eastern locale that Captain Patterson had presciently suggested became the focus of considerable attention. In 1931, Japan had invaded Manchuria (later Manchukuo), a move that led to the Second Sino-Japanese War and Japanese military operations against China. By late in the decade, full-scale warfare engulfed the region, events not unnoticed in *Terry and the Pirates*. American neutrality and a natural reticence in the "funny pages" did not allow for overt political commentary. Lest he be accused of warmongering, Caniff compromised and showed China at war, but called the Japanese "the invaders," although it is doubtful the ruse fooled many people. The "pirates," usually bandits, evil warlords, or rogue military units, of the title disappear, and *Terry and the Pirates* moves resolutely into the impending shadows of World War II. Almost alone among American comic strips of the later 1930s, it talks openly about war and loyalties and responsibilities. When the United State finally enters the Second World War, Terry Lee promptly joins the U.S. Army Air Force and stands poised to fight—no nameless enemies anymore, no "invaders," but the Axis powers—and *Terry and the Pirates* emerged as one of the most earnest and patriotic of all comic strips.

See also *The Gumps*; Illustrators; Movies; Newspapers; Race Relations & Stereotyping; Youth

SELECTED READING

Goulart, Ron. *The Adventurous Decade: Comic Strips in the Thirties*. New Rochelle, NY: Arlington House, 1975.

Tucker, Michael. "The Dragon Lady's Well-Favoured Children: The Transition from Corporatist to Individualist in Comic Strips of 1930s." http://etc.dal.ca/belphegor/vol4_no1/articles

Walker, Brian. *The Comics before 1945*. New York: Harry N. Abrams, 2004.

TOYS. From 1930 until 1933, sales for the toy industry fell, a reflection of reduced consumer spending. Shoppers continued to acquire low- and medium-price playthings, causing overall revenues to decline since customers purchased fewer expensive ones. In time, production slowed and some manufacturers went out of business. Industry leaders urged strategic changes in marketing and suggested discontinuing the traditional November and December seasonal approach to sales. Instead, they pushed for year-round promotion. Some companies heeded the recommendation and it helped.

While a number of firms struggled, a few thrived. The venerable Holgate Toy Company, which traces its history back to 1789, along with the Playskool Manufacturing Company, established in 1928, and Fisher-Price, which incorporated in 1930, successfully researched and developed wooden educational toys for preschool children throughout the decade. Holgate, led by toy designer Jarvis Rockwell (active 1920s–1950s), brother of famed illustrator **Norman Rockwell** (1894–1978), manufactured the successful Bingo Bed (1934). It offered children a small bench, or "bed," along with eight pegs and a small hammer. The company profited from the Rocky Color Cone, six colorful rings stacked on a rocking cone, and Playskool produced a hammer and peg table set, a basic toy for very young children that taught hand-eye coordination.

Fisher-Price, on the other hand, started with wooden pull toys—two ducks and a black and white dog. Granny Doodle (1931) waddled, bobbed her head, opened and closed her bill, and quacked. A 1932 adaptation, Granny Doodle & Family, employed the same features but added two baby ducks. Dr. Doodle (1931), yet another duck, quacked as he strutted along, neck rising and falling, bill opening and closing. Each of these toys had an original retail price of $1 (roughly $14.75 in contemporary dollars). The company's toy dog, Snoopy Sniffer, introduced in 1938, exceeded sales expectations and the company had difficulty keeping up with orders. Fisher-Price established a child research center in the 1930s and eventually created over 5,000 different toys for children up to five years of age.

Despite the educational value found in some toys, many people voiced concern about their safety. In the early 1930s, toy manufacturers formed a Safety Standards Committee that created the industry's first voluntary guidelines. This committee cooperated with the National Safety Council, an alliance that led to the formation of a national accident reporting service and a clearinghouse for toy injuries.

As manufacturers became more aware of safety, they took advantage of the business downturn caused by the Depression. Lumber, steel, and textile mills struggling to stay in business during the crisis eagerly accepted new customers. As a result, American toy companies stopped using auto scrap or inferior wood for their products and switched to top-grade components, a move that improved the overall quality and safety of American-made toys.

The changes in standards and construction materials could not, however, stop a flood of shoddy, foreign-made toys from entering the American market. Celluloid, a cheap, highly flammable substance once used in the making of motion picture film and shirt collars, and easily molded into any shape, served as the basis for baby rattles, Ping-Pong balls, and innumerable other toys throughout the 1930s. Japan became the world's leading exporter of inexpensive celluloid items, and Japanese companies mass-produced thousands of replicas of American comic strip characters, sports heroes, and movie stars.

Miniature tin and lead soldiers also enjoyed great popularity for boys at this time. In 1934, the Barclay Manufacturing Company emerged as the largest manufacturer of toy soldiers, producing nearly 500,000 soldiers, vehicles, airplanes, and other related items every week. Available at five-and-dime stores, these toy soldiers sold for a penny apiece (about 15 cents in contemporary money), making them easily affordable by most children. Despite the company's success during the 1930s, Barclay went out of business in 1971, a victim of the restrictions placed on the lead found in toys and other products.

While boys played with soldiers, girls entertained themselves with dolls. The doll industry struggled during the Depression years, but popular culture connections kept some companies solvent. In 1932, Effanbee Doll Company introduced the Patsy Doll Club as a marketing strategy. The club invited dolls, not their owners, to join and at its peak boasted 270,000 "members." Effanbee's Dy-Dee Baby and Ideal's Betsy Wetsy of 1934, facsimiles of real babies, required a mother's care for feeding and diapering. The Ideal Novelty and Toy Company in 1934 sold 1.5 million dolls fashioned after the popular child star **Shirley Temple** (b. 1928), and by 1935 Shirley Temple replicas of one kind or another accounted for almost one-third of all doll sales. In 1939, the Ideal Company added another item to its catalog based on a popular youthful movie star, its first **Judy Garland** (1922–1969) model.

The **movies** provided toymakers many other big sellers. **Walt Disney** (1901–1966) Studio characters, especially Mickey Mouse, served as models for stuffed dolls and other playthings; over 15 different Mickey Mouse toys came out in 1931 alone. By 1935, Mickey, along with Minnie, Donald Duck, Pluto, Goofy, the Three Little Pigs, and the Big Bad Wolf, made up the bulk of Disney's toy sales. The box office success of 1937's *Snow White and the Seven Dwarfs* added eight more characters to the toy world. In 1938, Macy's Department Store in New York City offered an in-store staged marionette production of the popular movie for children—five performances every day over a period of weeks.

Paper dolls, a mass-produced item in the United States since the early 1800s, afforded girls considerable pleasure. They appeared in *Jack and Jill Magazine*, a periodical published especially for children, and *Good Housekeeping* featured a series titled "Polly and Peter Perkin." Some see the 1930s as the beginning of a golden age of paper dolls with celebrities and movie stars serving as models. Fun for children, paper dolls conveyed the latest fashions and served as valuable teaching aids.

During the darkest days of the Depression, not all families could buy toys and many children, often with the help of their parents, constructed homemade toys from plans printed in **magazines** or **newspapers**. Some families created their own designs. Empty tin cans, baling wire, orange crates, rope, wooden spools, rubber bands, discarded tires, odd screws and nails, and countless other found objects allowed an imaginative child to build just about anything. Rubber-band guns, paper airplanes, whirligigs from jar lids, comb-and-paper kazoos, grass-blade violins, cigar-box banjos, and tin-can telephones rivaled many commercial toys.

Popular **radio** shows presented another source for inexpensive toys. Many programs, such as *Tom Mix*, **Little Orphan Annie**, *The Lone Ranger*, and *Jack Armstrong, the All-American Boy*, offered premiums like decoder rings, badges, and assorted trinkets that either came in a sponsor's box of cereal or were mailed upon receipt of proofs of purchase. Ventriloquist Edgar Bergen (1903–1978), along with Charlie McCarthy, his popular dummy, first appeared on National Broadcasting Company (NBC radio) affiliate stations in 1937. Soon thereafter, Charlie McCarthy, the real "star" of the act, became available in a myriad of promotional products. Wooden dolls, of course, led the lineup, but tin windup figures, radio sets (a reminder to listen to the show), costumes cut like Charlie's outfits, and playing cards bearing his picture also enjoyed considerable popularity. Finally, in an effort at crossover marketing, a child's book titled *Charlie McCarthy Meets Snow White* appeared on the market shortly after the movie's release.

Characters from newspaper **comic strips** like *Popeye* and *Buck Rogers* likewise inspired the creation of several toys. Popeye himself could be found as a doll, and in windup form he appeared as Popeye in a Rowboat, Popeye Express, Popeye Puncher, and Popeye the Pilot. The Buck Rogers Chemical Laboratory came out in 1937. The stalwart spaceman's likeness emblazoned a number of windup models that included a rocket ship, and he spawned a line of futuristic space pistols in 1934 from the Daisy Air Rifle Company. Daisy also manufactured BB guns that resembled Old West carbines found in another comic strip, Fred Harmon's (1902–1982) widely syndicated *Red Ryder*. **Flash Gordon**, **Blondie**, and **Dick Tracy** likewise made it to the toy world, as did **Superman**, the hero of many **comic books** in the late 1930s.

Some of the toys requested by children reflected grownup life and mimicked housekeeping tasks and adult jobs. Examples included miniature kitchen stoves, tea sets, tiny kitchen utensils, vacuum cleaners, and washing machines, miniature equipment and machines representing trades from baking to building. Children could undertake construction projects such as erecting their own skyscrapers or add-a-room doll houses. Garage and farm sets did well, and toy **trains** and **automobiles** broke playroom speed records.

Wooden wagons, available long before the 1930s, continued as a popular item. Radio Steel and Manufacturing Company, founded in 1923 and previously known as the Liberty Coaster Company, in 1930 daily produced more than 1,500 red steel wagons called Radio Flyers. The company constructed a 45-foot-tall display of Coaster Boy astride his Radio Flyer for Chicago's 1933–1934 **Century of Progress Exposition**. The model announced the wagon's popularity to all who passed by. Inside, a showroom featured the latest Radio Flyer products and visitors could buy a miniature wagon for 25 cents (about $3.75 in contemporary dollars). In the mid-1930s, Radio Steel expanded its line by introducing the Streak-o-Lite, a sleek coaster wagon with control dials and working headlights inspired by the Zephyr Streamlined locomotive. A few years later, the company introduced the Zep, a wagon with the flowing lines and fenders of a Chrysler Airflow, the nation's first Streamlined car.

Toy electric trains and track layouts had been introduced by the Lionel Manufacturing Company in 1900. The business boomed in the 1920s, but factory orders bottomed out by 1930 and the company flirted with bankruptcy. Expensive by any standard, many of their trains cost the same as a three-piece bedroom set or a used Model T automobile and thus did not sell. In an attempt to save the business, Lionel introduced a line of less costly electric train sets under the brand name of Winner Toy Corporation from 1930 to 1932. The starting price for a set was $3.25, including a transformer (about $43.00 in contemporary dollars).

Still struggling, Lionel's business rebounded when in 1934 it manufactured an authentic scale model of Union Pacific's The City of Salina, one of the early Streamliners. A second railroad-oriented item, a Mickey and Minnie Mouse windup hand car, proved even more successful and Lionel had difficulty meeting demand. In 1935, they expanded their products to include a large array of switches and transformers to operate bridges and cranes, load and unload freight cars, and uncouple units. Passenger coaches, complete with interior illumination, included Pullman cars with made-up berths, diners with auxiliary kitchens, club cars, and day coaches. Their freight trains, equally realistic, featured tank cars, flat cars loaded with lumber cut to scale, and coal, refrigerator, and cattle cars. In 1935, model trains boasted whistles, a final touch that completed the realistic effect.

Lionel introduced another highly successful toy during the mid-1930s, an electric airplane connected to a tower. In response to the heightened interest in **aviation**, it revolved around the tower and could perform maneuvers. The company also continued to produce its traditional locomotives and the decade ended with Lionel Corporation again on solid financial ground.

Lionel did not stand alone when it came to manufacturing electric trains. American Flyer, formed in 1907, introduced its first electric train in 1914, but struggled during and after the Depression. A. C. Gilbert, founded in 1909 and known as a manufacturer of supplies for magicians, as well as Erector Sets and toy microscopes, bought American Flyer in 1938 and competed directly with Lionel.

The yo-yo entered the American marketplace in 1929 when it went into mass-production under the guidance of Donald F. Duncan, Sr. (1899–1971). Together with Pedro Flores (active 1920s–1930s), another entrepreneur, they promoted the toy by sending out hundreds of "yo-yo men," usually Filipino nationals, who traveled the country demonstrating yo-yo tricks. Duncan even managed to make a deal with the Hearst chain of newspapers for free **advertising**. In exchange, he organized competitions in which the entrants were required to bring a certain number of new newspaper subscriptions as their entry fee. These ploys generated strong sales; celebrities could be seen with yo-yos, and several popular songs, some of them a bit risqué, celebrated the simple but clever toy.

See also Design; Education; Fashion; Illustrators; Streamlining

SELECTED READING

Cross, Gary. *Kids' Stuff: Toys and the Changing World of American Childhood.* Cambridge, MA: Harvard University Press, 1997.

Fisher-Price. http://www.shareholder.com/mattel/news/20041117–148538.cfm

O'Brien, Richard. *The Story of American Toys: From the Puritans to the Present.* New York: Abbeville Press, 1990.

O'Dell, John. *The Great American Depression Book of Fun.* New York: Harper & Row, 1981.

Toys. *New York Times,* 5 December 1930; 17 December 1932; 18 October 1938. *Historic New York Times.* Proquest, Lynchburg College Library, Lynchburg, VA.

Yo-yos. http://www.nationalyoyo.org/museum/youcanyo-yo.htm

TRAILERS. As **automobiles** grew in popularity during the early years of the twentieth century, a handful of imaginative travelers improvised various kinds of trailers to pull behind their cars. These home-built rooms on wheels provided an inexpensive means to adventure on the open road. Spending the evening beside a pasture, a stream, or myriad other places, the "tin can tourists," as people dubbed them, had the freedom to go almost anywhere the highway led. Trailer owners did not have to rely on the location of **hotels**, **motels**, or **auto camps**, nor did they have the expenses associated with such lodging. Enough individuals showed an interest in this form of **travel** that **newspapers** and **magazines** gave them considerable publicity.

With media coverage and the growing popularity of touring, some automobile manufacturers took notice and began producing both pulled and self-propelled house cars equipped for sleeping and dining. These creations unfortunately carried a price tag that made them affordable only to the wealthy. In the early 1920s, for example, Glenn Curtiss (1878–1930), an **aviation** pioneer and founder of Curtiss Aeroplane and Motor Company, manufactured luxury trailers, or "motor bungalows." Curtiss renamed his motor bungalow the Aerocar Land Yacht in 1928, and it was indeed an elegant and expensive yacht. Its interior reflected the styling of a private Pullman train car, including servants' quarters and two bathrooms. Other custom-built trailers frequently resembled **buses** and sometimes had actually been constructed from converted buses.

In 1928, Arthur Sherman (active 1920s and 1930s), a New England scientist, inventor, and handyman, designed a simple, inexpensive camping trailer for his family. Constructed on wheels, his 9×6×5-foot box, no taller than the family Buick, attached to the car for easy pulling and could be quickly set up for shelter each evening. Friends and neighbors expressed interest and soon Sherman had developed a small business building, assembling, and selling Sherman Covered Wagons to middle-class America.

Encouraged by his success, Sherman displayed his camper on wheels at the 1930 Detroit Auto Show and began an **advertising** campaign in *National Geographic* and *Field and Stream* magazines. *Scientific American* gave it national publicity in its February 1931 issue. By 1932, the company had sold 80 units, a figure that grew to 189 in 1933. With continued demand, Sherman by 1936 employed 1,100 people assembling "covered wagons" at the rate of 1,000 a month.

Sherman was not alone. Another early manufacturer, R. T. Baumberger's (active 1920s and 1930s) Columbia Trailer Company, built affordable trailers shaped like Pullman cars and painted in gypsy wagon color schemes. Baumberger in 1933 organized the first caravan tour for Americans with trailers. Industry competitors—Vagabonds, Indians, Kozy Coaches, Silver Domes, Split-Coaches, Aladdins, and a host of others—entered the business, and 1936 saw at least 700 commercial builders assembling units of one kind or another.

A distinct improvement over Sherman's original box, the new models averaged 17 feet in length and boasted amenities like complete kitchenettes, chemical toilets, self-contained water supplies, and increased storage. Most important, people could afford them. In response to the growing popularity of trailers, Montgomery Ward, a large retail and mail-order firm, announced in 1935 its intention to add a furnished house trailer to its catalog. In addition, Karl Hale Dixon (active 1920s and 1930s) published *Trailer Travel* magazine, a journal that provided enthusiasts information on camping locations.

That same year, Wally Byam (1896–1962), a California printer, closed his shop and turned to designing and building trailers. His plan incorporated aircraft construction methods that gave his creations an aerodynamic look. Byam described his vehicles as "cruising down the road like a stream of air" and named his business the Airstream Trailer Company. In 1936, shortly after Pan American Airlines had introduced its famous **China Clippers**, Byam's Clipper trailer made its debut. Manufactured from aluminum instead of the plywood and Masonite used in the original Airstreams, this expensive model qualified as the king of comfort. Features included sleeping space for four, an enclosed galley, electric lights, insulation, a ventilation system, air conditioning that used dry ice, and a dropped floor that allowed adults to stand upright. Although the Clipper carried an expensive price tag of $1,200 (roughly $17,500 in contemporary dollars), the company could not build them fast enough to meet demand. The Airstream Clipper would prove to be one of the most popular and enduring trailers of all time. Wally Byam had created an American icon.

Trailer popularity spread across the nation. At the 1936 National Automobile Show at New York City's Grand Central Palace Exhibition Hall, the fourth-floor trailer display attracted everyone. Visitors willingly stood in long lines to see them; many placed orders on the spot. Dealers at the show estimated a potential market for 200,000 to 300,000 trailers that year. Demand far exceeded production, and the major manufacturers, even working at capacity, produced just over 40,000. The Sherman Covered Wagon Company, for example, filled only one out of every five orders received.

Celebrities such as Wallace Beery (1885–1949), Gypsy Rose Lee (1911–1970), Buster Keaton (1895–1966), Ray Milland (1905–1986), Ginger Rogers (1911–1995), and W. C. Fields (1879–1946) let it be known that they owned trailers. Cowboy star Tom Mix (1880–1940) took delivery on an early Airstream. Trailers even became a part of politics when the Democrats equipped 50 snow-white Hayes trailers with loudspeakers and huge boxes of Roosevelt-Garner campaign buttons for the 1936 presidential race. Pulled by brand-new family sedans, the Roosevelt caravan campaigned across the country and, incidentally, showed the "trailer way" of traveling.

Fortune, Harper's, the *Nation,* and *Time* published articles on the trailer phenomenon. In 1937, *Life* Magazine ran three full pages of photojournalism about the Sherman Covered Wagon Company's travel trailers. A long-running episode that deals with trailer travel appeared in the popular *Ella Cinders,* a nationally syndicated newspaper comic strip drawn by Charlie Plumb (1900–1982) and written by Bill Conselman (1896–1940). Also, several **soap operas** then on **radio** had their heroines living the trailer life.

Trailers attracted a variety of Americans. More affluent citizens living in cold climates started taking their vacation units to warmer states to escape the severe winter weather. In the early years of the Depression, some economically oppressed Americans made them their homes, a practice that carried on after the worst days of the crash had passed. In 1936, Roger Ward Babson (1875–1967), a financial adviser who had predicted the market collapse of 1929, estimated that 300,000 to 500,000 people lived on wheels and predicted that within two decades one out of every two Americans would reside in a trailer.

Babson's prophecy turned out to be inaccurate, but thousands of families did move to trailer camps across the country. Florida's 17,000 sites, each accommodating about 100 trailers, led the nation, followed by California, with 6,000 camps, and Michigan, with 4,500. Every state in the union had facilities to accommodate the nomads who had found such living cheaper than residing in a conventional home.

The onset of an economic recession in 1937 forecast a gloomy future for many businesses, one that became a reality for the trailer industry. Also, editorial pages across the country moved from curiosity and praise to antitrailer journalism. They voiced concern about the absence of roots, about "gasoline gypsies" who appeared to lack a work ethic and threatened the traditional American home, and about impacts on the country's tax structure and property values. Some cities passed laws banning trailers completely or relegated them to ugly and noisy industrial areas.

The rapid growth of the trailer industry had saturated the market, and in late 1938 the trailer bubble burst. Even the successful and well-established Sherman Covered Wagons declared bankruptcy and reorganized; many other companies simply locked their doors. By the early 1940s the trailer manufacturers that had held on found themselves once again in a growth industry. Sales increased when American defense workers and military personnel utilized trailers as temporary housing. This use continued throughout World War II. At the close of the war, the industry moved into another expansionary period as trailers again gained popularity for both travel and permanent living.

See also Fred Astaire & Ginger Rogers; Comic Strips; Design; Gas Stations; Movies; Photography; Franklin Delano Roosevelt; Trains

SELECTED READING

Landau, Robert, and James Phillippi. *Airstream*. Salt Lake City, UT: Gibbs M. Smith, Peregrine Smith Books, 1984.

Thornburg, David A. *Galloping Bungalows: The Rise and Demise of the American House Trailer*. Hamden, CT: Archon Books, 1991.

White, Roger B. *Home on the Road: The Motor Home in America*. Washington, DC: Smithsonian Institution Press, 2000.

TRAINS. Following World War I, American railroads commenced a long, painful decline that would only be exacerbated during the Depression years. Before then, U.S. trains had boasted an unprecedented level of operating efficiency and carrying capacity, a vast **transportation** system that much of the world could envy. In 1920, domestic train **travel** hit a peak of 1.2 billion annual riders that accounted for 47 billion passenger miles. For the remainder of the decade, however, those heady figures fluctuated, usually downward. With the onset of the 1930s and the Great Depression, the totals had already fallen to 700 million annual train patrons and 27 billion passenger miles, or roughly half the ridership of just 10 years earlier. Except for a brief resurgence with the introduction of Streamlined trains around mid-decade, the slide continued, and 1939 recorded 454 million passengers riding 23 billion miles. To make matters worse, the number of operating American railroads also declined, from 775 in 1930 to 600 in 1939. As the decade drew to a close, much of the nation saw the glimmers of a modest economic recovery, but the railroads faced an uncertain future.

Almost from its beginnings, in addition to its freight business, the railroad industry had emphasized passenger service in two areas: intercity travel and vacation travel. The formula worked well until the 1920s, when significant increases in the number of registered **automobiles** had a profound negative effect on railroading. The use of trains for intercity transportation had dropped 18 percent by 1929 and usage continued to drop during the Depression. Americans preferred the privacy, flexibility, and perceived economy of their cars.

Early on, the railroads promoted train travel for "happy vacations" and provided service to many of the nation's parks. For example, Yellowstone Park, isolated from any major highways at the time, welcomed 45,000 rail visitors in 1915; only 7,500 tourists braved the journey by car. By 1930, with an improved road system, 195,000 people drove to Yellowstone, while a paltry 27,000 took the train. This pattern repeated itself across the land; despite the heavily advertised comfort and glamour of train travel, its use for vacations decreased. In addition to the competition from the automobile, developments in the airline industry, such as the **Douglas DC-3**, and the creation of comfortable long-distance bus services like Greyhound and Trailways, created new alternatives for tourists and commuters alike, and they came at the expense of rail travel.

At first, much of the railroad industry failed to recognize or respond to the loss of passengers caused by automobiles, **buses**, and airplanes. A few rail lines did grasp the extent of the competition and spent large amounts of money to create and maintain a few luxury trains in hopes of attracting more passengers. They cut fares and increased creature comforts for coach travelers, such as providing air conditioning in the all-parlor trains, improving lighting, and equipping lounge cars with radios. As a further inducement, advertisements and timetables often employed attractive paintings or photographs of a line's newest trains, showing happy patrons in a pleasant setting. These marketing efforts intended to connect potential passengers with specific companies and their services, but by 1935 more people rode buses than trains. The pretty ads did little to staunch the loss of customers to other modes of transportation.

Another ploy tried by the railroads involved Streamlined trains. The **design** concept known as **Streamlining**, an outgrowth of **Art Deco**, swept the country in the mid-1930s, especially in the area of industrial design. Everything, from pencil sharpeners to skyscrapers, exhibited elements of Streamlining, and the great steam engines and diesels that powered trains were no exception. Mechanical devices took on futuristic aerodynamic traits that suggested speed and efficiency. The Union Pacific Railroad encased its M-10,000, also known as Little Zip and later renamed the City of Salina, in a sleek covering, and the resultant Streamliner became an attraction at the 1933–1934 **Century of Progress Exposition** in Chicago.

The Burlington Railroad in like manner put a Streamlined casing over its Zephyr, and the train set out from Denver in May 1934 to go to Chicago and the fair in a record-breaking fashion. The train cut the traditional running time between Colorado and Illinois almost in half—from 25$^3/_4$ hours to slightly over 13 hours—and at times it reached a top speed of 104 miles per hour. Once the Zephyr arrived at the fair, Burlington put the engine on display for the remainder of the exposition. After the Century of Progress closed in the autumn of 1934, the locomotive went into service between Lincoln, Nebraska, and Kansas City, Missouri. To differentiate it from subsequent Zephyrs, Burlington renamed its record-breaking train the Pioneer Zephyr.

Because passenger numbers for these trains briefly increased, other railroads soon ordered their own Streamliners. People liked the look, and the trains did live up to their image of speed. Others included the New York Central's Commodore Vanderbilt (1934), the Gulf, Mobile, and Northern's Rebel (1934), the Milwaukee Road's Hiawatha (1935), the New York, New Haven and Hartford's Comet (1935), the Santa Fe Railroad's Super Chief (1936), and the New York Central's Mercury (1936). The Seaboard Railway inaugurated the Silver Meteor, which in 1939 trimmed 8 hours off the

33-hour run from New York City to Florida, a state rapidly becoming a tourist destination.

At the 1939–1940 **New York World's Fair**, Streamlined trains again proved a major attraction, just as they had at Chicago's extravaganza a few years earlier. Twenty-seven eastern railroads, in an attempt to prove their role in "building the world of tomorrow," collaborated by erecting the fair's largest freestanding structure, the Railroad Building. Divided into three sections—Railroads in Building, Railroads at Work, and Railroads on Parade, the last a one-hour pageant celebrating rail history—it housed the popular display of the Pennsylvania Railroad's huge engine called S1 6100, a long, elegant Streamliner created by the renowned designer Raymond Loewy (1893–1986). Placed on a specially constructed treadmill, engineers fired up the S1 6100's engine and allowed it to run at a continuous—but stationary—speed of 65 miles per hour. For many, this display signaled a bright future, and Streamlining promised to take the country there. After the fair closed in 1940, the S1 6100 entered service, but its enormous size and rigid frame limited its operation to relatively straight sections of track, since its length prevented it from negotiating curves. After just a few years, the Pennsylvania Railroad had to cut up the S1 6100 for scrap, a sad ending after such an optimistic introduction.

Since the earliest days of railroading, trains have exerted a romantic hold on the American imagination. Certainly the Zephyrs and their counterparts from the 1930s attempted to capitalize on this fantasy of speed, comfort, and escape. But the railroads were not the only ones to employ imagery and symbolism. The motion picture industry, dealing as it does with the visual aspects of life, from its inception has made effective use of trains, with cinematographers creating exciting shots of turning wheels, tracks stretching out to the horizon, or smoke pouring from a stack as a train races across the countryside. During the 1930s, **movies** like *Rome Express* (1932), *Streamline Express* (1936), *Last Train from Madrid* (1937), and *The Lady Vanishes* (1938) promoted the concept of trains as a glamorous and often exotic way to travel. In the hit 1934 film *Twentieth Century*, the plot unfolds during a railroad trip. Carole Lombard (1908–1942) and John Barrymore (1882–1942), two big stars of the era, bring sophistication to their roles, and the sets allow the audience to move with the characters throughout the train, from modern compartments to a sleek cocktail lounge.

Warner Brothers' classic Depression musical *42nd Street* (1933) also features images of train travel. With a great score by songsmiths Harry Warren (1893–1981) and Al Dubin (1891–1945), virtually the entire cast sings "Shuffle Off to Buffalo" in a scene showing a cutaway sleeper car. The original Burlington Zephyr had a significant role in 1934's *Silver Streak*, a story where a train must race against time in order to save lives. *Sweet Music* (1935) stars the popular crooner **Rudy Vallee** (1901–1986), along with a futuristic train with shiny curves and bullet shapes that suggests it is ready to break any and all speed records.

Finally, *Union Pacific* (1939), a big-budget Western directed by Cecil B. DeMille (1881–1959), has it all: building the transcontinental railroad, cowboys and Indians, the U.S. Cavalry, a love story, and a spectacular train wreck. A box office hit, *Union Pacific* delighted audiences with its sprawling, romanticized picture of railroad history and captured the continuing fascination Americans have for trains.

American **music**, particularly the blues, has long featured the aural imagery of trains, the relentless rhythm, the clickety-clack of the rails, and the lonesome whistle in the middle of the night, transferring these sounds to instrumental pictures. The lyrics that accompany this music also summon up images: hoboes riding the rails, endless lines of freight cars crossing the land, and trains separating—or perhaps uniting—lovers. With so many people unemployed in the 1930s, "hobo jungles" sprang up outside many cities, populated by destitute individuals who had hopped a train in search of work. Many songs, like "Freight Train Blues (c. 1935), "Hobo Bill's Last Ride" (c. 1930), and "Blow Your Whistle, Freight Train" (c. 1933) celebrated this life. Cheerier railroad songs included the up-tempo "Orange Blossom Special" (c. 1935) and "Honky Tonk Train Blues" (1924, but popularized in the 1930s). Even Streamlining received musical mention with "Special Streamline" (c. 1934). Dozens of rail-related songs came out in the 1930s, suggesting a continuing attachment for trains and the symbolism connected with them.

Several well-known performers of the era dipped into the railroading song bag for their inspiration. Jimmie Rodgers (1897–1933), who usually sported a railroader's cap in his public appearances, was called "the Singing Brakeman." He cut numerous records that dealt with life on and around the rails, such as "Train Whistle Blues" (1930) and "Southern Cannonball" (1933). **Woody Guthrie** (1912–1967) led a rather nomadic life himself and could sing of his experiences. Two numbers from the late 1930s typify his work, "Railroad Blues" and "Walking down That Railroad Line."

In the print genre, **pulp magazines** early on discovered the lore and the lure of trains. Adventure and intrigue color their tales as trains carry their characters to dangerous or exotic locales. *Railroad Man's Magazine*, founded in 1906, offered stories about railroad heroes. In 1932, the **magazine**'s name changed to *Railroad Stories*, but the stories retained their unique focus; it continued in publication until the 1950s.

The 1930s ended with the railroad industry still struggling against the combined forces of the Great Depression, the popularity of the automobile, and the increased use of buses and airplanes. Sleek, Streamlined trains did little to increase overall ridership, and the onset of World War II only postponed the day of reckoning for the once-mighty rail carriers.

See also Advertising; Aviation; Magazines; Musicals; Radio; Songwriters & Lyricists; Spectacle & Costume Drama Films

SELECTED READING

Douglas, George H. *All Aboard! The Railroad in American Life*. New York: Paragon House, 1992.

Historical Statistics of the United States, Colonial Times to 1970. Washington, DC: Bureau of the Census, U.S. Department of Commerce, 1975.

Runte, Alfred. *Trains of Discovery: Western Railroads and the National Parks*. Niwot, CO: Roberts Rinehart, 1990.

Stilgoe, John R. *Metropolitan Corridor: Railroads and the American Scene*. New Haven, CT: Yale University Press, 1983.

Stover, John F. *The Life and Decline of the American Railroad*. New York: Oxford University Press, 1970.

Streamliners. http://www.pbs.org/wgbh/amex/Streamliners/timelinetimeline2.html

TRANSPORTATION. During the 1930s, the basic structure of the public transportation system in the United States underwent profound changes. Although a handful of large cities boasted subway systems, most urban areas relied on surface streetcars and trolleys. Both of these carriers depend on tracks that have been placed atop city streets in elaborate patterns that interconnect and form routes for the streetcars and trolleys to follow. They employ a third rail or an overhead wire or cable connected to the carrier by a trolley pole for power, and had served as the primary means of mass transit in most communities. These systems proved efficient, safe, and clean, especially when compared with animals as the source of power and mobility. But streetcars and trolleys lost favor when alternative means of transportation became available, especially the increasingly affordable and dependable automobile.

In hopes of reclaiming a declining ridership, the streetcar and trolley industries in 1929 formed the Electric Railway Presidents Conference Committee, charging this prestigious group to **design** a truly modern trolley. The committee came back with the PCC, the President's Conference Car. It featured a smooth ride, quick acceleration, comfortable seats, and, in keeping with the times, a modern Streamlined body. The PCC trolleys enjoyed some limited success, and a few large cities continue their use even in the twenty-first century. The PCC, however, never emerged as a significant threat to other modes of transportation.

Mack Truck and J. G. Brill, along with several other truck and bus manufacturers, attempted to capture both the bus and trolley markets by producing a trolley bus, a wheeled carrier that featured a trolley pole and thus was not limited to preexisting track routes, but continued to be dependent on the routes created by power lines. By 1933, however, most streetcar and trolley companies had ceased operation, and cities and towns busily removed the tracks and electric wires that had once crisscrossed their locations and powered their fleets of vehicles.

The primary threat facing streetcars and trolleys remained the automobile. Many American families bought their first car in the 1920s. Passenger car registration jumped from 8 million vehicles in 1920 to 23 million by 1930, and it continued climbing, reaching 26 million in 1939. By the end of the decade, almost 90 percent of all **travel** (in miles) within the continental United States took place in **automobiles**, leaving the remainder to be divided among **trains**, streetcars, trolleys, **buses**, airplanes, and ships. The private automobile reigned supreme, and it has never relinquished that position.

The high rate of car ownership negatively affected the use of public transportation. The bus and railroad industries engaged in heavy **advertising** hoping to convince the American public that they offered unequalled economy, efficiency, and safety. In the early 1930s, the Burlington Railroad, the Union Pacific, the Great Northern, the New York Central, and the Pennsylvania Railroad all set up subsidiary bus lines or acquired stock in the existing Greyhound system. This unlikely alliance helped drive the final nail into the streetcar/trolley coffin, but neither buses nor railroads could make much headway against the popularity of the automobile. A new player also entered the field with the arrival of regularly scheduled commercial airlines. In its early days air travel had no noticeable impact on auto travel, but sleek airplanes did compete with railroad and bus lines in the ongoing battle for passengers.

Most cities of any size boasted at least a couple of taxi companies. The use of plush Packards, roomy Checkers, a De Soto with a sunroof, or a Hudson Terraplane, all with leather upholstery, provided a luxurious means to get around locally. During the 1920s and 1930s, the entry of new entrepreneurs into this all-cash business led to an oversupply of taxis. Too many cabs meant traffic congestion, fare-cutting wars, and reduced drivers' wages. The onset of the Great Depression hit the taxi business hard and many firms went under. Survivors such as the Yellow Cab Company, founded in 1915 by John Hertz (1879–1961), benefited when cities established limits on the number of taxicabs on their streets, since the familiar Yellow Cabs were usually part of existing fleets, not some upstarts trying to make a quick profit.

Movies like *Taxi* (1932) and *The Big City* (1937; also called *Skyscraper Wilderness*) etched an indelible portrait of the wisecracking, seen-it-all cabbie as part of the American urban scene. *Taxi*, in a bit of perfect casting, stars James Cagney (1899–1986) and his screen persona—the tough, swaggering wise guy—a role he took on with ease. *The Big City* uses another popular actor ready to trade verbal jabs with anyone, Spencer Tracy (1900–1967). And millions of fans listened on **radio** to the comedy adventures of **Amos 'n' Andy**, many of which revolve around the Fresh-Air Taxicab Company. In reality, with fares running around 20 cents a mile in the 1930s (about $2.80 a mile in contemporary money), cabs provided a relatively expensive way to travel, and only the fairly well-to-do could afford them. Hollywood made their drivers working-class heroes who usually served a wealthy clientele.

With more automobiles being used for commuting, errands, and leisure travel, taxis becoming a part of the fabric of city life, buses taking on Streamlined styling, and modern passenger planes flying higher and faster, the country faced new transportation challenges. The list included more and better roads, bridges and tunnels, and airports—and of course the money to build them. Earlier, the federal government had given its first tentative support toward constructing a national highway system with the passage of the Federal Aid Road Act in 1916. This bill matched federal money with state resources for building through streets and major highways. Some states imposed car registration fees and taxes on gasoline as a means of raising funds for building and maintaining such projects.

Two of President **Franklin D. Roosevelt**'s (1882–1945) **New Deal** programs specifically addressed these needs and made major contributions toward building an up-to-date transportation system. The Public Works Administration (PWA; 1933–1939) and the Works Progress Administration (WPA, 1935–1943; name changed to Work Projects Administration in 1939) spent large sums of federal money on transportation projects while offering much-needed jobs for unemployed workers.

The PWA provided funds and supervision for federal agencies and local governments to construct roads, dams, airports, bridges, subways, tunnels, and harbors. The greatest amount of PWA monies allotted for transportation projects—over $750 million—went for primary highways and roads; administrators broadened the definitions in 1934 to include work on urban segments of primary roads and in 1936 added secondary feeder roads.

The WPA tackled similar needs. Money from this department built 651,087 miles of highways, roads, and streets, including Chicago's 1937 Lake Shore Drive (originally called Leif Erickson Drive). These funds also covered work on 124,031 bridges and 853 airports, the most notable effort being New York's 1939 LaGuardia Field.

Realizing the growing traffic congestion in the urbanized areas of the East Coast, especially around New York City and its environs, several large-scale projects attempted to alleviate some of the more obvious problems. Led by **Robert Moses** (1888–1981), plans like the West Side Highway (1927–1931), the Triborough Bridge (1930–1936), the Belt Parkway (Circumferential Parkway; 1934), the Henry Hudson Bridge (1936–1938), and the Whitestone Expressway (1939) moved from the drawing board to fruition. Outside the city, the Westchester County Parks Commission in 1924 recommended construction of a north-south parkway, a scenic route for automobiles traveling between New York City and New England. One of the first such highways, officials named it the Hutchinson River Parkway. A short, 2-mile stretch had been completed by December 1927, with 11 more miles in the fall of 1928. The parkway finally reached the New York–Connecticut state line in 1937.

On the Connecticut side of things, groundbreaking occurred in 1934 for the limited access Merritt Parkway. Starting at the state line where the Hutchinson River Parkway ended, the new road went just west of New Haven. The first 17.5 miles opened in June 1938, and builders completed the full 38 miles in 1940. One of the nation's first highways that attempted to control vehicle access, the Merritt also featured an early cloverleaf intersection. The many bridges that cross the parkway have been recognized for their architecturally significant **Art Deco** and Streamlined detailing. In 1939, to meet rising costs, the state levied a 10-cent toll (about $1.50 in contemporary money) to travel the Merritt. The public strenuously objected to the construction of toll houses along the route, but to no avail.

These early parkways eased the increasing traffic flow north and east of New York City. On the south side of the city, workers carved out the Holland Tunnel. Opening late in 1927, it carried traffic under the Hudson River and into New Jersey and proved so successful that in 1930 the New York Port Authority announced plans for a second such tunnel. Workmen finished the Lincoln Tunnel in December 1937, and it recorded 1.8 million vehicles during its first year of operation.

Construction designed to accommodate increasingly heavy traffic occurred in other parts of the country as well. As early as 1910, engineers in Pennsylvania discussed ways to convert abandoned railroad tracks through the Allegheny Mountains so they could be used as the foundations for highways. The Pennsylvania Turnpike Commission, established in 1937, displayed at the 1939–1940 **New York World's Fair** a model of a proposed superhighway that would cross the state. The model became reality when a section of the Pennsylvania Turnpike opened to traffic in 1940; World War II temporarily delayed further expansion.

California witnessed the building of the Arroyo Seco Parkway, occasionally called the Pasadena Freeway, the first limited-access, high-speed divided road in the West. Constructed in three major stages from 1938 to 1953, it connected suburban Pasadena with metropolitan Los Angeles. Cars traveled the first segment, supported by the WPA, in 1939. Farther north, San Francisco served as the site for two important bridge-building projects. In 1933, ground-breaking took place for the San Francisco–Oakland Bay Bridge, and it opened to traffic a short three years later. At about the same time, ahead of schedule and under budget, the Golden Gate Bridge welcomed vehicles in 1937. These two great suspension bridges relieved congestion for commuters entering and exiting San Francisco.

Before the construction of the San Francisco–Oakland Bay Bridge, 35 million commuters annually crossed the bay by ferry. Until the end of the decade, bridge authorities and ferry boat owners waged a strident competition against one another to lure the public to use either the new bridge or the traditional ferry boats. In the age of the automobile, it proved a futile contest for the ferry owners; despite the public's nostalgia for an older way of life, by 1940 most of the ferries had gone out of business.

With significant federal and state assistance, the building and improvement of many components of the American transportation system assisted the country in its quest to come out of the Great Depression slump. During the 1930s, highway and parkway construction boomed, and automobiles soared in popularity. Buses and trains competed for passengers, and the air line industry emerged both as a new competitor and as a viable part of this network.

See also Aviation; Douglas DC-3; Gas Stations; Leisure & Recreation; Streamlining

SELECTED READING

Barger, Harold. *The Transportation Industries, 1889–1946: A Study of Output, Employment, and Productivity.* New York: National Bureau of Economic Research, 1951.

Cavin, Ruth. *Trolleys: Riding and Remembering the Electric Interurban Railways.* New York: Hawthorn Books, 1976.

Parkways. http://www.arroyofest.org/ParkwaysAccess.htm

Stover, John F. *The Life and Decline of the American Railroad.* New York: Oxford University Press, 1970.

Tunnels. http://lcweb2.loc.gov/cocoon/legacies/CT/200002790.html

———. http://www.nycroads.com/crossings/lincoln

TRAVEL. Inextricably linked to **transportation**, the means of getting somewhere have always been almost as important as the destination. For many Americans, travel during the 1930s had little to do with being "on the road" for fun. Countless citizens roamed the nation's rails and highways out of desperation; the worst days of the Great Depression saw about a million unemployed individuals drifting from town to town, always with the faint hope that the next stop might promise some work. Most of these transients knocked at back doors to ask for **food**, slept in abandoned buildings, or camped out, often alongside railroad tracks. They got from one community to the next by jumping onto a moving rail car or hitching rides with sympathetic drivers. Derisively called hoboes (the origins of this word remain unknown), these twentieth-century nomads bore mute testimony to the havoc brought into individual lives by the economic collapse.

Thrust into aimless wandering in search of work, hoboes came from towns and cities across the land, and many had held blue- or white-collar jobs. The Dust Bowl that plagued Midwestern farmers in the late 1920s and early 1930s put a different group on the road. John Steinbeck's (1902–1968) classic novel, *The Grapes of Wrath* (1939), chronicles the exodus of Oklahoma farmers from their devastated land. As these desperate families head for the promised land of California, their "travel" consists of using jalopies and wagons piled high with meager possessions. People had turned to the highway as a last resort; they camped along the way out of necessity, and hoped for a chance to begin anew.

Not everyone, however, faced such dire conditions. Despite the Depression, for many wealthy and middle-class families, summer meant travel of a completely different kind, often with mother and the children spending several weeks at a mountain or beachside resort. Father continued to work—not everyone was unemployed—and joined the family for the weekend. For others, travel might suggest short automobile or trolley excursions. Since the tracks often extended a considerable distance beyond the city limits in those

A poster urges Americans to travel to scenic destinations within the country. (Courtesy of the Library of Congress)

days, families without cars could go by streetcar or trolley to a countryside spot for a Sunday afternoon picnic or to a cabin at a nearby lake for the weekend.

The mountains and the seashore also beckoned, as did national monuments and historic sites. Families stayed in **auto camps** or **motels** along the way, or they undertook a train trip to a national park, or even a tour to Canada or Europe. A report from the Natural Resources Board in 1934 states that more than half the volume over U.S. highways during 1933, and 60 percent of the total use of American **automobiles**, involved recreational traffic.

Beginning in the 1920s, a gradual change in business attitudes also boosted such travel. Because of pressure from unions, along with efficiency and productivity studies promoting the idea, companies began providing employees with paid vacations, urging them to spend this time traveling. The idea caught on; in 1920, about 40 percent of white collar

A roadside stop for travelers in Ohio. (Courtesy of the Library of Congress)

workers received at least one week of paid vacation, and that figure doubled to 80 percent by 1930. A small number of companies also introduced paid vacations to hourly employees, a practice that would grow during the decade.

With the onset of the Depression, half the employers offering vacation plans dropped them. But many quickly reinstated the practice when they realized the benefits in terms of employee morale and productivity, and a substantial number of companies added such plans for the first time. As a result, the percentage of employees with paid vacations in the mid-1930s exceeded the figures for pre-Depression days. By the close of the decade, 95 percent of salaried employees and almost 37 percent of hourly workers received vacations of one kind or another.

Throughout the 1930s, popular **magazines** such as *Ladies' Home Journal, Popular Science Monthly*, and *Good Housekeeping* published articles discussing the value of travel when taking a vacation, even during economically depressed times. **Newspapers** also ran articles and editorials supporting family vacations. Topics ranged from the cost of roadside cabins, the popularity of camping and hiking, and the increased number of natural and historic sites to visit thanks to **New Deal** projects.

Responding to the growing popularity of vacations, the federal government, especially the National Park Service and New Deal programs, played an important role in the development and promotion of tourism. The Park Service, from its establishment in 1916, has urged citizens to "See America First." Twenty parks constituted the National Park Service system before 1930, with five additional parks—Carlsbad Caverns (1930), Isle Royale (1931), Everglades (1934), Big Bend (1935) and Olympic (1938)—joining the ranks during the Depression years.

National park directors secured private donations to support the upkeep and growth of the parks and to educate Americans about the value of visiting them. These successful campaigns included extensive newspaper and magazine coverage. For example, in 1930 newspaper articles across the country encouraged travel, whether by car, train, or bus, with headlines such as "Tourist Industry Great Aid to Business." National and state parks, national forests, and historic and military sites received high recommendations. They claimed to offer a combination of the best fun and relaxation for the family and a display of patriotism during an economic crisis.

Park officials worked with many groups—women's clubs, photographers, moviemakers, community and regional travel promotion associations, and automobile clubs—in an effort to increase the number of park visitors. During the 1920s, Park Service Director Stephen Mather (1867–1930) built a strong relationship with the railroad industry, inducing it to expand its **advertising** for tourism. From this came the "happy vacation travel" concept for **trains** that journeyed to the isolated national parks in the West. Colorful posters and brochures emphasized the spectacular scenery and the romance of steam locomotives as incentives. These efforts, bright and cheerful as they were, did not, however, overcome the growing popularity of the automobile. Despite the aura of romance and adventure, train travel decreased significantly during the 1930s.

The New Deal brought new energy and opportunities for the Park Service to broaden its appeal to a larger cross section of Americans. In 1934, an intensive publicity campaign under the slogan, "1934—A National Parks Year," encouraged travel to a national park. That year, the Federal Emergency Relief Administration (FERA, 1933–1935), through its Federal Surplus Relief Corporation, allocated $5 million (roughly $75 million in contemporary dollars) to the Service to acquire submarginal lands for conversion to recreational areas. The following chart shows the success of that campaign, a success that continued throughout the decade.

Visitors to National Parks, Monuments, & Historical Sites

Year	Number of Visitors to National Parks (in millions)	Number of Visitors to National Monuments (in millions)	Number of Visitors to Historical & Military Sites (in millions)
1929	2.7	.491	n/a
1930	2.7	.472	n/a
1931	3.1	.392	n/a
1932	2.9	.406	n/a
1933	2.8	.523	.91
1934	3.5	1.3	1.4
1935	4	1.3	2.3
1936	5.7	1.7	4.5
1937	6.7	2	6
1938	6.6	2.4	6.7
1939	6.8	2.6	5.4
1940	7.4	2.8	6

Source: *Historical Statistics of the United States, Colonial Times to 1970.*

Getting to and from the national parks—as well as any other destination—demanded adequate transportation facilities. During the 1930s, a surge in road building resulted not just in new highways to relieve traffic congestion, but also in a number of new roads designed for noncommercial, recreational use. This effort proved a boon for travelers.

These scenic highways had their origin in county and municipal undertakings such as the Westchester County Parkway in New York, built between 1913 and 1930. At the federal level, Congress authorized its first parkway project in 1913 with the 4-mile Rock Creek and Potomac Parkway in the District of Columbia. Congress ordered the construction of the Mount Vernon Memorial Highway in 1928 and renamed it, on the bicentennial of his birth, the George Washington (1732–1799) Memorial Parkway. This road, designed for **leisure and recreation**, connects historic sites while passing through scenic areas. It became a part of the National Park System in 1933. Outside the District of Columbia, Congress moved to create the Colonial Parkway in Virginia and construction began in 1931. It would link the historic towns of Williamsburg, Yorktown, and Jamestown.

The federal government also built the Skyline Drive and the Blue Ridge Parkway, two winding mountaintop roads that run for 469 miles through Virginia and North Carolina. The work began in 1933 at the depth of the Depression. Construction crews also tackled the Natchez Trace Parkway in 1937, a 444-mile road that runs from Natchez, Mississippi, to Nashville, Tennessee, and includes a bit of northwest Alabama. These massive projects, called "public works" during New Deal days, extended beyond the Depression era. Completion of the Blue Ridge Parkway did not occur until 1987, and the Natchez Trace Parkway remained under construction until 2005. Both parkways today serve as parts of the National Park system.

Much of the building of these two parkways fell under the auspices of the **Civilian Conservation Corps** (CCC; 1933–1942). This New Deal work program, aimed at putting unemployed **youth** to work, improved millions of acres of federal and state lands, constructed roads and parks, as well as countless campgrounds, picnic shelters, fireplaces, swimming pools, and restrooms.

Another Works Progress Administration (WPA, 1935–1943; renamed Work Projects Administration in 1939) program, the **Federal Writers' Project** (FWP; 1935–1943), commissioned jobless writers across the country to develop the *American Guide Series*. This project, which commenced in 1935, produced in-depth guidebooks for each of the 48 contiguous states and gave the nation a fresh, in-depth view of the country. Nestled among the contents of each guide were suggested automobile tours, along with places to see and things to do.

In 1937, the government organized the U.S. Travel Bureau. It shut down soon after the country's entry into World War II in 1941, but during its brief life this agency issued numerous newsletters, bulletins, research reports, and promotional aids to travel agencies, transportation companies, trade associations, and tour operators. Travel-related groups, such as the American Automobile Association (AAA), United Motor Courts, and International Motor Court Association, as well as private entrepreneurs like Duncan Hines (1880–1959) and Emmons Walker and Ray A. Walker (both active 1920s and 1930s), also published guides to sights, dining, and lodging.

A few of the hardier travelers of the day did not need recommendations about where to spend the night. They proudly pulled their own "cabins"—**trailers**—behind their cars. A number of media chronicled the trailer phenomenon. Articles could be found in widely read magazines such as *Harper's*, *Life*, *Popular Mechanics*, the **Saturday Evening Post**, and *Time*.

Americans and their automobile vacations created interesting variations in the expenditure of vacation dollars. Businesses as varied as garages; **gas stations**; roadside stands; diners; **restaurants**; overnight camps; **hotels**; amusement parks; beach, lake, and mountain resorts; **ice cream** and soft drink companies; souvenir manufacturers and vendors; and guidebook publishers and sellers benefited from vacationing Americans (see chart below).

Statistics Related to Vacation Travels during the 1930s

1	2	3	4	5	6	7
Year	Motor Vehicle Miles of Travel for the Nation (in billions)	Dollars Spent on Gas, Oil, & Other Vacation Car Operating Expenses (in millions)	Number of Lodging Establishments Other Than Hotels	Expenditures for Hotels, Restaurants, Vacation Clothing, & Travel Supplies (in millions)	Railroad Coach & Pullman Fares (in millions)	Hotel Occupancy Rates as Percent of Hotel Capacity
1927	n/a	n/a	5,000	n/a	n/a	n/a
1929	198	$1,102	n/a	$872	$201	70
1930	206	n/a	n/a	n/a	n/a	n/a
1931	216	n/a	n/a	n/a	n/a	n/a
1932	201	n/a	n/a	n/a	n/a	n/a
1933	201	$1,040	n/a	$444	$80	51
1934	216	n/a	n/a	n/a	n/a	56
1935	229	$1,331	15,000–20,000	n/a	n/a	n/a
1936	252	n/a	n/a	n/a	n/a	66
1937	270	n/a	n/a	n/a	n/a	n/a
1938	271	n/a	n/a	n/a	n/a	n/a
1939	285	n/a	n/a	n/a	n/a	n/a
1940	302	n/a	n/a	n/a	n/a	n/a

Source: *Historical Statistics of the United States, Colonial Times to 1970.*

A drop in money spent on railroad coach and Pullman fares from 1929 to 1933 (column 6) and the corresponding increase in motor vehicle miles of travel (column 2) clearly show a change in preference from rail to road travel. Column 3 suggests that the number of dollars spent on vacation travel related to the family car, such as gas and oil, varied little from 1929 to 1933, the year of greatest national unemployment (24 percent). The expenditures for hotels, restaurants, and clothing (column 5) and train fares (column 6) between 1929 and 1933 declined significantly. This information, along with the increase in the number of lodging establishments other than hotels (column 4) and the fall in hotel occupancy rates (column 7), suggests increased use of auto camps and, later, motor courts and motels. By 1935 the amount of vacation dollars spent had markedly increased.

Buses and trains struggled to retain current riders and secure additional vacation travelers. Greyhound and Trailways, the two dominant bus companies by the end of the decade, offered local, intercity, interstate, and transcontinental services, and urged everyone to "leave the driving to us." Greyhound, like the railroad industry, targeted families on vacation and marketed their 1936 Super Coach for family travel. Their glossy ads promoting Streamlined buses that offered comfort and convenience for vacationers did not succeed; the majority of bus passengers continued to be commercial travelers such as salesmen.

A select few did not confine their travel to the United States. Ocean liners operated by French and British companies moved back and forth between New York and Europe, carrying mostly American tourists. This mode of travel, limited as it was, received a great deal of play in the press and **movies**. Advertisements placed in general circulation magazines and newspapers, along with posters and billboards, guaranteed that millions would see and read about luxurious ocean travel, although few had the resources to enjoy it.

The motion picture industry did the best job of promoting ocean travel and reached the largest audience. England's *Queen Mary*, commissioned in 1936, presented a sleek symbol of the machine age, an image Hollywood fostered in many films. *Transatlantic* (1931), *Reaching for the Moon* (1931), *Transatlantic Merry-Go-Round* (1934), *Chained* (1934), and *The Princess Came Across* (1936) all feature ocean liners that display the latest in **Art Deco** stylishness. *Dodsworth* (1936), based on Sinclair Lewis's (1885–1951) 1929 novel of the same name, won an Academy Award for Set Decoration. Part of the story takes place on a splendid, modernistic liner. But the epitome of all the pictures associated with ocean liners has to be *The Big Broadcast of 1938* (1938). The movie boasts plenty of stars—W. C. Fields (1880–1946), Bob Hope (1903–2003), Dorothy Lamour (1914–1996), Martha Raye (1916–1994)—but it also features a Streamlined ship created by noted designer Norman Bel Geddes (1893–1958).

Either in the movies or in advertisements, the ocean liner, imagined or real, signaled glamour and luxury, efficiency and convenience. Although most of the movie audiences would never set foot on such a vessel, Streamlined or otherwise, the repetition of images created a popular acceptance of ocean travel that carried over into the mundane objects of everyday life. For example, a 1936 Coca-Cola bottling plant constructed in Los Angeles mimics the shape of a large, sleek ocean liner.

Ocean travel to Europe or South America may have been the privilege of the few, but Americans of modest economic means went cruising in considerably smaller craft along the shores of the United States during the latter years of the decade. The *New York Times* in 1937 proclaimed "the Winter Vacation Spreads" and described how winter vacations no longer belonged just to the wealthy but could be afforded by a cross section of Americans who could cruise to destinations that included Virginia and Florida.

After 1934, the economic picture brightened and more and more Americans began traveling. The paid vacation became a firmly entrenched benefit, and the amount of vacation time a company offered emerged as a hot topic in labor relations discussions. Car ownership grew, as did automotive tourism. The New Deal, through its many projects, set park and recreational development ahead by at least a decade and provided new travel and vacation opportunities for everyone.

See also Aviation; Design; Woody Guthrie; Photography; Soft Drinks; Streamlining

SELECTED READING

Belasco, Warren Jamers. *Americans on the Road: From Autocamp to Motel, 1910–1945*. Cambridge, MA: MIT Press, 1979

Berkowitz, Michael. "A 'New Deal' for Leisure: Making Mass Tourism during the Great Depression." In *Being Elsewhere: Tourism, Consumer Culture, and Identity in Modern Europe and North America*, ed. Shelley Baranowski and Ellen Furlough. Ann Arbor: University of Michigan Press, 2001, 185–212.

Historical Statistics of the United States, Colonial Times to 1970. Washington, DC: Bureau of the Census, U.S. Department of Commerce, 1975.

Parkways. http://www.cr.nps.gov/history/online_books/unrau-williss/adhi4j.htm

V

VALLEE, RUDY. A native of New England, Rudy Vallee (1901–1986) started out in life as Hubert Prior Vallee and acquired the nickname Rudy in high school. He entered the University of Maine in 1921, but transferred to Yale University the following year; there he formed a dance band, the Yale Collegians. This group played local clubs and gave him a grounding in live performing. Because of his strong interest in **music**, he dropped out of Yale and went to London to play with English dance orchestras. He also cut his first **recordings** while abroad, although few people in the United States ever heard them.

Vallee returned to American shores in 1925; he finally earned a degree from Yale and then enjoyed some limited regional success as a bandleader. In early 1928, he fronted a group called the Connecticut Yankees and landed a contract to play the Heigh-Ho Club, a popular nightspot in New York City. This engagement marked the beginning of Vallee's rise to national prominence.

Although he considered himself a saxophonist, Vallee began doing a few vocals with the Yankees. He had a thin, nasal voice that did not project well and began performing his vocal numbers through a large megaphone. In the days before electric amplification and quality microphones, the device allowed his reedy voice to be heard above background noise at the night club.

The novelty of the megaphone almost immediately became a standard prop, not just for Vallee but for other vocalists also. When reliable amplification became a reality, allowing even the weakest voices to be heard without distortion, Vallee retained the gimmick, although he no longer needed it. He eventually wired his megaphone for sound so audiences would hear him just as he sounded on similarly amplified recordings. A case of technology influencing artistic performance, Vallee exemplified a new, modern generation of performers who came to employ an array of electronic devices to carry their songs, instead of relying on sheer lung power.

Because he could sing softly into a microphone, fans and critics alike dubbed him a "crooner," a term that came to mean a soft-voiced vocalist, almost always male, who "crooned," intimately, to his listeners. Despite his admittedly weak voice, Vallee found an audience, especially with women. On recordings and over the **radio**, he sounded close and personal, as if he were singing directly to the listener. This approach also made some people uneasy; they viewed Vallee and his counterparts as effeminate, as "sissies" who did not project traditional masculinity into their music. But his legions of fans felt otherwise; they loved the image of a man musically revealing his deepest feelings in a romantic relationship.

Later in 1928, based on the success of his Heigh-Ho performances, the National Broadcasting Company (NBC radio) offered Vallee a contract for his own show. The result, considered by many to be the first great radio variety program, almost immediately became a network hit, and it set a standard for much subsequent programming. Called *The Fleischmann Yeast Hour*, the show lasted until 1936, when it changed sponsors and became *The Royal Gelatin Hour*. It continued on NBC in one form or another until 1950. As he did in his night club performances, Vallee opened his radio broadcasts with "Heigh ho, everybody," a not-so-veiled reference to the nightclub where his climb to fame began.

Acting as the genial host of *The Fleischmann Yeast Hour*, Vallee frequently appeared as a star in his own right. He usually included fellow musicians as his guests, although the show broke some new ground by allowing dramatic excerpts to be read by stage and film actors. These passages tended to be written for radio and not the theater or motion pictures, suggesting the growing importance given the medium and its unique characteristics. The success of his series heightened Vallee's popularity in other areas, especially recordings.

Throughout his radio days, Vallee enjoyed a continuing string of recorded hits. Numbers like "I'm Just a Vagabond Lover" (1929; theme song, words and music by Leon Zimmerman [active 1920s] and Rudy Vallee), "My Time Is Your Time" (1929; music by Leo Dance [active 1930s], lyrics by Eric Little [active 1930s]), "A Little Kiss Each Morning (A Little Kiss Each Night)" (1929; words and music by Harry Woods [1896–1970]), "I Guess I'll Have to Change My Plan" (the Blue Pajama Song)" (1929; music by Arthur Schwartz [1900–1984], lyrics by Howard Dietz [1896–1983]), "Maine Stein Song" (1930; original music by E. A. Fensted [active early 1900s] in 1901, words by Lincoln Colcord [active early 1900s]), "You're Driving Me Crazy! (What Did I Do?)" (1930; words and music by Walter Donaldson [1893–1947]), "Let's Put Out the Lights" (1932; words and music by Herman Hupfeld [1894–1951]), "Just an Echo in the Valley" (1932; words and music by Harry Woods, James Campbell [active 1930s], and Reg Connelly [1896–1963]), and "Everything I Have Is Yours" (1933; music by Burton Lane [1912–1997], lyrics by Harold Adamson [1906–1980]) kept him in the musical spotlight throughout the first years of the decade.

Success on radio and in recordings naturally led Vallee to Hollywood and **movies**. Studios at first cast him in short musical films, such as *Rudy Vallee and His Connecticut Yankees* (1929; debut picture), *Radio Rhythm* (1929), and *Campus Sweethearts* (1929). As his fame and popularity grew, however, he finally landed a role in a full-length feature, *The Vagabond Lover* (1929). Publicity agents had tacked the "vagabond lover" name on Vallee, and it briefly worked. His breathy, crooning style of singing sounded intimate and amorous on recordings and radio broadcasts, so the attempt to cast him as a romantic lead seemed logical. Visually, however, he lacked the rugged good looks and demeanor of most male stars, plus he showed more of an aptitude for light comedy than he did for emoting with starlets. In time, his screen persona changed from the strong leading man to the amiable sidekick who could also sing.

More films followed *The Vagabond Lover*, several of them shorts, and all of them **musicals**. In 1939, Vallee made his final screen appearance for the decade in *Second Fiddle*, a vehicle to showcase the ice-skating talents of the then-popular Sonja Henie (1912–1969). An appropriate title since Vallee plays second fiddle to Tyrone Power (1913–1958), both actors get billed after Henie and her skates. This picture's release marked the decline of Rudy Vallee as a movie star of the first rank, and although he would act in many films during the 1940s and 1950s, his roles became increasingly comedic.

Despite his failure to emerge as a force in Hollywood, Vallee's singing style set the pattern for other important vocalists of the 1930s. Fans always linked the tunes "I'm Just a Vagabond Lover," "Maine Stein Song" (with his alma mater's "Whiffenpoof Song" [traditional] on the flip side), and "My Time Is Your Time" to him. Vallee reigned as one of the top male stars in show business unchallenged until **Bing Crosby** (1903–1977) and to a lesser extent **Russ Columbo** (1908–1934) gained fame as crooners.

He favored simple songs that listeners could remember, often skipping the verse and going straight to the chorus—the melodic portion that people usually associate with a particular song. Among the first performers to feature singing as part of the band's package of dance music, Vallee put his primary emphasis on the lyrics, and his vocal solos frequently replaced what traditionally had been instrumental ones. In this way, the band took second stage to the singer, a shift in roles. For the first half of the 1930s, this approach to vocalizing dominated; only with the rise of **swing** and the importance placed on instrumentalists would the pendulum swing back toward the orchestra.

Radio turned out to be Vallee's medium: he got to do some singing, lead the Connecticut Yankees, and clown with celebrities of the day. In time, he came to be recognized more as a popular entertainer than merely a vocalist. His indelible contribution to crooning influenced much of the popular music of the 1930s, and most of the leading vocalists of the era owe a debt to him.

See also Ice Skating & Hockey; Radio Networks; Songwriters & Lyricists

SELECTED READING

Kaye, Lenny. *You Call It Madness: The Sensuous Song of the Croon.* New York: Villard, 2004.

Kiner, Larry F. *The Rudy Vallee Discography.* Westport, CT: Greenwood Press, 1985.

Pitts, Michael R., and Frank W. Hoffman. *The Rise of the Crooners.* Lanham, MD: Scarecrow Press, 2002.

Whitcomb, Ian. "The First Crooners, Volume One: The Twenties." http://www.picklehead.com/ian/ian_txt_first crooners1.html

———. "The First Crooners, Volume Two: 1930–1934." http://www.picklehead.com/ian/ian_txt_first crooners2.html

———. "The First Crooners, Volume Three: 1935–1940." http://www.picklehead.com/ian/ian_txt_first crooners3.html

W

WELLES, ORSON. A child prodigy, the Wisconsin-born Orson Welles (1915–1985) endured a difficult childhood. After being in a number of school plays, at the age of 16 he performed on stage in Dublin, Ireland. That experience launched a remarkable career. By 1934, and still a teenager, he had returned to the United States and begun work as a director and actor in commercial **radio**, as well as continuing to appear on stage. He also experimented with film, an aspect of his interests that would blossom in the 1940s. Regardless of medium—stage, radio, or motion pictures—during these early years Welles worked with many colleagues who would later join him in the development of his renowned repertory company, the Mercury Theatre.

In 1934, the young Welles met producer John Houseman (1902–1988); the two quickly discovered an artistic rapport and proceeded to work together on various endeavors. The following year, Houseman cast Welles in a production of poet and playwright Archibald MacLeish's (1892–1982) *Panic*. From there, they moved to the growing **Federal Theater Project** (FTP; 1935–1939), a government-sponsored effort to lend support to actors, producers, and other stage workers left unemployed by the Great Depression. A branch of the FTP, the Negro Theater Project, utilized their talents to stage a successful version of *Macbeth* with Haiti instead of Scotland as its locale. They next produced *Dr. Faustus*, which also received good notices.

Welles and Houseman collaborated on their most famous FTP effort, bringing the musical *The Cradle Will Rock*, by composer Marc Blitzstein (1905–1964), to the stage in June 1937. The story of getting *The Cradle Will Rock* before an audience remains something of a legend in the annals of American theater. A controversial play because of its prolabor, anticapitalist stance, Welles served as director while Houseman produced it. The musical's leftist leanings riled conservative members of Congress, and they tried to censor it.

Government agents blocked the show's New York theater on opening night, causing the cast and crew to search for a new venue. They found the small Venice Theatre, which stood empty at the time, so everyone paraded through Manhattan's streets to restage the show. At the last moment, the musician's union, in a squabble about pay, forbade its members to perform. But Broadway says "the show must go on," and so Blitzstein himself played a piano on the Venice stage while the actors, scattered about the theater, spoke their lines as a single spot searched them out. With all the resultant

Orson Welles (1915–1985), whose radio version of *The War of the Worlds* made history in 1938. (Courtesy of the Library of Congress)

publicity, *The Cradle Will Rock* eventually moved to the larger Windsor Theatre in early 1938, where it ran for 108 performances.

The curious success of *The Cradle Will Rock* helped establish the reputations of both Orson Welles and John Houseman. The furor, however, effectively removed them from further participation in the Federal Theatre Project, so Welles proposed they form their own performance group. From this came the Mercury Theatre, a serendipitous gathering of actors such as Ray Collins (1889–1965), Joseph Cotton (1905–1994), Martin Gabel (1912–1986), Agnes Moorhead (1900–1974), and Everett Sloane (1909–1965), among many others.

Already a presence in radio, Welles had been featured in **The March of Time** series and in September 1937 had taken the lead role of Lamont Cranston on *The Shadow*, a series carried by the Columbia Broadcasting System (CBS radio). His distinctive voice—"Who knows what evil lurks…?"—made him one of the most identifiable Shadows ever, and he retained the role of the invisible dispenser of justice for the next two seasons. *The Shadow* required little work on his part, since he almost never rehearsed but instead read his lines straight from the script while on the air. More importantly, the show also provided a steady income that allowed Welles to pursue other interests.

Those "other interests" meant the Mercury Theatre. He and Houseman mounted a production of Shakespeare's *Julius Caesar* soon after organizing the group. A critical success, several more plays followed, and in the summer of 1938, *The Mercury Theater on the Air* premiered on CBS. A weekly hourlong show, it kept the repertory company busy. The mix of volatile artistic personalities led to many arguments, concessions, and revisions, but somehow they put on a new production every seven days. With no sponsors—CBS carried it more for prestige than for money—the entourage felt free to experiment. They performed classic novels; did old chestnuts in modern settings; tinkered with sound effects; and generally stretched the limits of contemporary radio. Through it all, Houseman wrote most of the scripts and Welles directed and acted.

In the autumn of 1938, Welles and the Mercury Players decided on their boldest move yet: they would adapt *The War of the Worlds*, the 1898 **science fiction** classic by British novelist H. G. Wells (1866–1946), for radio. And instead of employing the late nineteenth century as their setting, they would use the present—Halloween 1938, to be exact. In what can arguably be called the most famous radio broadcast in history, listeners got both a trick and a treat. Despite repeated statements throughout the presentation that what people were hearing was a dramatization, many in the audience became convinced it was the real thing, an invasion from Mars. Presented as an innocuous **music** interlude, but one suddenly interrupted by a realistic sounding newscast, it all seemed authentic; Welles had cleverly camouflaged his warnings. For the inattentive, Martian invaders indeed roamed the swamps of New Jersey. *The War of the Worlds* gave a perfect demonstration of radio's imaginative impact, along with creating the potential for mass hysteria through polished production methods.

Because of the furor the broadcast evoked, the Federal Communications Commission (FCC) ruled against future productions that might frighten or dupe the public. The commission's move acknowledged the power of radio as a mass medium and demonstrated the need for rules so that power would not be abused. In the meantime, the production gave Welles a notoriety he relished, using it to further other projects that occupied his restless mind. In the meantime, the Campbell Soup Company agreed to sponsor the suddenly famous *Mercury Theater on the Air*. In December, the title changed to *The Campbell Playhouse*, and the Mercury Players found themselves relegated to supporting roles when the sponsor began to bring in guest stars for the leads. Welles left the show in 1940 to follow other pursuits, and the Mercury Theatre effectively came to an end, along with Welles' longtime partnership with John Houseman.

As the decade drew to a close, the boy genius of radio, or perhaps the enfant terrible, had become nationally famous. He had made his mark in broadcasting and theater, and all that remained was his earlier interest in **movies**. Fortunately, RKO Radio Pictures, an increasingly important Hollywood studio, offered Welles a contract in 1939. It stipulated that he direct three feature films and granted him considerable artistic license. By 1941, he had honored the first third of his contract with *Citizen Kane*, a film many say ranks as the greatest American motion picture of all time. The future held much more for Welles, and although he never again reached the heights he attained in the 1930s and early 1940s, a long and distinguished career lay ahead.

See also Musicals; New Deal; Pulp Magazines; Race Relations & Stereotyping; Radio Networks; Serials; Stage Productions

SELECTED READING

Dunning, John. *On the Air: The Encyclopedia of Old-Time Radio*. New York: Oxford University Press, 1998.

Naremore, James. *The Magic World of Orson Welles*. Dallas: Southern Methodist University Press, 1989.

Thomson, David. *Rosebud: The Story of Orson Welles*. New York: Vintage Books, 1996.

WESTERN FILMS. The Western remains one of the most durable film genres. Since the beginnings of movie making, the stories of cowboys, Indians, ranchers, outlaws, and wagon trains have been Hollywood staples. The 1930s proved no exception, although the decade never saw any Westerns achieve the success and influence of, say, a **Gone with the Wind** (1939) or **It Happened One Night** (1934). Some have called the 1930s the golden age of the B Western, the B designating a movie that is in the second rank. It may be competently made but usually stars lesser-known performers, skimps on production costs, and generally lacks the overall quality of an A, or first-run, feature. In an age of double features, B pictures filled the lower half of the bill.

Despite the relative success of the B Westerns, expensively mounted dramas about cowboys have long attracted Hollywood's attention. In 1931, RKO Radio Pictures released *Cimarron*, a sprawling tale of the days of the Oklahoma land rush that features Richard Dix (1893–1949) and Irene Dunne (1898–1990). An early big-budget Western, it garnered Best Picture, a rare feat for this genre of movie. The land rush scenes, expertly choreographed by director Wesley Ruggles (1889–1972), remain thrilling to this day.

In 1931, unable to afford anything approaching *Cimarron* in the midst of the Depression, filmmakers came back in 1936 with *The Plainsman*, another "big" movie, and one directed by the master of that sort of thing, Cecil B. DeMille (1881–1959). Paramount Pictures may have thought the presence of Gary Cooper (1901–1961) as Wild Bill Hickok and Jean Arthur (1900–1991) as Calamity Jane, along with lots of gunplay between cowboys 'n' Indians, would guarantee box office riches, but they were wrong. More DeMille hokum than frontier history, this lavish black-and-white epic struggles for almost two hours, but its often-silly story fails to instill much awe.

Since Paramount Pictures missed the boat with *The Plainsman*, that same year they tried new film technology to assure the success of *Trail of the Lonesome Pine*. Billed as the first "all-outdoor, all-Technicolor" movie, it boasts rich color throughout its 102-minute running time. A tale of feuding families and the coming of the railroad, it stars Fred MacMurray (1908–1991) and Henry Fonda (1905–1982). Not the greatest movie of its day, but the lush Technicolor helped assure the slow demise of black-and-white, although the bulk of B Westerns continued to use that cheaper format for a number of years.

As the decade wound down, a spate of lavishly produced Westerns came to the screen, exemplifying Hollywood's prosperity on the eve of World War II. *Union Pacific* and *Dodge City*, both released in 1939, signaled renewed interest in the Western as a film type and a willingness to spend large sums to mount them. The first, directed by Cecil B. DeMille, features Joel McCrea (1905–1990) and Barbara Stanwyck (1907–1990) in a tale that climaxes with a stupendous train wreck, one of the biggest in movie history. The second, directed by Michael Curtiz (1886–1962), features Errol Flynn (1909–1959) and Olivia de Havilland (b. 1916) as a romantically linked couple. Action fans, however, had little interest in romance; they wanted fists and guns, and *Dodge City* grants their wishes with a rough-and-tumble barroom fight unlike anything filmed before. If DeMille had the grandest train wreck, Curtiz rivaled him with the biggest, wildest, longest brawl. The big-budget Western had come of age.

Expensive, star-filled Westerns were the exception. Given the lower costs but reasonable profitability of B movies, studios cranked out hundreds of them between 1930 and 1940; only a handful ever achieved any lasting fame. Actors like Buck Jones (1889–1942; *Ridin' for Justice* [1932], *Border Brigands* [1935], many others), Ken Maynard (1895–1973; *Two-Gun Man* [1931], *Six-Shootin' Sheriff* [1938], others), and Tom Mix (1880–1940; *The Rider of Death Valley* [1932], *The Miracle Rider* [1935], others) successfully made the transition from silents to sound. Relative newcomers like Charles Starrett (1903–1986; *Code of the Range* [1936], *One-Man Justice* [1937], others), George O'Brien (1899–1985; *Hollywood Cowboy* [1937], *Arizona Legion* [1939], others), and John Wayne (1907–1979; *Arizona* [1931], *'Neath the Arizona Skies* [1934], many others) emerged as new Western stars in the sound era. Out of this grouping of B actors, few managed to achieve wider stardom, although John Wayne successfully moved to A pictures.

One film in particular advanced Wayne's career, director John Ford's (1894–1973) classic *Stagecoach*, a 1939 picture. Ford, already established as a reliable and innovative director, took Wayne and the cast and crew to Monument Valley on the Arizona-Utah border. There the director achieved a perfect blend of character and action. Ably assisted by the peerless work of Yakima Canutt (1896–1986), one of the great stunt men in

Behind the scenes of *Stagecoach*, a 1939 Western. (Courtesy of Photofest)

Hollywood history, he told a timeless story, how a mixed group of individuals could find redemption on the desert, in a stagecoach, pursued by Indians on much of the journey. Ford would go on to new heights in the years to come, and Wayne accompanied him on this journey as his own career soared.

Unlike John Wayne, William Boyd (1895–1972) labored in endless B features. A matinee idol in the 1920s, he had virtually disappeared from the **movies** by 1935, appearing mainly in a group of inferior action pictures as Bill Boyd. In 1935, however, his flagging career as a movie actor suddenly blossomed with the first of a long series of cheaply made Westerns in which he starred as Hop-Along Cassidy. By 1937, the hyphen had been dropped, and "Hopalong" became his character's recognized name. With one after another Hopalong Cassidy tales playing on screens everywhere, the series became a favorite of Western fans. Between 1935 and 1940, Boyd made 31 Hopalong movies, or some 5 new titles a year. He would appear in 35 additional films during the 1940s, and then he successfully transferred this large movie library over to the new medium of **television**, beginning in 1946. There, he would garner even more fame as a TV pioneer.

Dressed all in black, his prematurely gray hair carefully coiffed, and accompanied always by his white horse, Topper, Boyd presents a striking image. "Hoppy" always plays the good guy, one reluctant to draw his six-shooter but eager to see justice done. The Hopalong Cassidy stories follow an unchanging format, a device that allowed

Paramount Studios frequently to reuse footage from earlier films. Although they might never win any awards, these movies represent one of the most successful Western series in motion picture history. They also demonstrate how formularized the Western myths had become by the 1930s, and how audiences had expectations that these conventions would be followed, even if it invited repetition in plot and action.

A spin-off in the stylized Western genre involved the **singing cowboys**, a category that includes such favorites as Gene Autry (1907–1998) and Roy Rogers (1911–1998). Not until the 1940s, would the major studios fully rediscover the Western as a significant and profitable component of movie genres.

See also Musicals; Race Relations & Stereotyping; Trains

SELECTED READING

Baxter, John. *Hollywood in the Thirties*. New York: A. S. Barnes & Co., 1968.
Bergman, Andrew. *We're in the Money: Depression America and Its Films*. New York: Harper & Row [Colophon], 1971.
Fenin, George N., and William K. Everson. *The Western: From Silents to Cinerama*. New York: Orion Press, 1962.

WINCHELL, WALTER. One of the leading newspaper columnists and **radio** personalities of the 1930s, Walter Winchell (1897–1972) was born in New York City and would spend most of his life there. He became a vaudevillian while still in his teens, a vocation that led to a continuing interest in show business and its people. Winchell collected gossip about his fellow entertainers and as a young man wrote an informal newsletter concerning their activities, especially their private lives. This avocation led to newspaper work during the 1920s, first with the tabloid *New York Graphic* in 1924, and then an association with the *New York Mirror* that began in 1929 and endured until 1963.

While ensconced at the *Mirror*, Winchell perfected the arts of celebrity-watching and gossipmongering. His success led to a new kind of journalism, the gossip column, and no one could challenge his authority in that area. Over 2,000 newspapers carried his daily column, *On Broadway*, during his heyday, a period that covered, roughly, from the 1930s on into the 1950s. Undone by his own sense of self-importance and out of step with changing times, Winchell died a forgotten man, a sad figure who once could make or break show business careers.

As he solidified his power, Winchell in 1930 branched out into radio, a medium just coming into it own. He had a 15-minute show on the Columbia Broadcasting System (CBS radio) network called *Saks on Broadway*, a brief, innuendo-filled summary of who was seen with whom and when and where. Audiences responded favorably to the exposé format, and the National Broadcasting Company (NBC radio) network contracted him to do *The Jergens Journal*, a similar show that reached millions. He soon began introducing his broadcasts with the staccato tap-tap-tap of a telegraph key and then intoning, "Good evening, Mr. and Mrs. America, from border to border and coast to coast, and all the ships at sea. Let's go to press!" Those opening words (the borders and coasts later came out) quickly became a part of radio history, familiar to people everywhere. *The Jergens Journal* in time became one of the nation's top-rated programs, and remained on the air, with different sponsors after 1948, until 1957.

Hollywood, impressed by the colorful columnist, in 1932 made two fictional **movies** about a similar journalist, calling one *Blessed Event* and the other *Okay, America!* Lee Tracy (1898–1968) impersonates Winchell in *Blessed Event*, and Lew Ayres (1908–1996) has the honors in *Okay, America!* Four years later, MGM produced *Broadway Melody of 1936*, the second of four *Broadway Melodies* released from 1929 to 1940. In this picture, radio comedian Jack Benny (1894–1974) plays yet another Winchell-like columnist always hungry for a story. Over the course of the decade, six additional movies used Winchell as himself. Although all will doubtless be remembered as second-rank B features—they bear such titles as *I Know Everybody's Racket* (1933), *Hollywood Gad-About* (1934), and *Love and Hisses* (1937)—the fact that producers agreed to do them at all confirms the notoriety Winchell had achieved by the early 1930s.

Although collecting and publicizing gossip constitutes a gray area of journalism, Winchell nonetheless made his mark in American **newspapers** and broadcasting. His Winchellisms, breezy but distinctive expressions that caught the public's attention, abounded. If a couple "middle-aisled," that signified a wedding; "renovate," on the other hand, meant someone dissolved his

Columnist Walter Winchell (1897–1972). (Courtesy of the Library of Congress)

or her marriage in Reno, Nevada, a place where divorces could be easily obtained. "Infanticipate" suggested someone was pregnant. Many other phrases likewise entertained his huge audience, contributing further to his popularity.

Winchell saw himself not just as an investigative reporter, but also a champion for the underdog. He therefore strongly defended President **Franklin D. Roosevelt** (1882–1945) and the **New Deal**. As World War II drew near, he ardently opposed the Axis powers and fascism (or "ratzis," as he termed them), and any hints of Nazism within the United States drew his considerable wrath. Through his career of chronicling the doings and misdoings of the famous, Walter Winchell himself became a newsworthy personality, a celebrity journalist.

See also Radio Networks

SELECTED READING
Dunning, John. *On the Air: The Encyclopedia of Old-Time Radio.* New York: Oxford University Press, 1998.
Gabler, Neal. *Winchell: Gossip, Power, and the Culture of Celebrity.* New York: Vintage Books, 1995.

WIZARD OF OZ, THE. A movie that has enthralled millions since its premiere in 1939, *The Wizard of Oz* continues to invite audiences of all ages to follow the Yellow Brick Road. A combination of the real and the fantastic, this lavish Metro-Goldwyn-Mayer production made a major star of **Judy Garland** (1922–1969), and the memorable

The Tin Man, the Scarecrow, Dorothy, and the Cowardly Lion on the Yellow Brick Road in *The Wizard of Oz*. (Courtesy of Photofest)

score, composed by Harold Arlen (1905–1986, music), E. Y. Harburg (1896–1981, lyrics), and Herbert Stothart (1885–1949, scoring), took two Academy Awards.

The film opens in a drab sepia, but not for long. A fearsome tornado sweeps across the Midwestern countryside, picks up Dorothy, along with her faithful dog, Toto, and gently deposits them in a different locale. In one of the great moments in movie history, Dorothy opens the doors to her new surroundings and the screen goes from sepia to lush, saturated Technicolor. With that, the story moves down the fabled Yellow Brick Road, from reality to fantasy, from Kansas to Oz, undergirded by a firm foundation in myth, especially that of returning home to family and security. But the success of *The Wizard of Oz* depends not on ingenious color processing and special effects, nor on plot, stars, and **music**; it works because all these elements mesh perfectly. Director Victor Fleming (1889–1949) would never again achieve the sustained level of imagination he briefly enjoyed on that film, although he would, in the months following, share in the overall direction of **Gone with the Wind**, another MGM blockbuster that would entertain audiences for generations to come.

Loosely based on the Oz stories by L. Frank Baum (1856–1919), especially *The Wonderful Wizard of Oz* (1900), it might have struck a chord with some members of a 1939 audience since nine silent films had also attempted the tale. Faithful to the original plots, MGM's production contains some elements of the prairie populism that often crops up in Baum's writing. He had failed in several business ventures and exhibited a bitter side in his prose, but aside from a few glimpses of honorable poverty (Uncle Henry and Auntie Em's farm, for instance), the movie avoids anything topical. True, it presents the "real" world of Kansas in sepia and the "dream" world of Oz in vivid colors, one stark and the other fantastical.

Those visual shifts, however, do not necessarily carry with them subtle references about the Dust Bowl 1930s or failed agrarianism; they function as special effects that separate the real from the unreal. The one exception might involve the delightful sets designed by Edwin B. Willis (1893–1963). For the Oz portions of the story, he created an inspired blend of **Art Deco** and **Streamlining**; the towers of the gleaming Emerald City evoke an optimistic view of the future, far more so than the aesthetic mixes attempted earlier in films like *Just Imagine* (1930) and the many Warner Brothers **musicals** of the decade. In fact, the **New York World's Fair** (1939–1940) was up and running at the same time as the movie, and the similarities between the fair's World of Tomorrow and Oz's Emerald City appear to be more than coincidence. In its own Hollywood way, *The Wizard of Oz* reflects many of the forward-looking **design** concepts of the later 1930s.

As the story unfolds, Dorothy and Toto meet a zany trio of bumbling associates, good vaudevillians all: a cowardly lion (Bert Lahr, 1895–1967), a bumbling scarecrow (Ray Bolger, 1904–1987), and a rusting tin man (Jack Haley, 1898–1979). This unlikely group then encounters a wicked witch (Margaret Hamilton, 1902–1985), the wizard himself (Frank Morgan, 1890–1949), and assorted Munchkins and other creatures. But Dorothy, throughout the movie, remains levelheaded. She knows better than to blindly accept all the bizarre events occurring around her; she knows that dreams cannot last forever. And the dream does end, as does the Yellow Brick Road. The film reverts to its opening sepia, and Dorothy and Toto return to Kansas and family and good heartland sensibility.

See also Children's Films; Movies; Musicals; Songwriters & Lyricists; Spectacle & Costume Drama Films; Teenage & Juvenile Delinquency Films

SELECTED READING
Ebert, Roger. *The Great Movies*. New York: Broadway Books, 2002.
Fricke, John, Jay Scarfone, and William Stillman. *The Wizard of Oz: The Official 50th Anniversary Pictorial History*. New York: Warner Books, 1989.

WOOD, GRANT. Born on a farm near Anamosa, Iowa, artist Grant Wood (1891–1942) achieved most of his fame on the basis of one painting, **American Gothic**. Done in 1930, this portrait of a stern couple (father and daughter? husband and wife?) has come down to the present as arguably the best-known painting ever executed by an American artist. Generations of viewers have responded to the two enigmatic portraits, along with endless parodies, and *American Gothic* has become larger than itself, evolving into an American icon.

Despite the fame—some would say notoriety—of *American Gothic*, Wood deserves attention for his entire output, not just one picture. He acquired his primary **education** in the United States, studying art, crafts, and **design** at several institutions. In 1920, he made the first of three trips to Europe, earning money by teaching in Cedar Rapids during the school year. By the mid-1920s, Wood had begun to exhibit and pick up commissions. Although he at times showed a humorous side, sometimes presenting himself as a naive rural painter in overalls who had happened to turn out a memorable portrait, his artistic influences came from a variety of sources. In addition to serious academic study of the Old Masters, he also derived inspiration from **advertising** art, catalogs, Currier and Ives lithographs, old photographs, and magazine illustrations. Together, these influences gave Wood a distinctive, identifiable style, one formed in realism, but imaginative and stylized in its own right.

By the mid-1930s, Wood had become part of the established artistic community. He directed programs in the federally funded Public Works of Art Project (PWAP; 1933–1934), a precursor to the better-known **Federal Art Project** (FAP; 1935–1943). He undertook several assignments involving public murals, including 1937's *Breaking the Prairie* at Iowa State University in Ames. Active until the end, Grant Wood died in February 1942.

Wood's approach to his subjects made his fame. Many in his audience initially saw him as a satirist of American values, a kind of Midwestern H. L. Mencken (1880–1956) in oils. For example, *Daughters of Revolution* (1932), a portrait similar in a number of ways to *American Gothic*, presents three stern, self-satisfied women looking directly at the viewer. Presumably members of an Iowa branch of the Daughters of the American Revolution, this trio will brook no misbehavior in thought or deed. As if for reinforcement, in the background is a copy of Emanuel Leutze's (1816–1868) *Washington Crossing the Delaware*, a painting done in 1851 and a much prouder retelling of American history than anything these latter-day protectors might utter.

Grant Wood himself also looked to American myth for his inspiration. Thus in 1931's *Midnight Ride of Paul Revere* and 1939's *Parson Weems' Fable*, he takes two well-known stories and interprets them anew. A tiny Paul Revere (1735–1818) gallops through the Massachusetts night to deliver his warning, but the effect suggests children manipulating little toy figures, not larger-than-life deeds. In the other work, a bemused Parson Weems (1756–1825) pulls aside a curtain to show viewers a miniature, bewigged George Washington (1732–1799), just a boy, hatchet in hand, but bearing the iconic face painted in the famous Gilbert Stuart (1755–1828) portraits, the same one that appears on dollar bills. This little Washington may be telling his irked father he "cannot tell a lie," but the event looks so staged, so artificial, that it questions the whole mythology about the first president.

As if to show his versatility, another side of Grant Wood goes beyond the sardonic mockery he sometimes exhibited. Many of his paintings depict Iowa in full bloom, a land of trimmed trees and geometric fields. In paintings like *Stone City, Iowa* (1930), *Young Corn* (1931), *Arbor Day* (1932), and *Spring Turning* (1936), among numerous others, he positions himself squarely as a **Regionalist** artist, capturing on canvas the seasons, the land, and the people of the American Midwest. Good, hardworking farmers live here, and he clearly shows them, partners with the fertile land, as in *Dinner for Threshers* (1934) or *In the Spring* (1939). His love for this side of the Midwest becomes evident, and the small minds and prejudices of *Daughters of Revolution* can be forgotten.

A splendid technician, and a man of greater depth than a cursory glance at his paintings might reveal, Grant Wood presented both a Regionalist love for locale and American themes and a satirical, questioning side that challenged the small thinking and smug certainties found in the Midwest of the 1930s.

See also Thomas Hart Benton; Herbert Hoover; Edward Hopper; Illustrators; Magazines; Reginald Marsh; New Deal; Charles Sheeler; Social Realism; Toys

SELECTED READING

Corn, Wanda. *Grant Wood: The Regionalist Vision.* New Haven, CT: Yale University Press, 1983.

Dennis, James. *Grant Wood: A Study in American Art and Culture.* Columbia: University of Missouri Press, 1986.

Roberts, Brady M., James M. Dennis, James S. Horns, and Helen Mar Parkin. *Grant Wood: An American Master Revealed.* San Francisco: Pomegranate Artbooks, 1995.

WRIGHT, FRANK LLOYD. The man deemed the greatest U.S. architect of the twentieth century had been designing buildings for some 40 years when the 1930s began. Born in 1869, he launched his long and distinguished career in 1889 in Wisconsin. A colorful personality, and possessed of a tempestuous personal life, by the time he reached 60, some in the architectural community perhaps thought it time for him to retire. Wright did not count himself among them. Although he had a string of acknowledged masterpieces behind him, no one could have foretold that almost 30 more productive years lay ahead of him. Wright remained active until his death in 1959, and the 1930s rank among his most fruitful decades.

During those years, he oversaw the completion of no fewer than 27 structures, ranging from modest homes to large-scale office complexes, and some of his most admired and enduring buildings emerged from his drawing board. Among those accomplishments, the following designs deserve mention: the many Usonian homes (1930s–1940s), the Kaufman residence, Fallingwater (1935), the Johnson Wax Building (1936), and the Johnson residence, Wingspread (1937).

The term "Usonian," a Wright neologism, suggests "United States," or "U.S.," and also serves as an acronym, US + *onian*. He began using the word in the 1930s when he discussed low-cost, available housing for people of limited means. The effects of the Depression had crippled much of the housing industry, a reality that had impacted his own commissions, and he decided to create affordable, aesthetically pleasing residences. His Usonian houses make up over half of his completed works for the decade and depart from his larger, expansive Prairie House concepts.

Using wood as his primary building material, Wright opted for one-story dwellings featuring flat roofs with considerable, often cantilevered, overhangs that blended the interior spaces with the surrounding outdoors. Since most American homeowners had acquired an automobile by the 1930s, he incorporated that fact into his designs, conceiving—and naming—the carport, an inexpensive, minimal shelter for the ubiquitous vehicle. Usonian homes frequently employ an L-shaped floor plan that effectively separates bedrooms from other living areas, and maximizes available floor space. Although his Usonian dwellings did not stir the enthusiasm, nor the sales, he anticipated and hoped for, they nonetheless looked to, and influenced, the future housing developments that would dot the American landscape following World War II.

While he worked on creating a "home for all" with his Usonian concepts, Wright also completed one of his great masterpieces, the Kaufman House, or Fallingwater. Built on a rocky hillside in southwestern Pennsylvania, Fallingwater incorporates elements of the

International Style with its white, unadorned facades, as well as much of his Prairie Style thinking with open interiors and natural touches like exposed rock ledges and a cascading stream that become integral parts of the house. Boldly cantilevered, Fallingwater sums up much of Wright's thinking about a dwelling being but an extension of the surrounding environment, and it challenged a generation of architects. In Wright's words "a **design** for living," the Kaufman House proved costly both to build and to maintain. But it broke free of the sterility of the International Style and brought a new level of modernism to usually conservative home **architecture**.

The following year, 1936, Wright unveiled his Administration Building for the Johnson Wax Company of Racine, Wisconsin. Using an essentially treeless urban site, he eliminated corners and cornices to produce a light-filled office space that supplies its own "trees" with what he called "dendriforms," narrow, towering columns that flare open at the top in order to support the ceiling. This design allows the creation of a vast, airy arena for employees to do their work, a place that enjoys a certain harmony with nature.

The Administration Building, from the exterior, invites comparison with the popular International Style, especially its smooth brick walls and ribbons of windows. But the sinuous curves of the Johnson structure run counter to the sharp angularity of most other commercial buildings, giving it a warmth usually lacking in modernism.

Wright and Herbert F. Johnson (1900–1980), the president of Johnson Wax, enjoyed a special relationship. With the completion of the Administration Building, Johnson commissioned Wright to design a private home for a peninsula on the shore of Lake Michigan near Racine. In a burst of creativity, Wright responded in 1937 with Wingspread, a large, expensive house that again expresses his Prairie School aesthetic. Employing what Wright described as a "pinwheel design," the house features a central, three-story domed octagon that serves as the axis for four wings that extend across the site, creating in effect a pinwheel that suggests the four points on a compass. Although not as spectacular as the Kaufman house, which preceded it by just two years, Wingspread embodies many characteristics associated with the architect: the horizontality of the earlier prairie houses; a long, low silhouette; a cruciform plan; and a complete integration of site and structure.

An architect who contributed a unique vision to American building, Frank Lloyd Wright continued to produce significant works until his death. The 1930s, a time of retrenchment in the construction trades, saw him attempting to adjust to the economic crises of the period with his Usonian houses. Much contemporary residential architecture owes a debt to his vision.

See also Automobiles; Streamlining

SELECTED READING

Gill, Brendan. *Many Masks: A Life of Frank Lloyd Wright*. New York: G. P. Putnam's Sons, 1987.

Hoffman, Donald. *Understanding Frank Lloyd Wright's Architecture*. New York: Dover Publications, 1995.

Johnson, Donald Leslie. *Frank Lloyd Wright versus America: The 1930s*. Cambridge, MA: MIT Press, 1990.

Storrer, William Allin. *The Architecture of Frank Lloyd Wright: A Complete Catalog*. Cambridge, MA: MIT Press, 1978.

WYETH, N. C. Born in Needham, Massachusetts, Newell Convers Wyeth (1882–1945; through most of his life, he was known by the initials N. C.) early on displayed artistic talent, along with a fondness for literature and history. In 1902, he enrolled in classes taught by the distinguished American illustrator Howard Pyle (1853–1911) in Wilmington, Delaware. Founder of the so-called Brandywine School of Illustration, Pyle profoundly influenced Wyeth, especially in the areas of realism and narrative. These elements achieved paramount importance in Wyeth's illustrations. A year after his admission to Pyle's school, the **Saturday Evening Post**, at that time already one of the most popular mass-circulation **magazines** published in the United States, accepted a Wyeth painting of a bronco rider as the cover for a February 1903 issue. That accomplishment launched the 21-year-old into what would prove to be a great career.

By the onset of the 1930s, Wyeth had reached a pinnacle of success and public regard, and many considered him the dean of American **illustrators**. A prolific artist, he had executed over 2,000 drawings and paintings since that early *Saturday Evening Post* cover. Among his Depression-era magazine clients, he could count *Good Housekeeping, Ladies' Home Journal, McCall's, The Progressive Farmer, Redbook, Scribner's Magazine, Woman's Day,* and *Woman's Home Companion*. His **advertising** art at that time included such diverse companies as the American Tobacco Company (Lucky Strikes), Coca-Cola, Frankfort Distilleries (Paul Jones whiskey), the General Electric Company, Hercules Incorporated (chemicals), International Harvester, and John Morrell & Company (meat packing).

In addition to these commissions, Wyeth also managed to create a significant body of other artistic work during the decade. Brochures and newsletters, booklets and bulletins, posters and calendars—his signature could be found on all. He painted a number of murals for banks, life insurance companies, publishers, schools, and **hotels**, the majority featuring episodes from American history or religious themes. In 1936, he completed a triptych for the Washington Cathedral, an unusual commission in those dire economic times.

By now financially secure, Wyeth enjoyed the luxury of painting for its own sake and showed no lessening of his powers or prestige. He practiced his still life techniques, especially the uses of light, and explored tempera painting. For these personal compositions, he worked leisurely, in contrast to the hectic pace he had maintained in earlier decades. In acknowledgment of his renown and popularity, museums, galleries, and collectors strove to purchase his works, both old and new. Numerous exhibitions celebrating prominent illustrators displayed his paintings and drawings, and he had the honor of a one-man show—belatedly, some would argue—in 1939 at a gallery in New York City.

People perhaps best remember N. C. Wyeth for the paintings he executed for the publishing firm of Charles Scribner's Sons between 1911 and 1939. Called the Scribner Illustrated Classics, these attractive, well-bound books were aimed at younger readers and included many well-known titles. Wyeth's pictures adorn the jackets and pages of such favorites as *Treasure Island* (1911), *Kidnapped* (1913), *The Black Arrow* (1916), *The Boy's King Arthur* (1917), *The Last of the Mohicans* (1919), *The Deerslayer* (1925), and *The Yearling* (1939), the last in the series. The success of the Scribner Classics led to contracts with other publishers for similar work, and his illustrations can be found in histories, novels, and stories published by Harper's, Houghton Mifflin; David McKay; Cosmopolitan

Book Corporation; Little, Brown; and others. Many of these editions have remained in print, in no small measure because of Wyeth's evocative pictures.

N. C. Wyeth stayed active on into the 1940s, but a fatal accident in 1945 prematurely snuffed out his career, but not his fame. In addition, he fathered a veritable artistic dynasty; of his five children, three were painters who carried the Wyeth name forward for the remainder of the century: Henriette (1907–1997), Carolyn (1909–1994), and Andrew (b. 1917).

See also Best Sellers; Regionalism; Soft Drinks; Norman Rockwell

SELECTED READING

Allen, Douglas, and Douglas Allen, Jr. *N. C. Wyeth: The Collected Paintings, Illustrations, and Murals.* New York: Crown Publishers, 1972.

Ermoyan, Arpi. *Famous American Illustrators.* New York: Society of Illustrators, 1997.

Meyer, Susan E. *America's Great Illustrators.* New York: Galahad Books, 1978.

Michaelis, David. *N. C. Wyeth: A Biography.* New York: Alfred A. Knopf, 1998.

Y

YOUR HIT PARADE. On Saturday evening, April 20, 1935, a new and original show made its **radio** debut on the National Broadcasting Company (NBC radio) network. Calling itself *Your Lucky Strike Hit Parade*, it attempted, in the space of an hour, to rank the most popular current songs across the nation. Contrary to what most people recall, the format at first featured 15 songs played in random order; the idea of a "top 10" and the breathless counting down to "number one" came later. "We don't pick 'em, we just play 'em," and play 'em they did, making *Your Hit Parade* must listening for anyone who wanted to know what tunes led the way for any particular week.

Your Hit Parade—although the cigarette maker continued to sponsor the show, the "*Lucky Strike*" soon disappeared from the title—enjoyed sufficient popularity that in April 1936 the two leading **radio networks** shared broadcasting rights to the program. The Columbia Broadcasting System (CBS radio) scheduled it on Saturday evenings, and NBC aired it on Wednesdays. At the end of 1937, CBS gained exclusive rights to *Your Hit Parade* and retained them until 1947, when NBC recaptured the show. The program would remain on radio until 1957. A **television** version also covered the hits; it ran from 1950 until 1959, an unusual radio-television overlap.

The show's promoters claimed they could estimate, scientifically, the nation's popular preferences by surveying weekly record and **sheet music** sales, along with jukebox plays and disc jockey preferences, at selected outlets. *Hit Parade* staffers also contacted popular band leaders, questioning them about what musical numbers received the most requests from the dance floor, although any responses in that regard would have to be seen as subjective and less than reliable. The producers professed complete objectivity in their surveys—Broadway and Hollywood tunes, current hits, old standards, new releases—and claimed no favorites; whatever sold during the week they noted. After tabulating the results of their polling, they promised listeners the show would perform the 15 top-ranked songs for the preceding seven days.

That tabulating, done amid a rather contradictory mix of fanfare and secrecy by the American Tobacco Company's **advertising** agency, brought with it delightful suspense for the waiting audience. The results arrived, in time for rehearsals, at the networks' studios each week in an armored truck. Of course, such procedures generated considerable publicity, something everyone involved wanted. While listeners awaited the results, the orchestra and the singers worked diligently to come up with fresh weekly arrangements of the chosen songs. If a number lingered in the listings, they faced the challenge of repeating it while at the same time keeping it from getting repetitious or stale.

The show changed over time. The original 15 songs got cut to 7 in 1936. A year later, 7 went to 10, the figure most people remember. *Your Hit Parade* stayed with 10 songs until 1943, when the total dropped to 9. For the remainder of its run, the show's number of selections shifted periodically. By the time of its 1957 demise the band and singers were performing only 5 tunes. *Your Hit Parade* often gave audiences additional songs not in the official tabulations, calling these treats "Lucky Strike Extras."

The musicians and singers on *Your Hit Parade* changed almost as quickly as the latest hits they performed. The house band had no fewer than 14 different leaders fronting it between 1935 and 1940, most of whom appeared for only a few weeks at a time. The conductors ranged from fairly well-known figures like Lennie Hayton (1908–1971) in the summer of 1935, Harry Sosnik (1906–1996) in September 1936, and Raymond Scott (1908–1994), who led the band from November 1938 until July 1939, to relative unknowns like Richard Himber (1899–1966) in June 1937, and Peter Van Steeden (1904–1990) the following month. The vocalists of the 1930s likewise made for a mixed group, with 19 different singers interpreting the hits, although few achieved much fame. Kay Thompson (1908–1998) sang in 1935, Buddy Clark (1912–1949) in 1936, Georgia Gibbs (b. 1920; then known as Fredda Gibson) in 1938, Lanny Ross (1906–1988) in 1939, as well as "Wee" Bonnie Baker (1917–1990) and Bea Wain (b. 1917) that same year; together they remain the best-remembered performers for the 1930s.

Despite the constantly changing faces on the show, audiences loved the suspense and they got to hear some of their favorites performed each week. The proof of the formula came with the show's longevity: *Your Hit Parade* outlasted most **music** shows of any kind. It focused on the songs themselves, not the performers. "Number one" always meant a particular tune, although several interpretations of the same song by different artists might be competing in the marketplace.

With its large, enthusiastic listenership, a tantalizing question arises: How closely did the show reflect the public's tastes and how much did it influence them? Did *Your Hit Parade* serve as an accurate barometer of public preferences? No definitive answer has ever been given, but the show doubtless had an effect on both sides of the issue. Like many elements of popular culture, *Your Hit Parade* functioned as both an influence on and a reflector of public preferences.

See also Jukeboxes; Radio Networks; Recordings

SELECTED READING
Dunning, John. *On the Air: The Encyclopedia of Old-Time Radio.* New York: Oxford University Press, 1998.
Williams, John R. *This Was "Your Hit Parade."* Camden, ME: Courier-Gazette, 1973.

YOUTH. Before the onset of the Great Depression, most young people had tradition-ally entered the workforce when they reached their teen years. They found jobs on farms or in factories, and the terms "teenager" and "adolescent" usually signified those lucky ones who could go on to high school, a small elite group that did not have to find work. But the economic difficulties of the 1930s pushed youths out of the job market in order to guarantee more opportunities for adults seeking employment. Many teens chose to remain in school, creating the largest high school population in the nation's history. "Adolescents" now referred to an entire age group, not just a privileged socioeconomic class.

Even with a dramatic increase in school enrollment, perhaps as many as 3 million young people between the ages of 16 and 24 did not attend school, did not have a job, had no good reason to stay at home, and had no place to turn to for relief. In 1933, the U.S. Children's Bureau estimated that 23,000 adolescents (a figure that many ascribed as low), mostly males, aimlessly roamed the country with neither a dime nor a place to sleep, a condition that caught the attention of many Americans.

Franklin D. Roosevelt (1882–1945) assumed the presidency following a landslide victory in the 1932 election. Soon after his 1933 inauguration, and at his urging, Congress established the **Civilian Conservation Corps** (CCC, 1933–1942), a **New Deal** program that offered unemployed men between the ages of 18 and 25 meaningful work and healthy living in camps across the country. As conditions worsened, officials lowered the entry age to 17. For those who volunteered, the program quickly improved their lives, and their labor contributed to the betterment of the country.

But this stopgap measure primarily served young adults, not needy youth; therefore it failed to meet the wants of many younger Americans. Those teens who stayed in high school or college to pursue an **education** often struggled financially to do so. Also, the total number of youth not in school, unemployed, and ineligible for the CCC remained high. Many adults worried that these ranks would grow and that young people would become disillusioned and apathetic; some expressed concern about the potential for juvenile delinquency. The fear that unproductive and disgruntled youth would succumb to revolutionary politics also entered these discussions.

In May 1934, First Lady **Eleanor Roosevelt** (1884–1962) stepped forward as a champion of adolescents, saying that she lived in "real terror that we may be losing this generation. We have got to bring these young people into the active life of the community and make them feel that they are necessary." Shortly thereafter, student leaders and youth activists from across the country formed the American Youth Congress (AYC) to discuss the problems facing teenagers. AYC activity peaked between 1936 and 1939 as the group lobbied for racial justice, increased federal spending on education, and an end to mandatory participation in the Reserve Officers Training Corps (ROTC) for male college students. In 1936, the AYC issued a Declaration of the Rights of American Youth, a statement that recognized the growing impact that adolescents exerted in society.

Mrs. Roosevelt took a special interest in the politics undergirding the student movement. She worked closely with educators and convinced the president to sign an executive order establishing the National Youth Administration (NYA, 1935–1943), a division of the Works Progress Administration (WPA, 1935–1943; name changed to Work Projects Administration in 1939). The NYA, designed for young people between the ages of 16 and 25, aimed to combat the problem of youth unemployment on a long-term basis in two ways. First, it allocated grants to high school and college students in exchange for part-time work, usually within the educational institution. This income enabled them to continue their studies while at the same time reducing the number of unemployed youth. Second, it combined economic relief with on-the-job training for those not in school and unemployed, thereby giving them a better opportunity to find meaningful work.

President Roosevelt appointed Aubrey Willis Williams (1890–1965) to head the new agency, a position he held throughout the program's existence. By 1938, the NYA had enrolled more than 480,000 people, and, unlike the all-male CCC, it included women. Schools and colleges ran the student work program, making that sector relatively easy to manage. The component for individuals not attending school presented more difficulties. The first work projects, such as cleaning up public buildings, benefited communities, but they did not impart practical job skills. To correct this situation, the NYA introduced short-term courses to assist participants in acquiring permanent work skills.

In addition, the NYA courses supported traditional American values. Across all economic strata, social classes, and races, a majority of citizens during the 1930s saw a respectable life as one where women held the role of homemakers and men worked as breadwinners. Instruction in areas like child care, sewing, nutrition, and money management enabled girls to learn how to run their future homes efficiently and raise their children intelligently. The NYA also taught some out-of-home employment skills, such as those needed for secretarial positions. For boys, courses in car mechanics, basic shop, and commercial art provided them marketable skills in anticipation of their becoming the primary wage-earners for their future families.

Community groups also offered teenagers opportunities for worthwhile ways to spend their time. These groups organized activities that helped prepare them for their future lives as husbands and breadwinners, wives and homemakers, and responsible community residents and leaders. Organizations such as the Young Men's Hebrew Association (YMHA) and the Department of Agriculture's 4-H Clubs gained new members.

The Boy Scouts of America did well during the Depression, with membership surpassing 1 million by the early 1930s. Encouraged by this popularity, the organization launched a program for younger boys in 1930 called Cub Scouts. The Girl Scouts of America also engaged in active recruiting and experienced substantial growth. In the mid-1930s the organization inaugurated its annual nationwide cookie sale. Churches, YMCAs, and YWCAs, along with high school athletic programs, provided **leisure and recreation** resources with indoor tracks, **swimming** pools, gyms, game rooms, and hobby clubs.

As enrollments grew, high school became a shared experience for a majority of American adolescents, and with that a distinct youth culture developed. Teens began looking to one another, not to adults, for advice, information, and approval. They tried to make sense of their times, with the result that social science and history courses gained in popularity. Marxist study and discussion groups, such as the Young Socialists and the Young Communists, experienced membership increases, and an active student antiwar movement developed.

Three groups in particular appeared on college campuses: the Socialist League for Industrial Democracy (SLID), the National Student League (NSL), and the National Student Federation of America (NSFA). All three adapted the Oxford Pledge, an ideological movement that had its origins in England. Those who affirmed it promised not to support the government of the United States in any war it might conduct, and as early as 1933 the three groups coordinated an annual student strike against war. As the very real threat of world war loomed larger, these organizations openly demonstrated for peace and lobbied in Washington, D.C., to keep the nation out of foreign conflicts.

The business community, far less ideological and political than those student groups, addressed the youth issue in another way. Advertisers and merchants quickly zeroed in on this newly identified youth market. Sellers of school supplies and clothing aimed their ads directly at teenage consumers, not their parents. Products traditionally targeted at adults were found to possess new uses for this marketing group. For example, Fleischmann's Yeast promised to clear a pimply complexion, while Postum, a beverage substitute for caffeine and coffee, guaranteed young people pep and vitality.

Acceptability and popularity, always important for young people, became important components of a new concept, that of teenage rights. They increasingly demanded the right to dress and act the way they wanted to, along with the right to choose their own friends and run their own social lives. As the Depression waned, **magazines**, books, **movies**, and **radio** exploited these themes and, with the enthusiastic help of advertisers, began to create an image of the American teenager as an autonomous person possessing a private life that included a car, a telephone, an allowance, stylish clothes, and endless entertainment. For most adolescents and their parents, it may have been pie in the sky, but the image nonetheless took vigorous root.

Print media recognized the emerging adolescent subculture while simultaneously reinforcing character building and the accepted role differences of men and women. Publications such as *American Boy* and *Boy's Life* contained inspiring adventure stories of teenage heroes who could handle a gun, survive in the wilderness, and protect their families. These male-oriented articles admired bravery but cautioned that real men never took risks lightly and always upheld their responsibilities to others. Numerous authors extolled the value of earning a good living and even suggested ways for young men to make money, ranging from delivering **newspapers** to printing and distributing circulars.

On the other hand, magazines like *American Girl* and *Everygirls* taught that life improved with marriage and children. These periodicals urged girls to nurture their talents in order to create a beautiful home and raise healthy children. The magazines' articles stressed the importance of mastering the domestic skills of cooking, sewing, shopping, and housekeeping, and acknowledged the value of engaging in community service. Discussions of working outside the home appeared occasionally, with the exception of careers that would have been in direct competition with masculine goals, such as medicine and law.

In a bow to the manners and mores of past decades, dating remained restrictive during the 1930s; teenage autonomy still had its limits. Few young men could afford the costs of entertaining a girlfriend beyond maybe a movie or a soda. No doubt many girls and some boys felt their wardrobes inadequate for socializing. Along with innumerable **fashion** hints, the magazines for girls also emphasized that they should know proper etiquette and understand how dating and courtship worked in American society. Although both girl- and boy-oriented publications avoided frank discussions of sex, the ones directed at teenage girls did present the concept of "Mr. Right," along with the idea that one should wait to marry until "he" came along. Some women's magazines, such as the *Ladies' Home Journal*, along with a few newspapers, ran advice columns on modern dating behaviors. They stressed the girl's role of regulating male deportment and of practicing caution and restraint; nice girls kept their dates in line.

The boys' magazines did not carry comparable columns. Some of the more daring young males might sneak a glance at a newsstand copy of *Spicy Detective, Esquire*, or the *Police Gazette*, and some might discover the crude, cheaply printed cartoon booklets of pornographic material called "8-pagers," or "Tijuana Bibles" for titillation. Family-centered magazines, like *Parents*, encouraged adults to address their children's sexual development through frank father-son and mother-daughter talks that stressed responsibility and the need to prepare for a productive future before marrying and starting a family.

Pulp magazines and books also catered to the youth market. Girls could turn to a host of publications like *True Romance, True Lovers, True Experience*, and *True Story* to read about love and all its accompanying emotional anguish. For young males, the exploits of youthful heroes appeared in cheap periodicals like *Argosy, Doc Savage, Action Stories, The Shadow*, and innumerable others. Heroes for either gender could be found in **comic books** like *Detective Comics, Superman, Batman*, and dozens more.

As far as portraying adolescents, newspaper **comic strips** had a head start on rival media. Readers in the 1920s and 1930s enjoyed, among others, two humorous strips that focused on young people: *Freckles and His Friends* and *Harold Teen. Freckles and His Friends* debuted in 1915. Written and drawn by Merrill Blosser (1892–1983), it features Freckles, a kid about 7 or 8 years old. In the 1930s, Freckles overnight grows to be 16 and gets involved with girls, dating, and all the other rituals of adolescence. It would continue in newspapers until 1973, when it quietly faded away.

Harold Teen, created in 1919 by Carl Ed (1890–1959), boasted a strong readership from its inception. Harold uses contemporary slang, a teenage characteristic across all time periods, and the strip introduced a number of favorites during the 1930s—for example, "Yowsah!" and "pitch a li'l woo." Despite the popularity of the comic strip, two movie adaptations, *Harold Teen* (1928; remade in 1934 as a musical but with the same title) did little at the box office, once again proving that media crossovers have no guaranteed success. Harold's antics in newspapers ended with Carl Ed's death in 1959.

Other strips with adolescent characters often focused on adventure. Milton Caniff's (1907–1988) **Terry and the Pirates**, an immediate hit, premiered in 1934. Its likable young hero moves from one dangerous experience to another in the exotic Far East, matching up well with radio **serials** of the day. In fact, in 1937 Terry got his own late afternoon network time slot with the National Broadcasting Company (NBC radio).

Roy Powers, Eagle Scout, a series done by Frank Godwin (1889–1959), among others, in 1938 featured 17-year-old Roy as leader of the Beaver Patrol Troop in adventures around the neighborhood and later around the globe. For the five years of its run it served as the official strip of the Boy Scouts of America, a reflection of the popularity of scouting.

The Stratemeyer Syndicate, a large publishing firm that controlled many different fiction titles and series, specialized in mass producing formularized reading for youthful audiences. The firm released, with great success, 16 different Nancy Drew books during the 1930s. Starting with *The Secret of the Old Clock* (1930), and three others that first year, the syndicate created one of the most enduring teen heroines in literary history. Ghostwritten by several authors under the pseudonym Carolyn Keene, each featured Nancy Drew and her friends solving mysteries. Unlike most teenage girls of the 1930s, Nancy owns a sporty blue roadster and knows as much about engines and transmissions as any young man. In fact, she can do just about anything, important features for an adventure series. Mildred Wirt Benson (1905–2002) worked as one of the ghostwriters for the series, and she wrote most of the 1930s titles.

Given her success in print, Nancy Drew in time graduated to film. *Nancy Drew, Detective* (1938), the first in a series of four movies during the period, presented the story line of the 1933 novel *Password to Larkspur Lane*. Bonita Granville (1923–1988) starred in all, and she made a convincing Nancy Drew. Three more pictures came out in 1939: *Nancy Drew and the Hidden Staircase* carried the same story and title as its 1930 print counterpart; *Nancy Drew, Reporter* and *Nancy Drew, Troubleshooter* rounded out this rush of Depression-era films about the teenage detective.

In addition to magazines, books, and comic strips, other media, such as movies, radio, and **recordings**, became universal experiences for an increasing number of young people during the 1930s. Children and teenagers everywhere went to Saturday matinees and saw the same features, short subjects, newsreels, and serials, reinforcing national modes of behavior. As the teen culture developed, Hollywood struggled with how to portray adolescents; for most of the decade, many motion pictures focused on troubled youth caught up in petty **crime** and running in gangs. Initially, these movies served as hard-hitting studies of juvenile delinquency, a side of youthful behavior that concerned many adults, and they purported to demonstrate how economic and social forces conspired to wear down a neighborhood and turn innocent children into hardened criminals. Over time, however, these movies eroded into youthful shenanigans and slapstick comedy.

The films of the 1930s seldom depict adolescents in meaningful roles that clearly link them with any evolving subculture of youth. All that changed when Mickey Rooney (b. 1920) appeared in a succession of 17 Andy Hardy Films that commenced in 1937. The first, *A Family Affair*, casts him as the typical American male teenager. **Judy Garland** (1922–1969), soon to be a star herself, costars with Rooney in *Thoroughbreds Don't Cry* (1937—not an Andy Hardy film, but their first roles together), *Love Finds Andy Hardy* (1938), and *Babes in Arms* (1939) and quickly found herself cast as the model teenage girl, a role that would culminate with her playing Dorothy in 1939's **The Wizard of Oz**.

On weekdays, right after they got home from school, many young people turned on the radio. Early in the decade, the major networks began utilizing the 4 P.M. until 6 P.M. slot for serials aimed at the after-school crowd. In extended tales of good pitted against evil (with good always winning), the serials contained action, adventure, patriotism, and heroics that appealed to listeners from elementary through high school. *Jack Armstrong, the All-American Boy* (1933–1950), *The Lone Ranger* (1933–1955), *Jungle Jim* (1935–1952), *Smilin' Jack* (1935–1939), *Don Winslow of the Navy* (1937–1943), and *Captain Midnight* (1939–1949) ranked among the most popular.

Fan magazines, radio shows, and the movies provided teenagers an incredible amount of knowledge about the **music** of the 1930s and they quickly became connoisseurs, particularly in the area of **swing**. NBC's Saturday evening show **Your Hit Parade** premiered in April 1935 and attracted young listeners all over the country, another step toward creating a national teen culture. They bought millions of records and fed nickels into the innumerable **jukeboxes** found in soda shops and diners everywhere. The more they listened, the more they learned about the popular tunes of the era; in time, they challenged authorities who had traditionally dictated musical standards. This new generation of youthful critics brought about a refreshing openness. As educated fans, they knew the bands and sidemen, appreciated the hits, and saw in swing a new expression of their right of independence.

Much popular music in the 1930s encouraged both listening and dancing. For teenagers out of work and not in school, the popular dance marathons offered something to do along with the chance to make some money. Dance crazes abounded: the Shag, the Lindy Hop, the Big Apple, and the Suzy Q. But for most teenagers only one dance really mattered, the **jitterbug**. Dance halls and pavilions sprang up everywhere, as did jukeboxes, and in 1937 they even jitterbugged in the aisles of New York's Paramount Theater to the swing of **Benny Goodman**.

The economic crisis at the beginning of the 1930s clearly shaped the lives of children and youth. Despite the troubled times and the large number of uneducated and untrained transient youth during the Great Depression, the decade developed as one filled with promise for young people. Adolescence became a developmental period separate from childhood and adulthood; it possessed its own rituals and responsibilities, and demanded—for most youth—that they get a high school education. Finally, merchandisers, advertisers, and the popular media courted teenagers as a distinct, identifiable subculture.

See also Advertising; Automobiles; Desserts; Children's Films; Games; Hobbies; Marathon Dancing; Musicals; Race Relations & Stereotyping; Radio Networks; Soft Drinks; Teenage & Juvenile Delinquency Films; Toys

SELECTED READING

Davis, Maxine. *The Lost Generation: A Portrait of American Youth Today.* New York: Macmillan, 1936.

Palladino, Grace. *Teenagers, An American History.* New York: Basic Books, 1996.

Rollin, Lucy. *Twentieth-Century Teen Culture by the Decades: A Reference Guide.* Westport, CT: Greenwood Press, 1999.

Roosevelt, Eleanor. "'Blind Voting' Hit by Mrs. Roosevelt." *New York Times*, 8 May 1934. *Historic New York Times.* Proquest, Lynchburg College Library, Lynchburg, VA.

Selected Resources

Bibliographical Note. As the Internet grows in thoroughness, accuracy, and ever-easier access, the number of available resource tools will continue to increase. In any work, such as this encyclopedia, that stresses popular culture, familiarity with sources like the Internet Movie Database (http://www.imdb.com), the Internet Broadway Database (http://www.ibdb.com), and the bands-composers-lyricists database (http://info.net/index.html) will prove invaluable. Access to the National Archives and the Library of Congress, two treasure troves of information on just about anything connected with the United States, can be found at http://www.archives.gov and http://www.loc.gov/index.html. Monetary conversions are simple with http://www.minneapolisfed.org/research/data/us/calc. Literally hundreds of other websites offer information about the 1930s, and readers are encouraged to avail themselves of this research tool.

Adam, Henry. *Thomas Hart Benton: An American Original.* New York: Alfred A. Knopf, 1989.

Alcoholics Anonymous. 3rd ed. New York: Alcoholics Anonymous World Services, 1976.

Alcohol Statistics. http://www.niaaa.hih.gov/databases/consum01.txt

Aldrich, Nelson W., Jr. *Tommy Hitchcock: An American Hero.* New York: Margaret Mellon Hitchcock, 1984.

Allen, Douglas, and Douglas Allen Jr. *N. C. Wyeth: The Collected Paintings, Illustrations, and Murals.* New York: Crown Publishers, 1972.

Allen, E. John B. *From Skisport to Skiing: One Hundred Years of an American Sport, 1840–1940.* Amherst, MA: University of Massachusetts Press, 1993.

Almond, Steve. *Candyfreak: A Journey through the Chocolate Underbelly of America.* Chapel Hill, NC: Algonquin Books, 2004.

Altman, Rick, ed. *Genre: The Musical.* Boston: Routledge & Kegan Paul, 1981.

The American Heritage History of Flight. New York: Simon & Schuster, 1962.

American Musical Theater. 6 LPs. Smithsonian Collection of Recordings. R 036, 1989.

American Popular Song. 7 LPs. Smithsonian Collection of Recordings. R 031, 1984.

Anobile, Richard J., ed. *Why a Duck? Verbal and Visual Gems from the Marx Brothers Movies.* New York: Darien House, 1971.

Appelbaum, Stanley. *The New York World's Fair, 1939–1940.* New York: Dover Publications, 1977.

Armour, Richard. *Give Me Liberty.* New York: World Publishing Co., 1969.

Aron, Cindy S. *Working at Play: A History of Vacations in the United States.* New York: Oxford University Press, 1998.

Arwas, Victor. *Art Deco.* New York: Harry N. Abrams, 1992.

Aspinwall, Margaret, ed. *200 Years of American Sculpture*. New York: Whitney Museum of American Art, 1976.

Astaire, Fred. *Steps in Time*. New York: Harper & Brothers, 1959.

Atkinson, Brooks, and Albert Hirschfeld. *The Lively Years, 1920–1973*. New York: Association Press, 1973.

Augspurger, Michael. *An Economy of Abundant Beauty: Fortune Magazine and Depression America*. Ithaca, NY: Cornell University Press, 2004.

Austin, Joe, and Michael Nevin Willard, eds. *Generations of Youth: Youth Cultures and History in Twentieth-Century America*. New York: New York University Press, 1998.

Automobile Manufacturers Association. *Automobiles of America*. Detroit: Wayne State University Press, 1968.

Baby Foods. http://www.gerber.com/gerberbaby

Baeder, John. *Gas, Food, and Lodging*. New York: Abbeville Press, 1982.

Baigell, Matthew. *The American Scene: American Painting of the 1930s*. New York: Praeger, 1974.

———. *Thomas Hart Benton*. New York: Harry N. Abrams, 1975.

Baker, Aaron. *Contesting Identities: Sports in American Film*. Urbana: University of Illinois Press, 2003.

Balfour, Alan. *Rockefeller Center: Architecture as Theater*. New York: McGraw-Hill, 1978.

Balio, Tino. *Grand Design: Hollywood as a Modern Business Enterprise, 1930–1939*. Vol. 5 of *History of the American Cinema*. Charles Harpole, gen. ed. 10 vols. New York: Charles Scribner's Sons, 1993.

Ball, John, ed. *The Mystery Story*. San Diego: University of California, San Diego, 1976.

Barbour, Alan G. *Cliffhanger: A Pictorial History of the Motion Picture Serial*. New York: Lyle Stuart, 1979.

Barfield, Ray. *Listening to Radio, 1920–1950*. Westport, CT: Praeger, 1996.

Barger, Harold. *The Transportation Industries, 1889–1946: A Study of Output, Employment, and Productivity*. New York: National Bureau of Economic Research, 1951.

Barnet, Richard D., Bruce Nemerov, and Mayo R. Taylor. *The Story behind the Song: 150 Songs That Chronicle the 20th Century*. Westport, CT: Greenwood Press, 2004.

Barnouw, Erik. *A History of Broadcasting in the United States*. 3 vols. Vol. 1, *A Tower in Babel*. Vol. 2, *The Golden Web*. Vol. 3, *The Image Empire*. New York: Oxford University Press, 1966–1970.

———. *Tube of Plenty: The Evolution of American Television*. New York: Oxford University Press, 1982.

Baron, Stanley [Wade]. *Brewed in America: A History of Beer and Ale in the United States*. New York: Arno Press, 1972

Barrier, Michael, and Martin Williams, eds. *The Smithsonian Book of Comic-Book Comics*. Washington, DC: Smithsonian Institution Press, 1981.

Bascomb, Neal. *Higher: A Historic Race to the Sky and the Making of a City*. New York: Doubleday, 2003.

Basinger, Jeanine. *A Woman's View: How Hollywood Spoke to Women, 1930–1960*. New York: Alfred A. Knopf, 1993.

Batterberry, Michael, and Ariane Batterberry. *Fashion: The Mirror of History*. New York: Greenwich House, 1977.

Baughman, James L. *Henry R. Luce and the Rise of the American News Media*. Boston: Twayne, 1987.

Baur, Brian C. *Franklin D. Roosevelt and the Stamps of the United States, 1933–1945*. Sidney, OH: Amos Press, 1993.

Baxter, John. *Hollywood in the Thirties*. New York: A. S. Barnes & Co., 1968.

———. *Science Fiction in the Cinema*. New York: A. S. Barnes & Co., 1970.

Bealle, Morris A. *The Softball Story*. Washington, DC: Columbia Publishing Co., 1957.

Beck, Calvin Thomas. *Heroes of the Horrors*. New York: Macmillan, 1975.

Beer. http://www.beeradvocate.com/beer/101/history_american_beer.php

———. http://www.falstaffbrewing.com/interest.htm

Behlmer, Rudy. *America's Favorite Movies: Behind the Scenes*. New York: Frederick Ungar Publishing Co., 1982.

Belasco, Warren James. *Americans on the Road: From Autocamp to Motel, 1910–1945*. Cambridge, MA: MIT Press, 1979.

Belasco, Warren, and Philip Scranton, eds. *Food Nations: Selling Taste in Consumer Societies*. New York: Routledge, 2002.

Benshoff, Harry M., and Sean Griffin. *America on Film: Representing Race, Class, Gender, and Sexuality at the Movies*. Malden, MA: Blackwell Publishing, 2004.

Bergman, Andrew. *We're in the Money: Depression America and Its Films*. New York: Harper & Row [Colophon], 1971.

Bergreen, Lawrence. *As Thousands Cheer: The Life of Irving Berlin*. New York: Viking-Penguin, 1990.

Berkowitz, Michael. "A 'New Deal' for Leisure: Making Mass Tourism during the Great Depression." In *Being Elsewhere: Tourism, Consumer Culture, and Identity in Modern Europe and North America*, ed. Shelley Baranowski and Ellen Furlough. Ann Arbor: University of Michigan Press, 2001, 185–212.

Bernstein, Irving. *A Caring Society: The New Deal, the Worker, and the Great Depression*. Boston: Houghton Mifflin, 1985.

Bernstein, Matthew, ed. *Controlling Hollywood: Censorship and Regulation in the Studio Era*. New Brunswick, NJ: Rutgers University Press, 1999.

Best, Gary Dean. *The Nickel and Dime Decade: American Popular Culture during the 1930s*. Westport, CT: Praeger, 1993.

Biel, Steven. *American Gothic: A Life of America's Most Famous Painting*. New York: W. W. Norton, 2005.

Bigelow, Marybelle S. *Fashion in History: Western Dress, Prehistoric to Present*. Minneapolis: Burgess Publishing Co., 1979.

Big Little Books. http://www.biglittlebooks.com

Bindas, Kenneth J. *All of This Music Belongs to the Nation: The WPA's Federal Music Project and American Society*. Knoxville: University of Tennessee Press, 1995.

Bird, Caroline. *The Invisible Scar*. New York: David McKay, 1966.

Bird, William L., Jr. *"Better Living": Advertising, Media, and the New Vocabulary of Business Leadership, 1935–1955*. Evanston, IL: Northwestern University Press, 1999.

Birds Eye Foods. http://www.birdseyefoods.com/corp/about/clarenceBirdseye.asp

Bix, Amy Sue. *Inventing Ourselves Out of Jobs? America's Debate over Technological Unemployment, 1929–1981*. Baltimore: Johns Hopkins University Press, 2000.

Black, Allida M., ed. *Courage in a Dangerous World: The Political Writings of Eleanor Roosevelt*. New York: Columbia University Press, 1999.

Blanchard, Margaret A., ed. *History of the Mass Media in the United States, An Encyclopedia*. Chicago: Fitzroy-Dearborn, 1998.

Bleiler, Everett F., and Richard J. Bleiler. *Science-Fiction: The Gernsback Years*. Kent, OH: Kent State University Press, 1998.

Block, Geoffrey. *Enchanted Evenings: The Broadway Musical from Show Boat to Sondheim*. New York: Oxford University Press, 1997.

Blockade. http://www.classicfilmguide.com/index.php?s=links

Bloom, John. *A House of Cards: Baseball Card Collecting and Popular Culture*. Minneapolis: University of Minnesota Press, 1997.

Blum, Stella, ed. *Everyday Fashions of the Thirties: As Pictured in Sears Catalogs*. New York: Dover Publications, 1986.

Bogle, Donald. *Bright Boulevards, Bold Dreams: The Story of Black Hollywood*. New York: Ballantine Books, 2005.

———. *Toms, Coons, Mulattoes, Mammies, and Bucks: An Interpretive History of Blacks in American Films*. New York: Continuum, 1989.

Bojarski, Richard, and Kenneth Beale. *The Films of Boris Karloff*. Secaucus, NJ: Citadel Press, 1974.

Bondi, Victor, ed. *American Decades, 1930–1939*. New York: Gale Research, 1995.

Book-of-the-Month Club editors. *The First Forty Years of the Book-of-the-Month Club*. New York: Book-of-the-Month Club, 1966.

Borden, Bill, and Steve Posner. *The Big Book of Big Little Books*. San Francisco: Chronicle Books, 1997.

Bordman, Gerald. *American Theatre: A Chronicle of Comedy and Drama, 1930–1969*. New York: Oxford University Press, 1996.

———. *Jerome Kern: His Life and Music*. New York: Oxford University Press, 1980.

Botting, Douglas. *Dr. Eckener's Dream Machine: The Giant Zeppelin and the Dawn of Air Travel*. New York: Henry Holt, 2001.

Bourke-White, Margaret, and Erskine Caldwell. *You Have Seen Their Faces*. New York: Modern Age Books, 1937.

Braden, Donna R. *Leisure and Entertainment in America*. Dearborn, MI: Henry Ford Museum and Greenfield Village, 1988.

Brant, Marshall. *The Games*. New York: Proteus, 1980.

Brenner, Joel Glenn. *The Emperors of Chocolate: Inside the Secret World of Hershey and Mars*. New York: Random House, 1999.

Bridwell, E. Nelson. *Superman: From the Thirties to the Seventies*. New York: Bonanza Books, 1971.

Brinkley, Alan. "Prosperity, Depression, and War, 1920–1945." In *The New American History*, ed. Eric Foner. Philadelphia: Temple University Press, 1997, 133–158.

Brock, Charles. *Charles Sheeler: Across Media*. Berkeley: University of California Press, 2006.

Broekel, Ray. *The Chocolate Chronicles*. Lombard, IL: Wallace-Homestead Book Co., 1985.

———. *The Great American Candy Bar Book*. Boston: Houghton Mifflin, 1982.

Brooks, Lou. *Skate Crazy*. Philadelphia: Running Press, 2003.

Brosnan, John. *Movie Magic*. New York: St. Martin's Press, 1974.

Brown, Gene, ed. *Ethnic Groups in American Life*. New York: Arno Press, 1978.

Brown, Lorraine. "Federal Theatre, Melodrama, Social Protest, and Genius." http://memory.loc.gov/ammem/fedtp/ftbrwn00.html

Brown, Nigel. *Ice-Skating: A History*. New York: A. S. Barnes and Co., 1959.

Brown, Robert J. *Manipulating the Ether: The Power of Broadcast Radio in Thirties America*. Jefferson, NC: McFarland & Co., 1998.

Bruce, Scott, and Bill Crawford. *Cerealizing America: The Unsweetened Story of American Breakfast Cereal*. Boston: Faber and Faber, 1995.

Brunas, Michael, John Brunas, and Tom Weaver. *Universal Horrors: The Studio's Classic Films, 1931–1946*. Jefferson, NC: McFarland & Co., 1990.

Brunner, Edwin. *The Encyclopedia of the American Theatre, 1900–1975*. New York: A. S. Barnes & Co., 1980.

Buechner, Thomas S. *Norman Rockwell: Artist and Illustrator*. New York: Harry N. Abrams, 1970.

Bundy, Beverly. *The Century in Food: America's Fads and Favorites*. Portland, OR: Collectors Press, 2002.

Burk, Robert F. *Much More Than a Game: Players, Owners, and American Baseball since 1921*. Chapel Hill: University of North Carolina Press, 2001.

Burner, David. *Herbert Hoover: A Public Life*. New York: Alfred A. Knopf, 1979.

Burnham, Kenneth E. *God Comes to America: Father Divine and the Peace Mission Movement*. Boston: Lambeth Press, 1979.

Burns, Ric, James Sanders, and Lisa Ades. *New York: An Illustrated History*. New York: Alfred A. Knopf, 1999.

Bush, Donald J. *The Streamlined Decade*. New York: George Braziller, 1975.

Buxton, Frank, and Bill Owen. *The Big Broadcast, 1920–1950*. New York: Viking Press, 1972.

Calkins, Earnest Elmo. *Care and Feeding of Hobby Horses*. New York: Leisure League of America, 1934.

Campbell, Robert. *The Golden Years of Broadcasting: A Celebration of the First 50 Years of Radio and TV on NBC*. New York: Charles Scribner's Sons [Rutledge Book], 1976.

Candy. http://www.circushistory.org/Bandwagon/bw-candy.htm

———. http://www.uwm.edu/ano/project4.html

Cantor, Muriel G., and Suzanne Pingree. *The Soap Opera*. Beverly Hills, CA: Sage Publications, 1983.

Capp, Al. *The Best of* Li'l Abner. New York: Holt, Rinehart and Winston, 1978.

Capra, Frank. *The Name above the Title: An Autobiography*. New York: Macmillan, 1971.

Caro, Robert A. *The Power Broker: Robert Moses and the Fall of New York City*. New York: Vintage Books, 1975.

Carruth, Gordon, ed. *The Encyclopedia of American Facts and Dates*. New York: Thomas Y. Crowell, 1959.

Carter Family. http://www.pbs.org/wgbh/amex/carterfamily/timeline/index.html

Cary, Diana Serra. *Hollywood's Children: An Inside Account of the Child Star Era*. Dallas: Southern Methodist University Press, 1997.

Cassidy, Donna M. *Painting the Musical City: Jazz and Cultural Identity in American Art, 1910–1940*. Washington, DC: Smithsonian Institution Press, 1997.

Cavin, Ruth. *Trolleys: Riding and Remembering the Electric Interurban Railways*. New York: Hawthorn Books, 1976.

Chandler, Lester V. *America's Greatest Depression, 1929–1941*. New York: Harper & Row, 1970.

Chanin, Michael. *Repeated Takes: A Short History of Recording and Its Effects on Music*. New York: Verso, 1995.

Child Stars. http://www.classicmoviekids.com

China Clipper. http://www.aviation-history.com/martin/m130.html

———. http://www.pbs.org/kcet/chasingthesun/planes/clipper.html

Chiu, Tony. *CBS: The First 50 Years*. Santa Monica, CA: General Publishing Group, 1998.

Civilian Conservation Corps. http://www.cccalumni.org/history1.html

Clarens, Carlos, *Crime Movies: From Griffith to the Godfather and Beyond*. New York: W. W. Norton, 1980.

———. *An Illustrated History of the Horror Film*. New York: Capricorn Books, 1967.

Clark, Clifford Edward, Jr. *The American Home, 1800–1960*. Chapel Hill: University of North Carolina Press, 1986.

Clarke, Gerald. *Get Happy: The Life of Judy Garland*. New York: Random House, 2000.

———. "Pan Am's Clippers: The Revolutionary Planes That Transformed 1930s Travel." *Architectural Digest* 61:5 (May 2004): 280–285.

Cline, William C. *In the Nick of Time: Motion Picture Sound Serials*. Jefferson, NC: McFarland & Co., 1984.

Clurman, Harold. *The Fervent Years: The Story of the Group Theatre and the Thirties*. New York: Hill and Wang, 1957.

Clute, John, and Peter Nicolls. *The Encyclopedia of Science Fiction*. New York: St. Martin's Press, 1993.

Coffey, Frank, and Joseph Layden. *America on Wheels: The First 100 Years, 1896–1996*. Los Angeles: General Publishing Group, 1998.

Coffin, Tristam Potter. *The Old Ball Game: Baseball in Folklore and Fiction*. New York: Herder and Herder, 1971.

Cohen, Marilyn. *Reginald Marsh's New York: Paintings, Drawings, Prints, and Photographs*. New York: Dover Publications, 1983.

Cohen, Norm. *Long Steel Rail: The Railroad in American Folksong*. Urbana: University of Illinois Press, 1981.

Cohen, Paula Marantz. *Silent Film and the Triumph of the American Myth*. New York: Oxford University Press, 2001.

Cohen, Robert, ed. *Dear Mrs. Roosevelt: Letters from Children of the Great Depression*. Chapel Hill: University of North Carolina Press, 2002.

Cohn, Jan. *Creating America: George Horace Lorimer and the* Saturday Evening Post. Pittsburgh, PA: University of Pittsburgh Press, 1989.

Coleman, Emily R. *The Complete Judy Garland: The Ultimate Guide to Her Career in Films, Records, Concerts, Radio, and Television, 1935–1969*. New York: Harper & Row, 1990.

Collier, James Lincoln. *Benny Goodman and the Swing Era*. New York: Oxford University Press, 1989.

Collins, A. Frederick. *How to Ride Your Hobby*. New York: D. Appleton-Century, 1935.

———. *Money-Making Hobbies*. New York: World Publishing Co., 1938.

Collins, Max Allan. *The History of Mystery*. Portland, OR: Collectors Press, 2001.

Colmer, Michael. *Pinball: An Illustrated History*. London: Pierrot Publishing, 1976.

Congdon, Don, ed. *The Thirties: A Time to Remember*. New York: Simon & Schuster, 1962.

Conkin, Paul K. *The New Deal*. 2nd ed. Arlington Heights, IL: Harlan Davidson, 1975.

Cook, Sylvia Jenkins. *Erskine Caldwell and the Fiction of Poverty: The Flesh and the Spirit*. Baton Rouge, LA: Louisiana State University Press, 1991.

Cookies. http://www.whatscookingamerica.net/History/CookieHistory.htm

Coote, James. *A Picture History of the Olympics*. New York: Macmillan, 1972.

Copley-Graves, Lynn. *Figure Skating History: The Evolution of Dance on Ice*. Columbus, OH: Platoro Press, 1992.

Corn, Joseph J. *Imagining Tomorrow: History, Technology, and the American Future*. Cambridge, MA: MIT Press, 1986.

———. *The Winged Gospel: America's Romance with Aviation, 1900–1950*. New York: Oxford University Press, 1983.

Corn, Joseph J., and Brian Horrigan. *Yesterday's Tomorrows: Past Visions of the American Future*. New York: Summit Books, 1984.

Corn, Wanda. *Grant Wood: The Regionalist Vision*. New Haven, CT: Yale University Press, 1983.

Cornebise, Alfred Emile. *The CCC Chronicles: Camp Newspapers of the Civilian Conservation Corps, 1933–1942*. Jefferson, NC: McFarland & Co., 2004.

Couperie, Pierre, and Maurice C. Horn. *A History of the Comic Strip*. New York: Crown Publishers, 1968.

Cowgill, Donald Olen. *Mobile Homes: A Study of Trailer Life*. Washington, DC: American Council on Public Affairs, 1941.

Crafton, Donald. *The Talkies: American Cinema's Transition to Sound, 1926–1931*. Vol. 4 of *History of the American Cinema*. Charles Harpole, gen. ed. 10 vols. New York: Charles Scribner's Sons, 1997.

Craig, E. Quita. *Black Drama of the Federal Theatre Era: Beyond the Formal Horizons*. Amherst, MA: University of Massachusetts Press, 1980.

Craven, Wayne. *Sculpture in America*. New York: Thomas Y. Crowell, 1968.

Crawford, Richard. *America's Musical Life*. New York: W. W. Norton, 2001.

Croce, Arlene. *The Fred Astaire and Ginger Rogers Book*. New York: Outerbridge & Lazard, 1972.

Crosby, Bing. *Bing Crosby: It's Easy to Remember*. 4 CDs. Proper Records, 2001.

Cross, Gary. *Kids' Stuff: Toys and the Changing World of American Childhood*. Cambridge, MA: Harvard University Press, 1997.

Crumpacker, Bunny. *The Old-Time Brand-Name Cookbook*. New York: Smithmark, 1998.

———. *The Old-Time Brand-Name Desserts*. New York: Abradale Press, 1999.

Csida, Joseph, and June Bundy Csida. *American Entertainment: A Unique History of Popular Show Business*. New York: Watson-Guptil Publications, 1978.

Culhane, John. *The American Circus: An Illustrated History*. New York: Henry Holt, 1990.

Currell, Susan. *The March of Spare Time: The Problem and Promise of Leisure in the Great Depression*. Philadelphia: University of Pennsylvania Press, 2005.

Curtis, James. *Mind's Eye, Mind's Truth: FSA Photography Reconsidered*. Philadelphia: Temple University Press, 1989.

Curtis, Joshua James. *Sunkissed: Sunwear and the Hollywood Beauty, 1930–1950*. Portland, OR: Collectors Press, 2003.

Dairy Queen. http://www.davidsdairyqueen.com/history.html

D'Amico, Joan, and Karen Eich Drummond. *The U.S. History Cookbook*. New York: John Wiley & Sons, 2003.

Dance, Stanley. *The World of Count Basie*. New York: Charles Scribner's Sons, 1980.

———. *The World of Duke Ellington*. New York: Da Capo Press, 1970.

Daniels, Les. *Comix: A History of Comic Books in America*. New York: Bonanza Books, 1971.

Davis, Kingsley. *Youth in the Depression*. Chicago: University of Chicago Press, 1935.

Davis, Maxine. *The Lost Generation: A Portrait of American Youth Today*. New York: Macmillan, 1936.

Delamater, Jerome. *Dance in the Hollywood Musical*. Ann Arbor, MI: UMI Research Press, 1981.

Delong, Thomas A. *Radio Stars*. Jefferson, NC: McFarland & Co., 1996.

Denenberg, Thomas Andrew. *Wallace Nutting and the Invention of Old America*. New Haven, CT: Yale University Press, 2003.

Denison, Edward F. *Trends in American Economic Growth, 1929–1982*. Washington, DC: Brookings Institution, 1985.

Dennis, James. *Grant Wood: A Study in American Art and Culture*. Columbia: University of Missouri Press, 1986.

Derks, Scott. *Working Americans, 1880–1999*. Vol. 1, *The Working Class*. Vol. 2, *The Middle Class*. Lakeville, CT: Grey House Publishing Co., 2000, 2001.

Dettelbach, Cynthia Golumb. *In the Driver's Seat: The Automobile in American Literature and Popular Culture*. Westport, CT: Greenwood Press, 1976.

Dickinson, Leon A. "Ways to Yorktown." *New York Times*, 11 October 1931. *Historic New York Times*. Proquest, Lynchburg College Library, Lynchburg, VA.

Dickson, Paul. *The Worth Book of Softball: A Celebration of America's True National Pastime*. New York: Facts on File, 1994.

Dinnerstein, Leonard, Roger L, Nichols, and David M. Reimers. *Natives and Strangers: Ethnic Groups and the Building of America*. New York: Oxford University Press, 1979.

Dionne Quintuplets. http://www.city.north-bay.on.ca/quints/digitize/dqdpe.htm

———. http://www.quintland.com

Dirks, Tim. Synopsis of *Snow White and the Seven Dwarfs*. http://www.filmsite.org/snow3.html

Dooley, Dennis, and Gary Engle, eds. *Superman at Fifty! The Persistence of a Legend!* Cleveland: Octavia, 1987.

Dorner, Jane. *Fashion in the Twenties and Thirties*. New Rochelle, NY: Arlington House, 1973.

Douglas, George H. *All Aboard! The Railroad in American Life*. New York: Paragon House, 1992.

———. *The Smart Magazines*. New York: Anchor Books, 1991.

Douglas, Susan J. *Listening In: Radio and the American Imagination*. Minneapolis: University of Minnesota Press, 1999.

Douglas DC-3. http://www.douglasdc3.com

Downs, Robert B. *Famous American Books*. New York: McGraw-Hill, 1971.

Dr. Bob and the Good Oldtimers. New York: Alcoholics Anonymous World Services, 1980.

Duberman, Martin. *Paul Robeson: A Biography*. New York: New Press, 1989.

Dulles, Foster Rhea. *A History of Recreation: America Learns to Play*. Englewood Cliffs, NJ: Prentice-Hall, 1965.

Dunning, John. *On the Air: The Encyclopedia of Old-Time Radio*. New York: Oxford University Press, 1998.

Dupre, Judith. *Skyscrapers*. New York: Black Dog & Leventhal, 1996.

Durant, John, and Otto Bettmann. *Pictorial History of American Sports: From Colonial Times to the Present*. New York: A. S. Barnes and Co., 1965.

Durgnat, Raymond. *The Crazy Mirror: Hollywood Comedy and the American Image*. New York: Dell Publishing Co. [Delta], 1969.

Durham, Weldon B., ed. *American Theatre Companies, 1931–1986*. Westport, CT: Greenwood Press, 1989.

Earhart, Amelia. http://ellensplace.net/eae_intr.html

Ebert, Roger. *The Great Movies*. New York: Broadway Books, 2002.

Edelson, Edward. *Great Kids of the Movies*. Garden City, NY: Doubleday, 1979.

Edsforth, Ronald. *The New Deal: America's Response to the Great Depression*. Malden, MA: Blackwell Publishers, 2000.

Edwards, Anne. *Road to Tara: The Life of Margaret Mitchell*. New York: Ticknor & Fields, 1983.

Eells, George. *The Life That Late He Led: A Biography of Cole Porter*. New York: G. P. Putnam's Sons, 1967.

Ege, Lennart. *Balloons and Airships*. New York: Macmillan, 1974.

Elder, Glen H., Jr. *Children of the Great Depression*. Chicago: University of Chicago Press, 1974.

Election Results. http://www.uselectionatlas.org

Ellis, Edward Robb. *A Nation in Torment: The Great American Depression, 1929–1939*. New York: Kodansha America, 1995.

Ely, Melvin Patrick. *The Adventures of Amos 'n' Andy: The Social History of an American Phenomenon*. Charlottesville: University of Virginia Press, 1991.

Emery, Michael, Edwin Emery, and Nancy L. Roberts. *The Press and America: An Interpretive History of the Mass Media*. Boston: Allyn & Bacon, 1999.

Engen, Alan K. *For the Love of Skiing: A Visual History*. Salt Lake City, UT: Gibbs-Smith, 1998.

Epstein, Daniel Mark. *Sister Aimee*. New York: Harcourt, Brace, Jovanovich, 1993.

Erenberg, Lewis A. *Swingin' the Dream: Big Band Jazz and the Rebirth of American Culture*. Chicago: University of Chicago Press, 1998.

Ermoyan, Arpi. *Famous American Illustrators*. New York: Society of Illustrators, 1997.

Evans, Harold. *The American Century*. New York: Alfred A. Knopf, 1998.

Ewen, David. *All the Years of American Popular Music*. Englewood Cliffs, NJ: Prentice-Hall, 1977.

———. *Complete Book of the American Musical Theater*. New York: Henry Holt, 1959.

———. *A Journey to Greatness: The Life and Music of George Gershwin*. New York: Henry Holt, 1956.

———. *The Life and Death of Tin Pan Alley: The Golden Age of American Popular Music*. New York: Funk and Wagnalls, 1964.

———. *Panorama of American Popular Music*. Englewood Cliffs, NJ: Prentice-Hall, 1957.

Fausold, Martin L., ed. *The Hoover Presidency: A Reappraisal*. Albany: State University of New York Press, 1974.

Feather, Leonard. *The New Edition of the Encyclopedia of Jazz*. New York: Bonanza Books, 1962.

Federal Art Project. "WPA Artists Fight Police; 219 Ejected, Many Clubbed." *New York Times*, 2 December 1936. *Historic New York Times*. Proquest, Lynchburg College Library, Lynchburg, VA.

Fenin, George N., and William K. Everson. *The Western: From Silents to Cinerama*. New York: Orion Press, 1962.

Fielding, Raymond. *The March of Time, 1935–1951*. New York: Oxford University Press, 1978.

Fields, Dorothy. http://www.dorothyfields.co.uk/home.htm

Filler, Louis, ed. *The Anxious Years: America in the 1930s*. New York: Capricorn Books, 1963.

Finch, Christopher. *The Art of Walt Disney: From Mickey Mouse to the Magic Kingdoms*. New York: Harry N. Abrams, 1975.

———. *Norman Rockwell's America*. New York: Harry N. Abrams, 1975.

Findling, John E., and Kimberly D. Pelle, eds. *Historical Dictionary of World's Fairs and Expositions, 1851–1988*. Westport, CT: Greenwood Press, 1990.

Firestone, Ross. *Swing, Swing, Swing: The Life and Times of Benny Goodman*. New York: W. W. Norton, 1993.

Fisher, David E., and Marshall J. Fisher. *Tube: The Invention of Television*. Washington, DC: Counterpoint, 1996.

Fisher-Price. http://www.shareholder.com/mattel/news/20041117-148538.cfm

Flamini, Roland. *Scarlett, Rhett, and a Cast of Thousands: The Filming of* Gone with the Wind. New York: Macmillan, 1975.

Flanagan, Hallie. *Arena: The History of the Federal Theatre.* New York: Benjamin Blom, 1940.

Fleischhauer, Carl, ed. *Documenting America, 1935–1943.* Berkeley: University of California Press, 1988.

Foley, Mary Mix. *The American House.* New York: Harper & Row, 1980.

Food and Drug Administration (FDA). http://www.fda.gov/oc/history/historyoffda

Ford, James L. C. *Magazines for Millions: The Story of Specialized Publications.* Carbondale, IL: Southern Illinois University Press, 1969.

Fowler, Gene, and Bill Crawford. *Border Radio: Quacks, Yodelers, Pitchmen, Psychics, and Other Amazing Broadcasters of the American Airwaves.* Austin, TX: Texas Monthly Press, 1987.

Fowles, Jib. *Advertising and Popular Culture.* Thousand Oaks, CA: Sage Publications, 1996.

Fox, Stephen. *The Mirror Makers: A History of American Advertising and Its Creators.* New York: William Morrow, 1984.

Frank, Gerold. *Judy.* New York: Da Capo, 1999.

Fraser, Antonia. *A History of Toys.* New York: Delacorte Press, 1966.

Fraser, James. *The American Billboard: 100 Years.* New York: Harry N. Abrams, 1991.

Freedland, Michael. *All the Way: A Biography of Frank Sinatra.* New York: St. Martin's Press, 1998.

Freeland, Cynthia A. *The Naked and the Undead: Evil and the Appeal of Horror.* Boulder, CO: Westview Press, 2000.

Freeman, Larry, ed. *Yesterday's Games.* Watkins Glen, NY: Century House, 1970.

French, Warren G. *John Steinbeck.* New York: Twayne, 1985.

Fricke, John, Jay Scarfone, and William Stillman. *The Wizard of Oz: The Official 50th Anniversary Pictorial History.* New York: Warner Books, 1989.

Friedman, Martin. *Charles Sheeler.* New York: Watson-Guptill Publications, 1975.

Friedman, Martin, Bartlett Hayes, and Charles Millard. *Charles Sheeler.* Washington, DC: Smithsonian Institution Press, 1968.

Friedwald, Will. *Jazz Singing: America's Great Voices.* New York: Da Capo Press, 1996.

[Frozen foods industry.] "The Formative Years, 1930–1941." *Frozen Food Age* 46 (August 1997): 34–40.

———. "How It Began." *Frozen Food Age* 8 (April–May 1993): 74–99.

Fucini, Joseph J., and Suzy Fucini. *Entrepreneurs: The Men and Women behind Famous Brand Names and How They Made It.* Boston: G. K. Hall & Co., 1985.

Funderburg, Anne Cooper. *Chocolate, Strawberry, and Vanilla: A History of American Ice Cream.* Bowling Green, OH: Bowling Green State University Popular Press, 1995.

Gabler, Neal. *Winchell: Gossip, Power, and the Culture of Celebrity.* New York: Vintage Books, 1995.

Galbraith, John Kenneth. *The Great Crash, 1929.* Boston: Houghton Mifflin, 1961.

Gallo, Max. *The Poster in History.* New York: New American Library, 1972.

Gandt, Robert L. *China Clipper: The Age of the Great Flying Boats.* Annapolis, MD: Naval Institute Press, 1991.

Gardner, Erle Stanley. http://www.erlestanleygardner.com

———. http://hometown.aol.com/mg4273/Gardner.htm

Garraty, John A. *The Great Depression.* New York: Harcourt Brace Jovanovich, 1986.

Garwood, Darrell. *Artist in Iowa: A Life of Grant Wood.* New York: W. W. Norton, 1944.

Gebhard, David. *The National Trust Guide to Art Deco in America.* New York: John Wiley & Sons, 1996.

Gehring, Wes D., ed. *Handbook of American Film Genres.* Westport, CT: Greenwood Press, 1988.

Gelber, Steven M. "A Job You Can't Lose: Work and Hobbies in the Great Depression." *Journal of Social History* 24 (1991): 741–766.

Gelernter, David. *1939: The Lost World of the Fair.* New York: Avon Books, 1995.

Giddins, Gary. *Bing Crosby: A Pocketful of Dreams.* Vol. 1, *The Early Years, 1903–1940.* Boston: Little, Brown, 2001.

———. *Visions of Jazz: The First Century.* New York: Oxford University Press, 1998.

Gill, Brendan. *Many Masks: A Life of Frank Lloyd Wright.* New York: G. P. Putnam's Sons, 1987.

Gioia, Ted. *The History of Jazz.* New York: Oxford University Press, 1997.

Girl Scout Cookies. http://www.girlscouts.org/program/gs_cookies/cookie_history

Goddard, Stephen B. *Getting There: The Epic Struggle between Road and Rail in the American Century.* New York: Basic Books, 1994.

Godfrey, Donald C., and Frederic A. Leigh, eds. *Historical Dictionary of American Radio.* Westport, CT: Greenwood Press, 1998.

Golbey, Brian. *The Carter Family: Wildwood Flower.* CD. Liner notes. AJA 5323, 2000.

Golden Age Radio. *101 Old Radio Commercials.* CD. Plymouth, MN: Metacom, n.d.

Good Humor Ice Cream. http://www.icecreamusa.com/goodhumor/know.asp

Goodrich, Lloyd. *Edward Hopper.* New York: Harry N. Abrams, 1971.

———. *Reginald Marsh.* New York: Harry N. Abrams, 1972.

———. *Three Centuries of American Art.* New York: Praeger, 1966.

Goodrum, Charles, and Helen Dalrymple. *Advertising in America: The First 200 Years.* New York: Harry N. Abrams, 1990.

Gordon, Ian. *Comic Strips and Consumer Culture, 1890–1945.* Washington, DC: Smithsonian Institution Press, 1998.

Gordon, Lois, and Alan Gordon. *American Chronicle: Six Decades in American Life, 1920– 1980.* New York: Atheneum, 1987.

Gottfried, Herbert, and Jan Jennings. *American Vernacular Design, 1870–1940: An Illustrated Glossary.* New York: Van Nostrand Reinhold, 1985.

Goulart, Ron. *The Adventurous Decade: Comic Strips in the Thirties.* New Rochelle, NY: Arlington House, 1975.

———. *Cheap Thrills: An Informal History of the Pulp Magazines.* New Rochelle, NY: Arlington House, 1972.

———. *Over 50 Years of American Comic Books.* Lincolnwood, IL: Mallard Press, 1991.

———, ed. *The Encyclopedia of American Comics.* New York: Facts on File, 1990.

Gould, Chester. *The Celebrated Cases of Dick Tracy, 1931–1951.* Secaucus, NJ: Wellfleet Press, 1990.

———. *Dick Tracy, the Thirties: Tommy Guns and Hard Times.* New York: Chelsea House, 1978.

Gray, Harold. *Arf! The Life and Hard Times of Little Orphan Annie, 1935–1945.* New Rochelle, NY: Arlington House, 1970.

———. *Little Orphan Annie in the Great Depression.* New York: Dover Publications, 1979.

Green, Douglas B. *Singing in the Saddle: The History of the Singing Cowboy.* Nashville, TN: Vanderbilt University Press, 2002.

Green, Harvey. *Encyclopaedia of the Musical Film.* New York: Oxford University Press, 1981.

———. *Ring Bells! Sing Songs! Broadway Musicals of the 1930s.* New Rochelle, NY: Arlington House, 1971.

———. *The Uncertainty of Everyday Life, 1915–1945.* New York: HarperCollins, 1992.

Green, Stanley. *Broadway Musicals, Show by Show.* 4th ed. Milwaukee, WI: Hal Leonard Publishing Corp., 1994.

Greene, Suzanne Ellery. *Books for Pleasure: Popular Fiction, 1914–1945.* Bowling Green, OH: Bowling Green State University Popular Press, 1974.

Greenfield, Thomas Allen. *Radio: A Reference Guide.* Westport, CT: Greenwood Press, 1989.

Greif, Martin. *Depression Modern: The Thirties Style in America.* New York: Universe Books, 1975.

Grier, Katherine C. *Culture and Comfort: Parlor Making and Middle-Class Identity, 1850–1930.* Washington, DC: Smithsonian Institution Press, 1988.

Griffith, Richard, and Arthur Mayer. *The Movies.* New York: Simon and Schuster, 1970.

Grimsley, Will. *Golf: Its History, People, and Events.* Englewood Cliffs, NJ: Prentice-Hall, 1966.

———. *Tennis: Its History, People, and Events.* Englewood Cliffs, NJ: Prentice-Hall, 1971.

————, ed. *A Century of Sports by the Associated Press Sports Staff*. New York: Associated Press, 1971.

Grinfelds, Vesma, and Bonnie Hultstrand. *Right Down Your Alley: The Complete Book of Bowling*. West Point, NY: Leisure Press, 1985.

Gruber, Frank. *The Pulp Jungle*. Los Angeles: Sherbourne Press, 1967.

Guimond, James. *American Photography and the American Dream*. Chapel Hill: University of North Carolina Press, 1991.

Gurko, Leo. *The Angry Decade: American Literature and Thought from 1929 to Pearl Harbor*. New York: Harper & Row [Colophon], 1947.

Guthrie, Woody. *Bound for Glory*. New York: Penguin Books [Plume], 1943.

————. http://www.geocities.com/nashville/3448/dbball.html#bg

Guthrie, Woody, and the Carter Family. http://xroads.virginia.edu/1930s/radio/c_w/cw-front.html

Gutman, Richard J. S., and Elliott Kaufman. *American Diner*. New York: Harper & Row, 1979.

Guttmann, Allen. *The Olympics: A History of the Modern Games*. Urbana: University of Illinois Press, 1992.

Gwynn, David. Grocery Stores. http://www.groceteria.com/about/host.html

Hackett, Alice Payne. *60 Years of Best Sellers, 1895–1955*. New York: R. R. Bowker, 1956.

Hall, Ben M. *The Best Remaining Seats: The Story of the Golden Age of the Movie Palace*. New York: Bramhall House, 1961.

Hamm, Charles. Liner notes. "American Song during the Great Depression." *Brother, Can You Spare a Dime?* LP. New World Records, 1977.

————. *Yesterdays: Popular Song in America*. New York: W. W. Norton, 1979.

Hammond, John. *Hammond on Record*. New York: Ridge Press, 1977.

Hangen, Tona J. *Redeeming the Dial: Radio, Religion, and Popular Culture in America*. Chapel Hill: University of North Carolina Press, 2002.

Hanks, David A., and Anne H. Hoy. *American Streamlined Design: The World of Tomorrow*. Paris, France: Flammarion, 2005.

Hanna, Linda. *The Jigsaw Book*. New York: Dial Press, 1981.

Hanson, Elizabeth I. *Margaret Mitchell*. Boston: Twayne, 1991.

Harmon, Jim. *Jim Harmon's Nostalgia Catalogue*. Los Angeles: J. P. Tarcher, 1973.

Harrison, Helen A. *Dawn of a New Day: The New York World's Fair, 1939–1940*. New York: New York University Press, 1980.

Hart, Dorothy. *Thou Swell, Thou Witty: The Life and Lyrics of Lorenz Hart*. New York: Harper & Row, 1976.

Hart, James D. *The Popular Book: A History of America's Literary Taste*. Berkeley: University of California Press, 1950.

Harvey, Robert C. *Children of the Yellow Kid: The Evolution of the American Comic Strip*. Seattle, WA: Frye Art Museum, 1998.

Haskell, Barbara. *The American Century: Art and Culture, 1900–1950*. New York: Whitney Museum of American Art, 1999.

Haskins, Jim. *The Cotton Club*. New York: New American Library [Plume], 1977.

Hastings, Robert J. *A Nickel's Worth of Skim Milk: A Boy's View of the Great Depression*. Carbondale, IL: Southern Illinois University Press, 1972.

Hayden, Dolores. *Building Suburbia: Green Fields and Urban Growth, 1820–2000*. New York: Pantheon Books, 2003.

Hayes, Richard K. *Kate Smith: A Biography, with a Discography, Filmography, and List of Stage Appearances*. Jefferson, NC: McFarland & Co., 1995.

Hazzard-Gordon, Katrina. *Jookin': The Rise of Social Dance Formations in African-American Culture*. Philadelphia: Temple University Press, 1992.

Hearn, Charles R. *The American Dream and the Great Depression*. Westport, CT: Greenwood Press, 1977.

Heide, Robert, and John Gilman. *Dime-Store Dream Parade: Popular Culture, 1925–1955*. New York: E. P. Dutton, 1979.

Heidenry, John. *Theirs Was the Kingdom: Lila and DeWitt Wallace and the Story of the* Reader's Digest. New York: W. W. Norton, 1993.

Heimann, Jim. *Car Hops and Curb Service: A History of American Drive-In Restaurants, 1920–1960.* San Francisco: Chronicle Books, 1996.

———. *May I Take Your Order? American Menu Design, 1920–1960.* San Francisco: Chronicle Books, 1998.

Heller, Nancy, and Julia Williams. *Painters of the American Scene.* New York: Galahad Books, 1976.

Heller, Steven, and Seymour Chwast. *Jackets Required: An Illustrated History of American Book Jacket Design, 1920–1950.* San Francisco: Chronicle Books, 1995.

Heller, Steven, and Louise Fili. *Cover Story: The Art of American Magazine Covers, 1900–1950.* San Francisco: Chronicle Books, 1996.

Henderson, Amy, and Dwight Blocker Bowers. *Red, Hot, and Blue: A Smithsonian Salute to the American Musical.* Washington, DC: Smithsonian Institution Press, 1996.

Henderson, Mary C. *Broadway Ballyhoo.* New York: Harry N. Abrams, 1989.

Henderson, Sally, and Robert Landau. *Billboard Art.* San Francisco: Chronicle Books, 1981.

Hennessey, Maureen Hart, and Anne Knutson. *Norman Rockwell: Pictures for the American People.* New York: Harry N. Abrams, 1999.

Hesseltine, William B. *The Rise and Fall of Third Parties: From Anti-Masonry to Wallace.* Washington, DC: Public Affairs Press, 1948.

———. *Third-Party Movements in the United States.* Princeton, NJ: D. Van Nostrand, 1962.

Higby, Mary Jane. *Tune in Tomorrow.* New York: Cowles Education, 1968.

Higham, Charles. *The Art of the American Film, 1900–1971.* Garden City, NY: Anchor Press, 1973.

Hillenbrand, Laura. *Seabiscuit: An American Legend.* New York: Ballantine Books, 2001.

Hilliard, Robert L., and Michael C. Keith. *The Broadcast Century: A Biography of American Broadcasting.* Boston: Focal Press, 1992.

Hillier, Bevis. *The Style of the Century, 1900–1980.* New York: E. P. Dutton, 1983.

Hilmes, Michele. *Radio Voices: American Broadcasting, 1922–1952.* Minneapolis: University of Minnesota Press, 1997.

Himelstein, Morgan Y. *Drama Was a Weapon: Left-Wing Theatre in New York, 1929–1941.* Westport, CT: Greenwood Press, 1963.

Hine, Lewis W. *The Empire State Building.* New York: Prestel Publishing, 1998.

———. *Men at Work: Photographic Studies of Modern Men and Machines.* New York: Dover Publications, 1977.

Hine, Thomas. *The Rise and Fall of the American Teenager.* New York: Avon Books [Bard], 1999.

Hirsch, Jerrold. *Portrait of America: A Cultural History of the Federal Writers' Project.* Chapel Hill: University of North Carolina Press, 2003.

Hirschhorn, Clive. *The Warner Brothers Story.* New York: Crown Publishers, 1979.

Hirshhorn, Paul, and Steven Izenour. *White Towers.* Cambridge, MA: MIT Press, 1979.

Hischak, Thomas S. *Through the Screen Door: What Happened to the Broadway Musical When It Went to Hollywood.* Lanham, MD: Scarecrow Press, 2004.

Historical Statistics of the United States, Colonial Times to 1970. Washington, DC: Bureau of the Census, U.S. Department of Commerce, 1975.

Historic New York Times. Proquest, Lynchburg College Library, Lynchburg, VA.

History of the 20th Century, 1930–1939. Vol. 4. Dir. Richard A. Klein. Videocassette, 6 vols. ABC Video Enterprises, 1980.

Hitchcock, Henry-Russell, and Philip Johnson. *The International Style.* New York: W. W. Norton, 1932.

Hobson, Archie, ed. *Remembering America: A Sampler of the WPA American Guide Series.* New York: Columbia University Press, 1985.

Hoffman, Donald. *Understanding Frank Lloyd Wright's Architecture.* New York: Dover Publications, 1995.

Hoffman, Frank W., and William G. Bailey. *Sports and Recreation Fads*. New York: Haworth Press, 1991.

Hoff-Wilson, Joan, and Marjorie Lightman, eds. *Without Precedent: The Life and Career of Eleanor Roosevelt*. Bloomington: Indiana University Press, 1984.

Holme, Bryan. *The Art of Advertising*. London: Peerage Books, 1982.

Holtsmark, Erling B. *Edgar Rice Burroughs*. New York: Twayne, 1986.

Hooker, Richard J. *Food and Drink in America: A History*. Indianapolis, IN: Bobbs-Merrill, 1981.

Horan, James D. *The Desperate Years*. New York: Bonanza Books, 1962.

Horn, Maurice. *Women in the Comics*. New York: Chelsea House, 1977.

———, ed. *100 Years of American Newspaper Comics*. New York: Gramercy Books, 1996.

———. *The World Encyclopedia of Comics*. New York: Chelsea House, 1976.

Hornung, Clarence P., and Fridolf Johnson. *200 Years of American Graphic Art*. New York: George Braziller, 1976.

Horsham, Michael. *20s and 30s Style*. Secaucus, NJ: Chartwell Books, 1989.

Hoving, Thomas. *American Gothic: The Biography of Grant Wood's American Masterpiece*. New York: Chamberlain Bros., 2005.

Howell, Georgina. *In Vogue, 75 Years of Style*. London: Conde Nast Books, 1991.

Howard, Sidney. *GWTW, the Screenplay*. Ed. Richard Harwell. New York: Macmillan, 1980.

Hower, Ralph M. *The History of an Advertising Agency: N. W. Ayer & Son at Work, 1869–1939*. Cambridge, MA: Harvard University Press, 1939.

Hoyt, Edwin P. *The Tempering Years*. New York: Charles Scribner's Sons, 1963.

Hudson, Kenneth. *Air Travel: A Social History*. Totowa, NJ: Rowman and Littlefield, 1972.

Hughes, Dorothy B. *Erle Stanley Gardner: The Case of the Real Perry Mason*. New York: Morrow, 1978.

Hughes, Robert. *American Visions: The Epic History of Art in America*. New York: Alfred A. Knopf, 1997.

Hulick, Diana Emery, with Joseph Marshall. *Photography, 1900 to the Present*. Upper Saddle River, NJ: Prentice-Hall, 1998.

Hunt, William R. *Body Love: The Amazing Career of Bernarr Macfadden*. Bowling Green, OH: Bowling Green State University Popular Press, 1989.

Hurley, F. Jack. *Portrait of a Decade: Roy Stryker and the Development of Documentary Photography in the Thirties*. Baton Rouge, LA: Louisiana State University Press, 1972.

Huss, Roy, and T. J. Huss. *Focus on the Horror Film*. Englewood Cliffs, NJ: Prentice-Hall, 1972.

Hutchinson, Tom. *Horror and Fantasy in the Movies*. New York: Crown Publishers [Crescent], 1974.

Hyland, William G. *George Gershwin: A New Biography*. New York: Praeger, 2003.

———. *Richard Rodgers*. New Haven, CT: Yale University Press, 1998.

———. *The Song Is Ended: Songwriters and American Music*. New York: Oxford University Press, 1995.

Inge, M. Thomas. *Comics as Culture*. Jackson, MS: University Press of Mississippi, 1990.

———, ed. *Concise Histories of American Popular Culture*. Westport, CT: Greenwood Press, 1982.

———. *Handbook of American Popular Culture*. 3 vols. Westport, CT: Greenwood Press, 1981.

Inge, M. Thomas, and Dennis Hall, eds. *The Greenwood Guide to American Popular Culture*. 4 vols. Westport, CT: Greenwood Press, 2002.

Innes, Sherrie A. *Dinner Roles: American Women and Culinary Culture*. Iowa City, IA: University of Iowa Press, 2001.

Jablonski, Edward. *Gershwin*. New York: Doubleday, 1987.

Jackson, Carlton. *Hounds of the Road: A History of the Greyhound Bus Company*. Bowling Green, OH: Bowling Green State University Popular Press, 1984.

Jackson, Kathy Merlock. *Images of Children in American Film*. Metuchen, NJ: Scarecrow Press, 1986.

Jakle, John A. *City Lights: Illuminating the American Night*. Baltimore: Johns Hopkins University Press, 2001.

Jakle, John A., and Keith A Sculle. *The Gas Station in America*. Baltimore: Johns Hopkins University Press, 1994.

Jakle, John A., Keith A. Sculle, and Jefferson S. Rogers. *The Motel in America*. Baltimore: Johns Hopkins University Press, 1996.

Jandl, H. Ward. *Yesterday's Houses of Tomorrow: Innovative American Homes, 1850 to 1950*. Washington, DC: Preservation Press, 1991.

Janello, Amy, and Brennon Jones. *The American Magazine*. New York: Harry N. Abrams, 1991.

Jelly Beans. http://www.foodreference.com/html/fjellybeans.html

Jewell, Derek. *Duke: A Portrait of Duke Ellington*. New York: W. W. Norton, 1977.

Jigsaw Puzzles. http://www.puzzlehistory.com

Jodard, Paul. *Raymond Loewy*. New York: Taplinger Publishing Co., 1992.

Johnson, Bruce E. "Board Games: Affordable and Abundant, Boxed Amusements from the 1930s and 1940s Recall the Cultural Climate of an Era." *Country Living* 20:12 (December 1997): 50–54.

Johnson, Donald Leslie. *Frank Lloyd Wright versus America, the 1930s*. Cambridge, MA: MIT Press, 1990.

Johnson, J. Stewart. *American Modern, 1925–1940: Design for a New Age*. New York: Harry N. Abrams, 2000.

———. *The Modern American Poster*. New York: Museum of Modern Art, 1983.

Johnson, Lynn, and Michael O'Leary. *All Aboard! Images from the Golden Age of Rail Travel*. San Francisco: Chronicle Books, 1999.

Jonas, Susan, and Marilyn Nissenson. *Going, Going, Gone: Vanishing Americana*. San Francisco: Chronicle Books, 1994.

Jones, Gerard. *Men of Tomorrow: Geeks, Gangsters, and the Birth of the Comic Book*. New York: Basic Books, 2004.

Jones, Max, and John Chilton. *Louis: The Louis Armstrong Story*. Boston: Little, Brown, 1971.

Jordy, William H. *American Buildings and Their Architects: The Impact of European Modernism in the Mid-Twentieth Century*. Garden City, NY: Doubleday [Anchor Press], 1976.

Jukeboxes. http://www.nationaljukebox.com/history.htm

———. http://www.tomszone.com

Junker, Patricia. *John Steuart Curry: Inventing the Middle West*. New York: Hudson Hill Press, 1998.

Kammen, Michael. *American Culture, American Tastes: Social Change and the 20th Century*. New York: Alfred A. Knopf, 2000.

Kanfer, Stefan. "The Voodoo That He Did So Well." http://www.city-journal.org/html/13_1_urbanities-the_voodoo.html

Kaplan, Donald, and Alan Bellink. *Classic Diners of the Northeast*. Boston: Faber and Faber, 1980.

Kaye, Lenny. *You Call It Madness: The Sensuous Song of the Croon*. New York: Villard, 2004.

Kearney, James R. *Anna Eleanor Roosevelt: The Evolution of a Reformer*. Boston: Houghton Mifflin, 1968.

Kendall, Elizabeth. *The Runaway Bride: Hollywood Romantic Comedy of the 1930s*. New York: Alfred A. Knopf, 1990.

Kennedy, David M. *Freedom from Fear: The American People in Depression and War, 1929–1945*. New York: Oxford University Press, 1999.

Kennedy, Ludovic. *The Airman and the Carpenter*. New York: Viking Penguin, 1985.

Kenney, William Howland. *Recorded Music in American Life: The Phonograph and Popular Memory, 1890–1945*. New York: Oxford University Press, 1999.

Kern-Foxworth, Marilyn. *Aunt Jemima, Uncle Ben, and Rastus: Blacks in Advertising, Yesterday, Today, and Tomorrow*. Westport, CT: Greenwood Press, 1994.

Keyishian, Harry. *Screening Politics: The Politician in American Movies, 1931–2001*. Lanham, MD: Scarecrow Press, 2003.

Kidwell, Claudia B., and Margaret C. Christman. *Suiting Everyone: The Democratization of Clothing in America*. Washington, DC: Smithsonian Institution Press, 1974.

Kimball, Robert. *The Complete Lyrics of Cole Porter*. New York: Da Capo Press, 1992.

Kimball, Robert, and Richard M. Sudhalter. *You're the Top: Cole Porter in the 1930s*. 3 CDs. Indianapolis: Indiana Historical Society, 1992.

Kimmerle, Beth. *Candy: The Sweet History*. Portland, OR: Collectors Press, 2003.

Kiner, Larry F. *The Rudy Vallee Discography*. Westport, CT: Greenwood Press, 1985.

Kiple, Kenneth F., and Kriemhild Conee Ornalas, eds. *The Cambridge World History of Food*. 2 vols. Cambridge, UK: Cambridge University Press, 2000.

Kirchner, Bill, ed. *The Oxford Companion to Jazz*. New York: Oxford University Press, 2000.

Kirkendall, Richard. S. *The United States, 1929–1945: Years of Crisis and Change*. New York: McGraw-Hill, 1974.

Kisor, Henry. *Zephyr: Tracking a Dream across America*. New York: Random House, 1994.

Klein, Dan. *All Color Book of Art Deco*. London: Octopus Books, 1974.

Klingaman, William K. *1929, the Year of the Great Crash*. New York: Harper & Row, 1989.

Korda, Michael. *Making the List: A Cultural History of the American Bestseller, 1900–1999*. New York: Barnes & Noble Books, 2001.

Krebs, Roland. *Making Friends Is Our Business: 100 Years of Anheuser-Busch*. St. Louis, MO: Anheuser-Busch, 1953.

Kyvig, David E. *Daily Life in the United States, 1920–1940*. Chicago: Ivan R. Dee, 2004.

Lackmann, Ron. *The Encyclopedia of American Radio*. New York: Checkmark Books, 2000.

Laforse, Martin W., and James A. Drake. *Popular Culture and American Life*. Chicago: Nelson-Hall, 1981.

Lahue, Kalton C. *Continued Next Week: A History of the Moving Picture Serial*. Norman: University of Oklahoma Press, 1964.

Landau, Robert, and James Phillippi. *Airstream*. Salt Lake City, UT: Peregrine Smith Books, 1984.

Langdon, Philip. *Orange Roofs, Golden Arches: The Architecture of American Chain Restaurants*. New York: Alfred A. Knopf, 1986.

Laning, Edward. *The Sketchbooks of Reginald Marsh*. Greenwich, CT: New York Graphic Society, 1973.

Lanza, Joseph, and Dennis Penn. *Russ Columbo and the Crooner Mystique*. Los Angeles: Feral House, 2002.

Larkin, Colin, ed. *The Guinness Who's Who of Blues*. Middlesex, UK: Guinness Publishing, 1993.

Larkin, Oliver W. *Art and Life in America*. New York: Holt, Rinehart and Winston, 1960.

Larrabee, Eric, and Rolf Meyersohn, eds. *Mass Leisure*. Glencoe, IL: Free Press, 1958.

LaSalle, Mick. *Dangerous Man: Pre-Code Hollywood and the Birth of the Modern Man*. New York: St. Martin's Press, 2002.

Lash, Joseph P. *Eleanor and Franklin: The Story of Their Relationship Based on Eleanor Roosevelt's Private Papers*. New York: W. W. Norton, 1971.

Laubner, Ellie. *Collectible Fashions of the Turbulent Thirties*. Atglen, PA: Schiffer Publishing, 2000.

Lazo, Hector, and M. H. Bletz. *Who Gets Your Food Dollar?* New York: Harper & Brothers, 1938.

Lears, Jackson. *Fables of Abundance: A Cultural History of Advertising in America*. New York: Basic Books, 1994.

———. *Something for Nothing: Luck in America*. New York: Viking Books, 2003.

Lee, Alfred McClung. *The Daily Newspaper in America*. New York: Macmillan, 1937.

Lee, Charles. *The Hidden Public: The Story of the Book-of-the-Month Club*. Garden City, NY: Doubleday, 1958.

Lee, R. Alton. *The Bizarre Careers of John R. Brinkley*. Lexington, KY: University of Kentucky Press, 2002.

Leff, Leonard J., and Jerold L. Simmons. *The Dame in the Kimono: Hollywood, Censorship, and the Production Code from the 1920s to the 1960s*. New York: Grove Wiedenfeld, 1990.

Lehmann-Haupt, Hellmut. *The Book in America: A History of the Making and Selling of Books in the United States.* New York: R. R. Bowker, 1952.

Leighton, Isabel, ed. *The Aspirin Age, 1919–1941.* New York: Simon & Schuster [Clarion], 1949.

Leonard, Thomas C. *News for All: America's Coming-of-Age with the Press.* New York: Oxford University Press, 1995.

Lesser, Robert. *A Celebration of Comic Art and Memorabilia.* New York: Hawthorn Books, 1975.

———. *Pulp Art: Original Cover Paintings for the Great American Pulp Magazines.* Edison, NJ: Castle Books, 2003.

Leuchtenburg, William E. *Franklin D. Roosevelt and the New Deal.* New York: Harper & Row, 1963.

Levenstein, Harvey A. *Paradox of Plenty: A Social History of Eating in Modern America.* New York: Oxford University Press, 1993.

———. *Revolution at the Table: The Transformation of the American Diet.* New York: Oxford University Press, 1988.

Levin, Gail. *Edward Hopper as Illustrator.* New York: W. W. Norton, 1979.

———. *Edward Hopper: The Art and the Artist.* New York: W. W. Norton, 1980.

Levin, Gail, and Judith Tick. *Aaron Copland's America: A Cultural Perspective.* New York: Watson-Guptill Publications, 2000.

Levin, Martin, ed. *Hollywood and the Great Fan Magazines.* New York: Arbor House, 1970.

Lewis, Lucinda. *Roadside America: The Automobile and the American Dream.* New York: Harry N. Abrams, 2000.

Lewis, Tom. "'A Godlike Presence': The Impact of Radio on the 1920s and 1930s." *OAH Magazine of History* 6 (Spring 1992). http://oah.org/pubs/magazine/communication/lewis.html

Ley, Sandra. *Fashion for Everyone: The Story of Ready-to-Wear, 1870s–1970s.* New York: Charles Scribner's Sons, 1975.

Libby, Bill. *Great American Race Drivers.* Chicago: Cowles Book Co., 1970.

Liebs, Chester H. *Main Street to Miracle Mile: American Roadside Architecture.* Baltimore: Johns Hopkins University Press, 1985.

Lienhard, John H. *Inventing Modern: Growing Up with X-Rays, Skyscrapers, and Tailfins.* New York: Oxford University Press, 2003.

Liesner, Thelma. *Economic Statistics, 1900–1983.* New York: Facts on File, 1985.

Lifshey, Earl. *The Housewares Story.* Chicago: National Housewares Manufacturers Association, 1973.

Linton, Calvin D., ed. *The American Almanac.* New York: Thomas Nelson, 1977.

Lomax, Alan, ed. *Hard Hitting Songs for Hard-Hit People.* New York: Oak Publications, 1967.

Long, Elgen M., and Marie K. Long. *Amelia Earhart: The Mystery Solved.* New York: Simon & Schuster, 1999.

Lovegren, Sylvia. *Fashionable Food: Seven Decades of Food Fads.* New York: Macmillan, 1995.

Lucie-Smith, Edward. *American Realism.* New York: Harry N. Abrams, 1994.

———. *Visual Arts in the Twentieth Century.* New York: Harry N. Abrams, 1996.

Lukacs, Paul. *American Vintage: The Rise of American Wine.* New York: Houghton Mifflin, 2000.

Luke, William A. *Bus Industry Chronicle: U.S. and Canadian Experiences.* Spokane, WA: William A. Luke, 2000.

Lupoff, Dick, and Don Thompson, eds. *All in Color for a Dime.* New Rochelle, NY: Arlington House, 1970.

Lupton, Ellen. *Mechanical Brides: Women and Machines from Home to Office.* Princeton, NJ: Princeton Architectural Press, 1993.

Lynch, Vincent, and Bill Henkin. *Jukebox: The Golden Age.* Berkeley, CA: Lancaster-Miller, 1981.

Lynd, Robert, and Helen Lynd. *Middletown in Transition: A Study in Cultural Conflicts.* New York: Harcourt Brace, 1937.

Lynes, Russell. *The Lively Audience.* New York: Harper & Row, 1985.

Lyons, Eugene. *Herbert Hoover: A Biography.* Garden City, NY: Doubleday, 1964.

MacCambridge, Michael, ed. *ESPN Sports Century*. New York: Hyperion, 1999.

MacDonald, J. Fred. *Don't Touch That Dial! Radio Programming in American Life, 1920–1960*. Chicago: Nelson-Hall, 1979.

MacDougald, Duncan, Jr. "The Popular Music Industry." In *Radio Research 1941*, ed. Paul F. Lazarsfeld and Frank N. Stanton. New York: Duell, Sloan and Pearce, 1941, 65–109.

Madden, David, ed. *Proletarian Writers of the Thirties*. Carbondale, IL: Southern Illinois University Press, 1968.

Maddocks, Melvin. *The Great Liners*. Alexandria, VA: Time-Life Books, 1978.

Madison, Charles A. *Book Publishing in America*. New York: McGraw-Hill, 1966.

Magee, Jeffrey. *The Uncrowned King of Swing: Fletcher Henderson and Big Band Jazz*. New York: Oxford University Press, 2004.

Maltby, Richard. *Passing Parade: A History of Popular Culture in the Twentieth Century*. New York: Oxford University Press, 1989.

Maltin, Leonard. *The Disney Films*. Los Angeles: Disney Editions, 2000.

———. *The Great American Broadcast: A Celebration of Radio's Golden Age*. New York: New American Library, 2000.

———. *Of Mice and Magic: A History of American Animated Cartoons*. New York: McGraw-Hill, 1980.

Manchester, William. *The Glory and the Dream: A Narrative History of America, 1932–1972*. 2 vols. Boston: Little, Brown, 1974.

Mandelbaum, Howard, and Eric Myers. *Screen Deco*. New York: St. Martin's Press, 1985.

Mangione, Jerre. *The Dream and the Deal: The Federal Writers' Project, 1935–1943*. Boston: Little, Brown, 1972.

Manvell, Roger. *Films and the Second World War*. New York: Dell Publishing Co. [Delta Book], 1974.

Marchand, Roland. *Advertising the American Dream: Making Way for Modernity, 1920–1940*. Los Angeles: University of California Press, 1985.

———. *Creating the Corporate Soul: The Rise of Public Relations and Corporate Imagery in American Big Business*. Berkeley: University of California Press, 1998.

March of Time (radio show). http://xroads.virginia.edu/MA04/wood/mot/html

Margolies, John. *Home Away from Home: Motels in America*. Boston: Little, Brown, 1995.

———. *Pump and Circumstance: Glory Days of the Gas Station*. Boston: Little, Brown, 1993.

Margolies, John, and Emily Gwathmey. *Ticket to Paradise: American Movie Theaters and How We Had Fun*. Boston: Little, Brown, 1991.

Mariani, John. *America Eats Out*. New York: William Morrow, 1991.

———. *The Dictionary of American Food and Drink*. New Haven, CT: Ticknor & Fields, 1983.

Marling, Karal Ann. *Wall-to-Wall America: A Cultural History of Post Office Murals in the Great Depression*. Minneapolis: University of Minnesota Press, 1982.

Marquis, Alice G. *Hopes and Ashes: The Birth of Modern Times, 1929–1939*. New York: Free Press, 1986.

Marschall, Richard. *America's Great Comic-Strip Artists*. New York: Stewart, Tabori & Chang, 1997.

Marsden, Michael T, John G. Nachbar, and Sam L. Grogg Jr., eds. *Movies as Artifacts: Cultural Criticism of Popular Film*. Chicago: Nelson-Hall, 1982.

Marum, Andrew, and Frank Parise. *Follies and Foibles: A View of 20th-Century Fads*. New York: Facts on File, 1984.

Marx, Samuel, and Jan Clayton. *Rodgers and Hart: Bewitched, Bothered, and Bewildered*. New York: G. P. Putnam's Sons, 1976.

Mathews, Jane Dehart. *The Federal Theatre, 1935–1939: Plays, Relief, and Politics*. Princeton, NJ: Princeton University Press, 1967.

Mathews, Ryan. "1926–1936, Entrepreneurs and Enterprise: A Look at Industry Pioneers Like King Kullen and J. Frank Grimes, and the Institution They Created." *Progressive Grocer* 75:12 (December 1996): 39.

————. "1926–1936, the Mass Market Comes of Age: How the Great Depression, the Rise of Mass Media, and World War II Helped Create a Mass Consumer Market." *Progressive Grocer* 75:12 (December 1996): 47.

Mathy, Francois. *American Realism: A Pictorial Survey from the Early Eighteenth Century to the 1970s*. New York: Skira, 1978.

Mattfeld, Julius. *Variety Music Cavalcade, 1620–1961: A Chronology of Vocal and Instrumental Music Popular in the United States*. Englewood Cliffs, NJ: Prentice-Hall, 1962.

Matthew-Walker, Robert. *Broadway to Hollywood: The Musical and the Cinema*. London: Sanctuary Publishing, 1996.

Mayo, James M. *The American Grocery Store: The Business Evolution of an Architectural Space*. Westport, CT: Greenwood Press, 1993.

Mazo, Joseph H. *Prime Movers: The Makers of Modern Dance in America*. New York: William Morrow, 1977.

McArthur, Colin. *Underworld U.S.A.* New York: Viking Press, 1972.

McBrien, William. *Cole Porter: A Biography*. New York: Alfred A. Knopf, 1998.

McClintock, Inez, and Marshall McClintock. *Toys in America*. Washington, DC: Public Affairs Press, 1961.

McCoy, Horace. *They Shoot Horses, Don't They?* New York: Simon and Schuster, 1935.

McCracken, Allison. "'God's Gift to Us Girls': Crooning, Gender, and the Re-Creation of American Popular Song, 1928–1933." *American Music* (Winter 1999): 17:4. http://www.findarticles.com/p/articles/mi_g1epc/is_tov/ai_2419101008

McCutcheon, Marc. *The Writer's Guide to Everyday Life from Prohibition through World War II*. Cincinnati, OH: Writer's Digest Books, 1995.

McDermott, Catherine. *Book of 20th-Century Design*. New York: Overlook Press, 1998.

McDonogh, Gary W., Robert Gregg, and Cindy H. Wong, eds. *Encyclopedia of Contemporary American Culture*. New York: Routledge, 2001.

McElvaine, Robert S. *The Depression and the New Deal: A History in Documents*. New York: Oxford University Press, 2000.

————. *Down and Out in the Great Depression: Letters from the "Forgotten Man."* Chapel Hill: University of North Carolina Press, 1983.

————. *The Great Depression: America, 1929–1941*. New York: Times Books, 1961.

McGee, Mark Thomas, and R. J. Robertson. *The J.D. Films: Juvenile Delinquency in the Movies*. Jefferson, NC: McFarland & Co., 1982.

McKinzie, Richard D. *The New Deal for Artists*. Princeton, NJ: Princeton University Press, 1973.

McLanathan, Richard. *The American Tradition in the Arts*. New York: Harcourt, Brace & World, 1968.

McPherson, Aimee Semple. http://members.aol.com/XBCampbell/ASM/indexasm.htm

McShane, Clay. *Down the Asphalt Path: The Automobile and the American City*. New York: Columbia University Press, 1994.

Meeker, David. *Jazz in the Movies*. New York: Da Capo Press, 1981.

Meikle, Jeffrey L. *Twentieth Century Limited: Industrial Design in America, 1925–1939*. Philadelphia: Temple University Press, 1979.

Menten, Theodore. *The Art Deco Style*. New York: Dover Publications, 1972.

Mergen, Bernard. *Play and Playthings: A Reference Guide*. Westport, CT: Greenwood Press, 1982.

Merrill, Perry H. *Roosevelt's Forest Army: A History of the Civilian Conservation Corps, 1933–1942*. Montpelier, VT: Perry H. Merrill, 1981.

Meyer, Susan E. *America's Great Illustrators*. New York: Galahad Books, 1978.

Michaelis, David. *N. C. Wyeth: A Biography*. New York: Alfred A. Knopf, 1998.

Millard, Andre. *America on Record: A History of Recorded Sound*. New York: Cambridge University Press, 1995.

Miller, Dan B. *Erskine Caldwell: The Journey from Tobacco Road*. New York: Alfred A. Knopf, 1994.

Miller, Edward D. *Emergency Broadcasting and 1930s American Radio*. Philadelphia: Temple University Press, 2003.

Miniature Golf. http://www.mastersnationalchamps.com/history.html

Mintz, Steven, and Susan Kellogg. *Domestic Revolutions: A Social History of American Family Life.* New York: Free Press, 1988.

Mitchell, Curtis. *Cavalcade of Broadcasting.* Chicago: Benjamin Co./Rutledge Books, 1970.

Mitchell, Margaret. *Gone with the Wind.* New York: Macmillan, 1936.

Mixon, Wayne. *The People's Writer: Erskine Caldwell and the South.* Charlottesville: University of Virginia Press, 1995.

Modell, John. *Into One's Own: From Youth to Adulthood in the United States, 1920–1975.* Berkeley: University of California Press, 1989.

Molella, Arthur P., and Elsa M. Bruton. *FDR, the Intimate Presidency: Franklin Delano Roosevelt, Communication, and the Mass Media in the 1930s.* Washington, DC: National Museum of American History, 1982.

Moline, Mary. *Norman Rockwell Encyclopedia: A Chronological Catalog of the Artist's Work, 1910–1978.* Indianapolis, IN: Curtis Publishing Co., 1979.

Monopoly. http://www.hasbro.com/monopoly

———. http://tt.tf/gamehist/mon-index.html

Moquin, Wayne, ed. *The American Way of Crime: A Documentary History.* New York: Praeger, 1976.

Mordden, Ethan. *Sing for Your Supper: The Broadway Musical in the 1930s.* New York: Palgrave Macmillan, 2005.

Morella, Joe, Edward Z. Epstein, and John Griggs. *The Films of World War II.* Secaucus, NJ: Citadel Press, 1973.

Moreo, Dominic W. *Schools in the Great Depression.* New York: Garland Publishing, 1996.

Morgan, Winona. *The Family Meets the Depression.* Minneapolis: University of Minnesota Press, 1939.

Morris, Ronald L. *Wait until Dark: Jazz and the Underworld, 1880–1940.* Bowling Green, OH: Bowling Green State University Popular Press, 1980.

Motorsports. http://beta.motorsportsforum.com/ris01/legends.htm

Mott, Frank Luther. *American Journalism: A History, 1690–1960.* New York: Macmillan, 1962.

———. *Golden Multitudes: The Story of Best Sellers in the United States.* New York: R. R. Bowker Co., 1947.

———. *A History of American Magazines.* Vol. 5, *Sketches of 21 Magazines, 1905–1930.* Cambridge, MA: Harvard University Press, 1968. 5 vols.

Mount Rushmore. http://www.pbs.org/wgbh/amex/rushmore/peopleevents/p_lborglum.html

Mulvey, Kate, and Melissa Richards. *Decades of Beauty: The Changing Image of Women, 1890s–1990s.* New York: Checkmark Books, 1998.

Murdock, Catherine Gilbert. *Domesticating Drink: Women, Men, and Alcohol in America, 1870–1940.* Baltimore: Johns Hopkins University Press, 1998.

Mustazza, Leonard. *Frank Sinatra and Popular Culture.* Westport, CT: Greenwood Press, 1999.

———. *Ol' Blue Eyes: A Frank Sinatra Encyclopedia.* Westport, CT: Greenwood Press, 1999.

Mystery Movies. http://www.mysterymovies.com/index.htm

Nachman, Gerald. *Raised on Radio.* Berkeley: University of California Press, 1998.

Naison, Mark. "Lefties and Righties: The Communist Party and Sports during the Great Depression." In *Sport in America: New Historical Perspectives,* ed. Donald Spivey. Westport, CT: Greenwood Press, 1985, 128–144.

Naremore, James. *The Magic World of Orson Welles.* Dallas: Southern Methodist University Press, 1989.

Nasaw, David. *Going Out: The Rise and Fall of Public Amusements.* Cambridge, MA: Harvard University Press, 1993.

Nash, Anedith Jo Bond. "Death on the Highway: The Automobile Wreck in American Culture, 1920–1940." Ph.D. dissertation, University of Minnesota, 1983.

Nash, Eric P. *Manhattan Skyscrapers.* Princeton, NJ: Princeton Architectural Press, 1999.

Nash, Howard P., Jr. *Third Parties in American Politics.* Washington, DC: Public Affairs Press, 1959.

Naylor, David. *Great American Movie Theaters*. Washington, DC: Preservation Press, 1987.

Neal, Arthur G. *National Trauma and Collective Memory*. Armonk, NY: M. E. Sharpe, 1998.

Neuberg, Victor. *The Popular Press Companion to Popular Literature*. Bowling Green, OH: Bowling Green State University Popular Press, 1983.

Neuhaus, Jessamyn. *Manly Meals and Mom's Home Cooking*. Baltimore: Johns Hopkins University Press, 2003.

Neumeyer, Martin H., and Esther S. Neumeyer. *Leisure and Recreation*. New York: Ronald Press Co., 1958.

New York World's Fair. http://www.pmphoto.to/WorldsFairTour/Zone-6/189.htm

——. http://websyte.com/alan/nywf.htm

——. http://xroads.virginia.edu/1930s/DISPLAY/39wf/front.htm

Nye, David E. *American Technological Sublime*. Cambridge, MA: MIT Press, 1994.

——. *Electrifying America: Social Meanings of a New Technology, 1880–1940*. Cambridge, MA: MIT Press, 1991.

Nye, Russel, ed. *New Dimensions in Popular Culture*. Bowling Green, OH: Bowling Green State University Popular Press, 1972.

——. *The Unembarrassed Muse: The Popular Arts in America*. New York: Dial Press, 1970.

O'Brien, Ed, and Scott Savers. *Sinatra: The Man and His Music: The Recording Artistry of Francis Albert Sinatra, 1939–1992*. Austin, TX: TSD Press, 1992.

O'Brien, Richard. *The Story of American Toys: From the Puritans to the Present*. New York: Abbeville Press, 1990.

O'Conner, Francis V., comp. *Art for the Millions*. Greenwich, CT: New York Graphic Society, 1973.

——, ed. *The New Deal Art Projects: An Anthology of Memoirs*. Washington, DC: Smithsonian Institution Press, 1972.

O'Connor, John, and Lorraine Brown, eds. *Free, Adult, Uncensored: The Living History of the Federal Theatre Project*. Washington, DC: New Republic Books, 1978.

O'Dell, John. *The Great American Depression Book of Fun*. New York: Harper & Row, 1981.

Official Pictures of a Century of Progress Exposition: Photographs by Kaufmann & Fabry Co., Official Photographers. Chicago: Reuben H. Donnelley Corp., 1933.

Okrent, Daniel. *Fortune: The Art of Covering Business*. Salt Lake City, UT: Gibbs-Smith, 1999.

——. *Great Fortune: The Epic of Rockefeller Center*. New York: Viking, 2003.

Okrent, Daniel, and Harris Lewine, eds. *The Ultimate Baseball Book*. Boston: Houghton Mifflin, 1979.

Oliphant, Dave. *The Early Swing Era, 1930 to 1941*. Westport, CT: Greenwood Press, 2002.

Oliver, Paul. *Songsters and Saints: Vocal Traditions on Race Records*. New York: Cambridge University Press, 1984.

Olney, Ross R. *Great Moments in Speed*. Englewood Cliff, NJ: Prentice-Hall, 1970.

Olsen, Jack. *The Mad World of Bridge*. New York: Holt, Rinehart and Winston, 1960.

Olson, James Stuart. *The Ethnic Dimension in American History*. New York: St. Martin's Press, 1979.

Olympics, 1936, Germany. http://www.ushmm.org/museum/exhibit/online/olympics

O'Neal, Hank. *A Vision Shared: A Classic Portrait of America and Its People, 1935–1943*. New York: St. Martin's Press, 1976.

Oriad, Michael. *King Football: Sport and Spectacle in the Golden Age of Radio and Newsreels, Movies and Magazines, the Weekly and the Daily Press*. Chapel Hill: University of North Carolina Press, 2001.

O'Sullivan, Judith. *The Great American Comic Strip: One Hundred Years of Cartoon Art*. Boston: Little, Brown, 1990.

Pacelle, Mitchell. *Empire: A Tale of Obsession, Betrayal, and the Battle for an American Icon*. New York: John Wiley & Sons, 2001.

Pachter, Marc, ed. *Champions of American Sport*. New York: Harry N. Abrams, 1981.

Pack, Arthur Newton. *The Challenge of Leisure*. Washington, DC: National Recreation and Park Association, 1934.

Pagano, Grace. *Contemporary American Painting.* New York: Duell, Sloan and Pearce, 1945.

Palladino, Grace. *Teenagers: An American History.* New York: Basic Books, 1996.

Panati, Charles. *Extraordinary Origins of Everyday Things.* New York: Harper & Row, 1987.

———. *Panati's Parade of Fads, Follies, and Manias.* New York: HarperCollins, 1991.

Parini, Jay. *John Steinbeck: A Biography.* New York: Henry Holt, 1995.

Parish, James Robert, and Michael R. Pitts. *The Great Gangster Pictures.* Metuchen, NJ: Scarecrow Press, 1976.

Park, Marlene, and Gerald E. Markowitz. *Democratic Vistas: Post Offices and Public Art in the New Deal.* Philadelphia: Temple University Press, 1984.

Parkways. http://www.arroyofest.org/ParkwaysAccess.htm

———. http://www.cr.nps.gov/history/online_books/unrau-williss/adhi4j.htm

Parlett, David. *The Oxford Guide to Card Games.* New York: Oxford University Press, 1990.

Pashko, Pearl, and Stanley Pashko. *American Girl's Treasury of Sports, Hobbies, and Parties.* New York: Grosset & Dunlap, 1949.

Pashko, Stanley. *American Boy's Treasury of Sports, Hobbies, and Games.* New York: Grosset & Dunlap, 1945.

Patton, Phil. *Open Road: A Celebration of the American Highway.* New York: Simon and Schuster, 1986.

Paul Robeson: Here I Stand. Dir. St. Clair Bourne. Public Broadcasting System. Videocassette. 1999.

Peacock, John. *Fashion Sketchbook, 1920–1960.* New York: Avon Books, 1977.

———. *Twentieth-Century Fashion: The Complete Sourcebook.* London: Thames and Hudson, 1993.

Pease, Otis. *The Responsibilities of American Advertising: Private Control and Public Influence, 1920–1940.* New York: Arno Press, 1976.

Peeler, David P. *Hope among Us Yet: Social Criticism and Social Solace in Depression America.* Athens, GA: University of Georgia Press, 1987.

Pendergast, Sara, and Tom Pendergast, eds. *Bowling, Beatniks, and Bell-Bottoms: Pop Culture of 20th-Century America.* 5 vols. New York: Thomson Gale, 2002.

Pendergast, Tom. *Creating the Modern Man: American Magazines and Consumer Culture, 1900–1950.* Columbia, MO: University of Missouri Press, 2000.

Pendergrast, Mark. *For God, Country, and Coca-Cola.* New York: Charles Scribner's Sons, 1993.

———. *Uncommon Grounds: The History of Coffee and How It Transformed the World.* New York: Basic Books, 1999.

Penkower, Monty Noam. *The Federal Writers' Project: A Study in Government Patronage and the Arts.* Urbana: University of Illinois Press, 1977.

Peplow, Elizabeth. *Encyclopedia of the Horse.* San Diego: Thunder Bay Press, 1998.

Perkins, Dexter. *The New Age of Franklin Roosevelt, 1932–1945.* Chicago: University of Chicago Press, 1957.

Peterson, Richard A. *Creating Country Music: Fabricating Authenticity.* Chicago: University of Chicago Press, 1997.

Peterson, Theodore. *Magazines in the Twentieth Century.* Urbana: University of Illinois Press, 1964.

Phillips, Ann-Victoria. *The Complete Book of Roller Skating.* New York: Workman Publishing, 1979.

Phillips, Cabell. *The New York Times Chronicle of American Life: From the Crash to the Blitz, 1929–1939.* New York: Macmillan, 1969.

Pierce, Max. "Russ Columbo: Hollywood's Tragic Crooner." http://www.classicimages.com/1999/april99/columbo.html

Pierre, Berton. *The Dionne Years: A Thirties Melodrama.* New York: Penguin, 1977.

Pillsbury, Richard. *From Boarding House to Bistro: The American Restaurant Then and Now.* Boston: Unwin Hyman, 1990.

Pitts, Michael R., and Frank W. Hoffman. *The Rise of the Crooners.* Lanham, MD: Scarecrow Press, 2002.

Pitz, Henry. "N. C. Wyeth." *American Heritage* 16:6 (October 1965): 36–55.

————. *200 Years of American Illustration*. New York: Random House, 1977.

Poague, Leland A. *The Cinema of Frank Capra: An Approach to Film Comedy*. New York: A. S. Barnes and Co., 1975.

Porges, Irwin. *Edgar Rice Burroughs: The Man Who Created Tarzan*. Provo, UT: Brigham Young University Press, 1975.

Potter, David M. *People of Plenty: Economic Abundance and the American Character*. Chicago: University of Chicago Press, 1954.

Powers, Richard Gid. *G-Men: Hoover's FBI in American Popular Culture*. Carbondale, IL: Southern Illinois University Press, 1983.

Pyle, Ernie. "Gutzon Boglum Carves Mount Rushmore." In *Ernie's America: The Best of Ernie Pyle's Travel Dispatches*, ed. David Nichols. New York: Random House, 1989.

Pyron, Darden Asbury. *Southern Daughter: The Life of Margaret Mitchell*. New York: Oxford University Press, 1991.

————, ed. *Recasting:* Gone with the Wind *in American Culture*. Miami, FL: University Presses of Florida, 1984.

Quigley, Martin, Jr., and Richard Gertner. *Films in America, 1929–1969*. New York: Golden Press, 1970.

Rader, Benjamin G. *American Sports: From the Age of Folk Games to the Age of Televised Sports*. 3rd ed. Englewood Cliffs, NJ: Prentice-Hall, 1996.

Radio Flyer. http://www.radioflyer.com/history/heritage1930.html

Radway, Janice A. *A Feeling for Books: The Book-of-the-Month Club, Literary Taste, and Middle-Class Desire*. Chapel Hill: University of North Carolina Press, 1997.

Rae, John B. *The Road and the Car in American Life*. Cambridge, MA: MIT Press, 1971.

Randel, William Peirce. *The Evolution of American Taste*. New York: Crown Publishers, 1978.

Rawls, Walton, ed. *A Century of American Sculpture: Treasures from Brookgreen Gardens*. New York: Abbeville Press, 1988.

Raymond, Alex. *Flash Gordon: Mongo, the Planet of Doom*. Princeton, WI: Kitchen Sink Press, 1990.

Reed, Walt, and Roger Reed. *The Illustrator in America, 1880–1980*. New York: Society of Illustrators, 1984.

Reichey, A. James. *Life of the Parties: A History of American Political Parties*. New York: Simon & Schuster, 1992.

Reilly, John M. *Twentieth-Century Crime and Mystery Writers*. New York: St. Martin's Press, 1991

Religion. http://www.xroads.virginia.edu/UG02/NewYorker/religion.html

Renshaw, Patrick. *America in the Era of the Two World Wars, 1910–1945*. New York: Longman Group, 1996.

Requa, Richard S. *Inside Lights on the Building of San Diego's Exposition, 1935*. San Diego: Richard S. Requa, 1937.

Reynolds, R. C. *Stage Left: The Development of the American Social Drama in the Thirties*. Troy, NY: Whitson Publishing Co., 1986.

Rich, Doris L. *Amelia Earhart: A Biography*. Washington, DC: Smithsonian Institution Press, 1989.

Rideout, Walter B. *The Radical Novel in the United States, 1900–1954*. New York: Hill and Wang, 1956.

Riggs, Austen Fox. *Play: Recreation in a Balanced Life*. Garden City, NY: Doubleday, Doran & Co., 1935.

Roberts, Brady M., James M. Dennis, James S. Horns, and Helen Mar Parkin. *Grant Wood: An American Master Revealed*. San Francisco: Pomegranate Artbooks, 1995.

Roberts, Garyn G. *Dick Tracy and American Culture: Morality and Mythology, Text and Context*. Jefferson, NC: McFarland & Co., 1993.

Robertson, William H. P. *The History of Thoroughbred Racing in America*. Englewood Cliffs, NJ: Prentice-Hall, 1964.

Robeson, Paul. http://www.scc.rutgers.edu/njh/paulrobeson/index.htm

Robinson, Cervin, and Rosemarie Haag Bletter. *Skyscraper Style: Art Deco, New York*. New York: Oxford University Press, 1975.

Robinson, Jerry. *The Comics: An Illustrated History of Comic Strip Art*. New York: G. P. Putnam's Sons, 1974.

Roettger, Dorye. *Rivals of Rockwell*. New York: Crescent Books, 1992.

Roffman, Peter, and Jim Purdy. *The Hollywood Social Problem Film: Madness, Despair, and Politics from the Depression to the Fifties*. Bloomington: Indiana University Press, 1981.

Rogers, Agnes. *I Remember Distinctly: A Family Album of the American People in the Years of Peace, 1918 to Pearl Harbor*. New York: Harper & Brothers, 1947.

Rollin, Lucy. *Twentieth-Century Teen Culture by the Decades: A Reference Guide*. Westport, CT: Greenwood Press, 1999.

Romano, Frederick V. *The Boxing Filmography: American Features, 1920–2003*. Jefferson, NC: McFarland & Co., 2004.

Roosevelt, Eleanor. *The Autobiography of Eleanor Roosevelt*. New York: Harper & Brothers, 1958.
———. "'Blind Voting' Hit by Mrs. Roosevelt." *New York Times*, 8 May 1934. *Historic New York Times*. Proquest, Lynchburg College Library, Lynchburg, VA.

Roosevelt, Elliott, and James Brough. *A Rendezvous with Destiny: The Roosevelts of the White House*. New York: G. P. Putnam's Sons, 1975.

Root, Waverley, and Richard de Rochemont. *Eating in America: A History*. New York: William Morrow, 1976.

Rorty, James. *Our Master's Voice: Advertising*. New York: John Day Co., 1934.

Rose, Kenneth D. *American Women and the Repeal of Prohibition*. New York: New York University Press, 1996.

Rose, Nancy E. *Put to Work: Relief Programs in the Great Depression*. New York: Monthly Review Press, 1994.

Rosenberg, Deena. *Fascinating Rhythm: The Collaboration of George and Ira Gershwin*. New York: Penguin Books [Plume], 1991.

Rosow, Eugene. *Born to Lose: The Gangster Film in America*. New York: Oxford University Press, 1978.

Roth, Leland M. *A Concise History of American Architecture*. New York: Harper & Row, 1979.

Rothstein, Arthur. *The Depression Years*. New York: Dover Publications, 1978.

Rowsome, Frank, Jr. *They Laughed When I Sat Down*. New York: Bonanza Books, 1959.
———. *The Verse by the Side of the Road: The Story of Burma-Shave Signs and Jingles*. Lexington, MA: Stephen Greene Press, 1965.

Rubin, Joan Shelley. *The Making of Middlebrow Culture*. Chapel Hill: University of North Carolina Press, 1992.

Rubinstein, Ruth P. *Dress Codes: Meanings and Messages in American Culture*. Boulder, CO: Westview Press, 1995.

Ruehlmann, William. *Saint with a Gun: The Unlawful American Private Eye*. New York: New York University Press, 1984.

Runte, Alfred. *Trains of Discovery: Western Railroads and the National Parks*. Niwot, CO: Roberts Rinehart, 1990.

Rydell, Robert W., John E. Findling, and Kimberly D. Pelle. *Fair America: World's Fairs in the United States*. Washington, DC: Smithsonian Institution Press, 2000.

Saab, A. Joan. *For the Millions: American Art and Culture between the Wars*. Philadelphia: University of Pennsylvania Press, 2004.

Salzman, Jack, and Barry Wallenstein, eds. *Years of Protest: A Collection of American Writings of the 1930s*. New York: Pegasus Books, 1967.

Sammons, Jeffrey T. *Beyond the Ring: The Role of Boxing in American Society*. Urbana: University of Illinois Press, 1988.

Sanderson, Dwight. *Research Memorandum on Rural Life in the Depression*. New York: Arno Press, 1972.

Sanjek, Russell. *Pennies from Heaven: The American Popular Music Business in the Twentieth Century*. New York: Da Capo Press, 1996.

Sann, Paul. *Fads, Follies, and Delusions of the American People*. New York: Crown Publishers, 1967.

————. *The Lawless Decade*. New York: Crown Publishers, 1957.

Santelli, Robert, and Emily Davidson, eds. *Hard Travelin': The Life and Legacy of Woody Guthrie*. Hanover, NH: Wesleyan University Press, 1999.

Sasowsky, Norman. *The Prints of Reginald Marsh*. New York: Clarkson N. Potter, 1976.

Scanlan, Tom. *The Joy of Jazz: The Swing Era, 1935–1947*. Golden, CO: Fulcrum Publishing, 1996.

Scherman, David E., ed. *The Best of* Life. New York: Time-Life Books, 1973.

Schickel, Richard. *The Disney Version*. New York: Avon Books, 1968.

Schindler-Carter, Petra. *Vintage Snapshots: The Fabrication of a Nation in the W.P.A. American Guide Series*. Frankfurt, Germany: Peter Lang, 1999.

Schlachter, Gail, ed. *The Great Depression: A Historical Bibliography*. Santa Barbara, CA: ABC-Clio Information Services, 1984.

Schlesinger, Arthur M., Jr. *The Age of Roosevelt*. 3 vols. Vol. 1, *The Crisis of the Old Order, 1919–1933*. Vol. 2 *The Coming of the New Deal,1933–1935*. Vol. 3, *The Politics of Upheaval, 1935–1936*. New York: Houghton Mifflin, 1957, 1958, 1960.

————. *History of United States Political Parties*. New York: Chelsea House, 1987.

Schnurnberger, Lynn. *Let There Be Clothes*. New York: Workman Publishing, 1991.

Schoeffler, O. E., and William Gale. Esquire's *Encyclopedia of 20th-Century Men's Fashions*. New York: McGraw-Hill, 1973.

Schreiner, Samuel A., Jr. *The Condensed World of the* Reader's Digest. New York: Stein & Day, 1977.

Schudson, Michael. *Advertising, the Uneasy Persuasion: Its Dubious Impact on American Society*. New York: Basic Books, 1984.

————. *Discovering the News: A Social History of American Newspapers*. New York: Basic Books, 1978.

Schuller, Gunther. *The Swing Era: The Development of Jazz, 1930–1945*. New York: Oxford University Press, 1989.

Schwartz, Charles. *Cole Porter*. New York: Da Capo Press, 1992.

Schweitzer, Robert, and Michael W.R. Davis. *America's Favorite Homes: Mail-Order Catalogues as a Guide to Popular Early Twentieth-Century Houses*. Detroit: Wayne State University Press, 1990.

Science Fiction. http://www.magicdragon.com/UltimateSF/SF-Index.html

Scott, Quinta, and Susan Croce Kelly. *Route 66: The Highway and Its People*. Norman: University of Oklahoma Press, 1988.

Seabiscuit. Dir. Gary Ross. Universal Pictures, 2003.

Seabiscuit. Dir. Stephen Ives. PBS Home Video. DVD. 2002.

Sears, Stephen W. *The American Heritage History of the Automobile in America*. New York: American Heritage Publishing Co., 1977.

Seidman, David. *All Gone: Things That Aren't There Anymore*. Los Angeles: General Publishing Group, 1998.

Server, Lee. *Encyclopedia of Pulp Fiction Writers*. New York: Checkmark Books, 2002.

Settel, Irving. *A Pictorial History of Radio*. New York: Grosset & Dunlap, 1967.

Settel, Irving, and William Laas. *A Pictorial History of Television*. New York: Grosset & Dunlap, 1969.

7-Up. http://www.brandspeoplelove.com/csab/Brands/7UP/7UPFullHistory/tabid/148/Default.aspx

Seymour, Harold. *Baseball: The Golden Age*. New York: Oxford University Press, 1971.

Shaffer, Marguerite S. *See America First: Tourism and National Identity, 1880–1940*. Washington, DC: Smithsonian Institution Press, 2001.

Shannon, David A. *Between the Wars: America, 1919–1941*. Boston: Houghton Mifflin, 1979.

————, ed. *The Great Depression*. Englewood Cliffs, NJ: Prentice-Hall, 1960.

———. *Twentieth-Century America*. Vol. 2, *The Twenties and Thirties*. Chicago: Rand McNally College Publishing Co., 1974.

Shaw, Arnold. *Let's Dance: Popular Music in the 1930s*. New York: Oxford University Press, 1998.

Sheridan, Martin. *Comics and Their Creators*. Westport, CT: Hyperion Press, 1942.

Shestack, Melvin. *The Country Music Encyclopedia*. New York: Thomas Y. Crowell, 1974.

Shindler, Colin. *Hollywood in Crisis: Cinema and American Society, 1929–1939*. New York: Routledge, 1996.

Sikov, Ed. *Screwball: Hollywood's Madcap Romantic Comedies*. New York: Crown Publishers, 1985.

Silberman, Charles E. *Criminal Violence, Criminal Justice*. New York: Random House, 1978.

Silverman, Al, ed. *The Book of the Month: Sixty Years of Books in American Life*. Boston: Little, Brown, 1986.

Simon, George T. *The Big Bands*. New York: Macmillan, 1967.

———. *Glenn Miller and His Orchestra*. New York: Thomas Y. Crowell, 1974.

Simon, Mary. *Racing through the Century: The Story of Thoroughbred Racing in America*. Irvine, CA: Bowtie Press, 2002.

Simon, Rita James, ed. *As We Saw the Thirties*. Urbana: University of Illinois Press, 1967.

Sinclair, Andrew. *Era of Excess: A Social History of the Prohibition Movement*. New York: Harper Colophon Books, 1962.

Sklar, Robert. *Movie-Made America: A Cultural History of American Cinema*. New York: Vintage Books, 1994.

Smith, Andrew F., ed. *Oxford Encyclopedia of Food and Drink in America*. 2 vols. New York: Oxford University Press, 2004.

Smith, Bradley. *The USA: A History in Art*. Garden City, New York: Doubleday, 1975.

Smith, C. Ray. *Interior Design in Twentieth-Century America: A History*. New York: Harper & Row, 1987.

Smith, G. E. Kidder. *Source Book of American Architecture: 500 Notable Buildings from the 10th Century to the Present*. Princeton, NJ: Princeton Architectural Press, 1996.

Smith, Hal H. "Special Stamp Issues Yield Profit to Nation." *New York Times*, 10 June 1934. *Historic New York Times*. Proquest, Lynchburg College Library, Lynchburg, VA.

———. "Stamp Show Closes; Crowds Set Record." *New York Times*, 19 February 1934. *Historic New York Times*. Proquest, Lynchburg College Library, Lynchburg, VA.

Smith, Jane Webb. *Smoke Signals: Cigarettes, Advertising, and the American Way of Life*. Chapel Hill: University of North Carolina Press, 1990.

Smith, Sidney. *The Gumps*. New York: Charles Scribner's Sons, 1974.

Smith, Steven, and Steven L. Wright. *Iced Tea: The Distinctively American Beverage*. The Winthrop Group. http://www.teausa.com/general/icedtea.cfm

Smulyan, Susan. *Selling Radio: The Commercialization of American Broadcasting, 1920–1934*. Washington, DC: Smithsonian Institution Press, 1994.

Snyder, Robert W. *Voice of the City: Vaudeville and Popular Culture in New York*. New York: Oxford University Press, 1989.

Soft Drinks. http://www.bottlebooks.com/ACL%201937/Soda%20in%201937.htm

Soister, John T. *Of Gods and Monsters: A Critical Guide to Universal Studios' Science Fiction, Horror, and Mystery Films, 1929–1939*. Jefferson, NC: McFarland & Co., 1999.

Springer, John. *All Talking! All Singing! All Dancing! A Pictorial History of the Movie Musical*. Secaucus, NJ: Citadel Press, 1966.

Stanfield, Peter. *Horse Opera: The Strange History of the 1930s Singing Cowboy*. Urbana: University of Illinois Press, 2002.

Stearns, Marshall. *The Story of Jazz*. New York: Oxford University Press, 1958.

Stearns, Marshall, and Jean Stearns. *Jazz Dance: The Story of American Vernacular Dance*. New York: Macmillan, 1992.

Stedman, Raymond William. *The Serials: Suspense and Drama by Installment*. Norman: University of Oklahoma Press, 1971.

Steele, Richard W. *Propaganda in an Open Society: The Roosevelt Administration and the Media, 1933–1941*. Westport, CT: Greenwood Press, 1985.

Steinberg, Sally Levitt. *The Donut Book*. New York: Alfred A. Knopf, 1987.

Steiner, Jesse F. *Research Memorandum on Recreation in the Depression*. New York: Arno Press, 1972.

Sterling, Christopher H., and John M. Kittross. *Stay Tuned: A Concise History of American Broadcasting*. Belmont, CA: Wadsworth Publishing Co., 1990.

Sternau, Susan A. *Art Deco: Flights of Artistic Fancy*. New York: Todtri Book Publishers, 1997.

Stevenson, Katherine Cole, and H. Ward Jandl. *Houses by Mail: A Guide to Houses from Sears, Roebuck and Company*. Washington, DC: Preservation Press, 1986.

Stewart, Jeffrey C., ed. *Paul Robeson: Artist and Citizen*. New Brunswick, NJ: Rutgers University Press, 1999.

Stewart, Mark. *Hockey: A History of the Fastest Game on Ice*. New York: Franklin Watts, 1998.

Stiles, Bent B. "Sales Vast Every Year." *New York Times*, 17 July 1938. *Historic New York Times*. Proquest, Lynchburg College Library, Lynchburg, VA.

Stilgoe, John R. *Borderland: Origins of the American Suburb, 1820–1939*. New Haven, CT: Yale University Press, 1988.

———. *Metropolitan Corridor: Railroads and the American Scene*. New Haven, CT: Yale University Press, 1983.

Stoddard, Bob. *Pepsi:100 Years*. Los Angeles: General Publishing Group, 1997.

Stoltz, Donald R., and Marshall L. Stoltz. *Norman Rockwell and the* Saturday Evening Post. Vol. 2, *The Middle Years, 1928–1943*. 3 vols. Philadelphia: Saturday Evening Post Co., 1976.

Stoltz, Donald Robert, Marshall Louis Stoltz, and William B. Earle. *The Advertising World of Norman Rockwell*. New York: Madison Square Press, 1985.

Storrer, William Allin. *The Architecture of Frank Lloyd Wright: A Complete Catalog*. Cambridge, MA: MIT Press, 1978.

Stott, William. *Documentary Expression and Thirties America*. New York: Oxford University Press, 1973.

Stover, John F. *The Life and Decline of the American Railroad*. New York: Oxford University Press, 1970.

Stowe, David W. *Swing Changes: Big-Band Jazz in New Deal America*. Cambridge, MA: Harvard University Press, 1994.

Strasser, Susan. *Never Done: A History of American Housework*. New York: Pantheon Books, 1982.

———. *Satisfaction Guaranteed: The Making of the American Mass Market*. Washington, DC: Smithsonian Institution Press, 1989.

Stravitz, David. *The Chrysler Building: Creating a New York Icon, Day by Day*. Princeton, NJ: Princeton Architectural Press, 2002.

———. *New York, Empire City, 1920–1945*. New York: Harry N. Abrams, 2004.

Streamliners: America's Lost Trains. Dir. Thomas Ott. http://www.pbs.org/wgbh/amex/streamliners/timeline/index.html

Sudhalter, Richard M. *Stardust Melody: The Life and Music of Hoagy Carmichael*. New York: Oxford University Press, 2002.

Suehsdorf, A. D. *The Great American Baseball Scrapbook*. New York: Random House [Rutledge Books], 1978.

Sugar, Bert Randolph. *100 Years of Boxing*. New York: Galley Press, 1982.

Summers, Harrison B. *A Thirty-Year History of Programs Carried on National Radio Networks in the United States, 1926–1956*. Columbus: Ohio State University Press, 1958.

Suskin, Steven. *Show Tunes: The Songs, Shows, and Careers of Broadway's Major Composers*. 3rd ed. New York: Oxford University Press, 2000.

Susman, Warren. *Culture as History: The Transformation of American Society in the Twentieth Century*. New York: Pantheon Books, 1984.

Swados, Harvey, ed. *The American Writer and the Great Depression*. Indianapolis, IN: Bobbs-Merrill, 1966.

Swanberg, W. A. *Luce and His Empire*. New York: Charles Scribner's Sons, 1972.

Sweeney, Russell C. *Coming Next Week: A Pictorial History of Film Advertising*. New York: Castle Books, 1973.

Swing That Music! The Big Bands, the Soloists, and the Singers. Smithsonian Collection of Recordings. 4 CDs. RD 102, 1993.

Symons, Julian. *Bloody Murder: From the Detective Story to the Crime Novel*. New York: Viking-Penguin, 1985.

Tauranac, John. *Empire State Building: The Making of a Landmark*. New York: St. Martin's Press, 1997.

Taylor, David A. "Ring King." *Smithsonian Magazine*, March 1998, 20, 22, 24.

Taylor, John W. R., and Kenneth Munson. *History of Aviation*. New York: Crown Publishers, 1972.

Taylor, Joshua. *America as Art*. Washington, DC: Smithsonian Institution Press, 1976.

Tchudi, Stephen N. *Soda Poppery: The History of Soft Drinks in America*. New York: Charles Scribner's Sons, 1986.

Tea. http://www.fda.gov/fdac/features/296_tea.html

Tebbel, John. *The American Magazine: A Compact History*. New York: Hawthorn Books, 1969.

———. *George Horace Lorimer and the Saturday Evening Post*. New York: Doubleday, 1948.

———. *A History of Book Publishing in the United States*. Vol. 3, *The Golden Age between Two Wars, 1920–1940*. New York: R. R. Bowker, 1978.

Tebbel, John, and Mary Ellen Zuckerman. *The Magazine in America, 1741–1990*. New York: Oxford University Press, 1991.

Tennyson, Jeffrey. *Hamburger Heaven: The Illustrated History of the Hamburger*. New York: Hyperion, 1993.

Terkel, Studs. *Hard Times: An Oral History of the Great Depression*. New York: Random House [Pantheon], 1970.

Tesher, Elle. *The Dionnes*. New York: Doubleday, 1999.

Thomas, Bob. *Walt Disney: An American Original*. New York: Disney Editions, 1994.

Thompson, Don, and Dick Lupoff, eds. *The Comic-Book Book*. New Rochelle, NY: Arlington House, 1973.

Thomson, David. *Rosebud: The Story of Orson Welles*. New York: Vintage Books, 1996.

Thornburg, David A. *Galloping Bungalows: The Rise and Demise of the American House Trailer*. Hamden, CT: Archon Books, 1991.

Tierney, Tom. *American Family of the 1930s: Paper Dolls in Full Color*. New York: Dover Publications, 1991.

———. *Great Fashion Designs of the Thirties: Paper Dolls in Full Color*. New York: Dover Publications, 1984.

Time-Life Books. *This Fabulous Century*. Vol. 3, *1920–1930*. Vol. 4, *1930–1940*. Vol. 5, *1940–1950*. New York: Time-Life Books, 1969.

Tobey, Ronald C. *Technology as Freedom: The New Deal and the Electrical Modernization of the American Home*. Berkeley: University of California Press, 1996.

Toland, John. *The Great Dirigibles: Their Triumphs and Disasters*. New York: Dover Publications, 1972.

Toll, Robert C. *The Entertainment Machine: American Show Business in the Twentieth Century*. New York: Oxford University Press, 1982.

———. *On with the Show: The First Century of Show Business in America*. New York: Oxford University Press, 1976.

Torricelli, Robert, and Andrew Carol, eds. *In Our Own Words: Extraordinary Speeches of the American Century*. New York: Washington Square Press, 1999.

Toys. *New York Times*, 5 December 1930; 17 December 1932; 18 October 1938. *Historic New York Times*. Proquest, Lynchburg College Library, Lynchburg, VA.

Trent, Paul. *Those Fabulous Movie Years: The Thirties*. Barre, MA: Barre Publishing, 1975.

Trotter, Joe William. *From a Raw Deal to a New Deal: African Americans, 1929–1945*. New York: Oxford University Press, 1996.

The True Story of Seabiscuit. Dir. David Butler. Warner Brothers, 1949.

Tsujimoto, Karen. *Images of America: Precisionist Painting and Modern Photography*. Seattle: University of Washington Press, 1982.

Tucker, Mark, ed. *The Duke Ellington Reader*. New York: Oxford University Press, 1993.

Tucker, Michael. "The Dragon Lady's Well-Favoured Children: The Transition from Corporatist to Individualist in Comic Strips of 1930s." http://etc.dal.ca/belphegor/vol4_no1/articles/04_01_Tucker_ragon_en.html

Tunnels. http://lcweb2.loc.gov/cocoon/legacies/CT/200002790.html

———. http://www.nycroads.com/crossings/lincoln

Turner, William W. *Hoover's FBI: The Men and the Myth*. Los Angeles: Sherbourne Press, 1970.

Twitchell, James B. *Adcult USA: The Triumph of Advertising in American Culture*. New York: Columbia University Press, 1996.

———. *Lead Us into Temptation: The Triumph of American Materialism*. New York: Columbia University Press, 1999.

———. *Twenty Ads That Shook the World*. New York: Crown Publishers, 2000.

Ulanov, Barry. *A History of Jazz in America*. New York: Da Capo Press, 1952.

Unstead, R. J. *The Thirties: An Illustrated History in Colour, 1930–1939*. London: Macdonald Educational, 1974.

U.S. Department of Commerce. *Coffee Consumption in the United States, 1920–1965*. Washington, DC: U.S. Government Printing Office, 1960.

Uys, Errol Lincoln. *Riding the Rails: Teenagers on the Move during the Depression*. New York: TV Books, 1999.

Valentine, Maggie. *The Show Starts on the Sidewalk: An Architectural History of the Movie Palace, Starring S. Charles Lee*. New Haven, CT: Yale University Press, 1994.

Van Dover, J. Kenneth. *Murder in the Millions: Erle Stanley Gardner, Mickey Spillane, and Ian Fleming*. New York: Frederick Ungar Publishing Co., 1984.

The Variety History of Show Business. New York: Harry N. Abrams, 1993.

Vermyle, Jerry. *The Films of the Thirties*. Secaucus, NJ: Citadel Press, 1982.

Verney, Kevern. *African Americans and U.S. Popular Culture*. New York: Routledge, 2003.

Vertrees, Alan David. *Selznick's Vision: Gone with the Wind and Hollywood Filmmaking*. Austin, TX: University of Texas Press, 1997.

Vieira, Mark A. *Hollywood Horror: from Gothic to Cosmic*. New York: Harry N. Abrams, 2003.

Wainwright, Loudon. *The Great American Magazine: An Inside History of Life*. New York: Alfred A. Knopf, 1986.

Wald, Carol. *Myth America: Picturing American Women, 1865–1945*. New York: Pantheon Books, 1975.

Waldau, Roy S. *Vintage Years of the Theatre Guild, 1928–1939*. Cleveland: Press of Case Western Reserve University, 1972.

Walker, Brian. *The Comics before 1945*. New York: Harry N. Abrams, 2004.

Wallace, Aurora. *Newspapers and the Making of Modern America: A History*. Westport, CT: Greenwood Press, 2005.

Waller, George. *Kidnap: The Story of the Lindbergh Case*. New York: Dial Press, 1961.

Walsh, Tim. *The Playmakers: Amazing Origins of Timeless Toys*. Sarasota, FL: Keys Publishing Co., 2003.

Waples, Douglas. *Research Memorandum on Social Aspects of Reading in the Depression*. New York: Arno Press, 1972.

Ward, Geoffrey C., and Ken Burns. *Jazz: A History of America's Music*. New York: Alfred A. Knopf, 2000.

Ware, Susan. *Holding Their Own: American Women in the 1930s*. Boston: Twayne, 1982.

Washburne, Carolyn Kott. *America in the Twentieth Century, 1930–1939*. New York: Marshall Cavendish, 1995.

Watkins, Julius Lewis. *The 100 Greatest Advertisements: Who Wrote Them and What They Did*. New York: Dover Publications, 1959.

Watkins, T. H. *The Great Depression: America in the 1930s*. Boston: Little, Brown, 1993.

———. *The Hungry Years: America in an Age of Crisis, 1929–1939.* New York: Henry Holt, 1999.

Watters, Pat. *Coca-Cola: An Illustrated History.* Garden City, New York: Doubleday, 1978.

Watterson, John Sayle. *College Football: History, Spectacle, Controversy.* Baltimore: Johns Hopkins University Press, 2000.

Waugh, Coulton. *The Comics.* New York: Luna Press, 1947.

Wecter, Dixon. *The Age of the Great Depression, 1929–1941.* Chicago: Quadrangle Books, 1948.

We Had Everything But Money. Greendale, WI: Reminisce Books, 1992.

Weisberger, Bernard, A., ed. *The WPA Guide to America: The Best of 1930s America as Seen by the Federal Writers' Project.* New York: Pantheon Books of Random House, 1985.

Weiskopf, Herman. *The Perfect Game: The World of Bowling.* Englewood Cliffs, NJ: Prentice-Hall [Rutledge Books], 1978.

West, Elliott. *Growing Up in Twentieth-Century America: A History and Reference Guide.* Westport, CT: Greenwood Press, 1996.

West, James L. W., III. *American Authors and the Literary Marketplace since 1900.* Philadelphia: University of Pennsylvania Press, 1988.

Whedon, Julia. *The Fine Art of Ice Skating.* New York: Harry N. Abrams, 1988.

Whiffen, Marcus. *American Architecture since 1780: A Guide to the Styles.* Cambridge, MA: MIT Press, 1992.

Whitcomb, Ian. *After the Ball: Pop Music from Rag to Rock.* Baltimore: Penguin Books, 1972.

———. "The First Crooners, Volume One: The Twenties." http://www.picklehead.com/ian/ian_txt_first crooners1.html

———. "The First Crooners, Volume Two, 1930–1934." http://www.picklehead.com/ian/ian_txt_first crooners2.html

———. "The First Crooners, Volume Three, 1935–1940." http://www.picklehead.com/ian/ian_txt_first crooners3.html

White, David Manning, and Robert H. Abel, eds. *The Funnies: An American Idiom.* New York: Free Press, 1963.

White, G. Edward. *Creating the National Pastime: Baseball Transforms Itself, 1903–1955.* Princeton, NJ: Princeton University Press, 1996.

White, Mark. *"You Must Remember This … ": Popular Songwriters, 1900–1950.* New York: Charles Scribner's Sons, 1985.

White, Roger B. *Home on the Road: The Motor Home in America.* Washington, DC: Smithsonian Institution Press, 2000.

Whittingham, Richard. *Saturday Afternoon: College Football and the Men Who Made the Day.* New York: Workman Publishing, 1985.

Wilder, Alec. *American Popular Song: The Great Innovators, 1900–1950.* New York: Oxford University Press, 1972.

Williams, Anne D. *The Jigsaw Puzzle: Piecing Together a History.* New York: Berkley Penguin, 2004.

Williams, John R. *This Was "Your Hit Parade."* Camden, ME: Courier-Gazette, 1973.

Williamson, J. W. *Hillbillyland: What the Movies Did to the Mountains and What the Mountains Did to the Movies.* Chapel Hill: University of North Carolina Press, 1995.

Wilson, Elizabeth. *Adorned in Dreams: Fashion and Modernity.* Berkeley: University of California Press, 1985.

Wilson, Kristina. *Livable Modernism: Interior Decorating and Design during the Great Depression.* New Haven, CT: Yale University Press, 2004.

Wilson, Richard Guy, Dianne H. Pilgrim, and Dickran Tashjian. *The Machine Age in America, 1918–1941.* New York: Harry N. Abrams, 1986.

Winer, Deborah Grace. *On the Sunny Side of the Street: The Life and Lyrics of Dorothy Fields.* New York: Schirmer Books, 1997.

Winfield, Betty Houchin. *FDR and the News Media.* Urbana: University of Illinois Press, 1990.

Witzel, Michael Karl. *The American Drive-In.* Osceola, WI: Motorbooks International, 1994.

———. *The American Gas Station.* New York: Barnes & Noble Books, 1999.

Wolfe, Charles K. *A Good-Natured Riot: The Birth of the Grand Ole Opry.* Nashville, TN: Country Music Foundation Press, 1999.

Wood, Donald F. *American Buses.* Osceola, WI: MBI Publishing Co., 1998.

Wood, James Playsted. *Magazines in the United States.* New York: Ronald Press Co., 1956.

———. *The Story of Advertising.* New York: Ronald Press Co., 1958.

Woodham, Jonathan M. *Twentieth-Century Design.* New York: Oxford University Press, 1997.

WPA Circus Project. *New York Times,* 3 November 1935, "WPA Circus Ready for Uptown Debut"; 1 August 1938, "2,500,000 in Year Viewed WPA Plays." *Historic New York Times.* Proquest, Lynchburg College Library, Lynchburg, VA.

Wulffson, Don. *Toys: Amazing Stories behind Some Great Inventions.* New York: Henry Holt, 2000.

Yanow, Scott. *Swing.* San Francisco: Miller Freeman Books, 2000.

Yaquinto, Marilyn. *Pump 'em Full of Lead: A Look at Gangsters on Film.* New York: Twayne, 1998.

Yenne, Bill. *The American Brewery: From Colonial Evolution to Microbrew Revolution.* St. Paul, MN: MBI Publishing Co., 2003.

Young, Dean, and Rick Marschall. *Blondie and Dagwood's America.* New York: Harper & Row, 1981.

Young, Walter G. *Stamp Collecting A to Z.* New York: A. S. Barnes & Co., 1981.

Young, William H. "The Serious Funnies: Adventure Comics during the Depression." *Journal of Popular Culture* (Winter 1969): 404–427.

———. "That Indomitable Redhead: Little Orphan Annie." *Journal of Popular Culture* (Fall 1974): 309–316.

Young, William H., and Nancy K. Young. *Music of the Great Depression: American History through Music.* Westport, CT: Greenwood Press, 2005.

———. *The 1930s: American Popular Culture through History.* Westport, CT: Greenwood Press, 2002.

Yo-yos. http://www.nationalyoyo.org/museum/youcanyo-yo.htm

Zierold, Norman J. *The Child Stars.* New York: Coward-McCann, 1965.

Zinsser, William. *Easy to Remember: The Great American Songwriters and Their Songs.* Jaffrey, NH: David R. Godine, 2000.

Zucker, Harvey Marc, and Lawrence J. Babich. *Sports Films: A Complete Reference.* Jefferson, NC: McFarland & Co., 1987.

Zuckerman, Mary Ellen. *A History of Popular Women's Magazines in the United States, 1792–1995.* Westport, CT: Greenwood Press, 1998.

Zwonitzer, Mark, with Charles Hirshberg, *Will You Miss Me When I'm Gone? The Carter Family and Their Legacy in American Music.* New York: Simon & Schuster, 2002.

Index

Fox trot (dance), 530
France, William, Sr., 38
Franchises, 316–17, 424, 492
Franco, Francisco, 370
Frankenstein (film), **188–90**, 246
Frankl, Paul, 123
Franklin Institute, Philadelphia, 462
Fraser, James Earle, 462
Freckles and His Friends (comic strip), 594
Fred Waring and the Pennsylvanians, 376
Freeman, Douglas Southall, 62
Freleng, Fritz, 130
Fremont Canning Co., 182
Frey, Albert, 24
Fried cakes. *See* Doughnuts
Friendly's Ice Cream Co., 254–55
Friml, Rudolf, 363, 364, 499, 504
Froman, Jane, 434
From Spirituals to Swing (concert), 326–27
"From the Bottom of My Heart" (song), 475
Front Page, The (film), 356
Frosted Foods Co., 190
Frozen foods, 181, **190–91**, 253, 423
FTP. *See* Federal Theatre Project
Fugitive Lovers (film), 76
Fuller, R. Buckminster, 23–24
Funding reductions, 160–61, 167, 169
Funnies on Parade (comic book), 104
Furniture, 122–25, 400, 524
Future: advertising, 2; Century of Progress Exposition, 86; New York World's Fair, **356–59**; science fiction, 456
Futurist, home design, 23–24
FWP. *See* Federal Writers' Project

Gable, Clark, 44, 203, 214, 263–65, 509, 513
Gallant Fox (racehorse), 247
Gallup, George, 3
Galvin Corp., 35
Gambling, 194
Games, 111–12, **193–96**, 284, 311, 312
Games of chance, 193–95
Gang Busters (radio program), 162
Gangster films, 128, 163, **197–98**, 382, 540; *Little Caesar*, 295–97
Gangsters, 114
Gannet, Lewis, 172
Garages, 26–27
Garbo, Greta, 12, 154
Gardening, 235
Gardner, Erle Stanley, **199–201**, 343
Gargantua the Great (gorilla), 95
Garland, Joe, 503

Garland, Judy, **201–4**, 249, 436, 496, 539, 595
Garrick Gaieties (musical), 434
Gaskill, Clarence, 103
Gasoline, 204
Gasoline Alley (comic strip), 26–27, 36
Gasoline pumps, 204
Gasoline taxes, 205
Gas stations, 36–37, **204–8**, 264; architecture, 22–23; residential, 206
Gatty, Harold, 41
Gay Divorce (musical), 376
Gay Divorcee, The (film), 376
Gehrig, Lou, 45
General Electric Co., 407, 542
General Foods Corp., 99, 101, 190
General Houses, Inc., 24
General Mills, 178, 190
General Motors Corp., 38, 75, 204, 358
General Seafoods Co., 190
George VI, King of Great Britain, 183
George Washington Parkway, 566
George White Scandals, The (musical), 73
Georgia, 486, 515
Gerber, Dorothy, 182
Gerber Foods, 182
Germany, 9, 277, 361–63, 385
Gernsback, Hugo, 454
Gershwin, George, **208–11**, 327, 358, 431, 498–99; *Porgy and Bess*, 374–75
Gershwin, Ira, **208–11**, 355, 358, 374, 499, 500, 505
Gettysburg (opera), 166
Giant Food Stores, 223
Gibson, Walter B., 525
Gifford, Gene, 505
Gilbert, A. C., 552
Gilbert, Cass, 92, 462
Gillis, Ann, 298
Gimbel Brothers Department Store, 195
Girl Crazy (film), 210
Girl Crazy (musical), 209
Girls, 156, 539, 544, 550, 592, 593–94; Scottsboro Case and rape of white, 399–400
Girl Scout cookies, 126
Girl Scout Council of Greater Philadelphia, 126
Girl Scout Federation of Greater New York, 126
Girl Scouts of America, 481, 592
Glass Key, The (Hammett), 341
Gleason, James, 55
Glen Island Casino, 310

About the Authors

WILLIAM H. YOUNG is a freelance writer and independent scholar. He retired in 2000 after 36 years from Lynchburg College, where he taught American Studies and popular culture. Young has published books and articles on various aspects of popular culture, including three Greenwood volumes co-written with his wife, Nancy K. Young.

NANCY K. YOUNG is a researcher and independent scholar. She retired in 2005 after 26 years from a career in management consulting. With her husband, William H. Young, she has co-written three recent Greenwood titles, *The 1930s*, *The 1950s*, and *Music of the Great Depression*.